THE SACRED BOOKS OF THE EAST

Translated by
VARIOUS ORIENTAL SCHOLARS

Edited by
F. MAX MÜLLER

VOLUME 2

THE SACRED LAWS OF THE ÂRYAS

As Taught in the School of
ÂPASTAMBA, GAUTAMA, VASISHTHA
AND BAUDHÂYANA

Translated by
GEORG BÜHLER

Part I
ÂPASTAMBA AND GAUTAMA

MOTILAL BANARSIDASS PUBLISHERS
PRIVATE LIMITED • DELHI

*Reprint: Delhi, 1965, 1969, 1975, 1986, 1992, 2001, **2007***
First published by the Clarendon Press, 1879

ISBN: 978-81-208-0103-5

MOTILAL BANARSIDASS
41 U.A. Bungalow Road, Jawahar Nagar, Delhi 110 007
8 Mahalaxmi Chamber, 22 Bhulabhai Desai Road, Mumbai 400 026
203 Royapettah High Road, Mylapore, Chennai 600 004
236, 9th Main III Block, Jayanagar, Bangalore 560 011
Sanas Plaza, 1302 Baji Rao Road, Pune 411 002
8 Camac Street, Kolkata 700 017
Ashok Rajpath, Patna 800 004
Chowk, Varanasi 221 001

UNESCO COLLECTION OF REPRESENTATIVE WORKS— Indian Series
This book has been accepted in the Indian Translation Series of the UNESCO Collection of Representative Works, jointly sponsored by the United Nations Educational Scientific and Cultural Organization (UNESCO) and the Government of India

PRINTED IN INDIA

BY JAINENDRA PRAKASH JAIN AT SHRI JAINENDRA PRESS,
A-45 NARAINA, PHASE-I, NEW DELHI 110 028
AND PUBLISHED BY NARENDRA PRAKASH JAIN FOR
MOTILAL BANARSIDASS PUBLISHERS PRIVATE LIMITED,
BUNGALOW ROAD, DELHI 110 007

RASHTRAPATI BHAVAN,
NEW DELHI-4
June 10, 1962

I am very glad to know that the Sacred Books of the East, published years ago by the Clarendon Press, Oxford, which have been out-of-print for a number of years, will now be available to all students of religion and philosophy. The enterprise of the publishers is commendable and I hope the books will be widely read.

S. RADHAKRISHNAN

PUBLISHER'S NOTE

First, the man distinguished between eternal and perishable. Later he discovered within himself the germ of the Eternal. This discovery was an epoch in the history of the human mind and the *East was the first to discover it.*

To watch in the Sacred Books of the East the dawn of this religious consciousness of man, must always remain one of the most inspiring and hallowing sights in the whole history of the world. In order to have a solid foundation for a comparative study of the Religions of the East, we must have before all things, complete and thoroughly faithful translation of their Sacred Books in which some of the ancient sayings were preserved because they were so true and so striking that they could not be forgotten. They contained eternal truths, expressed for the first time in human language.

With profoundest reverence for Dr. S. Radhakrishnan, President of India, who inspired us for the task; our deep sense of gratitude for Dr. C. D. Deshmukh & Dr. D. S. Kothari, for encouraging assistance; esteemed appreciation of UNESCO for the warm endorsement of the cause; and finally with indebtedness to Dr. H. Rau, Director, Max Müller Bhawan, New Delhi, in procuring us the texts of the Series for reprint, we humbly conclude.

PREFATORY NOTE TO THE NEW EDITION

Since 1948 the United Nations Educational, Scientific and Cultural Organization (UNESCO), upon the recommendation of the General Assembly of the United Nations, has been concerned with facilitating the translation of the works most representative of the culture of certain of its Member States, and, in particular, those of Asia.

One of the major difficulties confronting this programme is the lack of translators having both the qualifications and the time to undertake translations of the many outstanding books meriting publication. To help overcome this difficulty in part, UNESCO's advisers in this field (a panel of experts convened every other year by the International Council for Philosophy and Humanistic Studies), have recommended that many worthwhile translations published during the 19th century, and now impossible to find except in a limited number of libraries, should be brought back into print in low-priced editions, for the use of students and of the general public. The experts also pointed out that in certain cases, even though there might be in existence more recent and more accurate translations endowed with a more modern apparatus of scholarship, a number of pioneer works of the greatest value and interest to students of Eastern religions also merited republication.

This point of view was warmly endorsed by the Indian National Academy of Letters (Sahitya Akademi), and the Indian National Commission for UNESCO.

It is in the spirit of these recommendations that this work from the famous series "Sacred Books of the East" is now once again being made available to the general public as part of the UNESCO Collection of Representative Works.

CONTENTS.

INTRODUCTION

TO

ÂPASTAMBA.

FOR all students of Sanskrit philology and Indian history Âpastamba's aphorisms on the sacred law of the Âryan Hindus possess a special interest beyond that attaching to other works of the same class. Their discovery enabled Professor Max Müller, forty-seven years ago, to dispose finally of the Brahmanical legend according to which Hindu society was supposed to be governed by the codes of ancient sages, compiled for the express purpose of tying down each individual to his station, and of strictly regulating even the smallest acts of his daily life[1]. It enabled

---

[1] Max Müller, History of Ancient Sanskrit Literature, p. 133 seq.

The following letter, addressed to the late W. H. Morley, and published by him in his Digest of Indian Cases, 1850, may be of interest as connected with the first discovery of the Âpastamba-sûtras:—

9, *Park Place, Oxford, July* 29, 1849.

MY DEAR MORLEY,—I have been looking again at the law literature, in order to write you a note on the sources of Manu. I have treated the subject fully in my introduction to the Veda, where I have given an outline of the different periods of Vaidik literature, and analysed the peculiarities in the style and language of each class of Vaidik works. What I consider to be the sources of the Mânava-dharma-*s*âstra, the so-called Laws of Manu, are the Sûtras. These are works which presuppose the development of the prose literature of the Brâhma*n*as (like the Aitareya-brâhma*n*a, Taittirîya-brâhma*n*a, &c.) These Brâhma*n*as, again, presuppose, not only the existence, but the collection and arrangement of the old hymns of the four Sa*m*hitâs. The Sûtras are therefore later than both these classes of Vaidik works, but they must be considered as belonging to the Vaidik period of literature, not only on account of their intimate connection with Vaidik subjects, but also because they still exhibit the irregularities of the old Vaidik language. They form indeed the last branch of Vaidik literature; and it will perhaps be possible to fix some of these works chronologically, as they are contemporary with the first spreading of Buddhism in India.

Again, in the whole of Vaidik literature there is no work written (like the Mânava-dharma-*s*âstra) in the regular epic *S*loka, and the continuous employment of this metre is a characteristic mark of post-Vaidik writings.

One of the principal classes of Sûtras is known by the name of Kalpa-sûtras,

him not only to arrive at this negative result, but also to substitute a sounder theory the truth of which subsequent investigations have further confirmed, and to show that the sacred law of the Hindus has its source in the teaching of the Vedic schools, and that the so-called revealed law codes are, in most cases, but improved metrical editions of older

---

or rules of ceremonies. These are avowedly composed by human authors, while, according to Indian orthodox theology, both the hymns and Brâhma*n*as are to be considered as revelation. The Sûtras generally bear the name of their authors, like the Sûtras of Â*s*valâyana, Kâtyâyana, &c., or the name of the family to which the Sûtras belonged. The great number of these writings is to be accounted for by the fact that there was not one body of Kalpa-sûtras binding on all Brahmanic families, but that different old families had each their own Kalpa-sûtras. These works are still very frequent in our libraries, yet there is no doubt that many of them have been lost. Sûtras are quoted which do not exist in Europe, and the loss of some is acknowledged by the Brahmans themselves. There are, however, lists of the old Brahmanic families which were in possession of their own redaction of Vaidik hymns (Sa*m*hitâs), of Brâhma*n*as, and of Sûtras. Some of these families followed the Rig-veda, some the Ya*g*ur-veda, the Sâma-veda, and Atharva-veda; and thus the whole Vaidik literature becomes divided into four great classes of Brâhma*n*as and Sûtras, belonging to one or the other of the four principal Vedas.

Now one of the families following the Ya*g*ur-veda was that of the Mânavas (cf. *K*ara*n*avyûha). There can be no doubt that that family, too, had its own Sûtras. Quotations from Mânava-sûtras are to be met with in commentaries on other Sûtras; and I have found, not long ago, a MS. which contains the text of the Mânava-*s*rauta-sûtras, though in a very fragmentary state. But these Sûtras, the *S*rauta-sûtras, treat only of a certain branch of ceremonies connected with the great sacrifices. Complete Sûtra works are divided into three parts: 1. the first (*S*rauta), treating on the great sacrifices; 2. the second (G*ri*hya), treating on the Sa*m*skâras, or the purificatory sacraments; 3. the third (Sâmayâ*k*ârika or Dharma-sûtras), treating on temporal duties, customs, and punishments. The last two classes of Sûtras seem to be lost in the Mânava-sûtra. This loss is, however, not so great with regard to tracing the sources of the Mânava-dharma-*s*âstra, because whenever we have an opportunity of comparing Sûtras belonging to different families, but following the same Veda, and treating on the same subjects, the differences appear to be very slight, and only refer to less important niceties of the ceremonial. In the absence, therefore, of the Mânava-sâmayâ*k*ârika-sûtras, I have taken another collection of Sûtras, equally belonging to the Ya*g*ur-veda, the Sûtras of Âpastamba. In his family we have not only a Brâhma*n*a, but also Âpastamba *S*rauta, G*ri*hya, and Sâmayâ*k*ârika-sûtras. Now it is, of course, the third class of Sûtras, on temporal duties, which are most likely to contain the sources of the later metrical Codes of Law, written in the classical *S*loka. On a comparison of different subjects, such as the duties of a Brahma*k*ârin, a G*ri*hastha, laws of inheritance, duties of a king, forbidden fruit, &c., I find that the Sûtras contain generally almost the same words which have been brought into verse by the compiler of the Mânava-

prose works which latter, in the first instance, were destined to be committed to memory by the young Âryan students, and to teach them their duties. This circumstance, as well as the fact that Âpastamba's work is free from any suspicion of having been tampered with by sectarians or modern editors, and that its intimate connection with the manuals teaching the performance of the great and small sacrifices, the *S*rauta and G*ri*hya-sûtras, which are attributed to the same author, is perfectly clear and indisputable, entitle it, in spite of its comparatively late origin, to the first place in a collection of Dharma-sûtras.

The Âpastambîya Dharma-sûtra forms part of an enormous Kalpa-sûtra or body of aphorisms, which digests the teaching of the Veda and of the ancient *Ri*shis regarding the performance of sacrifices and the duties of twice-born men, Brâhma*n*as, Kshatriyas, and Vai*s*yas and which, being chiefly based on the second of the four Vedas, the Ya*g*ur-veda in the Taittirîya recension, is primarily intended for the benefit of the Adhvaryu priests in whose families the study of the Ya*g*ur-veda is hereditary.

The entire Kalpa-sûtra of Âpastamba is divided into

---

dharma-*s*âstra. I consider, therefore, the Sûtras as the principal source of the metrical Sm*ri*tis, such as the Mânava-dharma-*s*âstra, Yâ*gñ*avalkya-dharma-*s*âstra, &c., though there are also many other verses in these works which may be traced to different sources. They are paraphrases of verses of the Sa*m*hitâs, or of passages of the Brâhma*n*as, often retaining the same old words and archaic constructions which were in the original. This is indeed acknowledged by the author of the Mânava-dharma-*s*âstra, when he says (B. II, v. 6), 'The roots of the Law are the whole Veda (Sa*m*hitâs and Brâhma*n*as), the customs and traditions of those who knew the Veda (as laid down in the Sûtras), the conduct of good men, and one's own satisfaction.' The Mânava-dharma-*s*âstra may thus be considered as the last redaction of the laws of the Mânavas. Quite different is the question as to the old Manu from whom the family probably derived its origin, and who is said to have been the author of some very characteristic hymns in the Rig-veda-sa*m*hitâ. He certainly cannot be considered as the author of a Mânava-dharma-*s*âstra, nor is there even any reason to suppose the author of this work to have had the same name. It is evident that the author of the metrical Code of Laws speaks of the old Manu as of a person different from himself, when he says (B. X, v. 63), 'Not to kill, not to lie, not to steal, to keep the body clean, and to restrain the senses, this was the short law which Manu proclaimed amongst the four castes.'—Yours truly, M. M.

thirty sections, called Prasnas, literally questions[1]. The first twenty-four of these teach the performance of the so-called Srauta or Vaitânika sacrifices, for which several sacred fires are required, beginning with the simplest rites, the new and full moon offerings, and ending with the complicated Sattras or sacrificial sessions, which last a whole year or even longer[2]. The twenty-fifth Prasna contains the Paribhâshâs or general rules of interpretation[3], which are valid for the whole Kalpa-sûtra, the Pravara-khanda, the chapter enumerating the patriarchs of the various Brahmanical tribes, and finally the Hautraka, prayers to be recited by the Hotraka priests. The twenty-sixth section gives the Mantras or Vedic prayers and formulas for the Grihya rites, the ceremonies for which the sacred domestic or Grihya fire is required, and the twenty-seventh the rules for the performance of the latter[4]. The aphorisms on the sacred law fill the next two Prasnas; and the Sulva-sûtra[5], teaching the geometrical principles, according to which the altars necessary for the Srauta sacrifices must be constructed, concludes the work with the thirtieth Prasna.

The position of the Dharma-sûtra in the middle of the collection at once raises the presumption that it originally formed an integral portion of the body of Sûtras and that it is not a later addition. Had it been added later, it would either stand at the end of the thirty Prasnas or altogether outside the collection, as is the case with some other treatises attributed to Âpastamba[6]. The Hindus are, no doubt, unscrupulous in adding to the works of famous teachers But such additions, if of considerable extent, are usually not embodied in the works themselves which they are intended to supplement. They are mostly given

[1] Burnell, Indian Antiquary, I, 5 seq.

[2] The Srauta-sûtra, Pr. I–XV, has been edited by Professor R. Garbe in the Bibliotheca Indica, and the remainder is in the press.

[3] See Professor Max Müller's Translation in S. B. E., vol. xxx.

[4] The Grihya-sûtra has been edited by Dr. Winternitz, Vienna, 1887.

[5] On the Sulva-sûtras see G. Thibaut in 'the Pandit,' 1875, p. 292.

[6] Burnell, loc. cit.

as *s*eshas or pari*s*ish*t*as, tacked on at the end, and generally marked as such in the MSS.

In the case of the Âpastamba Dharma-sûtra it is, however, not necessary to rely on its position alone, in order to ascertain its genuineness. There are unmistakable indications that it is the work of the same author who wrote the remainder of the Kalpa-sûtra. One important argument in favour of this view is furnished by the fact that Pra*s*na XXVII, the section on the G*ri*hya ceremonies, has evidently been made very short and concise with the intention of saving matter for the subsequent sections on the sacred law. The Âpastambîya G*ri*hya-sûtra contains nothing beyond a bare outline of the domestic ceremonies, while most of the other G*ri*hya-sûtras, e.g. those of Â*s*valâyana, *S*âṅkhâyana, Gobhila, and Pâraskara, include a great many rules which bear indirectly only on the performance of the offerings in the sacred domestic fire. Thus on the occasion of the description of the initiation of Âryan students, Â*s*valâyana inserts directions regarding the dress and girdle to be worn, the length of the studentship, the manner of begging, the disposal of the alms collected, and other similar questions [1]. The exclusion of such incidental remarks on subjects that are not immediately connected with the chief aim of the work, is almost complete in Âpastamba's G*ri*hya-sûtra, and reduces its size to less than one half of the extent of the shorter ones among the works enumerated above. It seems impossible to explain this restriction of the scope of Pra*s*na XXVII otherwise than by assuming that Âpastamba wished to reserve all rules bearing rather on the duties of men than on the performance of the domestic offerings, for his sections on the sacred law.

A second and no less important argument for the unity of the whole Kalpa-sûtra may be drawn from the cross-references which occur in several Pra*s*nas. In the Dharma-sûtra we find that on various occasions, where the performance

[1] Â*s*valâyana G*ri*hya-sûtra I, 19, ed. Stenzler.

of a ceremony is prescribed, the expressions yathoktam, 'as has been stated,' yathopadesam, 'according to the injunction,' or yathâ purastât, 'as above,' are added. In four of these passages, Dh. I, 1, 4, 16; II, 2, 3, 17; 2, 5, 4; and 7, 17, 16, the Grihya-sûtra is doubtlessly referred to, and the commentator Haradatta has pointed out this fact. On the other hand, the Grihya-sûtra refers to the Dharma-sûtra, employing the same expressions which have been quoted from the latter. Thus we read in the beginning of the chapter on funeral oblations, Grihya-sûtra VIII, 21, 1, mâsisrâddhasyâparapakshe yathopadesam kâlâh, 'the times for the monthly funeral sacrifice (fall) in the latter (dark) half of the month according to the injunction.' Now as neither the Grihya-sûtra itself nor any preceding portion of the Kalpa-sûtra contains any injunction on this point, it follows that the long passage on this subject which occurs in the Dharma-sûtra II, 7, 16, 4–22 is referred to. The expression yathopadesam is also found in other passages of the Grihya-sûtra, and must be explained there in a like manner[1]. There are further a certain number of Sûtras which occur in the same words both in the Prasna on domestic rites, and in that on the sacred law, e.g. Dh. I, 1, 1, 18; I, 1, 2, 38; I, 1, 4, 14. It seems that the author wished to call special attention to these rules by repeating them. Their recurrence and literal agreement may be considered an additional proof of the intimate connection of the two sections.

Through a similar repetition of, at least, one Sûtra it is possible to trace the connection of the Dharma-sûtra with the Srauta-sûtra. The rule ritve vâ gâyâm, 'or (he may have conjugal intercourse) with his wife in the proper season,' is given, Dh. II, 2, 5, 17, with reference to a householder who teaches the Veda. In the Srauta-sûtra it occurs twice, in the sections on the new and full moon sacrifices III, 17, 8, and again in connection with the Kâturmâsya offerings, VIII, 4, 6, and it refers both times

[1] See the details, given by Dr. Winternitz in his essay, Das altindische Hochzeitsrituell, p. 5 (Denkschr. Wiener Akademie, Bd. 40).

to the sacrificer. In the first passage the verb, upeyât, is added, which the sense requires; in the second it has the abbreviated form, which the best MSS. of the Dharma-sûtra offer. The occurrence of the irregular word, *ri*tve for *ri*tvye, in all the three passages, proves clearly that we have to deal with a self-quotation of the same author. If the Dharma-sûtra were the production of a different person and a later addition, the Pseudo-Âpastamba would most probably not have hit on this peculiar irregular form. Finally, the G*ri*hya-sûtra, too, contains several cross-references to the *S*rauta-sûtra, and the close agreement of the Sûtras on the Vedic sacrifices, on the domestic rites, and on the sacred, both in language and style, conclusively prove that they are the compositions of one author[1].

Who this author really was, is a problem which cannot be solved for the present, and which probably will always remain unsolved, because we know his family name only. For the form of the word itself shows that the name Âpastamba, just like those of most founders of Vedic schools, e.g. Bhâradvâ*g*a, Â*s*valâyana, Gautama, is a patronymic. This circumstance is, of course, fatal to all attempts at an identification of the individual who holds so prominent a place among the teachers of the Black Ya*g*ur-veda.

But we are placed in a somewhat better position with respect to the history of the school which has been named after Âpastamba and of the works ascribed to him. Regarding both, some information has been preserved by tradition, and a little more can be obtained from inscriptions and later works, while some interesting details regarding the time when, and the place where the Sûtras were composed, may be elicited from the latter themselves. The data, obtainable from these sources, it is true, do not enable us to determine with certainty the year when the Âpastambîya school was founded, and when its Sûtras were composed. But they make it possible to ascertain the position of the school and of its Sûtras in Vedic litera-

[1] See Dr. Winternitz, loc. cit.

ture, their relative priority or posteriority as compared with other Vedic schools and works, to show with some amount of probability in which part of India they had their origin, and to venture, at least, a not altogether unsupported conjecture as to their probable antiquity.

As regards the first point, the *K*ara*n*avyûha, a supplement of the White Ya*g*ur-veda which gives the lists of the Vedic schools, informs us that the Âpastambîya school formed one of the five branches of the Khâ*nd*ikîya school, which in its turn was a subdivision of the Taittirîyas, one of the ancient sections of Brâhma*n*as who study the Black Ya*g*ur-veda. Owing to the very unsatisfactory condition of the text of the *K*ara*n*avyûha it is unfortunately not possible to ascertain what place that work really assigns to the Âpastambîyas among the five branches of the Khâ*nd*ikîyas. Some MSS. name them first, and others last. They give either the following list, 1. Kâleyas (Kâletas), 2. Sâ*t*yâyanins, 3. Hira*n*yake*s*ins, 4. Bhâradvâ*g*ins, and 5. Âpastambins, or, 1. Âpastambins, 2. Baudhâyanins or Bodhâyanins, 3. Satyâshâ*dh*ins, 4. Hira*n*yake*s*ins, 5. Aukheyas [1]. But this defect is remedied to a certain extent by the now generally current, and probably ancient tradition that the Âpastambîyas are younger than the school of Baudhâyana, and older than that of Satyâshâ*dh*a Hira*n*yake*s*in. Baudhâyana, it is alleged, composed the first set of Sûtras connected with the Black Ya*g*ur-veda, which bore the special title 'prava*k*ana,' and he was succeeded by Bhâradvâ*g*a, Âpastamba, and Satyâshâ*dh*a Hira*n*yake*s*in, who all founded schools which bear their names [2].

---

[1] Max Müller, Hist. Anc. Sansk. Lit , p. 371. A MS. of the *K*ara*n*avyûha with an anonymous commentary, in my possession, has the following passage: कांडिकेयानां पंच भेदा भवंति। आपस्तंबी बोधायनी सत्याषाढी हिरण्यकेशी औखेयी चेति.

[2] Max Müller, Hist. Anc. Sansk. Lit., p. 194. These statements occur in the introduction of Mahâdeva's commentary on the *S*rauta-sûtra of Hira*n*yake*s*in (Weber, Hist. Sansk. Lit., p. 110, 2nd ed.) and in an interpolated passage of Bhâradvâ*g*a's G*ri*hya-sûtra (Winternitz, op. cit., p. 8, note 1), as well as, with the omission of Bhâradvâ*g*a's name, in interpolated passages of

This tradition has preserved two important pieces of information. First, the Âpastamba school is what Professor Max Müller appropriately calls a Sûtra*k*ara*n*a, i. e. a school whose founder did not pretend to have received a revelation of Vedic Mantras or of a Brâhma*n*a text, but merely gave a new systematic arrangement of the precepts regarding sacrifices and the sacred law. Secondly, the Sûtras of Âpastamba occupy an intermediate position between the works of Baudhâyana and Hira*n*yake*s*in. Both these statements are perfectly true, and capable of being supported by proofs, drawn from Âpastamba's own and from other works.

As regards the first point, Professor Max Müller has already pointed [1] out that, though we sometimes find a Brâhma*n*a of the Âpastambîyas mentioned, the title Âpastamba-brâhma*n*a is nothing but another name of the Taittirîya-brâhma*n*a, and that this Brâhma*n*a, in reality, is always attributed to Tittiri or to the pupils of Vai*s*ampâyana, who are said to have picked up the Black Ya*g*urveda in the shape of partridges (tittiri). The same remark applies to the collection of the Mantras of the Black Ya*g*urveda, which, likewise, is sometimes named Âpastamba-sa*m*hitâ. The *K*ara*n*avyûha states explicitly that the five branches of the Khâ*nd*ikîya school, to which the Âpastambîyas belong, possess one and the same recension of the revealed texts, consisting of 7 Kâ*nd*as, 44 Pra*s*nas, 651 Anuvâkas, 2198 Pannâsîs, 19290 Padas [2], and 253,868 syllables, and indicates thereby that all these five schools were Sûtra*k*ara*n*as.

If we now turn to Âpastamba's own works, we find still

Baudhâyana's Dharma-sûtra (II, 5, 9, 14) and of the same author's G*ri*hya-sûtra (Sacred Books of the East, vol. xiv, p. xxxvi, note 1). Adherents of a Prava*k*ana-sûtra, no doubt identical with that of Baudhâyana, the Prava*k*anakartâ (Sacred Books of the East, vol. xiv, p. xxxvi), are mentioned in a land grant, originally issued by the Pallava king Nandivarman in the beginning of the eighth century A. D., see Hultzsch, South Indian Inscriptions, vol. ii, p. 361 seqq.; see also Weber, Hist. Sansk. Lit., p. 110, 2nd ed.

[1] Max Müller, op. cit., p. 195.

[2] See also Weber, Ind. Lit., p. 98, 2nd ed.

clearer proof that he laid no claim to the title *R*ishi, or inspired seer of Vedic texts. For (Dharma-sûtra I, 2, 5, 4-5) he says distinctly that on account of the prevalent transgression of the rules of studentship no *R*ishis are born among the Avaras, the men of later ages or of modern times, but that some, by virtue of a residue of the merit which they acquired in former lives, become similar to *R*ishis by their knowledge of the Veda. A man who speaks in this manner, shows that he considers the holy ages during which the great saints saw with their mind's eye the uncreated and eternal texts of the Veda to be past, and that all he claims is a thorough acquaintance with the scriptures which had been handed down to him. The same spirit which dictated this passage is also observable in other portions of the Dharma-sûtra. For Âpastamba repeatedly contrasts the weakness and sinfulness of the Avaras, the men of his own times, with the holiness of the ancient sages, who, owing to the greatness of their 'lustre,' were able to commit various forbidden acts without diminishing their spiritual merit [1]. These utterances prove that Âpastamba considered himself a child of the Kali Yuga, the age of sin, during which, according to Hindu notions, no *R*ishis can be born. If, therefore, in spite of this explicit disclaimer, the Sa*m*hitâ and the Brâhma*n*a of the Black Ya*g*ur-veda are sometimes called Âpastamba or Âpastambîya, i. e. belonging to Âpastamba, the meaning of this expression can only be, that they were and are studied and handed down by the school of Âpastamba, not that its founder was their author, or, as the Hindus would say, saw them.

The fact that Âpastamba confined his activity to the composition of Sûtras is highly important for the determination of the period to which he belonged. It clearly shows that in his time the tertiary or Sûtra period of the Ya*g*ur-veda had begun. Whether we assume, with Professor Max Müller, that the Sûtra period was one and the same for all the four Vedas, and fix its limits with him

[1] Dharma-sûtra II, 6, 13, 1-10; II, 10, 27, 4.

between 600–200 B.C., or whether we believe, as I am inclined to do, that the date of the Sûtra period differed for each Veda, still the incontestable conclusion is that the origin of the Âpastambîya school cannot be placed in the early times of the Vedic period, and probably falls in the last six or seven centuries before the beginning of the Christian era.

The correctness of the traditional statement that Âpastamba is younger than Baudhâyana may be made very probable by the following considerations. First, Baudhâyana's and Âpastamba's works on Dharma have a considerable number of Sûtras in common. Thus in the chapter on Penances not less than seven consecutive Sûtras, prescribing the manner in which outcasts are to live and to obtain readmission into the Brahmanical community for their children, occur in both treatises[1]. Besides this passage, there are a number of single Sûtras[2] which agree literally. Taken by itself this agreement does not prove much, as it may be explained in various ways. It may show either that Baudhâyana is older than Âpastamba, and that the latter borrowed from the former, or that the reverse was the case. It may also indicate that both authors drew from one common source. But if it is taken together with two other facts, it gains a considerable importance. First, Âpastamba holds in several cases doctrines which are of a later origin than those held by Baudhâyana. With respect to this point the puritan opinions which Âpastamba puts forward regarding the substitutes for legitimate sons and regarding the appointment of widows (niyoga), and his restriction of the number of marriage-rites, may be adduced as examples. Like many other ancient teachers, Baudhâyana permits childless Âryans to satisfy their craving for representatives bearing their name, and to allay their fears of falling after death into the regions of torment through a failure of the funeral oblations, by the affiliation

[1] Baudh. Dh. II, 1, 2, 18–23 = Âp. Dh. I, 10, 29, 8–14.

[2] E.g. Âp. Dh. I, 1, 2, 30; I, 2, 6, 8-9; I, 5, 15, 8 correspond respectively to Baudh. Dh. I, 2, 3, 39–40; I, 2, 3, 38; I, 2, 3, 29.

of eleven kinds of substitutes for a legitimate son. Illegitimate sons, the illegitimate sons of wives, the legitimate and illegitimate offspring of daughters, and the children of relatives, or even of strangers who may be solemnly adopted, or received as members of the family without any ceremony, or be acquired by purchase, are all allowed to take the place and the rights of legitimate sons [1]. Âpastamba declares his dissent from this doctrine. He allows legitimate sons alone to inherit their father's estate and to follow the occupations of his caste, and he explicitly forbids the sale and gift of children [2].

In like manner he protests against the custom of making over childless widows to brothers-in-law or other near relatives in order to obtain sons who are to offer the funeral oblations to the deceased husband's manes, while Baudhâyana has as yet no scruple on the subject [3]. Finally, he omits from his list of the marriage-rites the Pai*s*â*k*a vivâha, where the bride is obtained by fraud [4]; though it is reluctantly admitted by Baudhâyana and other ancient teachers. There can be no doubt that the law which placed the regular continuance of the funeral oblations above all other considerations, and which allowed, in order to secure this object, even a violation of the sanctity of the marriage-tie and other breaches of the principles of morality, belongs to an older order of ideas than the stricter views of Âpastamba. It is true that, according to Baudhâyana's own statement [5], before his time an ancient sage named Aupa*g*anghani, who is also mentioned in the *S*atapatha-brâhma*n*a, had opposed the old practice of taking substitutes for a legitimate son. It is also very probable that for a long time the opinions of the Brâhma*n*a teachers, who lived in different parts of India and belonged to different schools, may have been divided on this subject. Still it seems very improbable that of two authors who both belong to the same Veda and to the same school, the

[1] Baudh. Dh. II, 2, 3, 17 seqq.
[2] Âp. Dh. II, 5, 13, 1–2, 11.
[3] Âp. Dh. II, 10, 27, 2–7.
[4] Âp. Dh. II, 5, 11 and 12.
[5] Baudh. Dh. II, 2, 3, 33.

earlier one should hold the later doctrine, and the later one the earlier opinion. The contrary appears the more probable assumption. The same remarks apply to the cases of the Niyoga and of the Pais*âk*a marriage [1].

The second fact, which bears on the question how the identity of so many Sûtras in the two Dharma-sûtras is to be explained, affords a still stronger proof of Âpastamba's posteriority to Baudhâyana. For on several occasions, it appears, Âpastamba controverts opinions which Baudhâyana holds, or which may be defended with the help of the latter's Sûtras. The clearest case of this kind occurs in the chapter on Inheritance, where the treatment of the eldest son on the division of the estate by the father is discussed. There Âpastamba gives it as his own opinion that the father should make an equal division of his property 'after having gladdened the eldest son by some (choice portion of his) wealth,' i. e. after making him a present which should have some value, but should not be so valuable as to materially affect the equality of the shares [2]. Further on he notices the opinions of other teachers on this subject, and states that the practice advocated by some, of allowing the eldest alone to inherit, as well as the custom prevailing in some countries, of allotting to the eldest all the father's gold, or the black cows, or the black iron and grain, is not in accordance with the precepts of the Vedas. In order to prove the latter assertion he quotes a passage of the Taittirîya Sa*m*hitâ, in which it is declared that 'Manu divided his wealth among his sons,' and no difference in the treatment of the eldest son is prescribed. He adds that a second passage occurs in the same Veda, which declares that 'they distinguish the eldest son by (a larger portion of) the heritage,' and which thus apparently countenances the partiality for the first-born. But this second passage, he contends, appealing to the

[1] For another case, the rules, referring to the composition for homicide, regarding which Âpastamba holds later views than Baudhâyana, see the Festgruss an R. von Roth, pp. 47-48.

[2] Âp. Dh. II, 6, 13, 13, and II, 6, 14, 1.

opinion of the Mîmâmsists, is, like many similar ones, merely a statement of a fact which has not the authority of an injunction[1]. If we now turn to Baudhâyana, we find that he allows of three different methods for the distribution of the paternal estate. According to him, either an equal share may be given to each son, or the eldest may receive the best part of the wealth, or, also, a preferential share of one tenth of the whole property. He further alleges that the cows, horses, goats, and sheep respectively go to the eldest sons of Brâhmanas, Kshatriyas, Vaisyas and Sûdras. As authority for the equal division he gives the first of the two Vedic passages quoted above; and for the doctrine that the eldest is to receive the best part of the estate, he quotes the second passage which Âpastamba considers to be without the force of an injunction[2]. The fact that the two authors' opinions clash is manifest, and the manner in which Âpastamba tries to show that the second Vedic passage possesses no authority, clearly indicates that before his time it had been held to contain an injunction. As no other author of a Dharma-sûtra but Baudhâyana is known to have quoted it, the conclusion is that Âpastamba's remarks are directed against him. If Âpastamba does not mention Baudhâyana by name, the reason probably is that in olden times, just as in the present day, the Brahmanical etiquette forbad a direct opposition against doctrines propounded by an older teacher who belongs to the same spiritual family (vidyâvamsa) as oneself.

A similar case occurs in the chapter on Studentship[3], where Âpastamba, again appealing to the Mîmâmsists, combats the doctrine that pupils may eat forbidden food, such as honey, meat, and pungent condiments, if it is given to them as leavings by their teacher. Baudhâyana gives no explicit rule on this point, but the wording of his Sûtras is not opposed to the doctrine and practice, to which Âpastamba objects. Baudhâyana says that students

[1] Âp. Dh. II, 6, 14, 6-13.
[2] Baudh. Dh. II, 2, 3, 2-7.
[3] Âp. Dh. I, 1, 4, 5-7.

shall avoid honey, meat, pungent condiments, &c.; he further enjoins that pupils are to obey their teachers except when ordered to commit crimes which cause loss of caste (patanîya); and he finally directs them to eat the fragments of food given to them by their teachers. As the eating of honey and other forbidden substances is not a crime causing loss of caste, it is possible that Baudhâyana himself may have considered it the duty of a pupil to eat any kind of food given by the teacher, even honey and meat. At all events the practice and doctrine which Âpastamba blames, may have been defended by the wording of Baudhâyana's rules [1].

The three points which have been just discussed, viz. the identity of a number of Sûtras in the works of the two authors, the fact that Âpastamba advocates on some points more refined or puritan opinions, and, especially, that he labours to controvert doctrines contained in Baudhâyana's Sûtras, give a powerful support to the traditional statement that he is younger than that teacher. It is, however, difficult to say how great the distance between the two really is. Mahâdeva, as stated above, places between them only Bhâradvâ*g*a, the author of a set of Sûtras, which as yet have not been completely recovered. But it seems to me not likely that the latter was his immediate predecessor in the vidyâva*ms*a or spiritual family to which both belonged. For it cannot be expected that two successive heads of the school should each have composed a Sûtra and thus founded a new branch-school. It is

[1] Cases, in which Âpastamba's G*ri*hya-sûtra appears to refer to, or to controvert, Baudhâyana's G*ri*hya-sûtra, have been collected by Dr. Winternitz, op. cit., p. 8. Dr. Burnell, Tanjore Catalogue, p. 34, too, considers Baudhâyana to be older than Âpastamba, because his style is so much simpler. With this remark may be compared Dr. Winternitz's very true assertion that Baudhâyana's style resembles sometimes, especially in the discussion of disputed points, that of the Brâhma*n*as. On the other hand, Dr. R. G. Bhâ*nd*ârkar, Second Report on the Search for Sanskrit MSS., p. 34, believes Baudhâyana to be later than Âpastamba and Bhâradvâ*g*a, because he teaches other developments of sacrificial rites, unknown to the other two Sûtrakâras. This may be true, but it must not be forgotten that every portion of Baudhâyana's Sûtras, which has been subjected to a critical enquiry, has turned out to be much interpolated and enlarged by later hands.

more probable that Baudhâyana and Bhâradvâ*g*a, as well as the latter and Âpastamba, were separated by several intervening generations of teachers, who contented themselves with explaining the works of their predecessors. The distance in years between the first and the last of the three Sûtrakâras must, therefore, I think, be measured rather by centuries than by decades [1].

As regards the priority of Âpastamba to the school of Satyâshâ*dh*a Hira*n*yake*s*in, there can be no doubt about the correctness of this statement. For either Hira*n*yake*s*in himself, or, at least, his immediate successors have appropriated Âpastamba's Dharma-sûtra and have inserted it with slight modifications in their own collection. The alterations consist chiefly in some not very important additions, and in the substitution of more intelligible and more modern expressions for difficult and antiquated words [2]. But they do not extend so far as to make the language of the Dharma-sûtra fully agree with that of the other sections of the collection, especially with the G*ri*hya-sûtra. Numerous discrepancies between these two parts are observable. Thus we read in the Hira*n*yake*s*i

---

[1] The subjoined pedigree of the Sûtrakâras of the Black Ya*g*ur-veda will perhaps make the above remarks and my interpretation of the statements of Mahâdeva and the other authorities mentioned above more intelligible :—

Khâ*nd*ika, taught the Taittirîya recension of the Black Ya*g*ur-veda.

(Successors of Khâ*nd*ika, number unknown, down to)

Baudhâyana, Prava*k*anakartâ, i. e. 1st Sûtrakâra, and founder of Baudhâyana-*k*ara*n*a.

(Successors of Baudhâyana down to fellow-pupil of Bhâradvâ*g*a, number unknown.)
(Successors of Baudhâyana after the schism down to the present day.)

Bhâradvâ*g*a, 2nd Sûtrakâra, and founder of Bhâradvâ*g*a-*k*ara*n*a.

(Successors of Bhâradvâ*g*a down to fellow-pupil of Âpastamba, number unknown.)
(Successors after the schism down to the present day.)

Âpastamba, 3rd Sûtrakâra, and founder of Âpastamba-*k*ara*n*a.

(Successors of Âpastamba down to fellow-pupil of Satyâshâ*dh*a Hira*n*yake*s*in, number unknown.)
(Successors of Âpastamba down to the present day.)

Satyâshâ*dh*a Hira*n*yake*s*in, 4th Sûtrakâra, and founder of Hira*n*yake*s*i-*k*ara*n*a.

(Successors of Satyâshâ*dh*a Hira*n*yake*s*in down to the present day.)

After the schism of Satyâshâ*dh*a Hira*n*yake*s*in the pedigree has not been continued, though Mahâdeva asserts that several other Sûtrakâras arose. But to work it out further would be useless.

[2] See Appendix II to Part I of my second edition of Âpastamba's Dharma-sûtra, p. 117 seqq.

Grihya-sûtra that a Brâhmana must, ordinarily, be initiated in his seventh year, while the rule of the Dharma-sûtra, which is identical with Âp. Dh. I, 1, 1, 18, prescribes that the ceremony shall take place in the eighth year after conception. The commentators, Mâtridatta on the Grihya-sûtra and Mahâdeva on the Dharma-sûtra, both state that the rule of the Grihya-sûtra refers to the seventh year after birth, and, therefore, in substance agrees with the Dharma-sûtra. They are no doubt right. But the difference in the wording shows that the two sections do not belong to the same author. The same inference may be drawn from the fact that the Hiranyakesi Grihya-sûtra, which is much longer than Âpastamba's, includes a considerable amount of matter which refers to the sacred law, and which is repeated in the Dharma-sûtra. According to a statement which I have heard from several learned Brâhmanas, the followers of Hiranyakesin, when pronouncing the samkalpa or solemn pledge to perform a ceremony, declare themselves to be members of the Hiranyakesi school that forms a subdivision of Âpastamba's (âpastambântargatahiranyakesisâkhâdhyâyî . . . aham). But I have not been able to find these words in the books treating of the ritual of the Hiranyakesins, such as the Mahesabhattî. If this assertion could be further corroborated, it would be an additional strong proof of the priority of Âpastamba, which, however, even without it may be accepted as a fact[1]. The distance in time between the two teachers is probably not so great as that between Âpastamba and Baudhâyana, as Mahâdeva mentions no intermediate Sûtrakâra between them. Still it is probably not less than 100 or 150 years.

The results of the above investigation which show that the origin of the Âpastamba school falls in the middle of the Sûtra period of the Black Yagur-veda, and that its Sûtras belong to the later, though not to the latest products of Vedic literature, are fully confirmed by an

[1] Compare also Dr. Winternitz's remarks on the dependence of the Grihya-sûtra of the Hiranyakesins on Âpastamba's, op. cit., p. 6 seqq., and the second edition of the Âp. Dh., Part I, p. xi.

examination of the quotations from and references to Vedic and other books contained in Âpastamba's Sûtras, and especially in the Dharma-sûtra. We find that all the four Vedas are quoted or referred to. The three old ones, the *Ri*k, Ya*g*us, and Sâman, are mentioned both separately and collectively by the name trayî vidyâ, i. e. threefold sacred science, and the fourth is called not Atharvâṅgirasa*h*, as is done in most ancient Sûtras, but Atharva-veda[1]. The quotations from the *Ri*k and Sâman are not very numerous. But a passage from the ninth Ma*nd*ala of the former, which is referred to Dh. I, 1, 2, 2, is of some extent, and shows that the recension which Âpastamba knew, did not differ from that which still exists. As Âpastamba was an adherent of the Black Ya*g*ur-veda, he quotes it, especially in the *S*rauta-sûtra, very frequently, and he adduces not only texts from the Mantra-sa*m*hitâ, but also from the Taittirîya-brâhma*n*a and Âra*n*yaka. The most important quotations from the latter work occur Dh. II, 2, 3, 16–II, 2, 4, 9, where all the Mantras to be recited during the performance of the Bali-offerings are enumerated. Their order agrees exactly with that in which they stand in the sixty-seventh Anuvâka of the tenth Prapâ*th*aka of the recension of the Âra*n*yaka which is current among the Ândhra Brâhma*n*as[2]. This last point is of considerable importance, both for the history of the text of that book and, as we shall see further on, for the history of the Âpastambîya school.

The White Ya*g*ur-veda, too, is quoted frequently in the *S*rauta-sûtra and once in the section on Dharma by the title Vâ*g*asaneyaka, while twice its Brâhma*n*a, the Vâ*g*asaneyi-brâhma*n*a, is cited. The longer one of the two passages, taken from the latter work, Dh. I, 4, 12, 3, does, however, not fully agree with the published text of the Mâdhyandina recension. Its wording possesses just sufficient resemblance to allow us to identify the passage which Âpastamba meant, but differs from the *S*atapatha-

[1] Âp. Dh. II, 11, 29, 12.

[2] The Taittirîya Âra*n*yaka exists in three recensions, the Kar*n*â*t*a, Drâvi*d*a, and the Ândhra, the first of which has been commented on by Sâya*n*a.

brâhma*n*a in many details[1]. The cause of these discrepancies remains doubtful for the present[2]. As regards the Atharva-veda, Âpastamba gives, besides the reference mentioned above and a second to the Âṅgirasa-pavitra[3], an abstract of a long passage from Atharva-veda XV, 10–13, regarding the treatment of a Vrâtya, i. e. a learned mendicant Brâhma*n*a, who really deserves the title of an atithi, or guest[4]. It is true that Âpastamba, in the passage referred to, does not say that his rule is based on the Atharva-veda. He merely says that a Brâhma*n*a is his authority. But it seems, nevertheless, certain that by the expression a Brâhma*n*a, the Brâhma*n*a-like fifteenth book of the Atharva-veda is meant, as the sentences to be addressed by the host to his guest agree literally with those which the Atharva-veda prescribes for the reception of a Vrâtya. Haradatta too, in his commentary, expresses the same opinion. Actual quotations from the Atharva-veda are not frequent in Vedic literature, and the fact that Âpastamba's Dharma-sûtra contains one, is, therefore, of some interest.

Besides these Vedic texts[5], Âpastamba mentions, also, the Aṅgas or auxiliary works, and enumerates six classes, viz. treatises on the ritual of the sacrifices, on grammar, astronomy, etymology, recitation of the Veda, and metrics[6]. The number is the same as that which is considered the correct one in our days[7].

As the Dharma-sûtra names no less than nine teachers in connection with various topics of the sacred law, and frequently appeals to the opinion of some (eke), it follows that a great many such auxiliary treatises must have existed in Âpastamba's time. The Â*k*âryas mentioned are Eka, Ka*n*va, Kâ*n*va, Ku*n*ika, Kutsa, Kautsa, Push-

[1] Compare on this point Professor Eggeling's remarks in Sacred Books of the East, vol. xii, p. xxxix seqq.

[2] See the passage from the *K*ara*n*avyûhabhâshya given below, ver. 10.

[3] Âp. Dh. I, 2, 2, 2. [4] Âp. Dh. II, 3, 7, 12–17.

[5] Some more are quoted in the *S*rauta-sûtra, see Professor Garbe in the Gurupû*g*âkaumudî, p. 33 seqq.

[6] Âp. Dh. II, 4, 8, 10.

[7] See also Max Müller, Hist. Anc. Sansk. Lit., p. 111.

karasâdi, Vârshyâya*n*i, *S*vetaketu, and Hârîta[1]. Some of these persons, like Hârîta and Ka*n*va, are known to have composed Sûtras on the sacred law, and fragments or modified versions of their works are still in existence, while Kâ*n*va, Kautsa, Pushkarasâdi or Paushkarasâdi, as the grammatically correct form of the name is, and Vârshyâya*n*i are quoted in the Nirukta, the Prâti*s*âkhyas, and the Vârttikas on Pâ*n*ini as authorities on phonetics, etymology, and grammar[2]. Kâ*n*va, finally, is considered the author of the still existing Kalpa-sûtras of the Kâ*n*va school connected with the White Ya*g*ur-veda. It seems not improbable that most of these teachers were authors of complete sets of Aṅgas. Their position in Vedic literature, however, except as far as Kâ*n*va, Hârîta, and *S*vetaketu are concerned, is difficult to define, and the occurrence of their names throws less light on the antiquity of the Âpastambîya school than might be expected. Regarding Hârîta it must, however, be noticed that he is one of the oldest authors of Sûtras, that he was an adherent of the Maitrâya*n*îya *S*âkhâ[3], and that he is quoted by Baudhâyana, Âpastamba's predecessor. The bearing of the occurrence of *S*vetaketu's name will be discussed below.

Of even greater interest than the names of the teachers are the indications which Âpastamba gives, that he knew two of the philosophical schools which still exist in India, viz. the Pûrvâ or Karma Mîmâ*m*sâ and the Vedânta. As regards the former, he mentions it by its ancient name, Nyâya, which in later times and at present is usually applied to the doctrine of Gautama Akshapâda. In two passages[4] he settles contested points on the authority of those who know the Nyâya, i. e. the Pûrvâ Mîmâ*m*sâ, and

---

[1] Âp. Dh. I, 6, 19, 3-8; I, 10, 28, 1-2; I, 4, 13, 10; I, 6, 18, 2; I, 6, 19, 12; I, 10, 28, 5, 16; I, 10, 29, 12-16.

[2] Max Müller, loc. cit., p. 142.

[3] A Dharma-sûtra, ascribed to this teacher, has been recovered of late, by Mr. Vâman Shâstrî Islâmpurkar. Though it is an ancient work, it does not contain Âpastamba's quotations, see Grundriss d. Indo-Ar. Phil. und Altertumsk., II, 8, 8.

[4] Âp. Dh. II, 4, 8, 13; II, 6, 14, 13.

in several other cases he adopts a line of reasoning which fully agrees with that followed in *G*aimini's Mîmâ*m*sâ-sûtras. Thus the arguments [1], that 'a revealed text has greater weight than a custom from which a revealed text may be inferred,' and that 'no text can be inferred from a custom for which a worldly motive is apparent,' exactly correspond with the teaching of *G*aimini's Mîmâ*m*sâ-sûtras I, 3, 3-4. The wording of the passages in the two works does not agree so closely that the one could be called a quotation of the other. But it is evident, that if Âpastamba did not know the Mîmâ*m*sâ-sûtras of *G*aimini, he must have possessed some other very similar work. As to the Vedânta, Âpastamba does not mention the name of the school. But Kha*nd*as 22, 23 of the first Pa*t*ala of the Dharma-sûtra unmistakably contain the chief tenets of the Vedântists, and recommend the acquisition of the knowledge of the Âtman as the best means for purifying the souls of sinners. Though these two Kha*nd*as are chiefly filled with quotations, which, as the commentator states, are taken from an Upanishad, still the manner of their selection, as well as Âpastamba's own words in the introductory and concluding Sûtras, indicates that he knew not merely the unsystematic speculations contained in the Upanishads and Âra*n*yakas, but a well-defined system of Vedântic philosophy identical with that of Bâdarâya*n*a's Brahma-sûtras. The fact that Âpastamba's Dharma-sûtra contains indications of the existence of these two schools of philosophy, is significant as the Pûrvâ Mîmâ*m*sâ occurs in one other Dharma-sûtra only, that attributed to Vasish*th*a, and as the name of the Vedânta school is not found in any of the prose treatises on the sacred law.

Of non-Vedic works Âpastamba mentions the Purâ*n*a. The Dharma-sûtra not only several times quotes passages from 'a Purâ*n*a' as authorities for its rules [2], but names in one case the Bhavishyat-purâ*n*a as the particular Purâ*n*a from which the quotation is taken [3]. References to the

[1] Âp. Dh. I, 1, 14, 8, 9-10.

[2] Âp. Dh. I, 6, 19, 13; I, 10, 29, 7.

[3] Âp. Dh. II, 9, 24, 6.

Purâ*n*a in general are not unfrequent in other Sûtras on the sacred law, and even in older Vedic works. But Âpastamba, as far as I know, is the only Sûtrakâra who specifies the title of a particular Purâ*n*a, and names one which is nearly or quite identical with that of a work existing in the present day, and he is the only one, whose quotations can be shown to be, at least in part, genuine Paurâ*n*ic utterances.

Among the so-called Upa-purâ*n*as we find one of considerable extent which bears the title Bhavishya-purâ*n*a or also Bhavishyat-purâ*n*a[1]. It is true that the passage quoted in the Dharma-sûtra from the Bhavishyat-purâ*n*a is not to be found in the copy of the Bhavishya-purâ*n*a which I have seen. It is, therefore, not possible to assert positively that Âpastamba knew the present homonymous work. Still, considering the close resemblance of the two titles, and taking into account the generally admitted fact that most if not all Purâ*n*as have been remodelled and recast[2], it seems to me not unlikely that Âpastamba's

[1] Aufrecht, Catalogus Catalogorum, p. 400.

[2] Max Müller, Hist. Anc. Sansk. Lit., pp. 40–42. Weber, Literaturgeschichte, pp. 206–208. Though I fully subscribe to the opinion, held by the most illustrious Sanskritists, that, in general, the existing Purâ*n*as are not identical with the works designated by that title in Vedic works, still I cannot believe that they are altogether independent of the latter. Nor can I agree to the assertion that the Purâ*n*as known to us, one and all, are not older than the tenth or eleventh century A. D. That is inadmissible, because Bêrûnî (India, I, 131) enumerates them as canonical books. And his frequent quotations from them prove that in 1030 A. D. they did not differ materially from those known to us (see Indian Antiquary, 19, 382 seqq.). Another important fact bearing on this point may be mentioned here, viz. that the poet Bâ*n*a, who wrote shortly after 600 A. D., in the *S*rîharsha*k*arita, orders his Paurâ*n*ika to recite the Pavanaprokta-purâ*n*a, i. e. the Vâyu-purâ*n*a (Harsha*k*arita, p. 61, Calcutta ed.). Dr. Hall, the discoverer of the life of Harsha, read in his copy Yavanaprokta-purâ*n*a, a title which, as he remarks, might suggest the idea that Bâ*n*a knew the Greek epic poetry. But a comparison of the excellent Ahmadâbâd and Benares Devanâgarî MSS. and of the Ka*s*mîr *S*âradâ copies shows that the correct reading is the one given above. The earlier history of the Purâ*n*as, which as yet is a mystery, will only be cleared up when a real history of the orthodox Hindu sects, especially of the *S*ivites and Vish*n*uites, has been written. It will, then, probably become apparent that the origin of these sects reaches back far beyond the rise of Buddhism and Jainism. It will also be proved

authority was the original on which the existing Upapurâ*n*a is based. And in favour of this view it may be urged that passages, similar to Âpastamba's quotation, actually occur in our Paurâ*n*ic texts. In the *G*yotishpra*k*âra section of several of the chief Purâ*n*as we find, in connection with the description of the Path of the Manes (pit*ri*yâ*n*a)[1], the assertion that the pious sages, who had offspring and performed the Agnihotra, reside there until the general destruction of created things (â bhûtasa*m*plavât), as well as, that in the beginning of each new creation they are the propagators of the world (lokasya sa*m*tânakarâ*h*) and, being re-born, re-establish the sacred law. Though the wording differs, these passages fully agree in sense with Âpastamba's Bhavishyat-purâ*n*a which says, 'They (the ancestors) live in heaven until the (next) general destruction of created things. At the new creation (of the world) they become the seed.' In other passages of the Purâ*n*as, which refer to the successive creations, we find even the identical terms used in the quotation. Thus the Vâyup., Adhy. 8, 23, declares that those beings, which have gone to the *G*analoka, 'become the seed at the new creation' (puna*h* sarge . . . bîgârtha*m* tâ bhavanti hi).

These facts prove at all events that Âpastamba took his quotation from a real Purâ*n*a, similar to those existing. If it is literal and exact, it shows, also, that the Purâ*n*as of his time contained both prose and verse.

Further, it is possible to trace yet another of Âpastamba's quotations from 'a Purâ*n*a.' The three Purâ*n*as, mentioned above, give, immediately after the passages referred to, enlarged versions of the two verses[2] regarding the sages, who begot offspring and obtained 'burial-grounds,' and

that the orthodox sects used Purâ*n*as as text books for popular readings, the Purâ*n*apâ*th*ana of our days, and that some, at least, of the now existing Purâ*n*as are the latest recensions of those mentioned in Vedic books.

[1] Vâyup., Adhy. 50, 208 seqq.; Matsyap., Adhy. 123, 96 seqq.; Vish*n*up. II, 8. 86–89; H. H. Wilson, Vish*n*up., vol. ii, pp. 263–268 (ed. Hall).

[2] Âp. Dh. II, 9, 23, 4–5.

regarding those who, remaining chaste, gained immortality[1]. In this case Âpastamba's quotation can be restored almost completely, if certain interpolations are cut out. And it is evident that Âpastamba has preserved genuine Paurâ*n*ic verses in their ancient form. A closer study of the unfortunately much neglected Purâ*n*as, no doubt, will lead to further identifications of other quotations, which will be of considerable interest for the history of Indian literature.

There is yet another point on which Âpastamba shows a remarkable agreement with a theory which is prevalent in later Sanskrit literature. He says (Dh. II, 11, 29, 11-12), 'The knowledge which *S*ûdras and women possess, is the completion of all study,' and 'they declare that this knowledge is a supplement of the Atharva-veda.' The commentator remarks with reference to these two Sûtras, that 'the knowledge which *S*ûdras and women possess,' is the knowledge of dancing, acting, music, and other branches of the so-called Artha*s*âstra, the science of useful arts and of trades, and that the object of the Sûtras is to forbid the study of such matters before the acquisition of sacred learning. His interpretation is, without doubt, correct, as similar sentiments are expressed by other teachers in parallel passages. But, if it is accepted, Âpastamba's remark that 'the knowledge of *S*ûdras and women is a supplement of the Atharva-veda,' proves that he knew the division of Hindu learning which is taught in Madhusûdana Sarasvatî's Prasthânabheda[2]. For Madhusûdana allots to each Veda an Upa-veda or supplementary Veda, and asserts that the Upa-veda of the Atharva-veda is the Artha*s*âstra. The agreement of Âpastamba with the modern writers on this point, furnishes, I think, an additional argument that he belongs to the later Vedic schoolmen.

In addition to this information regarding the relative position of the Âpastambîya school in ancient Sanskrit literature, we possess some further statements as to the

[1] An abbreviated version of the same verses, ascribed to the Paurâ*n*ikas, occurs in *S*aṅkarâ*k*ârya's Comm. on the *Kh*ândogya Up., p. 336 (Bibl. Ind.).

[2] Weber, Ind. Stud. I, 1-24.

part of India to which it belongs, and these, as it happens, are of great importance for fixing approximately the period in which the school arose. According to the Brahmanical tradition, which is supported by a hint contained in the Dharma-sûtra and by information derivable from inscriptions and the actual state of things in modern India, the Âpastambîyas belong to Southern India, and their founder probably was a native of or resided in the Ândhra country. The existence of this tradition, which to the present day prevails among the learned Brahmans of Western India and Benares, may be substantiated by a passage from the above-mentioned commentary of the *K*ara*n*avyûha[1], which,

---

[1] *K*ara*n*avyûhabhâshya, fol. 15ª, l. 4 seqq. :—

तत्र प्राच्योदीच्यां नैर्ऋत्यां नैर्ऋत्यास्तत्र (?) वाजसनेयानां पञ्चदश भेदा भवन्ति । प्राच्योदीच्यनैर्ऋत्यास्तिस्रो दिशायां (?) वाजसनेयवेदोत्पत्तिः ऋग्रे वक्ष्यामः (?) । इतरदेशेषु वेदशाखयोर्विभाग उच्यते । स च महार्णवे ।

पृथिव्या मध्यरेखा च नर्मदा परिकीर्तिता ।
दक्षिणोत्तरयोर्भागे शाखाभेदाश्च [दश्च] उच्यते ॥१॥
नर्मदा दक्षिणे भागे (sic) आपस्तम्ब्याश्वलायनी ।
राणायणी पिप्पला च यज्ञकन्याविभागिनः ॥२॥
माध्यन्दिनी शाखा[शाङ्खा]यनी कौथुमी शौनकी तथा ।
नर्मदोत्तरभागे च यज्ञकन्याविभागिनः ॥३॥
तुङ्गा कृष्णा तथा गोदा सह्याद्रिशिखरावधि ।
आन्ध्रदेशपर्यन्तं बह्वृचश्चाश्वलायनी ॥४॥
उत्तरे गुर्जरे देशे बह्वृचकीर्तितः [चाः परिकीर्तिताः] ।
कौषीतकी [कि] ब्राह्मणं च शाखा शाङ्खायनी स्थिता ॥५॥
आन्ध्रादिदक्षिणाग्नेयीगोदासागर आवधि (sic) ।
यजुर्वेदस्तु तैत्तियों आपस्तम्बी प्रतिष्ठिता ॥६॥
सह्याद्रिपर्वतारम्भाद्दिशां नैऋत्यसागरात् (sic) ।
हिरण्यकेशी[शि]शाखा पर्शुरामस्य (sic) संनिधौ ॥७॥
मयूरपर्वताच्चैव यावद्गुर्जरदेशतः ।
व्याप्ता व्या[वा]यव्यदेशात्तु मैत्रायणी प्रतिष्ठिता ॥८॥
अङ्गवङ्गकलिङ्गाश्च कानीमो (?) गुर्जरास्तथा (sic) ।
वाजसनीय [नेय] शाखा च माध्यंदिनी प्रतिष्ठिता ॥९॥
ऋषिणा याज्ञवल्क्येन सर्वदेशेषु विस्तृता ।
वाजसनीय [नेय] वेदस्य प्रथमा कण्व[काण्व]संज्ञकेति ॥१०॥

though written in barbarous Sanskrit, and of quite modern origin, possesses great interest, because its description of the geographical distribution of the Vedas and Vedic schools is not mentioned elsewhere. The verses from a work entitled Mahâr*n*ava, which are quoted there, state that the earth, i.e. India, is divided into two equal halves by the river Narmadâ (Nerbudda), and that the school of Âpastamba prevails in the southern half (ver. 2). It is further alleged (ver. 6) that the Ya*g*ur-veda of Tittiri and the Âpastambîya school are established in the Ândhra country and other parts of the south and south-east up to the mouth of the Godâvarî (godâsâgara-âvadhi). According to the Mahâr*n*ava the latter river marks, therefore, the northern frontier of the territory occupied by the Âpastambîyas, which comprises the Marâ*th*a and Kâ*n*ara districts of the Bombay Presidency, the greater part of the Nizâm's dominions, Berar, and the Madras Presidency, with the exception of the northern Sirkârs and the western coast. This assertion agrees, on the whole, with the actual facts which have fallen under my observation. A great number of the De*s*astha-brâhma*n*as in the Nâsik, Pu*n*a, Ahmadnagar, Sâtârâ, Sholâpur, and Kolhâpur districts, and of the Kâ*n*arâ or Kar*n*â*t*aka-brâhma*n*as in the Belgâm, Dhârvâ*d*, Kalâ*d*ghî, and Karvâ*d* collectorates, as well as a smaller number among the *K*ittapâvanas of the Koṅka*n*a are Âpastambîyas. Of the Nizâm's dominions and the Madras Presidency I possess no local knowledge. But I can say that I have met many followers of Âpastamba among the Teliṅgana-brâhma*n*as settled in Bombay, and that the frequent occurrence of MSS. containing the Sûtras of the Âpastambîya school in the Madras Presidency proves that the *K*ara*n*a there must count many adherents. On the other hand, I have never met with any Âpastambîyas among the ancient indigenous subdivisions of the Brahmanical community dwelling north of the Marâ*th*â country and north of the Narmadâ. A few Brâhma*n*as of this school, no doubt, are scattered over Gu*g*arât and Central India, and others are found in the great places of pilgrimage in Hindustan proper. The former mostly have immigrated during the last century, following the Marâ*th*â chieftains who conquered large portions of those countries, or have been imported in the present century by the Marâ*th*â rulers of Gwalior, Indor, and Baroda. The settlers in Benares, Mathurâ, and other sacred cities also, have chiefly come in modern times, and not unfrequently live on the bounty of the Marâ*th*â princes. But all of them consider themselves and are considered by the Brâhma*n*as, who are indigenous in those districts and towns, as aliens, with whom intermarriage and commensality are not permitted. The indigenous sections of the Brâhma*n*as of Gu*g*arât, such as the Nâgaras, Khe*d*âvals, Bhârgavas, Kapilas, and Motâlâs, belong, if they are adherents of the Ya*g*ur-veda, to the Mâdhyandina or Kâ*n*va schools of the White Ya*g*ur-veda. The same is the case with the Brâhma*n*as of Ra*g*putâna, Hindustan, and the Pa*ñg*ab. In Central India, too, the White Ya*g*ur-veda prevails; but, besides the two schools mentioned above, there are still some colonies of Maitrâya*n*îyas or Mânavas[1]. It seems, also, that the restriction of the Âpastambîya school to the south of India, or rather to those subdivisions of the Brahmanical community which for a long time have been settled in the south and are generally considered as natives of the south, is not of recent date. For it is a significant fact that the numerous ancient landgrants which have been found all over India indicate exactly the same state of things. I am not aware that in any grant issued by a king of a northern dynasty to Brâhma*n*as who are natives of the northern half of India, an Âpastambîya is mentioned as donee. But among the southern landgrants there are several on which the name of the school appears. Thus in a *s*âsana of king Harihara of Vidyânagara, dated *S*akasa*m*vat 1317 or 1395 A.D., one of the recipients of the royal bounty is 'the learned Ananta Dîkshita, son of Râmabha*tt*a, chief

[1] See Bhâû Dâ*g*î, Journ. Bombay Br. Roy. As. Soc. X, 40. Regarding the Maitrâya*n*îyas in Gu*g*arât, of whom the *K*ara*n*avyûha speaks, compare my Report on the Search for Sanskrit MSS., 1879–80, p. 3.

of the Âpastambya (read Âpastambîya) *s*âkhâ, a scion of the Vasish*th*a gotra[1].' Further, the eastern *K*âlukya king Vi*g*ayâditya II[2], who ruled, according to Dr. Fleet, from A.D. 799-843, presented a village to six students of the Hira*n*yake*s*i-sûtra and to eighteen students of the Apastamba, *recte* the Âpastamba-sûtra. Again, in the above-mentioned earlier grant of the Pallava king Nandivarman, there are forty-two students of the Âpastambha-sûtra[3] among the 108 sharers of the village of Udaya*k*andramaṅgalam. Finally, on an ancient set of plates written in the characters which usually are called cave-characters, and issued by the Pallava king Si*m*havarman II, we find among the donees five Âpastambhîya Brâhma*n*as, who, together with a Haira*n*yakesa, a Vâ*g*asaneya, and a Sâma-vedî, received the village of Maṅgadûr, in Veṅgŏrâsh*t*ra[4]. This inscription is, to judge from the characters, thirteen to fourteen hundred years old, and on this account a very important witness for the early existence of the Âpastambîyas in Southern India.

Under the circumstances just mentioned, a casual remark made by Âpastamba, in describing the *S*râddhas or funeral oblations, acquires considerable importance. He says (Dh. II, 7, 17, 17) that the custom of pouring water into the hands of Brâhma*n*as invited to a *S*râddha prevails among the northerners, and he indicates thereby that he himself does not belong to the north of India. If this statement is taken together with the above-stated facts, which tend to show that the Âpastambîyas were and are restricted to the south of India, the most probable construction which can be put on it is that Âpastamba declares himself to be a southerner. There is yet another indication to the same effect contained in the Dharma-sûtra. It has been pointed

[1] Colebrooke, Essays, II, p. 264, ver. 24 (Madras ed.)

[2] See Hultzsch, South Indian Inscriptions, vol. i, p. 31 seqq., and Indian Antiquary, ol. xx, p. 414 seqq.

[3] Âpastambha may be a mistake for Âpastamba. But the form with the aspirate occurs also in the earlier Pallava grant and in Devapâla's commentary on the Kâ*th*aka G*ri*hya-sûtra.

[4] Ind. Ant. V, 135.

out above that the recension of the Taittirîya Âra*n*yaka which Âpastamba recognises is that called the Ândhra text or the version current in the Ândhra country, by which term the districts in the south-east of India between the Godâvarî and the K*ri*sh*n*â have to be understood[1]. Now it seems exceedingly improbable that a Vedic teacher would accept as authoritative any other version of a sacred work except that which was current in his native country. It would therefore follow, from the adoption of an Ândhra text by Âpastamba, that he was born in that country, or, at least, had resided there so long as to have become naturalised in it. With respect to this conclusion it must also be kept in mind that the above-quoted passage from the Mahâr*n*ava particularly specifies the Ândhra country (ândhrâdi) as the seat of the Âpastambîyas. It may be that this is due to an accident. But it seems to me more probable that the author of the Mahâr*n*ava wished to mark the Ândhra territory as the chief and perhaps as the original residence of the Âpastambîyas.

This discovery has, also, a most important bearing on the question of the antiquity of the school of Âpastamba. It fully confirms the result of the preceding enquiry, viz. that the Âpastambîyas are one of the later *K*ara*n*as. For the south of India and the nations inhabiting it, such as Kaliṅgas, Dravi*d*as, Andhras, *K*olas, and Pâ*nd*yas, do not play any important part in the ancient Brahmanical traditions and in the earliest history of India, the centre of both of which lies in the north-west or at least north of the Vindhya range. Hitherto it has not been shown that the south and the southern nations are mentioned in any of the Vedic Sa*m*hitâs. In the Brâhma*n*as and in the Sûtras they do occur, though they are named rarely and in a not complimentary manner. Thus the Aitareya-brâhma*n*a gives the names of certain degraded, barbarous tribes, and among them that of the Andhras[2], in whose country, as

[1] See Cunningham, Geography, p. 527 seqq.; Burnell, South Ind. Pal., p. 14, note 2.

[2] Aitareya-brâhma*n*a VII, 18.

has been shown, the Âpastambîyas probably originated. Again, Baudhâyana, in his Dharma-sûtra I, 1, quotes some verses in which it is said that he who visits the Kaliṅgas must purify himself by the performance of certain sacrifices in order to become fit for again associating with Aryans. The same author, also, mentions distinctive forbidden practices (â*k*âra) prevailing in the south (loc. cit.). Further, Pâ*n*ini's grammatical Sûtras and Kâtyâyana's Vârttikas thereon contain rules regarding several words which presuppose an acquaintance with the south and the kingdoms which flourished there. Thus Pâ*n*ini, IV, 2, 98, teaches the formation of dâkshi*n*âtya in the sense of 'belonging to or living in the south or the Dekhan,' and a Vârttika of Kâtyâyana on Pâ*n*ini, IV, 1, 175, states that the words *K*ola and Pâ*nd*ya are used as names of the princes ruling over the *K*ola and Pâ*nd*ya countries, which, as is known from history, were situated in the extreme south of India. The other southern nations and a fuller description of the south occur first in the Mahâbhârata [1]. While an acquaintance with the south can thus be proved only by a few books belonging to the later stages of Vedic literature, several of the southern kingdoms are named already in the oldest historical documents. A*s*oka in his edicts [2], which date from the second half of the third century B.C., calls the *K*olas, Pâ*nd*yas, and the Keralaputra or Ketalaputra his pratyantas (pra*k*antâ) or neighbours. The same monarch informs us also that he conquered the province of Kaliṅga and annexed it to his kingdom [3], and his remarks on the condition of the province show that it was thoroughly imbued with the Aryan civilisation [4]. The same fact is attested still more clearly by the annals of the *K*eta king of Kaliṅga, whose thirteenth year fell in the 165th year of the Maurya era or about 150 B.C. [5] The early

[1] Lassen, Ind. Alterthumskunde, I, 684, 2nd ed.

[2] Edict II, Epigraphia Indica, vol. ii, pp. 449–450, 466.

[3] Edict XIII, op. cit., pp. 462–465, 470–472.

[4] See also Indian Antiquary, vol. xxiii, p. 246.

[5] Actes du 6ième Congrès Int. d. Orient., vol. iii, 2, 135 seqq., where, however, the beginning of the Maurya era is placed wrongly in the eighth year of A*s*oka.

spread of the Aryan civilisation to the eastern coast-districts between the Godâvarî and the Kr*i*sh*n*â is proved by the inscriptions on the Bha*tt*iprolu relic caskets, which probably belong to the period of 200 B.C.[1] Numerous inscriptions in the Buddhist caves of Western India[2], as well as coins, prove the existence during the last centuries before, and the first centuries after, the beginning of our era of a powerful empire of the Andhras, the capital of which was probably situated near the modern Amarâvatî on the lower Kr*i*sh*n*â. The princes of the latter kingdom, though great patrons of the Buddhist monks, appear to have been Brahmanists or adherents of the ancient orthodox faith which is founded on the Vedas. For one of them is called Vedisiri (vedi*s*rî), 'he whose glory is the Vedi,' and another Yañasiri (ya*g*ña*s*rî), 'he whose glory is the sacrifice,' and a very remarkable inscription on the Nânâghât[3] contains a curious catalogue of sacrificial fees paid to priests (dakshi*n*â) for the performance of *S*rauta sacrifices. For the third and the later centuries of our era the information regarding Southern India becomes fuller and fuller. Very numerous inscriptions, the accounts of the Buddhist chroniclers of Ceylon, of the Greek geographers, and of the Chinese pilgrims, reveal the existence and give fragments, at least, of the history of many kingdoms in the south, and show that their civilisation was an advanced one, and did not differ materially from that of Northern India.

There can be no doubt that the south of India has been conquered by the Aryans, and has been brought within the pale of Brahmanical civilisation much later than India north of the Vindhya range. During which century precisely that conquest took place, cannot be determined for the present. But it would seem that it happened a considerable time before the Vedic period came to an end, and it certainly was an accomplished fact, long before the

---

[1] Epigraphia Indica, vol. ii, p. 323 seqq.

[2] See Burgess, Arch. Surv. Reports, West India, vol. iv, pp. 104-114 and vol. v, p. 75 seqq.

[3] Op. cit., vol. v, p. 39 seqq. Its date probably falls between 150-140 B.C.

authentic history of India begins, about 500 B.C., with the Persian conquest of the Pañgab and Sindh. It may be added that a not inconsiderable period must have elapsed after the conquest of the south, before the Aryan civilisation had so far taken root in the conquered territory, that, in its turn, it could become a centre of Brahmanical activity, and that it could produce new Vedic schools.

These remarks will suffice to show that a Vedic *K*ara*n*a which had its origin in the south, cannot rival in antiquity those whose seat is in the north, and that all southern schools must belong to a comparatively recent period of Vedic history. For this reason, and because the name of Âpastamba and of the Âpastambîyas is not mentioned in any Vedic work, not even in a Kalpa-sûtra, and its occurrence in the older grammatical books, written before the beginning of our era, is doubtful [1], it might be thought advisable to fix the terminus a quo for the composition of the Âpastambîya-sûtras about or shortly before the beginning of the era, when the Brahmanist Ândhra kings held the greater part of the south under their sway. It seems to me, however, that such a hypothesis is not tenable, as there are several points which indicate that the school and its writings possess a much higher antiquity. For, first, the Dharma-sûtra contains a remarkable passage in which its author states that *S*vetaketu, one of the Vedic teachers who is mentioned in the *S*atapatha-brâhma*n*a and in the *Kh*ândogya Upanishad, belongs to the Avaras, to the men of later, i.e. of his own times. The passage referred to, Dh. I, 2, 5, 4–6, has been partly quoted above in order to show that Âpastamba laid no claim to the title *Ri*shi, or seer of revealed texts. It has been stated that according to Sûtra 4, 'No *Ri*shis are born among the Avaras, the men of later ages, on account of the prevailing transgression of the rules of studentship;' and that according to Sûtra 5,

[1] The name Âpastamba occurs only in the ga*n*a vidâdi, which belongs to Pâ*n*ini IV, 1, 104, and the text of this ga*n*a is certain only for the times of the Kâ*s*ikâ, about 650 A.D. The *S*rauta-sûtra of Âpastamba is mentioned in the nearly contemporaneous commentary of Bhart*ri*hari on the Mahâbhâshya, see Zeitschr. d. Deutschen Morg. Ges., vol. xxxvi, p. 654.

'Some in their new birth become similar to *Ri*shis by their knowledge of the Veda (*s*rutarshi) through a residue of merit acquired in former existences.' In order to give an illustration of the latter case, the author adds in Sûtra 6, 'Like *S*vetaketu.' The natural, and in my opinion, the only admissible interpretation of these words is, that Âpastamba considers *S*vetaketu to be one of the Avaras, who by virtue of a residue of merit became a *S*rutarshi. This is also the view of the commentator Haradatta, who, in elucidation of Sûtra 6, quotes the following passage from the *Kh*ândogya Upanishad (VI, 1, 1–2):

'1. Verily, there lived *S*vetaketu, a descendant of Aru*n*a. His father spake unto him, "O *S*vetaketu, dwell as a student (with a teacher); for, verily, dear child, no one in our family must neglect the study of the Veda and become, as it were, a Brâhma*n*a in name only."

'Verily, he (*S*vetaketu) was initiated at the age of twelve years, and when twenty-four years old he had learned all the Vedas; he thought highly of himself and was vain of his learning and arrogant.'

There can be no doubt that this is the person and the story referred to in the Dharma-sûtra. For the fact which the Upanishad mentions, that *S*vetaketu learned all the Vedas in twelve years, while the Sm*ri*tis declare forty-eight years to be necessary for the accomplishment of that task, makes Âpastamba's illustration intelligible and appropriate. A good deal more is told in the *Kh*ândogya Upanishad about this *S*vetaketu, who is said to have been the son of Uddâlaka and the grandson of Aru*n*a (âru*n*eya). The same person is also frequently mentioned in the *S*atapatha-brâhma*n*a. In one passage of the latter work, which has been translated by Professor Max Müller[1], it is alleged that he was a contemporary of Yâ*gñ*avalkya, the promulgator of the White Ya*g*ur-veda, and of the learned king *G*anaka of Videha, who asked him about the meaning of the Agnihotra sacrifice. Now, as has been shown above, Âpastamba knew and quotes the White Ya*g*ur-veda and

[1] Hist. Anc. Sansk. Lit., p. 421 seq.

the *S*atapatha-brâhma*n*a. The passage of the latter work, which he quotes, is even taken from the same book in which the story about *S*vetaketu and *G*anaka occurs. The fact, therefore, that Âpastamba places a teacher whom he must have considered as a contemporary of the promulgator of the White Ya*g*ur-veda among the Avaras, is highly interesting and of some importance for the history of Vedic literature. On the one hand it indicates that Âpastamba cannot have considered the White Ya*g*ur-veda, such as it has been handed down in the schools of the *K*â*n*vas and Mâdhyandinas, to belong to a remote antiquity. On the other hand it makes the inference which otherwise might be drawn from the southern origin of the Âpastambîya school and from the non-occurrence of its name in the early grammatical writings, viz. that its founder lived not long before the beginning of our era, extremely improbable. For even if the term Avara is not interpreted very strictly and allowed to mean not exactly a contemporary, but a person of comparatively recent times, it will not be possible to place between *S*vetaketu and Âpastamba a longer interval than, at the utmost, two or three hundred years. *S*vetaketu and Yâ*gñ*avalkya would accordingly, at the best, find their places in the fourth or fifth century B. C., and the *S*atapatha-brâhma*n*a as well as all other Vedic works, which narrate incidents from their lives, must have been composed or at least edited still later. Though little is known regarding the history of the Vedic texts, still it happens that we possess some information regarding the texts in question. For we know from a statement made by Kâtyâyana in a Vârttika on Pâ*n*ini IV, 3, 105, and from Patañ*g*ali's commentary on his words that the Brâhma*n*a proclaimed by Yâ*gñ*avalkya, i.e. the *S*atapatha-brâhma*n*a of the White Ya*g*ur-veda, was considered to have been promulgated by one of the Ancients, in the times of these two writers, i.e. probably in the fourth and second centuries B. C.[1]

[1] This famous Vârttika has been interpreted in various ways; see Max Müller, Hist. Anc. Sansk. Lit., pp. 360–364; Goldstücker, Pâ*n*ini, pp. 132–140; Weber,

These considerations will show that it is necessary to allow for Âpastamba a much higher antiquity than the first century B.C.

The same inference may also be drawn from another series of facts, viz. the peculiarities of the language of his Sûtras. The latter are very considerable and very remarkable. They may be classed under four heads. In the Âpastambîya Dharma-sûtra we have, first, archaic words and forms either occurring in other Vedic writings or formed according to the analogy of Vedic usage; secondly, ancient forms and words specially prescribed by Pâ*n*ini, which have not been traced except in Âpastamba's Sûtras; thirdly, words and forms which are both against Vedic usage and against Pâ*n*ini's rules, and which sometimes find their analogies in the ancient Prakrits; and fourthly, anomalies in the construction of sentences. To the first class belong, kravyâdas, I, 7, 21, 15, carnivorous, formed according to the analogy of *ris*âdas; the frequent use of the singular dâra, e.g. II, 1, 1, 17–18, a wife, instead of the plural dârâ*h*; salâv*ri*kî, I, 3, 10, 19, for sâlav*ri*kî; the substitution of *l* for *r* in pleṅkha, I, 11, 31, 14; occa-

Ind. Stud. V, 65–74; XIII, 443, 444. As regards the explanation of Kâtyâyana's and Pata*ñg*ali's words, I side with Kaiya*t*a and Professor Goldstücker. But I am unable to follow the latter in the inferences which he draws from the fact, that Kâtyâyana and Pata*ñg*ali declare Yâg*ñ*avalkya and other sages to be as ancient as those whose Brâhma*n*as and Kalpas are designated by the plural of adjectives formed by the addition of the affix in to the names of the promulgators. Though Pâ*n*ini asserts, IV, 3, 105, that only those Brâhma*n*as which are known by appellations like Bhâllavina*h*, Kaushîtakina*h*, &c., have been proclaimed by ancient sages, and though Kâtyâyana and the author of the Great Commentary add that this rule does not hold good in the case of the work called Yâg*ñ*avalkâni Brâhma*n*âni, it does not necessarily follow, as Professor Goldstücker thinks, that an extraordinarily long interval lies between Pâ*n*ini and Kâtyâyana—so long a period that what Pâ*n*ini considered to be recent had become ancient in Kâtyâyana's time. Professor Weber has rightly objected to this reasoning. The difference between the statements of the two grammarians may have been caused by different traditions prevailing in different schools, or by an oversight on the part of Pâ*n*ini, which, as the scene of Yâg*ñ*avalkya's activity seems to have been Videha in eastern India, while Pâ*n*ini belonged to the extreme north-west, is not at all improbable. As regards the two dates, I place, following, with Professor Max Müller. the native tradition, Kâtyâyana in the fourth century B.C., and Pata*ñg*ali, with Professors Goldstücker, Kern, and Bhâ*nd*arkar, between 178–140 B.C.

sional offences against the rules of internal and external Sandhi, e.g. in agrihyamânakâranah, I, 4, 12, 8; in sku'ptvâ, I, 11, 31, 22, the irregular absolutive of skubh or of sku; in pâdûna, I, 1, 2, 13; in adhâsanasâyin, I, 1, 2, 21; and in sarvatopeta, I, 6, 19, 8; the neglect of the rule requiring vriddhi in the first syllable of the name Pushkarasâdi, I, 10, 28, 1; the irregular instrumentals vidyâ, I, 11, 30, 3, for vidyayâ, and nihsreyasâ, II, 7, 16, 2, for nihsreyasena; the nominatives dual âvam, I, 7, 20, 6, for âvâm, and kruñkakrauñka, I, 5, 17, 36 for °krauñkau; and the potentials in îta, such as prakshâlayîta, I, 1, 2, 28; abhiprasârayîta, I, 2, 6, 3, &c.

Among the words mentioned by Pânini, but not traced except in the Dharma-sûtra, may be enumerated the verb strih, to do damage, I, 11, 31, 9; the verb srinkh, to sneeze, from which srinkhânikâ, I, 5, 16, 14, and nihsrinkhana, II, 2, 5, 9, are derived; and the noun vedâdhyâya, I, 9, 24, 6; II, 4, 8, 5, in the sense of a student of the Veda. Words offending against rules given by Pânini, without being either archaic or Prakritic, are e.g. sarvânnin, I, 6, 18, 33, one who eats anybody's food, which, according to Pânini V, 2, 9, should be sarvânnîna; sarpasîrshin, I, 5, 17, 39; annasamskartri, a cook, II, 3, 6, 16; dhârmya, righteous, for dharmya, I, 2, 7, 21, and elsewhere; dîvitri, a gambler, II, 10, 25, 13, for devitri, the very remarkable form prâsñâti, I, 1, 4, 1, for prâsnâti, finds an analogy in the Vedic snyaptre for snaptre[1] and in Pali, pañha from prasña for prasna; and the curious compounds avâṅgagra, I, 1, 2, 38, parâṅgâvritta, II, 5, 10, 11, where the first parts show the forms of the nominative instead of the base, and pratisûryamatsyah, I, 3, 11, 31, which as a copulative compound is wrong, though not without analogies in Prakrit and in later Sanskrit[2]. The irregular forms caused by the same tendencies as those which effected the formation of the

[1] Wackernagel, Altindische Grammatik, vol. i, p. xxxiii.

[2] See Zeitschr. d. Deutschen Morg. Ges., vol. xl, p. 539 seq.; Epigraphia Indica, vol. i, p. 3.

Prakrit languages, are, avipraktramina, II, 2, 5, 2, for avipraktramana, where an *a* standing in thesi has been changed to *i*; sâmvrittih, II, 3, 6, 13, sâmvartete, II, 5, 11, 20, and paryânta, I, 3, 9, 21, and I, 3, 11, 33 (compare Marâthî âmt for antah), in each of which *a* standing before a nasal has been lengthened; anika, I, 6, 19, 1, the initial *a* of which stands for *ri*, if it really has the meaning of rinika, as some commentators asserted; anulepana, I, 3, 11, 13; I, 11, 32, 5, with the Prakritic change of na to na; vyupagâva, I, 2, 8, 15, with va for pa; ritve for ritvye, where *y* seems to have been absorbed by the following *e*; apassayîta, I, 11, 32, 16, for apâsrayîta, and bhatrivyatikrama, I, 10, 28, 20, where *r* has been assimilated to the preceding, or has been lost before the following consonant. The irregularities in the construction are less frequent. But in two Sûtras, I, 3, 10, 2, and I, 3, 11, 31, some words which ought to stand in the locative case have the terminations of the nominative, and it looks as if the author had changed his mind about the construction which he meant to use. In a third passage II, 10, 26, 20, sisnakkhedanam savrishanasya, the adjective which is intended to qualify the noun sisna has been placed in the genitive case, though the noun has been made the first part of a compound.

The occurrence of so many irregularities[1] in so small a treatise as the Dharma-sûtra is, proves clearly that the author did not follow Pânini's grammar, and makes it very unlikely that he knew it at all. If the anomalous forms used by Âpastamba all agreed with the usage of the other Sûtrakâras, known to us, it might be contended that, though acquainted with the rules of the great grammarian, he had elected to adopt by preference the language of the Vedic schools. But this is by no means the case. The majority of the irregular forms are peculiar to Âpastamba. As it is thus not probable that Âpastamba employed his peculiar expressions in obedience to the tradition of the

[1] Many more may be collected from the other divisions of the body of Sûtras. See Winternitz, op. cit., p. 13 seqq.; Gurupûgâkaumudî, p. 34 seq.

Vedic schools or of his particular school, he must have either been unacquainted with Pâ*n*ini or have considered his teachings of no great importance. In other words, he must either have lived earlier than Pâ*n*ini or before Pâ*n*ini's grammar had acquired general fame throughout India, and become the standard authority for Sanskrit authors. In either case so late a date as 150 B.C. or the first century B.C. would not fit. For Pata*ñg*ali's Mahâbhâshya furnishes abundant proof that at the time of its composition, in the second century B.C., Pâ*n*ini's grammar occupied a position similar to that which it holds now, and has held since the beginning of our era in the estimation of the learned of India. On linguistic grounds it seems to me Âpastamba cannot be placed later than the third century B.C., and if his statement regarding *S*vetaketu is taken into account, the lower limit for the composition of his Sûtras must be put further back by 150–200 years.

But sufficient space has already been allotted to these attempts to assign a date to the founder of the Âpastambîya school, the result of which, in the present state of our knowledge of the ancient history of India, must remain, I fear, less certain and less precise than is desirable. It now is necessary to say, in conclusion, a few words about the history of the text of the Dharma-sûtra, and about its commentary, the U*gg*valâ V*ri*tti of Haradatta. The oldest writer with a known date who quotes the Âpastambîya Dharma-sûtra is *S*ankarâ*k*ârya[1], c. 800 A.D. Even somewhat earlier Kumârila, c. 750, refers repeatedly to a law-book by Âpastamba[2]. But it is improbable that he had our Dharma-sûtra before him. For he says, p. 138, that Âpastamba expressly sanctions local usages, opposed to the teaching of the Vedas, for the natives of those districts where they had prevailed since ancient times. Now, that is just an opinion, which our Dharma-sûtra declares to be wrong and refutes repeatedly[3]. As it seems

[1] See Deussen, Vedânta, p. 35.

[2] Tantravârttika, pp. 138, 139, 142, 174, 175, 179, Benares ed.

[3] Âp. Dh. I, 1, 14, 8, 9–10; II, 6, 14, 10–13; II, 6, 15, 1.

hazardous to impute to a man, like Kumârila, ignorance or spite against Âpastamba, I am inclined to assume that the great Mîmâ*m*saka refers to some other work, attributed to Âpastamba, perhaps the metrical Âpastamba-sm*ri*ti which Aparârka quotes very frequently[1]. Among the commentators on Sm*ri*tis the oldest, who quote the Dharma-sûtra, are Medhâtithi, the author of the Manubhâshya, and Vi*gñ*âne*s*vara, who composed the Mitâksharâ, the well-known commentary on Yâ*gñ*avalkya's Dharma-*s*âstra during the reign of the *K*âlukya king Vikramâditya VI, of Kalyâ*n*a towards the end of the eleventh century. From that time downwards Âpastamba is quoted by almost every writer on law. But the whole text, such as it is given in my edition[2], is vouched for only by the commentator Haradatta, who wrote his U*gg*valâ V*ri*tti, at the latest, in the fifteenth century A.D. or possibly 100 years earlier[3]. Haradatta was, however not the first commentator of the Dharma-sûtra. He frequently quotes the opinions of several predecessors whom he designates by the general expressions anya*h* or apara*h*, i.e. another (writer). The fact that the U*gg*valâ was preceded by earlier commentaries which protected the text from corruption, also speaks in favour of the authenticity of the latter, which is further attested by the close agreement of the Hira*n*yake*s*i Dharma-sûtra, mentioned above.

As regards the value of the U*gg*valâ for the explanation of Âpastamba's text, it certainly belongs to the best com-

[1] Âp. Dh., Introd., p. x.

[2] Âpastambîya Dharma-sûtram, second edition, Part i, Bombay, 1892; Part ii, Bombay, 1894.

[3] It seems not doubtful that Haradatta, the author of the U*gg*valâ, is the same person who wrote the Anâkulâ V*ri*tti on the Âpastambîya G*ri*hya-sûtra, an explanation of the Âpastambîya G*ri*hya-mantras (see Burnell, Ind. Ant. I, 6), and the Mitâksharâ V*ri*tti on the Dharma-sûtra of Gautama. From the occurrence in the latter work of Tamil words, added in explanation of Sanskrit expressions, it follows that Haradatta was a native of the south of India. I am not in a position to decide if our author also wrote the Padama*ñg*arî V*ri*tti on the Kâ*s*ikâ of Vâmana and *G*ayâditya. This is Professor Aufrecht's opinion, Catalogus Catalogorum, p. 754 seq. See also my remarks in the Introd. to the second ed., p. viii.

mentaries existing. Haradatta possessed in the older V*ri*ttis abundant and good materials on which he could draw; he himself apparently was well versed in Hindu law and in Sanskrit grammar, and distinguished by sobriety and freedom from that vanity which induces many Indian commentators to load their works with endless and useless quotations. His explanations, therefore, can mostly be followed without hesitation, and, even when they appear unacceptable, they deserve careful consideration.

INTRODUCTION

TO

GAUTAMA.

COMPARED with the information collected above regarding the origin and the history of Âpastamba's Dharma-sûtra, the facts which can be brought to bear on Gautama's Institutes are scanty and the conclusions deducible from them somewhat vague. There are only two points, which, it seems to me, can be proved satisfactorily, viz. the connection of the work with the Sâma-veda and a Gautama *K*ara*n*a, and its priority to the other four Dharma-sûtras which we still possess. To go further appears for the present impossible, because very little is known regarding the history of the schools studying the Sâma-veda, and because the Dharma*s*âstra not only furnishes very few data regarding the works on which it is based, but seems also, though not to any great extent, to have been tampered with by interpolators.

As regards its origin, it was again Professor Max Müller, who, in the place of the fantastic statements of a fabricated tradition, according to which the author of the Dharma*s*âstra is the son or grandson of the sage Utathya, and the grandson or great-grandson of U*s*anas or *S*ukra, the regent of the planet Venus, and the book possessed generally binding force in the second or Tretâ Yuga [1], first put forward a rational explanation which, since, has been adopted by all other writers on Sanskrit literature. He says, Hist. Anc. Sansk. Lit., p. 134, 'Another collection of Dharma-sûtras, which, however, is liable to critical doubts, belongs

---

[1] Manu III, 19; Colebrooke, Digest of Hindu Law, Preface, p. xvii Madras ed); Anantayag*v*an in Dr. Burnell's Catalogue of Sanskrit MSS., (p. 57; Pârâ*s*ara, Dharma*s*âstra I, 22 (Calcutta ed.)

to the Gautamas, a *K*ara*n*a of the Sâma-veda.' This assertion agrees with Kumârila's statement, that the Dharma*s*âstra of Gautama and the *Gri*hya-sûtra of Gobhila were (originally) accepted (as authoritative) by the *Kh*andogas or Sâmavedins alone[1]. Kumârila certainly refers to the work known to us. For he quotes in other passages several of its Sûtras[2].

That Kumârila and Professor Max Müller are right, may also be proved by the following independent arguments. Gautama's work, though called Dharma*s*âstra or Institutes of the Sacred Law, closely resembles, both in form and contents, the Dharma-sûtras or Aphorisms on the Sacred Law, which form part of the Kalpa-sûtras of the Vedic schools of Baudhâyana, Âpastamba, and Hira*n*yake*s*in. As we know from the *K*ara*n*avyûha, from the writings of the ancient grammarians, and from the numerous quotations in the Kalpa-sûtras and other works on the Vedic ritual, that in ancient times the number of Vedic schools, most of which possessed *S*rauta, *Gri*hya, and Dharma-sûtras, was exceedingly great, and that the books of many of them have either been lost or been disintegrated, the several parts being torn out of their original connection, it is not unreasonable to assume that the aphoristic law-book, usually attributed to the *Ri*shi Gautama, is in reality a manual belonging to a Gautama *K*ara*n*a. This conjecture gains considerably in probability, if the fact is taken into account that formerly a school of Sâma-vedîs, which bore the name of Gautama, actually existed. It is mentioned in one of the redactions of the *K*ara*n*avyûha[3] as a subdivision of the Râ*n*âyanîya school. The Va*ms*a-brâhma*n*a of the Sâma-veda, also, enumerates four members of the Gautama family among the teachers who handed down the third Veda, viz. Gât*ri* Gautama, Sumantra Bâbhrava

---

[1] Tantravârttika, p. 179 (Benares ed.), तद्यथा गौतमीयगोभिलीये छन्दोगैरेव च परिगृहीते ॥

[2] Viz. Gautama I, 2 on p. 143; II, 45-46 on p. 112, and XIV, 45-46 on p. 109.

[3] Max Müller, Hist. Anc. Sansk. Lit., p. 374.

Gautama, Sa*m*kara Gautama, and Râdha Gautama[1], and the existing *S*rauta and G*ri*hya-sûtras frequently appeal to the opinions of a Gautama and of a Sthavira Gautama[2]. It follows, therefore, that at least one, if not several Gautama *K*ara*n*as, studied the Sâma-veda, and that, at the time when the existing Sûtras of Lâ*t*yâyana and Gobhila were composed, Gautama *S*rauta and G*ri*hya-sûtras formed part of the literature of the Sâma-veda. The correctness of the latter inference is further proved by Dr. Burnell's discovery of a Pit*ri*medha-sûtra, which is ascribed to a teacher of the Sâma-veda, called Gautama[3].

The only link, therefore, which is wanting in order to complete the chain of evidence regarding Gautama's Aphorisms on the sacred law, and to make their connection with the Sâma-veda perfectly clear, is the proof that they contain special references to the latter. This proof is not difficult to furnish. For Gautama has borrowed one entire chapter, the twenty-sixth, which contains the description of the K*rikkh*ras or difficult penances from the Sâmavidhâna, one of the eight Brâhma*n*as of the Sâma-veda[4]. The agreement of the two texts is complete except in the Mantras (Sûtra 12) where invocations of several deities, which are not usually found in Vedic writings, have been introduced. Secondly, in the enumeration of the purificatory texts, XIX, 12, Gautama shows a marked partiality for the Sâma-veda. Among the eighteen special texts mentioned, we find not less than nine Sâmans. Some of the latter, like the B*ri*hat, Rathantara, *G*yesh*th*a, and Mahâdivâkîrtya chants, are mentioned also in works belonging to the *Ri*g-veda and the Ya*g*ur-veda, and are considered by Brâhma*n*as of all schools to possess great efficacy. But others, such as the Purushagati, Rauhi*n*a, and Mahâvairâ*g*a Sâmans, have hitherto not been met with anywhere but in books belonging to the Sâma-veda, and

[1] See Burnell, Va*ms*a-brâhma*n*a, pp. 7, 9, 11, and 12.

[2] See the Petersburg Dictionary, s. v. Gautama; Weber, Hist. Ind. Lit., p. 77 (English ed.); Gobhila G*ri*hya-sûtra III, 10, 6.

[3] Weber, Hist. Ind. Lit., p. 84, note 89 (English ed.)

[4] See below, pp. 292–296.

do not seem to have stood in general repute. Thirdly, in two passages, I, 50 and XXV, 8, the Dharmaśâstra prescribes the employment of five Vyâh*ri*tis, and mentions in the former Sûtra, that the last Vyâh*ri*ti is satyam, truth. Now in most Vedic works, three Vyâh*ri*tis only, bhû*h*, bhuva*h*, sva*h*, are mentioned; sometimes, but rarely, four or seven occur. But in the Vyâh*ri*ti Sâman, as Haradatta points out [1], five such interjections are used, and satyam is found among them. It is, therefore, not doubtful, that Gautama in the above-mentioned passages directly borrows from the Sâma-veda. These three facts, taken together, furnish, it seems to me, convincing proof that the author of our Dharmaśâstra was a Sâma-vedî. If the only argument in favour of this conclusion were, that Gautama appropriated a portion of the Sâmavidhâna, it might be met by the fact that he has also taken some Sûtras (XXV, 1–6), from the Taittirîya Âra*n*yaka. But his partiality for Sâmans as purificatory texts and the selection of the Vyâh*ri*tis from the Vyâh*ri*ti Sâman as part of the Mantras for the initiation (I, 50), one of the holiest and most important of the Brahmanical sacraments, cannot be explained on any other supposition than the one adopted above.

Though it thus appears that Professor Max Müller is right in declaring the Gautama Dharmaśâstra to belong to the Sâma-veda, it is, for the present, not possible to positively assert, that it is the Dharma-sûtra of that Gautama *K*ara*n*a, which according to the *K*ara*n*avyûha, quoted in the *S*abdakalpadruma of Râdhâkanta, formed a subdivision of the Râ*n*âya*n*îyas. The enumeration of four Â*k*âryas, bearing the family-name Gautama, in the Va*ms*a-brâhma*n*a, and Lâ*t*yâyana's quotations from two Gautamas, make it not unlikely, that several Gautama *K*ara*n*as once existed among the Sâma-vedî Brâhma*n*as, and we possess no means for ascertaining to which our Dharmaśâstra must be attributed. Further researches into the history of the schools of the Sâma-veda must be awaited until we can do more. Probably the living tradition of the Sâma-vedîs of

[1] See Gautama I, 50, note.

Southern India and new books from the South will clear up what at present remains uncertain.

In concluding this subject I may state that Haradatta seems to have been aware of the connection of Gautama's law-book with the Sâma-veda, though he does not say it expressly. But he repeatedly and pointedly refers in his commentary to the practices of the *Kh*andogas, and quotes the G*ri*hya-sûtra of the *G*aiminîyas [1], who are a school of Sâma-vedîs, in explanation of several passages. Another southern author, Govindasvâmin (if I understand the somewhat corrupt passage correctly), states directly in his commentary on Baudhâyana I, 1, 2, 6, that the Gautamîya Dharma*s*âstra was originally studied by the *Kh*andogas alone [2].

In turning now to the second point, the priority of Gautama to the other existing Dharma-sûtras, I must premise that it is only necessary to take into account two of the latter, those of Baudhâyana and Vasish*th*a. For, as has been shown above in the Introduction to Âpastamba, the Sûtras of the latter and those of Hira*n*yake*s*in Satyâshâ*dh*a are younger than Baudhâyana's. The arguments which allow us to place Gautama before both Baudhâyana and Vasish*th*a are, that both those authors quote Gautama as an authority on law, and that Baudhâyana has transferred a whole chapter of the Dharma*s*âstra to his work, which Vasish*th*a again has borrowed from him.

As regards the case of Baudhâyana, his references to Gautama are two, one of which can be traced in our Dharma*s*âstra. In the discussion on the peculiar customs prevailing in the South and in the North of India (Baudh. Dh. I, 2, 1-8) Baudhâyana expresses himself as follows:

---

[1] A G*ri*hya-sûtra of the *G*aiminîyas has been discovered by Dr. Burnell with a commentary by *S*rînivâsa. He thinks that the *G*aiminîyas are a Sûtra-*s*âkhâ of the *S*â*t*yâyana-Talavakâras.

[2] My transcript has been made from the MS. presented by Dr. Burnell, the discoverer of the work, to the India Office Library. The passage runs as follows: Yathâ vâ bodhâyanîya*m* dharma*s*âstra*m* kai*sk*id eva pa*th*yamâna*m* sarvâdhikâram bhavati tathâ gautamîye gobhilîye (?) *kh*andogair eva pa*th*yate || vâsish*th*a*m* tu bahv*rik*air eva ||

'1. There is a dispute regarding five (practices) both in the South and in the North.

'2. We shall explain those (peculiar) to the South.

'3. They are, to eat in the company of an uninitiated person, to eat in the company of one's wife, to eat stale food, to marry the daughter of a maternal uncle or of a paternal aunt.

'4. Now (the customs peculiar) to the North are, to deal in wool, to drink rum, to sell animals that have teeth in the upper and in the lower jaws, to follow the trade of arms and to go to sea.

'5. He who follows (these practices) in (any) other country than the one where they prevail commits sin.

'6. For each of these practices (the rule of) the country should be (considered) the authority.

'7. Gautama declares that this is false.

'8. And one should not take heed of either (set of practices), because they are opposed to the tradition of those learned (in the sacred law[1]).'

From this passage it appears that the Gautama Dharma-sûtra, known to Baudhâyana, expressed an opinion adverse to the authoritativeness of local customs which might be opposed to the tradition of the *S*ish*t*as, i. e. of those who really deserve to be called learned in the law. Our Gautama teaches the same doctrine, as he says, XI, 20, 'The laws of countries, castes, and families, which are not opposed to the (sacred) records, have also authority.'

---

[1] पञ्चधा विप्रतिपत्तिर्दक्षिणतस्तथोत्तरतः ॥१॥
यानि दक्षिणतस्तानि व्याख्यास्यामः ॥२॥
यथैतदनुपेतेन सह भोजनं स्त्रिया सह भोजनं पर्युषितभोजनं मातुलपितृष्वसृदुहितृगमनमिति ॥३॥
अथोत्तरत ऊर्णाविक्रयः सीधुपानमुभयतोदद्भिर्व्यवहार आयुधीयकं समुद्रयानमिति ॥४॥
इतरदितरस्मिन्कुर्वन्दुष्यति ॥५॥
तत्रतत्र देशप्रामाण्यमेव स्यात् ॥६॥
मिथ्यैतदिति गौतमः ॥७॥
उभयं चैव नाद्रियेत शिष्टस्मृतिविरोधदर्शनात् ॥८॥

As clear as this reference, is the case in which Baudhâyana has borrowed a whole chapter of our Dharmasâstra. The chapter in question is the nineteenth, which in Gautama's work forms the introduction to the section on penances and expiation. It is reproduced with a number of various readings[1] in the third Prasna of Baudhâyana's Dharma-sûtra, where it forms the tenth and last Adhyâya. Its contents, and especially its first Sûtra which connects the section on penances with the preceding ones on the law of castes and orders, make it perfectly clear that its proper position can only be at the beginning of the rules on expiation, not in the middle of the discussion, as Baudhâyana places it[2]. This circumstance alone would be sufficient to prove that Baudhâyana is the borrower, not Gautama, even if the name of the latter did not occur in Baudhâyana's Dharma-sûtra. But the character of many of Baudhâyana's readings, especially of those in Sûtras 2, 10, 11, 13, and 15, which, though supported by all the MSS. and Govindasvâmin's commentary, appear to have arisen chiefly through clerical mistakes or carelessness, furnishes

[1] Baudhâyana's various readings are the following: Gaut. XIX, 1 = Baudh. III, 10, 1, वर्णधर्मश्चा°. Gaut. XIX, 2 = Baudh. III, 10, 2, कर्मणा मिथ्या वाचरत्ययाज्यं वा याजयत्यप्रतिग्राह्यस्य वा प्रतिगृह्णात्यनाश्यान्नस्य वान्नमश्नात्यचरणीयेन वा चरति. Gaut. XIX, 4 left out. Gaut. XIX, 6 = Baudh. III, 10, 5, कुर्यादित्येव. Gaut. XIX, 7 = Baudh. III, 10, 6, पुनस्तोमेन यजेत; विज्ञायते left out. Gaut. XIX, 8 left out. Gaut. XIX, 9 = Baudh. III, 10, 7, अथाप्युदाहरन्ति तरति. Gaut. XIX, 10 = Baudh. III, 10, 8, °नो यजेत. Gaut. XIX, 12 = Baudh. III, 10, 10, वेदादयो वेदान्ताः; कूष्माण्डः. Gaut. XIX, 13 = Baudh. III, 10, 11, उपसंन्यायेन पयोव्रतता. Gaut. XIX, 14 = Baudh. III, 10, 12, ऋषिनिकेतनानि; गोष्ठक्षेत्रपरि°. Gaut. XIX, 15 = Baudh. III, 10, 13, अहिंसा सत्यमस्तैन्यं सवनोपस्पर्शनं गुरुशुश्रूषणं ब्रह्मचर्यमधःशयनमेकवस्त्रताना°. Gaut. XIX, 17 = Baudh. III, 10, 15, त्र्यहोरात्रमेकाह इति कालाः. Gaut. XIX, 18 = Baudh. III, 10, 16, विकल्पेन left out. Gaut. XIX, 20 = Baudh. III, 10, 18, सर्वप्रायश्चित्तिः.

[2] Baudhâyana's treatment of the subject of penances is very unmethodical. He devotes to them the following sections: II, 1–2; II, 2, 3, 48–53; II, 2, 4; III, 5–10; and the greater part of Prasna IV.

even an additional argument in favour of the priority of Gautama's text. It must, however, be admitted that the value of this point is seriously diminished by the fact that Baudhâyana's third Pra*s*na is not above suspicion and may be a later addition[1].

As regards Baudhâyana's second reference to Gautama, the opinion which it attributes to the latter is directly opposed to the teaching of our Dharma*s*âstra. Baudhâyana gives II, 2, 4, 16 the rule that a Brâhma*n*a who is unable to maintain himself by teaching, sacrificing, and receiving gifts, may follow the profession of a Kshatriya, and then goes on as follows[2]:

'17. Gautama declares that he shall not do it. For the duties of a Kshatriya are too cruel for a Brâhma*n*a.'

As the commentator Govindasvâmin also points out, exactly the opposite doctrine is taught in our Dharma*s*âstra, which (VII, 6) explicitly allows a Brâhma*n*a to follow, in times of distress, the occupations of a Kshatriya. Govindasvâmin explains this contradiction by assuming that in this case Baudhâyana cites the opinion, not of the author of our Dharma*s*âstra, but of some other Gautama. According to what has been said above[3], the existence of two or even more ancient Gautama Dharma-sûtras is not very improbable, and the commentator may possibly be right. But it seems to me more likely that the Sûtra of Gautama (VII, 6) which causes the difficulty is an interpolation, though Haradatta takes it to be genuine. My reason for considering it to be spurious is that the permission to follow the trade of arms is opposed to the sense of two other rules of Gautama. For the author states at the end of the same chapter on times of distress, VII, 25, that 'even a Brâhma*n*a may take up arms when his life is in danger.' The meaning of these words can only be, that a Brâhma*n*a must not fight under any other circumstances.

---

[1] See Sacred Books of the East, vol. xiv, p. xxxiv seq.

[2] Baudh. Dh. II, 2, 4, 17.

नेति गौतमोऽत्युग्रो हि क्षत्रधर्मो ब्राह्मणस्य ॥

[3] See p. lii.

But according to Sûtra 6 he is allowed to follow the occupations of a Kshatriya, who lives by fighting. Again, in the chapter on funeral oblations, XV, 18, those Brâhma*n*as 'who live by the use of the bow' are declared to defile the company at a funeral dinner. It seems to me that these two Sûtras, taken together with Baudhâyana's assertion that Gautama does not allow Brâhma*n*as to become warriors, raise a strong suspicion against the genuineness, of VII, 6, and I have the less hesitation in rejecting the latter Sûtra, as there are several other interpolated passages in the text received by Haradatta[1]. Among them I may mention here the Mantras in the chapter taken from the Sâmavidhâna, XXVI, 12, where the three invocations addressed to *S*iva are certainly modern additions, as the old Sûtrakâras do not allow a place to that or any other Paurâ*n*ic deity in their works. A second interpolation will be pointed out below.

The Vâsish*th*a Dharma-sûtra shows also two quotations from Gautama; and it is a curious coincidence that, just as in the case of Baudhâyana's references, one of them only can be traced in our Dharma*s*âstra. Both the quotations occur in the section on impurity, Vâs. IV, where we read as follows[2]:

'33. If an infant aged less than two years, dies, or in the case of a miscarriage, the impurity of the Sapi*nd*as (lasts) for three (days and) nights.

'34. Gautama declares that (they become) pure at once (after bathing).

'35. If (a person) dies in a foreign country and (his Sapi*nd*as) hear (of his death) after the lapse of ten days, the impurity lasts for one (day and) night.

'36. Gautama declares that if a person who has kindled the sacred fire dies on a journey, (his Sapi*nd*as) shall again

[1] In some MSS. a whole chapter on the results of various sins in a second birth is inserted after Adhyâya XIX. But Haradatta does not notice it; see Stenzler, Gautama, Preface, p. iii.

[2] In quoting the Vâsish*th*a Dh. I always refer to the Benares edition, which is accompanied by the commentary of K*ri*sh*n*apa*nd*ita Dharmâdhikârin, called Vidvanmodinî.

celebrate his obsequies, (burning a dummy made of leaves or straw,) and remain impure (during ten days) as (if they had actually buried) the corpse.'

The first of these two quotations or references apparently points to Gautama Dh. XIV, 44, where it is said, that 'if an infant dies, the relatives shall be pure at once.' For, though Vasish*th*a's Sûtra 34, strictly interpreted, would mean, that Gautama declares the relatives to be purified instantaneously, both if an infant dies and if a miscarriage happens, it is also possible to refer the exception to one of the two cases only, which are mentioned in Sûtra 33. Similar instances do occur in the Sûtra style, where brevity is estimated higher than perspicuity, and the learned commentator of Vasish*th*a does not hesitate to adopt the same view. But, as regards the second quotation in Sûtra 36, our Gautama contains no passage to which it could possibly refer. Govindasvâmin, in his commentary on the second reference to Gautama in Baudhâyana's Dharma*s*âstra II, 2, 71, expresses the opinion that this Sûtra, too, is taken from the 'other' Gautama Dharma-sûtra, the former existence of which he infers from Baudhâyana's passage. And curiously enough the regarding the second funeral actually is found in the metrical V*ri*ddha-Gautama [1] or Vaish*n*ava Dharma-*s*âstra, which, according to Mr. Vâman Shâstrî Islâmpurkar [2], forms chapters 94–115 of the A*s*vamedha-parvan of the Mahâbhârata in a Malayâlam MS. Nevertheless, it seems to me very doubtful if Vasish*th*a did or could refer to this work. As the same rule occurs sometimes in the *S*rauta-sûtras [3], I think it more probable that the *S*rauta-sûtra of the Gautama school is meant. And it is significant that the V*ri*ddha-Gautama declares its teaching to be kalpa*k*odita 'enjoined in the Kalpa or ritual.'

Regarding Gautama's nineteenth chapter, which appears in the Vâsish*th*a Dharma*s*âstra as the twenty-second, I have

[1] Dharma*s*âstra sa*m*graha (*G*îbânand), p. 627, Adhy. 20, 1 seqq.
[2] Parâ*s*ara Dharma Sa*m*hitâ (Bombay Sansk. Series, No. xlvii), vol. i, p. 9.
[3] See e. g. Âp. *S*r. Sû.

already stated above that it is not taken directly from Gautama's work, but from Baudhâyana's. For it shows most of the characteristic readings of the latter. But a few new ones also occur, and some Sûtras have been left out, while one new one, a well-known verse regarding the efficacy of the Vaisvânara vratapati and of the Pavitresh*t*i, has been added. Among the omissions peculiar to Vasish*th*a, that of the first Sûtra is the most important, as it alters the whole character of the chapter, and removes one of the most convincing arguments as to its original position at the head of the section on penances. Vasish*th*a places it in the beginning of the discussion on penances which are generally efficacious in removing guilt, and after the rules on the special penances for the classified offences.

These facts will, I think, suffice to show that the Gautama Dharmasâstra may be safely declared to be the oldest of the existing works on the sacred law[1]. This assertion must, however, not be taken to mean, that every single one of its Sûtras is older than the other four Dharma-sûtras. Two interpolations have already been pointed out above[2], and another one will be discussed presently. It is also not unlikely that the wording of the Sûtras has been changed occasionally. For it is a suspicious fact that Gautama's language agrees closer with Pâ*n*ini's rules than that of Âpastamba and Baudhâyana. If it is borne in mind that Gautama's work has been torn out of its original connection, and from a school-book has become a work of general authority, and that for a long time it has been studied by Pandits who were brought up in the traditions of classical grammar, it seems hardly likely that it could retain much of its ancient peculiarities of language. But I do not think that the interpolations and alterations can have affected the general character of the book very much. It is too methodically planned and too carefully arranged to admit of any very great changes. The fact, too, that in

[1] Professor Stenzler, too, had arrived independently at this conclusion, see Grundriss der Indo-Ar. Phil. und Altertumsk., vol. ii, Pt. 8, p. 5.

[2] See p. lvii.

the chapter borrowed by Baudhâyana the majority of the variae lectiones are corruptions, not better readings, favours this view. Regarding the distance in time between Gautama on the one hand, and Baudhâyana and Vasish*th*a on the other, I prefer not to hazard any conjecture, as long as the position of the Gautamas among the schools of the Sâma-veda has not been cleared up. So much only can be said that Gautama probably was less remote from Baudhâyana than from Vasish*th*a. There are a few curious terms and rules in which the former two agree, while they, at the same time, differ from all other known writers on Dharma. Thus the term bhikshu, literally a beggar, which Gautama [1] uses to denote an ascetic, instead of the more common yati or sannyâsin, occurs once also in Baudhâyana's Sûtra. The same is the case with the rule, III, 13, which orders the ascetic not to change his residence during the rains. Both the name bhikshu and the rule must be very ancient, as the *G*ainas and Buddhists have borrowed them, and have founded on the latter their practice of keeping the Vasso, or residence in monasteries during the rainy season.

As the position of the Gautamas among the Sâman schools is uncertain, it will, of course, be likewise inadvisable to make any attempt at connecting them with the historical period of India. The necessity of caution in this respect is so obvious that I should not point it out, were it not that the Dharma*s*âstra contains one word, the occurrence of which is sometimes considered to indicate the terminus a quo for the dates of Indian works. The word to which I refer is Yavana. Gautama quotes, IV, 21, an opinion of 'some,' according to which a Yavana is the offspring of a *S*ûdra male and a Kshatriya female. Now it is well known that this name is a corruption of the Greek 'Ιαϝων, an Ionian, and that in India it was applied, in ancient times, to the Greeks, and especially to the early Seleucids who kept up intimate relations with the first Mauryas, as well as later to the Indo-Bactrian and Indo-Grecian kings who from the beginning of the second century B. C. ruled

[1] Gaut. Dh. III, 2, 11; see also Weber, Hist. Ind. Lit., p. 327 (English ed.)

over portions of north-western India. And it has been occasionally asserted that an Indian work, mentioning the Yavanas, cannot have been composed before 300 B.C., because Alexander's invasion first made the Indians acquainted with the name of the Greeks. This estimate is certainly erroneous, as there are other facts, tending to show that at least the inhabitants of north-western India became acquainted with the Greeks about 200 years earlier[1]. But it is not advisable to draw any chronological conclusions from Gautama's Sûtra, IV, 21. For, as pointed out in the note to the translation of Sûtra IV, 18, the whole section with the second enumeration of the mixed castes, IV, 17–21, is probably spurious.

The information regarding the state of the Vedic literature, which the Dharma*s*âstra furnishes, is not very extensive. But some of the items are interesting, especially the proof that Gautama knew the Taittirîya Âra*n*yaka, from which he took the first six Sûtras of the twenty-fifth Adhyâya; the Sâmavidhâna Brâhma*n*a, from which the twenty-sixth Adhyâya has been borrowed; and the Atharva*s*iras, which is mentioned XIX, 12. The latter word denotes, according to Haradatta, one of the Upanishads of the Atharva-veda, which usually are not considered to belong to a high antiquity. The fact that Gautama and Baudhâyana knew it, will probably modify this opinion. Another important fact is that Gautama, XXI, 7, quotes Manu, and asserts that the latter declared it to be impossible to expiate the guilt incurred by killing a Brâhma*n*a, drinking spirituous liquor, or violating a Guru's bed. From this statement it appears that Gautama knew an ancient work on law which was attributed to Manu. It probably was the foundation of the existing Mânava Dharma*s*âstra[2]. No other teacher on law, besides Manu, is mentioned by name. But the numerous references to the opinions of 'some' show that Gautama's work was not the first Dharma-sûtra.

[1] See my Indian Studies, No. iii, p. 26, note 1.

[2] Compare also Sacred Books of the East, vol. xxv, p. xxxiv seq.

In conclusion, I have to add a few words regarding the materials on which the subjoined translation is based. The text published by Professor Stenzler for the Sanskrit Text Society has been used as the basis [1]. It has been collated with a rough edition, prepared from my own MSS. P and C, a MS. belonging to the Collection of the Government of Bombay, bought at Belgâm, and a MS. borrowed from a Puna Sâstrî. But the readings given by Professor Stenzler and his division of the Sûtras have always been followed in the body of the translation. In those cases, where the variae lectiones of my MSS. seemed preferable, they have been given and translated in the notes. The reason which induced me to adopt this course was that I thought it more advisable to facilitate references to the printed Sanskrit text than to insist on the insertion of a few alterations in the translation, which would have disturbed the order of the Sûtras. The notes have been taken from the above-mentioned rough edition and from my MSS. of Haradatta's commentary, called Gautamîyâ Mitâksharâ, which are now deposited in the India Office Library, Sansk. MSS. Bühler, Nos. 165-67.

[1] The Institutes of Gautama, edited with an index of words by A. F. Stenzler, London, 1876.

ÂPASTAMBA,

APHORISMS ON THE SACRED LAW OF THE HINDUS.

ÂPASTAMBA,

APHORISMS ON THE SACRED LAW OF THE HINDUS.

PRASNA I, PATALA 1, KHANDA 1.

1. Now, therefore, we will declare the acts productive of merit which form part of the customs of daily life, as they have been settled by the agreement (of those who know the law).

2. The authority (for these duties) is the agreement of those who know the law,

3. And (the authorities for the latter are) the Vedas alone.

4. (There are) four castes—Brâhma*n*as, Kshatriyas, Vai*s*yas, and *S*ûdras.

5. Amongst these, each preceding (caste) is superior by birth to the one following.

6. (For all these), excepting *S*ûdras and those who have committed bad actions, (are ordained) the initiation, the study of the Veda, and the kindling of

---

1. 1. Samaya, 'agreement, decision,' is threefold. It includes injunction, restriction, and prohibition.

Dharma, 'acts productive of merit,' usually translated by 'duty or law,' is more accurately explained as an act which produces the quality of the soul called apûrva, the cause of heavenly bliss and of final liberation.

2. Manu II, 6, 12; Yâ*gñ*. I, 7; Gautama I, 1.

6. Manu II, 35.

the sacred fire; and (their) works are productive of rewards (in this world and the next).

7. To serve the other (three) castes (is ordained) for the *S*ûdra.

8. The higher the caste (which he serves) the greater is the merit.

9. The initiation is the consecration in accordance with the texts of the Veda, of a male who is desirous of (and can make use of) sacred knowledge.

10. A Brâhma*n*a declares that the Gâyatrî is learnt for the sake of all the (three) Vedas.

11. (Coming) out of darkness, he indeed enters darkness, whom a man unlearned in the Vedas, initiates, and (so does he) who, without being learned in the Vedas, (performs the rite of initiation.) That has been declared in a Brâhma*n*a.

12. As performer of this rite of initiation he shall seek to obtain a man in whose family sacred learning is hereditary, who himself possesses it, and who is devout (in following the law).

13. And under him the sacred science must be

---

7. Manu I, 91, VIII, 410, and IX, 334; Yâg*ñ*. I, 120.

9. The use of the masculine in the text excludes women. For though women may have occasion to use such texts as 'O fire, lord of the dwelling,' &c. at the Agnihotra, still it is specially ordained that they shall be taught this and similar verses only just before the rite is to be performed.

10. The object of the Sûtra is to remove a doubt whether the ceremony of initiation ought to be repeated for each Veda, in case a man desires to study more than one Veda. This repetition is declared to be unnecessary, except, as the commentator adds, in the case of the Atharva-veda, for which, according to a passage of a Brâhma*n*a, a fresh initiation is necessary. The latter rule is given in the Vaitâna-sûtra I, 1, 5.

13. Haradatta: 'But this (latter rule regarding the taking of

studied until the end, provided (the teacher) does not fall off from the ordinances of the law.

14. He from whom (the pupil) gathers (âkinoti) (the knowledge of) his religious duties (dharmân) (is called) the Âkârya (teacher).

15. Him he should never offend.

16. For he causes him (the pupil) to be born (a second time) by (imparting to him) sacred learning.

17. This (second) birth is the best.

18. The father and the mother produce the body only.

19. Let him initiate a Brâhmana in spring, a Kshatriya in summer, a Vaisya in autumn, a Brâhmana in the eighth year after conception, a Kshatriya in the eleventh year after conception, (and) a Vaisya in the twelfth after conception.

20. Now (follows the enumeration of the years

another teacher) does not hold good for those who have begun to study, solemnly binding themselves to their teacher. How so? As he (the pupil) shall consider a person who initiates and instructs him his Âkârya, and a pupil who has been once initiated cannot be initiated again, how can another man instruct him? For this reason it must be understood that the study begun with one teacher may not be completed with another, if the first die.' Compare also Haradatta on I, 2, 7, 26, and the rule given I, 1, 4, 26. In our times also pupils, who have bound themselves to a teacher by paying their respects to him and presenting a cocoa-nut, in order to learn from him a particular branch of science, must not study the same branch of science under any other teacher.

14. Manu II, 69; Yâgñ. I, 15.

15. Manu II, 144.

16. Manu II, 146–148.

17. 'Because it procures heavenly bliss and final liberation.'—Haradatta.

18. Manu II, 147.

19. Yâgñ. I, 14; Manu II, 36; Âsvalâyana Gri. Sû. I, 19, 1, 4; Weber, Ind. Stud. X, 20 seq.

to be chosen) for the fulfilment of some (particular) wish.

21. (Let him initiate) a person desirous of excellence in sacred learning in his seventh year,

22. A person desirous of long life in his eighth year,

23. A person desirous of manly vigour in his ninth year,

24. A person desirous of food in his tenth year,

25. A person desirous of strength in his eleventh year,

26. A person desirous of cattle in his twelfth year.

27. There is no dereliction (of duty, if the initiation takes place), in the case of a Brâhma*n*a before the completion of the sixteenth year, in the case of a Kshatriya before the completion of the twenty-second year, in the case of a Vai*s*ya before the completion of the twenty-fourth year. (Let him be initiated at such an age) that he may be able to perform the duties, which we shall declare below.

28. If the proper time for the initiation has passed, he shall observe for the space of two months

---

21. Manu II, 37.

22–26. Â*s*v. G*ri*. Sû. I, 19, 5, 7; Weber, Ind. Stud. X, 21.

27. The meaning of the Sûtra is, that the initiation shall be performed as soon as the child is able to begin the study of the Veda. If it is so far developed at eight years, the ceremony must then be performed; and if it be then neglected, or, if it be neglected at any time when the capacity for learning exists, the expiation prescribed in the following Sûtras must be performed. The age of sixteen in the case of Brâhma*n*as is the latest term up to which the ceremony may be deferred, in case of incapacity for study only. After the lapse of the sixteenth year, the expiation becomes also necessary. Manu II, 38; Yâ*gñ*. I, 37.

28. The meaning is, he shall keep all the restrictions imposed upon a student, as chastity, &c., but that he shall not perform

the duties of a student, as observed by those who are studying the three Vedas.

29. After that he may be initiated.

30. After that he shall bathe (daily) for one year.

31. After that he may be instructed.

32. He, whose father and grandfather have not been initiated, (and his two ancestors) are called 'slayers of the Brahman.'

33. Intercourse, eating, and intermarriage with them should be avoided.

34. If they wish it (they may perform the following) expiation;

35. In the same manner as for the first neglect (of the initiation, a penance of) two months (was) prescribed, so (they shall do penance for) one year.

36. Afterwards they may be initiated, and then they must bathe (daily),

Prasna I, Patala 1, Khanda 2.

1. For as many years as there are uninitiated persons, reckoning (one year) for each ancestor (and the person to be initiated himself),

2. (They should bathe daily reciting) the seven

---

fire-worship or service to a teacher, nor study. Manu II, 39; XI, 192; Yâgñ. I, 38; Weber, Ind. Stud. X, 101.

30. 'If he is strong, he shall bathe three times a day—morning, midday, and evening.'—Haradatta.

32. Brahman, apparently, here means 'Veda,' and those who neglect its study may be called metaphorically 'slayers of the Veda.'

33. Manu II, 40; Âsv. Gri. Sû. I, 19, 8, 9; Weber, Ind. Stud. X, 21.

35. Compare above, I, 1, 1, 28.

2. 2. The seven Pâvamânîs are seven verses which occur Rig-veda IX, 67, 21-27. Yagushpavitra = Taitt. Samh. I, 2, 1, 1. The Sâmapavitra is found Sâma-veda I, 2, 2, 3, 5. Âṅgirasapavitra = Rig-veda IV, 40, 5.

Pâvamânîs, beginning with 'If near or far,' the Yagushpavitra, ('May the waters, the mothers purify us,' &c.) the Sâmapavitra, ('With what help assists,' &c.), and the Âṅgirasapavitra ('A swan, dwelling in purity'),

3. Or also reciting the Vyâhritis (om, bhûh, bhuvah, suvah).

4. After that (such a person) may be taught (the Veda).

5. But those whose great-grandfather's (grandfather's and father's) initiation is not remembered, are called 'burial-grounds.'

6. Intercourse, dining, and intermarriage with them should be avoided. For them, if they like, the (following) penance (is prescribed). (Such a man) shall keep for twelve years the rules prescribed for a student who is studying the three Vedas. Afterwards he may be initiated. Then he shall bathe, reciting the Pâvamânîs and the other (texts mentioned above, I, 1, 2, 2).

7. Then he may be instructed in the duties of a householder.

8. He shall not be taught (the whole Veda), but only the sacred formulas required for the domestic ceremonies.

9. When he has finished this (study of the Grihyamantras), he may be initiated (after having performed the penance prescribed) for the first neglect (I, 1, 1, 28).

10. Afterwards (everything is performed) as in the case of a regular initiation.

10. The commentator observes that for those whose great-great-grandfather or remoter ancestors were not initiated, no penance is prescribed, and that it must be fixed by those who know the law.

11. He who has been initiated shall dwell as a religious student in the house of his teacher,

12. For forty-eight years (if he learns all the four Vedas),

13. (Or) a quarter less (i. e. for thirty-six years),

14. (Or) less by half (i. e. for twenty-four years),

15. (Or) three quarters less (i.e. for twelve years),

16. Twelve years (should be) the shortest time (for his residence with his teacher).

17. A student who studies the sacred science shall not dwell with anybody else (than his teacher).

18. Now (follow) the rules for the studentship.

19. He shall obey his teacher, except (when ordered to commit) crimes which cause loss of caste.

20. He shall do what is serviceable to his teacher, he shall not contradict him.

21. He shall always occupy a couch or seat lower (than that of his teacher).

---

11. Manu II, 164.

12. Manu III, 1, and Yâgñ. I, 36; Weber, Ind. Stud. X, 125.

16. The commentator declares that in Manu III, 1, the expression 'until he has learnt it,' must be understood in this sense, that the pupil may leave his teacher, if he has learnt the Veda, after twelve years' study, never before. But compare also Âsv. Gri. Sû. I, 22, 3.

17. The commentator states that this rule refers only to a temporary, not to a professed student (naishthika). He also gives an entirely different explanation to the Sûtra, which, according to some, means, 'A student who learns the sacred science shall not fast in order to obtain heaven.' This rendering also is admissible, as the word para may mean either a 'stranger' or 'heaven,' and upavâsa, 'dwelling' or 'fasting.'

19. Regarding the crimes which cause loss of caste (patanîya), see below, I, 7, 21, 7.

20. Manu II, 108, and Yâgñ. I, 27.

21. Manu II, 108, 198; Weber, Ind. Stud. X, 123 and 124.

22. He shall not eat food offered (at a sacrifice to the gods or the Manes),

23. Nor pungent condiments, salt, honey, or meat.

24. He shall not sleep in the day-time.

25. He shall not use perfumes.

26. He shall preserve chastity.

27. He shall not embellish himself (by using ointments and the like).

28. He shall not wash his body (with hot water for pleasure).

29. But, if it is soiled by unclean things, he shall clean it (with earth or water), in a place where he is not seen by a Guru.

30. Let him not sport in the water whilst bathing; let him swim (motionless) like a stick.

31. He shall wear all his hair tied in one braid.

32. Or let him make a braid of the lock on the crown of the head, and shave the rest of the hair.

---

23. Regarding the meaning of kshâra, 'pungent condiments,' see Haradatta on II, 6, 15, 15. Other commentators explain the term differently.—Manu II, 177; Yâ*gñ*. I, 33; and Weber, Ind. Stud. X, 123. Â*s*v. G*ri*. Sû. I, 22, 2.

25. Manu II, 177; Yâ*gñ*. I, 33.

26. Manu II, 180.

27. Manu II, 178; Yâ*gñ*. I, 33.

29. 'Here, in the section on the teacher, the word guru designates the father and the rest also.'—Hara*d*atta.

30. Another version of the first portion of this Sûtra, proposed by Haradatta, is, 'Let him not, whilst bathing, clean himself (with bathing powder or the like).' Another commentator takes Sûtra 28 as a prohibition of the daily bath or washing generally ordained for Brâhma*n*as, and refers Sûtra 29 to the naimittika snâna or 'bathing on certain occasions,' and takes Sûtra 30 as a restriction of the latter.

31. Manu II, 219.

33. The girdle of a Brâhma*n*a shall be made of Mu*ñg*a grass, and consist of three strings; if possible, (the strings) should be twisted to the right.

34. A bowstring (should be the girdle) of a Kshatriya,

35. Or a string of Mu*ñg*a grass in which pieces of iron have been tied.

36. A wool thread (shall be the girdle) of a Vai*s*ya,

37. Or a rope used for yoking the oxen to the plough, or a string made of Tamala-bark.

38. The staff worn by a Brâhma*n*a should be made of Palâ*s*a wood, that of a Kshatriya of a branch of the Banian tree, which grows downwards, that of a Vai*s*ya of Bâdara or Udumbara wood. Some declare, without any reference to caste, that the staff of a student should be made of the wood of a tree (that is fit to be used at the sacrifice).

39. (He shall wear) a cloth (to cover his nakedness).

40. (It shall be made) of hemp for a Brâhma*n*a, of flax (for a Kshatriya), of the skin of a (clean) animal (for a Vai*s*ya).

41. Some declare that the (upper) garment (of a Brâhma*n*a) should be dyed with red Lodh,

---

33. Manu II, 42–44; Yâ*gñ*. I, 29; Â*s*v. G*ri*. Sû. I, 19, 12; Weber, Ind. Stud. X, 23.

38. Manu II, 45; Yâ*gñ*. I, 29; Â*s*v. G*ri*. Sû. I, 19, 13; 20, 1; Weber, Ind. Stud. X, 23.

Haradatta gives no commentary on this Sûtra, but refers back to the G*ri*hya-sûtra, 11, 16–17, where the same words occur.

39. The word forms a Sûtra by itself, in order to show that every one must wear this cloth.

40. Manu II, 41. 'Clean' means here and everywhere else, if applied to animals or things, 'fit to be used at the sacrifice.'

41. Â*s*v. G*ri*. Sû. I, 19, 11; Weber, Ind. Stud. X, 22.

Prasna I, Patala 1, Khanda 3.

1. And that of a Kshatriya dyed with madder,

2. And that of a Vaisya dyed with turmeric.

3. (The skin) worn by a Brâhmana shall be that of a common deer or of a black doe.

4. If he wears a black skin, let him not spread it (on the ground) to sit or lie upon it.

5. (The skin worn) by a Kshatriya shall be that of a spotted deer.

6. (The skin worn) by a Vaisya shall be that of a he-goat.

7. The skin of a sheep is fit to be worn by all castes,

8. And a blanket made of wool.

9. He who wishes the increase of Brâhmana power shall wear skins only; he who wishes the increase of Kshatriya power shall wear cloth only; he who wishes the increase of both shall wear both (skin and cloth). Thus says a Brâhmana.

10. But (I, Âpastamba, say), let him wear a skin only as his upper garment.

11. Let him not look at dancing.

12. Let him not go to assemblies (for gambling, &c.), nor to crowds (assembled at festivals).

---

3. 3. Manu II, 41; Yâgñ. I, 29; Âsv. Gri. Sû. I, 19, 10.

9. See also Gopatha-brâhmana I, 2, 4.

10. According to I, 1, 2, 39—I, 1, 3, 10, the rule of dress for students is the following:—According to Âpastamba, a student shall wear a piece of cloth to cover his nakedness (langoti); and a skin as upper garment. Other teachers allow, besides, an upper dress of cloth, coloured differently for the different castes, with or without the addition of a deer-skin.

11. Manu II, 178.

12–13. Manu II, 179; Yâgñ. I, 33.

13. Let him not be addicted to gossiping.

14. Let him be discreet.

15. Let him not do anything for his own pleasure in places which his teacher frequents.

16. Let him talk with women so much (only) as his purpose requires.

17. (Let him be) forgiving.

18. Let him restrain his organs from seeking illicit objects.

19. Let him be untired in fulfilling his duties;

20. Modest;

21. Possessed of self-command;

22. Energetic;

23. Free from anger;

24. (And) free from envy.

25. Bringing all he obtains to his teacher, he shall go begging with a vessel in the morning and in the evening, (and he may) beg (from everybody) except low-caste people unfit for association (with Âryas) and Abhi*s*astas.

---

15. 'Anything for his own pleasure,' i.e. keeping conversations with friends, making his toilet, &c.

19. The explanations of the last two terms, *s*ânta (Sûtra 18) and dânta (Sûtra 19), are different from those given usually. *S*ama is usually explained as 'the exclusive direction of the mind towards God,' and dama as 'the restraining of the senses.'

23. Manu II, 178.

25. Regarding the explanation of the term Abhi*s*asta, see below, I, 7, 21, 17. Haradatta: 'Apapâtras are called those born from a high-caste mother and a low-caste father, such as washermen. For their cooking vessels &c. are unfit for the use of the four castes. . . . Since Âpastamba says, "In the evening and in the morning, food obtained in the evening must not be used for the morning meal, nor food obtained in the morning for the evening meal."' Manu II, 182, 183, 185; Â*s*v. G*ri*. Sû. I, 22, 4. See also Gopatha-brâhma*n*a I, 2, 6.

26. A Brâhma*n*a declares: Since a devout student takes away from women, who refuse (to give him alms, the merit gained) by (*S*rauta)-sacrifices, by gifts, (and) by burnt-offerings (offered in the domestic fire), as well as their offspring, their cattle, the sacred learning (of their families), therefore, indeed, (a woman) should not refuse (alms) to the crowd of students; for amongst those (who come to beg), there might be one of that (devout) kind, one who thus (conscientiously) keeps his vow.

27. Alms (shall) not (be considered) leavings (and be rejected) by inference (from their appearance), but on the strength of ocular or oral testimony (only).

28. A Brâhma*n*a shall beg, prefacing (his request) by the word 'Lady';

29. A Kshatriya (inserting the word) 'Lady' in the middle (between the words 'give alms');

30. A Vai*s*ya, adding the word 'Lady' (at the end of the formula).

31. (The pupil) having taken those (alms) shall place them before his teacher and offer them to him.

32. He may eat (the food) after having been ordered to do so by his teacher.

---

27. To eat the residue of the meal of any person except that left by the teacher and other Gurus, is not permitted to a student; see also below, I, 1, 4, 1 seq.; Manu II, 56; Yâg*ñ*. I, 33.

28. The formula to be used by a Brâhma*n*a is, 'Lady, give alms;' that to be used by a Kshatriya, 'Give, lady, alms;' and that used by a Vai*s*ya, 'Give alms, lady.' Manu II, 49; Yâg*ñ*. I, 30; Â*s*v. G*ri*. Sû. I, 22, 8.

31. The words with which he announces the alms are, Idam ittham âh*ri*tam, 'this much have I received.' Manu II, 51; Yâg*ñ*. I, 27; Â*s*v. G*ri*. Sû. I, 22, 10.

32. The answer of the teacher is, Saumya tvameva bhuṅkshva, 'friend, eat thou.'

33. If the teacher is absent, the pupil (shall offer the food) to (a member of) the teacher's family.

34. If the (family of the teacher) is (also) absent, the pupil (may offer the food) to other learned Brâhma*n*as (*S*rotriyas) also (and receive from them the permission to eat).

35. He shall not beg for his own sake (alone).

36. After he has eaten, he himself shall clean his dish.

37. And he shall leave no residue (in his dish).

38. If he cannot (eat all that he has taken in his dish), he shall bury (the remainder) in the ground;

39. Or he may throw it into the water;

40. Or he may place (all that remains in a pot), and put it down near an (uninitiated) Ârya;

41. Or (he may put it down) near a *S*ûdra slave (belonging to his teacher).

42. If (the pupil) is on a journey, he shall throw

---

34. Regarding the term *S*rotriya, see below, II, 3, 6, 4.

35. 'The meaning of this Sûtra is, that the rule given, Sûtra 42 (below), for a pupil who is on a journey, shall hold good also for a pupil who is at home, if (in the absence of his teacher) no *S*rotriyas are to be found (from whom he can receive the permission to eat).'—Haradatta.

36. 'He commits no sin, if he has the alms-pot cleaned by somebody else. Some say that the Sûtra refers to both vessels (the alms-pot and his own dish).'

40. An Ârya is a person belonging to one of the first three castes (see below). The Ârya must be a boy who is not initiated, because children are kâmabhakshâ*h*, i.e. allowed to eat what they like, even leavings.

42. This rule holds good if no *S*rotriyas are near. If *S*rotriyas are to be found, Sûtra 34 applies. Agni, the god of fire, is considered to be of the Brahminical caste, and hence he takes the place of the teacher or of the *S*rotriyas. See also Manu II, 247,

a part of the alms into the fire and eat (the remainder).

43. Alms are declared to be sacrificial food. In regard to them the teacher (holds the position which) a deity (holds in regard to food offered at a sacrifice).

44. And (the teacher holds also the place which) the Âhavanîya fire occupies (at a sacrifice, because a portion of the alms is offered in the fire of his stomach).

45. To him (the teacher) the (student) shall offer (a portion of the alms),

PRASNA I, PATALA 1, KHANDA 4.

1. And (having done so) eat what is left.

2. For this (remnant of food) is certainly a remnant of sacrificial food.

3. If he obtains other things (besides food, such as cattle or fuel, and gives them to his teacher) as he obtains them, then those (things hold the place of) rewards (given to priests for the performance of a sacrifice).

4. This is the sacrifice to be performed daily by a religious student.

5. And (the teacher) shall not give him anything that is forbidden by the revealed texts, (not even as) leavings,

6. Such as pungent condiments, salt, honey, or meat (and the like).

248, and the passages collected from the Brâhmanas, by Prof. Weber, Ind. Stud. IX, 39.

44. Manu II, 231.

4. 6. See above, I, 1, 2, 23.

7. By this (last Sûtra it is) explained (that) the other restrictions (imposed upon a student, such as abstinence from perfumes, ointments, &c., are likewise not to be broken).

8. For (explicit) revealed texts have greater force than custom from which (the existence of a permissive passage of the revelation) may be inferred.

9. Besides (in this particular case) a (worldly) motive for the practice is apparent.

---

7. See above, I, 1, 2, 24 seq.:—According to Haradatta, teachers were in the habit of giving ointments and the like forbidden substances to their pupils, and Âpastamba gives this rule in order to show his dissent from the practice.

8. 'Ânumânika means "proper to be inferred from." For the existence of a text of the revelation or tradition (Sm*ri*ti) is inferred from custom. A visible text of the revelation is (however) of greater weight than a custom from which the existence of a text may be inferred. It is impossible to infer (the existence of a text) which is opposed to such (a visible text), on account of the maxim "an inference (can be made only, if it is) not opposed (by ocular proof)." (Âpastamba), by speaking thus, ("For revealed texts," &c.,) shows that the rule forbidding a student to eat pungent condiments, salt &c. is based on the existing text of a Brâhma*n*a.'—Haradatta.

9. 'Though the text forbidding the use of pungent condiments, salt, and the like refers to such substances if they are not leavings, still it is improper to assert, on the ground of the custom, from which a permissive text may be inferred, that it (the existing text), which is general, must be restricted (to those cases only) where the forbidden substances are not leavings given by the teacher. (If an opponent should answer that) certainly there are also texts which contradict each other, such as "he takes" and "he does not take," and that therefore there is no reason why a text restricted (to the case in which forbidden substances are leavings of the teacher) should not be inferred. In order to answer (that plea), he (Âpastamba) says (Sûtra 9), "True, that would be right if no motive whatever could be discovered for that custom (to eat forbidden food which is given by the teacher). But a reason for this course of action exists."'—Haradatta.

10. For pleasure is obtained (by eating or using the forbidden substances).

11. A residue of food left by a father and an elder brother, may be eaten.

12. If they act contrary to the law, he must not eat (their leavings).

13. In the evening and in the morning he shall fetch water in a vessel (for the use of his teacher).

14. Daily he shall fetch fuel from the forest, and place it on the floor (in his teacher's house).

15. He shall not go to fetch firewood after sunset.

16. After having kindled the fire, and having swept the ground around (the altar), he shall place

10. 'What is that (reason)? [Sûtra 10] For to eat pungent condiments, salt, &c. gives pleasure to the eater, and therefore according to the maxim, I, 4, 12, 11, "That in case a custom has pleasure for its motive, there is no text of the holy law to authorise it," no text restricting (the prohibition of forbidden substances to the case in which a Brahma*k*ârin does not receive them as leavings from his teacher) can be inferred (from the practice of eating such leavings).'—Haradatta.

12. Another explanation of this Sûtra is given by Haradatta: 'If by eating their leavings he should commit a sin (because the food contains salt &c.), he shall not do it.'

13. Manu II, 182.

14. The reason for placing the fuel on the ground is, according to Haradatta, the fear lest, if placed on some shelf or the like, it should tumble down and injure the teacher's children. Others, however, are of opinion that the wood which the pupil fetches daily, is not to be used by the teacher for cooking, but for the performance of the pupil's daily fire-offering. The reason for this interpretation is, that in the G*ri*hya-sûtra, 11, 24, the daily offering of fuel is enjoined with the same words. See Weber, Ind. Stud. X, 123; Manu II, 186.

16. Some explain, instead of 'after having swept the ground around the altar,' &c., 'after having raked the scattered brands into a heap.'—Haradatta.

the sacred fuel on the fire every morning and evening, according to the prescription (of the Gr*i*hya-sûtra).

17. Some say that the fire is only to be worshipped in the evening.

18. He shall sweep the place around the fire after it has been made to burn (by the addition of fuel), with his hand, and not with the broom (of Ku*s*a grass).

19. But, before (adding the fuel, he is free to use the broom) at his pleasure.

20. He shall not perform non-religious acts with the residue of the water employed for the fire-worship, nor sip it.

21. He shall not sip water which has been stirred with the hand, nor such as has been received into one hand only.

22. And he shall avoid sleep (whilst his teacher is awake).

23. Then (after having risen) he shall assist his teacher daily by acts tending to the acquisition of spiritual merit and of wealth.

24. Having served (his teacher during the day in this manner, he shall say when going to bed): I have protected the protector of the law (my teacher).

18. Âp. Gr*i*. Sû. 11, 22.

20. During the fire-worship water is wanted for sprinkling the altar in various ways.

23. Acts tending to the acquisition of merit are here—collecting sacred fuel, Ku*s*a grass, and flowers for sacrifices. Acts tending to the acquisition of wealth are—gathering fuel for cooking, &c. Manu II, 182; Weber, Ind. Stud. X, 123 and 124.

24. Another explanation of the words spoken by the student is, 'O law, I have protected him; protect thou me.' See also Gopatha-brâhma*n*a I, 2, 4.

25. If the teacher transgresses the law through carelessness or knowingly, he shall point it out to him privately.

26. If (the teacher) does not cease (to transgress), he himself shall perform the religious acts (which ought to be performed by the former);

27. Or he may return home.

28. Now of him who rises before (his teacher) and goes to rest after (him), they say that he does not sleep.

29. The student who thus entirely fixes his mind there (in the teacher's family), has thereby performed all acts which yield rewards (such as the *G*yotish*t*oma), and also those which must be performed by a householder.

PRA*S*NA I, PA*T*ALA 2, KHA*ND*A 5.

1. The word 'austerity' (must be understood to apply) to (the observance of) the rules (of studentship).

2. If they are transgressed, study drives out the knowledge of the Veda acquired already, from the (offender) and from his children.

---

26. Compare above, I, 1, 1, 13.

29. The Sûtra refers to a naish*th*ika brahma*k*ârin or professed student, who never leaves his teacher's family, and never enters any other order; and it declares his merit to be equal to that of one who becomes a householder. Manu II, 243, 244; Yâ*gñ*. I, 49, 50.

5. 1. Manu II, 164.

2. The meaning of the phrase, 'Study drives out the Veda, which has already been learnt from him who studies transgressing the rules prescribed for the student,' is, 'The Veda recited at the Brahmaya*gñ*a (daily study), and other religious rites, produces no effect, i.e. gains no merit for the reciter.' Manu II, 97. Hara-

3. Besides he will go to hell, and his life will be shortened.

4. On account of that (transgression of the rules of studentship) no *Ri*shis are born amongst the men of later ages.

5. But some in their new birth, on account of a residue of the merit acquired by their actions (in former lives), become (similar to) *Ri*shis by their knowledge (of the Veda),

6. Like *S*vetaketu.

7. And whatever else, besides the Veda, (a student) who obeys the rules learns from his teacher, that brings the same reward as the Veda.

8. Also, if desirous to accomplish something (be

---

datta gives also the following three explanations of this Sûtra, adopted by other commentators:—

a. If these (rules) are transgressed, he loses his capacity for learning, because the Brahman forsakes him, &c.

b. If these rules are transgressed, the capacity for learning and the Brahman leave him, &c.

c. From him who studies whilst transgressing these rules, the Brahman goes out, &c.

4. 'Amongst the avaras means "amongst the men of modern times, those who live in the Kaliyuga." No *Ri*shis are born means "there are none who see (receive the revelation of) Mantras, Vedic texts."'—Haradatta.

5. 'How is it then that men in our days, though they transgress the rules prescribed for students, learn the four Vedas with little trouble? (The answer is), By virtue of a residue of the reward (due) for the proper observance of those rules (of studentship) in a former Yuga. Therefore Âpastamba says, Sûtra 6, "But some," &c. New existence means "new birth (life)."'—Haradatta.

6. An example of this (follows, Sûtra 6): 'Like *S*vetaketu. For *S*vetaketu learned the four Vedas in a short time; as we read in the *Kh*ândogya Upanishad (Prapâ*th*aka VI, 1).'—Haradatta.

7. 'Whatever else besides the Veda, such as poison-charms and the like.'—Haradatta.

it good or evil), he thinks it in his mind, or pronounces it in words, or looks upon it with his eye, even so it will be; thus teach (those who know the law).

9. (The duties of a student consist in) acts to please the spiritual teacher, the observance (of rules) conducive to his own welfare, and industry in studying.

10. Acts other than these need not be performed by a student.

11. A religious student who retains what he has learned, who finds pleasure in the fulfilment of the law, who keeps the rules of studentship, who is upright and forgiving, attains perfection.

12. Every day he shall rise in the last watch of the night, and standing near his teacher, salute him with (this) salutation: I, N. N., ho! (salute thee.)

13. And (he shall salute) before the morning meal also other very aged (learned Brâhma*n*as) who may live in the same village.

14. If he has been on a journey, (he shall salute

---

9. 'Acts to please the teacher are—washing his feet and the like; observance (of rules) conducive to welfare are—obedience to the prohibition to cross a river swimming, to eat pungent condiments, and obedience to the injunction to beg.'—Haradatta.

10. 'Acts other than these, such as pilgrimages and the like.'—Haradatta.

11. 'What this "perfection" is has been declared in Sûtras 7, 8.'—Haradatta.

12. Manu II, 122 and 124.

14. This salutation is to be performed only when the occasion requires it. The formerly-mentioned salutation (Sûtras 12, 13) is to be performed daily. In the next Sûtra follows that by which the fulfilment of a wish may be obtained.—Haradatta. Manu II, 121; Yâg*ñ*. I, 26.

the persons mentioned) when he meets them on his return.

15. (He may also salute the persons mentioned at other times), if he is desirous of heaven and long life.

16. A Brâhma*n*a shall salute stretching forward his right arm on a level with his ear, a Kshatriya holding it on a level with the breast, a Vai*s*ya holding it on a level with the waist, a *S*ûdra holding it low, (and) stretching forward the joined hands.

17. And when returning the salute of (a man belonging) to the first (three) castes, the (last syllable of the) name (of the person addressed) is produced to the length of three moras.

18. But when he meets his teacher after sunrise (coming for his lesson), he shall embrace (his feet).

19. On all other occasions he shall salute (him in the manner described above).

20. But some declare that he ought to embrace the (feet of his) teacher (at every occasion instead of saluting him).

21. Having stroked the teacher's right foot with his right hand below and above, he takes hold of it and of the ankle.

22. Some say, that he must press both feet, each with both hands, and embrace them.

23. He shall be very attentive the whole day

16. 'A Vai*s*ya shall salute stretching forth his arm on a level with his middle, i.e. the stomach; others say, on a level with his thigh; the *S*ûdra stretching it forth low, i.e. on a level with his feet.'—Haradatta.

17. See also Manu II, 125.

18. Manu II, 71.

22. Manu II, 72.

23. Manu II, 191.

long, never allowing his mind to wander from the lesson during the (time devoted to) studying.

24. And (at other times he shall be attentive) to the business of his teacher.

25. And during the time for rest (he shall give) his mind (to doubtful passages of the lesson learnt).

26. And he shall study after having been called by the teacher (and not request the teacher to begin the lesson).

Prasna I, Patala 2, Khanda 6.

1. Every day he shall put his teacher to bed after having washed his (teacher's) feet and after having rubbed him.

2. He shall retire to rest after having received (the teacher's permission).

3. And he shall not stretch out his feet towards him.

4. Some say, that it is not (sinful) to stretch out the feet (towards the teacher), if he be lying on a bed.

5. And he shall not address (the teacher), whilst he himself is in a reclining position.

6. But he may answer (the teacher) sitting (if the teacher himself is sitting or lying down).

7. And if (the teacher) stands, (he shall answer him,) after having risen also.

---

26. Yâg*ñ*. I, 27; Manu II, 191.

6. 1. Manu II, 209.

2. Manu II, 194.

4. 'But, in Âpastamba's opinion, it is sinful even in this case.'—Haradatta.

5. Manu II, 195.

6. Manu II, 196.

8. He shall walk after him, if he walks.

9. He shall run after him, if he runs.

10. He shall not approach (his teacher) with shoes on his feet, or his head covered, or holding (implements) in his hand.

11. But on a journey or occupied in work, he may approach him (with shoes on, with his head covered, or with implements in his hand),

12. Provided he does not sit down quite near (to his teacher).

13. He shall approach his teacher with the same reverence as a deity, without telling idle stories, attentive and listening eagerly to his words.

14. (He shall not sit near him) with his legs crossed.

15. If (on sitting down) the wind blows from the pupil towards the master, he shall change his place.

16. (He shall sit) without supporting himself with his hands (on the ground),

17. Without leaning against something (as a wall or the like).

18. If the pupil wears two garments, he shall wear the upper one after the fashion of the sacred thread at the sacrifices.

19. But, if he wears a (lower) garment only, he shall wrap it around the lower part of his body.

20. He shall turn his face towards his teacher though the latter does not turn his towards him.

21. He shall sit neither too near to, nor too far (from the teacher),

---

15. Manu II, 203.

18. At sacrifices the sacred thread passes over the left shoulder and under the right arm. Manu II, 63, and Taitt. Âr. II, 1, 3.

20. Manu II, 197.

22. (But) at such a distance, that (the teacher) may be able to reach him with his arms (without rising).

23. (He shall not sit in such a position) that the wind blows from the teacher, towards himself.

24. (If there is) only one pupil, he shall sit at the right hand (of the teacher).

25. (If there are) many, (they may sit) as it may be convenient.

26. If the master (is not honoured with a seat and) stands, the (pupil) shall not sit down.

27. (If the master is not honoured with a couch) and sits, the (pupil) shall not lie down on a couch.

28. And if the teacher tries (to do something), then (the pupil) shall offer to do it for him, if it is in his power.

29. And, if his teacher is near, he shall not embrace (the feet of) another Guru who is inferior (in dignity);

30. Nor shall he praise (such a person in the teacher's presence) by (pronouncing the name of) his family.

31. Nor shall he rise to meet such an (inferior Guru) or rise after him,

32. Even if he be a Guru of his teacher.

33. But he shall leave his place and his seat, (in order to show him honour.)

---

23. See Sûtra 15 and Manu quoted there.

29. The term Guru includes a father, maternal uncle, &c. (see above), and these are inferior to the teacher. Manu II, 205.

31-32. 'The pupil is not to show the mentioned marks of respect to any of his own inferior Gurus, even if the person is the Guru, e.g. the maternal uncle, of his teacher.'—Haradatta.

34. Some say, that (he may address) a pupil of his teacher by (pronouncing) his name, if he is also one of his (the pupil's) own Gurus.

35. But towards such a person who is generally revered for some other reason than being the teacher (e.g. for his learning), the (student) should behave as towards his teacher, though he be inferior in dignity to the latter.

36. After having eaten in his (teacher's) presence, he shall not give away the remainder of the food without rising.

37. Nor shall he sip water (after having eaten in the presence of his teacher without rising).

38. (He shall rise) addressing him (with these words), 'What shall I do?'

Prasna I, Patala 2, Khanda 7.

1. Or he may rise silently.

2. Nor shall he (in going away) move around his teacher with his left hand turned towards him; he shall go away after having walked around him with his right side turned towards him.

3. He shall not look at a naked woman.

4. He shall not cut the (leaves or flowers) of herbs or trees, in order to smell at them.

---

34. 'But Âpastamba's own opinion is that he ought not to address by name a (maternal uncle or other) Guru (who visits his teacher).'—Haradatta.

36. According to I, 1, 3, 40 seq., a student shall give what he is unable to eat to a child, or to a slave. If he has eaten in the presence of his teacher, he shall not give the food away without rising for the purpose.

7. 3. Manu IV, 53; Yâgñ. I, 135.

4. Gopatha-brâhmana I, 2, 2.

5. He shall avoid (the use of) shoes, of an umbrella, a chariot, and the like (luxuries).

6. He shall not smile.

7. If he smiles, he shall smile covering (the mouth with his hand); thus says a Brâhma*n*a.

8. He shall not touch a woman with his face, in order to inhale the fragrance of her body.

9. Nor shall he desire her in his heart.

10. Nor shall he touch (a woman at all) without a particular reason.

11. A Brâhma*n*a declares, 'He shall be dusty, he shall have dirty teeth, and speak the truth.'

12. Those teachers, who instructed his teacher in that science which he (the pupil) studies with him, (are to be considered as) spiritual teachers (by the pupil).

13. But if (a teacher), before the eyes of his (pupil), embraces the feet of any other persons, then he (the pupil also) must embrace their feet, (as long as he remains) in that (state of studentship).

---

5. Manu II, 178.

10. Manu II, 179.

11. 'Though both (these first two precepts) have been given in Sûtra I, 1, 2, 27, still they are repeated, in order to show that a *S*rauta penance for the breach of them, is enjoined by a revealed text.'—Haradatta.

12. The term va*m*sya, 'ancestor,' for the teacher's teacher is explained by the circumstance, that Hindus consider a 'school,' consisting of a succession of teachers and pupils, as a spiritual family, and call it a vidyâva*m*sa, vidyâparamparâ. Manu II, 205.

13. 'Another (commentator) says, "He, the pupil, must embrace their feet (at every meeting) from that time (when he first saw his teacher do it)." Because the word "but" is used in the Sûtra, he must do so even after he has returned home (on completion of his studies).'—Haradatta.

14. If (a pupil) has more than one teacher, the alms (collected by him) are at the disposal of him to whom he is (just then) bound.

15. When (a student) has returned home (from his teacher), he shall give (whatever he may obtain by begging or otherwise) to his mother.

16. The mother shall give it to her husband;

17. (And) the husband to the (student's) teacher.

18. Or he may use it for religious ceremonies.

19. After having studied as many (branches of) sacred learning as he can, he shall procure in a righteous manner the fee for (the teaching of) the Veda (to be given to his teacher), according to his power.

20. But, if the teacher has fallen into distress, he may take (the fee) from an Ugra or from a *S*ûdra.

21. But some declare, that it is lawful at any time to take the money for the teacher from an Ugra or from a *S*ûdra.

---

14. 'More than one teacher,' i.e. several, who have taught him the several Vedas. Each Brahman generally knowing one Veda only.

This passage shows, that the young Brahmans in olden time, just as now, went from one teacher to the other, learning from each what he knew. The rules, which seemingly enjoin a pupil to stay with one and the same teacher, refer only to the principle, that the pupil must stay with his teacher, until he has learnt the subject which he began with him.

18. 'Religious ceremonies, i.e. the wedding and the like. For them he may use it optionally. He, i.e. on failure of the teacher; the father, on failure of the father; the mother, on failure of all (the pupil) himself.'—Haradatta.

19. Manu II, 245 and 246; Yâ*gñ*. I, 51; Weber, Ind. Stud. X, 125.

20. 'The word Ugra denotes either the offspring of a Vai*s*ya and of a *S*ûdra woman, or a twice-born man, who perpetrates dreadful deeds.'—Haradatta.

22. And having paid (the fee), he shall not boast of having done so.

23. And he shall not remember what he may have done (for his teacher).

24. He shall avoid self-praise, blaming others, and the like.

25. If he is ordered (by his teacher to do something), he shall do just that.

26. On account of the incompetence of his teacher, (he may go) to another (and) study (there).

27. He shall behave towards his teacher's wife as towards the teacher himself, but he shall not embrace her feet, nor eat the residue of her food.

28. So also (shall he behave) towards him who teaches him at (the teacher's) command,

29. And also to a fellow-student who is superior (in learning and years).

30. He shall behave to his teacher's son (who is superior to himself in learning or years) as to his teacher, but not eat the residue of his food.

31. Though he may have returned home, the

---

24. Manu II, 179.

26. See above, I, 1, 1, 13, and note. Here also Haradatta states that the permission to leave the teacher is to be restricted to those who have not solemnly bound themselves to their teacher by allowing him to perform the ceremony of initiation.

27. Manu II, 208–212.

28. 'The use of the present "adhyâpayati," shows that this rule holds good only for the time during which he is taught by such a man.'—Haradatta.

29. 'Because (an older fellow-student) is of use to him, according to the verse: One-fourth (of his learning) a pupil receives from his teacher, one-fourth he acquires by his own intelligence, one-fourth from his fellow-students, one-fourth he is taught by time.'—Haradatta.

30. Manu II, 207–209.

behaviour towards his (teacher and the rest) which is prescribed by the rule of conduct settled by the agreement (of those who know the law, must be observed by him to the end),

PRASNA I, PATALA 2, KHANDA 8.

1. Just as by a student (actually living with his teacher).

2. He may wear garlands, anoint his face (with sandal), oil his hair and moustaches, smear his eyelids (with collyrium), and (his body) with oil, wear a turban, a cloth round his loins, a coat, sandals, and wooden shoes.

3. Within the sight of his (teacher or teacher's relations) he shall do none of those (actions, as putting on a garland), nor cause them to be done.

4. Nor (shall he wear garlands &c. whilst performing) acts for his pleasure,

5. As, for instance, cleaning his teeth, shampooing, combing the hair, and the like.

6. And the teacher shall not speak of the goods of the (pupil) with the intention to obtain them.

7. But some declare, that, if a pupil who has bathed (after completing his studies) is called by his teacher or has gone to see him, he shall not take off

---

8. 1. Haradatta does not connect this Sûtra with the preceding one. He explains it by itself: '(We will now declare) how a student (who has left his teacher, but is not married) ought to behave.'

6. 'If the teacher comes to the house of his (former) pupil (who has become a householder), he shall, for instance, not say, "Oh, what a beautiful dish!" in such a manner, that his desire to obtain it becomes apparent.'—Haradatta.

7. This opinion is contrary to Âpastamba's view given in Sûtras 2 and 3 above.

that (garland or other ornaments) which he wears according to the law at the time (of that ceremony).

8. He shall not sit on a seat higher (than that of his teacher),

9. Nor on a seat that has more legs (than that of his teacher),

10. Nor on a seat that stands more firmly fixed (on the ground than that of his teacher),

11. Nor shall he sit or lie on a couch or seat which is used (by his teacher).

12. If he is ordered (by his teacher), he shall on a journey ascend a carriage after him.

13. (At his teacher's command) he shall also enter an assembly, ascend a roller (which his teacher drags along), sit on a mat of fragrant grass or a couch of straw (together with his teacher).

14. If not addressed by a Guru, he shall not speak to him, except (in order to announce) good news.

15. He shall avoid to touch a Guru (with his finger), to whisper (into his ear), to laugh (into his face), to call out to him, to pronounce his name or to give him orders and the like (acts).

---

10. 'When he gives to his teacher a wooden seat (with legs), he shall not sit on a cane-seat (without legs), for the latter touches the ground on all sides.'—Haradatta.

11. Manu II, 119.

12. This rule is an exception to I, 2, 7, 5. Manu II, 204.

13. 'The roller is an implement used by husbandmen, with which the ploughed land is made even. If one person ascends it and another drags it along, the ground becomes even. If that is dragged by the teacher, the pupil shall ascend it at his command. He shall not disobey from fear of the unseemliness of the action.'—Haradatta.

15. Manu II, 199; regarding the term Guru, see above, I, 2, 6, 29.

16. In time of need he may attract attention (by any of these acts).

17. If (a pupil) resides (in the same village) with (his teacher after the completion of his studies), he shall go to see him every morning and evening, without being called.

18. And if he returns from a journey, he shall (go to) see him on the same day.

19. If his teacher and his teacher's teacher meet, he shall embrace the feet of his teacher's teacher, and then show his desire to do the same to his teacher.

20. The other (the teacher) shall (then) forbid it.

21. And (other marks of) respect (due to the teacher) are omitted in the presence of the (teacher's teacher).

22. And (if he does not live in the same village), he shall go frequently to his teacher's residence, in order to see him, and bring him some (present), with his own hand, be it even only a stick for cleaning the teeth. Thus (the duties of a student have been explained).

23. (Now) the conduct of a teacher towards his pupil (will be explained).

24. Loving him like his own son, and full of attention, he shall teach him the sacred science, without hiding anything in the whole law.

25. And he shall not use him for his own purposes to the detriment of his studies, except in times of distress.

---

17. This and the following Sûtras refer to a person who has finished his studentship, while the preceding ones, from Sûtra 8, apply to the time of studentship also.

24. Weber, Ind. Stud. X, 126.

26. That pupil who, attending to two (teachers), accuses his (principal and first) teacher of ignorance, remains no (longer) a pupil.

27. A teacher also, who neglects the instruction (of his pupil), does no (longer) remain a teacher.

28. If the (pupil) commits faults, (the teacher) shall always reprove him.

29. Frightening, fasting, bathing in (cold) water, and banishment from the teacher's presence are the punishments (which are to be employed), according to the greatness (of the fault), until (the pupil) leaves off (sinning).

30. He shall dismiss (the pupil), after he has performed the ceremony of the Samâvartana and has finished his studentship, with these words, 'Apply thyself henceforth to other duties.'

Prasna I, Patala 3, Khanda 9.

1. After having performed the Upâkarma for studying the Veda on the full moon of the month *S*râva*n*a (July–August), he shall for one month not study in the evening.

---

26. 'Another commentator says, "That pupil who offends his teacher in word, thought, or deed, and directs his mind improperly, i.e. does not properly obey, does not (any longer) remain a pupil."'—Haradatta.

29. But see also Manu VIII, 299, where corporal punishment is permitted.

9. 1. The Upâkarma is the ceremony which is performed every year at the beginning of the course of study. It is in fact the solemn opening of the Brahmanic term. 'Because Âpastamba uses the word evening (i.e. first part of the night) it is not sinful to study later in the night.'—Haradatta. Manu IV, 95; Yâg*ñ*. I, 142, 143; Weber, Ind. Stud. X, 130 and 134.

2. On the full moon of the month of Pausha (December–January), or under the constellation Rohinî, he shall leave off reading the Veda.

3. Some declare, (that he shall study) for four months and a half.

4. He shall avoid to study the Veda on a high-road.

5. Or he may study it (on a high-road), after having smeared (a space) with cowdung.

6. He shall never study in a burial-ground nor anywhere near it within the throw of a Samyâ.

7. If a village has been built over (a burial-ground) or its surface has been cultivated as a field, the recitation of the Veda (in such a place) is not prohibited.

8. But if that place is known to have been (a burial-ground), he shall not study (there).

---

2. The term lasts therefore for five months; (i.e. latter half of Srâvana, Bhâdrapada, Âsvina, Kârttika, Mârgasîrsha, and the first half of Pausha.) The Rohinî-day of Pausha is meant.

3. 'According to this latter opinion the Upâkarma should be performed on the full moon of Bhâdrapada, as has been taught in another work (Manu IV, 95); the (time of the) Utsargana, (the solemn closing of the term) should be advanced; and after the Utsargana has been performed, one may study the Veda during the light nights of each month until the full moon of Srâvana, in order to fix in one's mind the part learned already; and in the dark fortnight of each month one may study the Vedâṅgas, i.e. grammar and the rest (Manu IV, 98). On the full moon of Srâvana the Upâkarma should be performed once more, and that part of the Veda should be studied which has not yet been learned.'—Haradatta.

4. Nigamâh, 'high-roads,' are squares and the like.—Haradatta.

6. The Samyâ is either the pin in the bullock's yoke or the round stick, about a foot and a half in length, which is used for the preparation of the Vedi. Manu IV, 116; Yâgñ. I, 148.

8. 'Nor anywhere near it within the throw of a Samyâ.' This must be understood from Sûtra 6.

9. A *S*ûdra and an outcast are (included by the term) burial-ground, (and the rule given, Sûtra 6, applies to them).

10. Some declare, that (one ought to avoid only, to study) in the same house (where they dwell).

11. But if (a student and) a *S*ûdra woman merely look at each other, the recitation of the Veda must be interrupted,

12. Likewise, if (a student and) a woman, who has had connexion with a man of a lower caste, (look at each other).

13. If he, who is about to study the Veda, wishes to talk to a woman during her courses, he shall first speak to a Brâhma*n*a and then to her, then again speak to a Brâhma*n*a, and afterwards study. Thereby the children (of that woman) will be blessed.

14. (He shall not study in a village) in which a corpse lies;

15. Nor in such a one where *K*â*nd*âlas live.

16. He shall not study whilst corpses are being carried to the boundary of the village,

17. Nor in a forest, if (a corpse or *K*â*nd*âla) is within sight.

18. And if outcasts have entered the village, he shall not study on that day,

---

9. Yâ*gñ*. I, 148.

13. The last part of the Sûtra may also be interpreted: 'Thus she will be blessed with children.'—Haradatta.

14. Manu IV, 108; Yâ*gñ*. I, 148.

18. Haradatta explains Bâhya, 'outcasts,' by 'robbers, such as Ugras and Nishâdas.' But, I think, it means simply such outcasts as live in the forest or outside the village in the Vâ*d*î, like the *Dh*ers, Mahârs, Mângs of the present day. Most of these tribes, however, are or were given to thieving. See Kullûka on Manu X, 28, and the Petersburg Dict. s. v.

19. Nor if good men (have come).

20. If it thunders in the evening, (he shall not study) during the night.

21. If lightning is seen (in the evening, he shall not study during that night), until he has slept.

22. If lightning is seen about the break of dawn, or at the time when he may distinguish at the distance of a *S*amyâ-throw, whether (a cow) is black or red, he shall not study during that day, nor in the following evening.

23. If it thunders in the second part of the third watch of the night, (he shall not study during the following day or evening).

24. Some (declare, that this rule holds good, if it thunders), after the first half of the night has passed.

25. (Nor shall he study) whilst the cows are prevented from leaving (the village on account of thieves and the like),

26. Nor (on the imprisonment of criminals) whilst they are being executed.

27. He shall not study whilst he rides on beasts (of burden).

28. At the new moon, (he shall not study) for two days and two nights.

---

19. Yâ*gñ*. I, 150.

20. Manu IV, 106; Yâ*gñ*. I, 145. 'This rule refers to the rainy season. (For thunder) at other (seasons) he orders below a longer (cessation).'—Haradatta.

27. Manu IV, 120; Yâ*gñ*. I, 151.

28. '"For two days," i.e. on the day of the new moon and the preceding one, the fourteenth of the half month.'—Haradatta. Manu IV, 113; Yâ*gñ*. I, 146.

PRASNA I, PATALA 3, KHANDA 10.

1. (Nor shall he study) on the days of the full moons of those months in which the *K*âturmâsya-sacrifice may be performed (nor on the days preceding them).

2. At the time of the Vedotsarga, on the death of Gurus, at the Ash*t*akâ-*S*râddha, and at the time of the Upâkarma, (he shall not study) for three days;

3. Likewise if near relations have died.

4. (He shall not study) for twelve days, if his mother, father, or teacher have died.

5. If these (have died), he must (also) bathe for the same number of days.

6. Persons who are younger (than the relation deceased), must shave (their hair and beard).

---

10. 1. The three full-moon days are Phâlgunî (February–March), Âshâ*dh*î (June–July), Kârttikî (October–November).

2. The construction is very irregular, the first noun standing in the nominative and the rest in the locative. A similar irregularity occurs below, I, 3, 11, 31. The Vedotsarga is the ceremony which is performed at the end of the Brahmanic term, in January. 'In the case of the death of a Guru, the vacation begins with the day on which the death occurs. On the other occasions mentioned he shall not study on the day preceding (the ceremony), on the day (of the ceremony), nor on the day following it.'—Haradatta. Manu IV, 119; Yâ*gñ*. I, 144. 'The Gurus' intended here, are fathers-in-law, uncles, &c.

3. 'This rule applies to a student only. It is known from another work that those who have been infected by impurity (on the death of a relation), must not study whilst the impurity lasts.'—Haradatta. Yâ*gñ*. I, 144.

6. The word anubhâvina*h*, interpreted by Haradatta as 'persons who are younger than the deceased,' is explained in different ways by others; firstly, as 'the mourners,' and secondly, as 'Samânodakas or gentiles beyond the sixth degree.' In the latter case the Sûtra ought to be translated thus: 'On the death of gentiles beyond the sixth degree, (the head) ought to be shaved.'

7. Some declare, that students who have returned home on completion of their studentship, shall never shave, except if engaged in the initiation to a *S*rauta-sacrifice.

8. Now a Brâhma*n*a also declares, 'Verily, an empty, uncovered (pot) is he, whose hair is shaved off entirely; the top-lock is his covering.'

9. But at sacrificial sessions the top-lock must be shaved off, because it is so enjoined in the Veda.

10. Some declare, that, upon the death of the teacher, (the reading should be interrupted) for three days and three nights.

11. If (he hears of) the death of a learned Brâhma*n*a (*S*rotriya) before a full year (since the death) has elapsed, (he shall interrupt his reading) for one night (and day).

12. Some declare, (that the deceased *S*rotriya must have been) a fellow-student.

13–14. If a learned Brâhma*n*a (*S*rotriya) has arrived and he is desirous of studying or is actually studying, (or if he is desirous of teaching or is teach-

---

7. Regarding the Dîkshâ 'initiation,' see Aitareya-brâhma*n*a I, 1, and Max Müller's History of Ancient Sanskrit Literature, p. 309 seq.

8. Hence it follows that the top-lock should not be shaved off, except in the case mentioned in the following Sûtra.

9. Sattras, 'sacrificial sessions,' are sacrifices which last longer than twelve days.

10. 'But in his opinion it should be twelve days, as declared above, Sûtra 4.'—Haradatta. It appears, therefore, that this Sûtra is to be connected with Sûtra 4.

11. 'Because the word "death" is used here, death only is the reason (for stopping the reading), in the case of Gurus and the rest (i.e. the word "died" must be understood in Sûtra 2 and the following ones).'—Haradatta.

ing,) he may study or teach after having received permission (to do so from the *S*rotriya).

15–16. He may likewise study or teach in the presence of his teacher, if (the latter) has addressed him (saying), 'Ho, study! (or, Ho, teach!)'

17. When a student desires to study or has finished his lesson, he shall at both occasions embrace the feet of his teacher.

18. Or if, whilst they study, another person comes in, he shall continue his recitation, after those words ('Ho, study!') have been pronounced (by the new-comer).

19. The barking of (many) dogs, the braying of (many) asses, the cry of a wolf or of a solitary jackal or of an owl, all sounds of musical instruments, of weeping, and of the Sâman melodies (are reasons for discontinuing the study of the Veda).

20. If another branch of the Veda (is being recited in the neighbourhood), the Sâman melodies shall not be studied.

21. And whilst other noises (are being heard, the recitation of the Veda shall be discontinued), if they mix (with the voice of the person studying).

15–16. Manu II, 73.

17. Manu II, 73.

18. Haradatta states rightly, that the plural ('they study') is useless. According to him, the use of the verb in the singular may be excused thereby, that the advice is addressed to each of the persons engaged in study. Manu IV, 122.

19. The ekas*ri*ka, 'solitary jackal,' is now called Bâlu or Pheough, and is considered to be the constant companion of a tiger or panther. Its unharmonious cry is, in the present day also, considered to be an evil omen. Yâ*gñ*. I, 148; Manu IV, 108, 115 and 123.

21. Manu IV, 121.

22. After having vomited (he shall not study) until he has slept.

23. Or (he may study) having eaten clarified butter (after the attack of vomiting).

24. A foul smell (is a reason for the discontinuance of study).

25. Food turned sour (by fermentation), which he has in his stomach, (is a reason for the discontinuance of the recitation, until the sour rising ceases).

26. (Nor shall he study) after having eaten in the evening,

27. Nor as long as his hands are wet.

28. (And he shall discontinue studying) for a day and an evening, after having eaten food prepared in honour of a dead person (for whom the Sapi*nd*î-kara*n*a has not yet been performed),

29. Or until the food (eaten on that occasion) is digested.

30. But he shall (always) eat in addition (to the meal given in honour of a dead person), food which has not been given at a sacrifice to the Manes.

---

22. Manu IV, 121.

24. Manu IV, 107; Yâg*ñ*. I, 150.

25. Manu IV, 121.

26. 'Therefore he shall sup, after having finished his study.'—Haradatta.

27. Manu IV, 121; Yâg*ñ*. I, 149.

28. Manu IV, 112; Yâg*ñ*. I, 146.

29. 'If that food has not been digested by the end of that time (i.e. in the evening), he shall not study until it has been digested.'—Haradatta.

30. 'Because in this Sûtra the expression "food not given at a *S*râddha" occurs, some think that the preceding Sûtra refers to "food eaten at a *S*râddha."'—Haradatta. This explanation is not at all improbable.

PRASNA I, PATALA 3, KHANDA 11.

1. (The recitation of the Veda shall be interrupted for a day and evening if he has eaten), on beginning a fresh Kâ*nd*a (of his Veda), food given by a motherless person,

2. And also if he has eaten, on the day of the completion of a Kâ*nd*a, food given by a fatherless person.

3. Some declare, that (the recitation shall be interrupted for the same space of time), if he has eaten at a sacrifice offered in honour of gods who were formerly men.

4. Nor is the recitation interrupted, if he has eaten rice received the day before, or raw meat (though these things may have been offered in honour of the dead),

5. Nor (if he has eaten at a funeral dinner) roots or fruits of herbs and trees.

6. When he performs the ceremony for beginning a Kâ*nd*a, or when he studies the index of the Anu-

---

11. 1. The Black Ya*g*ur-veda, to which Âpastamba belongs, is divided throughout into books called Kâ*nd*as.

3. Haradatta names as such gods, Nandîsvara and Kubera. Other commentators, however, explain Manushyaprak*ri*ti by Manushyamukha, 'possessing human faces.' A similar rule occurs Gautama XVI, 34, where a Manushyaya*gñ*a is mentioned as a cause for discontinuing the recitation of the Veda. In his commentary on Gautama, also, Haradatta is in doubt. He first refers the term to the sacraments like the Sîmantonnayana, and then adds, that some explain it to mean 'a sacrifice to gods who formerly were men.'

4. This Sûtra is an exception to I, 3, 10, 28.

6. Haradatta's commentary on this Sûtra is very meagre, and he leaves the word anuvâkyam unexplained. I am not certain that my explanation is correct. But it is countenanced by the statements of the G*ri*hya-sûtras regarding the order of studying. Weber, Ind. Stud. X, 132.

vâkas of a (Kâ*nd*a), he shall not study that (Kâ*nd*a) on that day (nor in that night).

7. And if he performs the ceremonies prescribed on beginning or ending the recitation of one entire Veda, he shall not study that Veda (during that day).

8. If the wind roars, or if it whirls up the grass on the ground, or if it drives the rain-drops forward during a rain-shower, (then the recitation shall be interrupted for so long a time as the storm lasts).

9. (Nor shall he study) on the boundary between a village and forest,

10. Nor on a highway.

11. If (some of his) fellow-students are on a journey, he shall not study during that day, (the passage) which they learn together.

12. And whilst performing acts for his pleasure,

13. Such as washing his feet, shampooing or anointing himself,

14. He shall neither study nor teach, as long as he is thus occupied.

---

7. Yâ*gñ*. I, 145. This Sûtra is a *Gñ*âpaka or 'such a one which indicates the existence of a rule not expressly mentioned.' Above (I, 3, 9, 1) the yearly performance of the Upâkarma and Utsarga ceremonies for the beginning and end of the Brahmanic term has been prescribed. In this Sûtra the performance of the Upâkarma and Utsarga at the beginning and completion of the Pârâya*n*a or the vow to go through a whole Veda is incidentally mentioned. Thence it may be inferred that these ceremonies must be likewise performed on the latter occasions, though no absolute rule to this effect has been given. Such *Gñ*âpakas are of frequent occurrence in all Sûtras, and constitute one of the chief difficulties of their interpretation.

8. Yâ*gñ*. I, 149; Manu IV, 102, 122.

11. Others explain the Sûtra thus: 'If he meets fellow-students, after they have come home from a journey, he shall not study with them on that day.'

15. (He shall not study or teach) in the twilight,

16. Nor whilst sitting on a tree,

17. Nor whilst immersed in water,

18. Nor at night with open doors,

19. Nor in the day-time with shut doors.

20. During the spring festival and the festival (of Indra), in the month of Âshâ*dh*a (June–July), the study of an Anuvâka is forbidden.

21. (The recitation) of the daily portion of the Veda (at the Brahmaya*gñ*a is likewise forbidden if done) in a manner differing from the rule (of the Veda).

22. (Now follows) the rule (for the daily recitation) of that (Brahmaya*gñ*a).

23. Before taking his morning-meal, he shall go to the water-side, and having purified himself, he shall recite aloud (a portion of the Veda) in a pure

---

15. Yâ*gñ*. I, 145; Manu IV, 113.

16. Yâ*gñ*. I, 151; Manu IV, 120.

20. According to Haradatta, Âpastamba uses the word Anuvâka in order to indicate that smaller portions of the Veda may be studied. Others think, that by Anuvâka, the Sa*m*hitâ and the Brâhma*n*a are meant, and that the study of the Aṅgas is permitted. The Vasantotsava, or spring-festival, which, according to the Dramas, was, in olden times, kept all over India, falls, according to Haradatta, on the thirteenth of the first half of *K*aitra, about the beginning of April.

21. 'Hence, if one has forgotten it and eaten one's breakfast, a penance, not the Brahmaya*gñ*a, must be performed.'—Haradatta.

23. See Taittirîya Âra*n*yaka II, 11, 1 and 11; Â*s*v. G*ri*. Sû. III, 2, 1–2. In our days this rule is usually not observed. Brâhma*n*as mostly recite at the daily Brahmaya*gñ*a, 'Veda-offering,' one particular formula, which symbolically comprises the whole Veda. A few learned Brâhma*n*a friends, however, have assured me, that they still recite the whole of their *S*âkhâ every year according to this rule of Âpastamba.

place, leaving out according to (the order of the) texts (what he has read the day before).

24. If a stoppage of study is enjoined (for the day, he shall recite the daily portion) mentally.

25. If lightning flashes without interruption, or, thunder rolls continually, if a man has neglected to purify himself, if he has partaken of a meal in honour of a dead person, or if hoarfrost lies on the ground, (in these cases) they forbid the mental recitation (of the daily portion of the Veda).

26 Some forbid it only in case one has eaten a funeral dinner.

27. Where lightning, thunder, and rain happen together out of season, the recitation shall be interrupted for three days.

28. Some (declare, that the recitation shall stop) until the ground is dry.

29. If one or two (of the phenomena mentioned in Sûtra 27 appear, the recitation shall be interrupted) from that hour until the same hour next day.

30. In the case of an eclipse of the sun or of the moon, of an earthquake, of a whirlwind, of the fall of a meteor, or of a fire (in the village), at whatever time these events happen, the recitation of all the sacred sciences (Vedas and Aṅgas) must be interrupted from that hour until the same hour next day.

31. If a cloud appears out of season, if the sun or the moon is surrounded by a halo, if a rainbow, a parhelion or a comet appears, if a (high) wind (blows),

25. Yâ*gñ*. I, 149; Manu IV, 106, 120, 127; Taitt. Âr. II, 15, 1.

26. Manu IV, 109, 116.

27. Manu IV, 103 and 104.

30. Yâ*gñ*. I, 145; Manu IV, 105, 118.

31. Manu IV, 104, and see above.

a foul smell (is observed), or hoarfrost (lies on the ground, at all these occasions (the recitation of all the sacred sciences must be interrupted) during the duration (of these phenomena).

32. After the wind has ceased, (the interruption of the recitation continues) for one muhûrta.

33. If (the howl of) a wolf or of a solitary jackal (has been heard, he shall stop the reading) until he has slept.

34. At night (he shall not study) in a wood, where there is no fire nor gold.

35. Out of term he shall not study any part of the Veda which he has not learnt before.

36. Nor (shall he study during term some new part of the Veda) in the evening.

37. That which has been studied before, must never be studied (during the vacation or in the evening).

38. Further particulars (regarding the interruption

---

32. One muhûrta = 48 minutes.

36. Other commentators interpret the Sûtra in a different sense. They take it to mean: 'And during the night (from the twelfth to the thirteenth of each half of the month, he shall not study at all, be it in or out of term).'

37. 'What has been studied before, must not be studied (again) at any time in the vacation nor in the evening.'—Haradatta.

38. Haradatta thinks that by 'Parishad,' Manu's and other Dharma-*s*âstras are meant. This explanation is, however, not exact. Parishad, 'assemblage,' means, in the language of the *S*âstras, either a Pa*ñk*, an assemblage of learned Brahmans called together to decide some knotty point of law, or a Brahminical school, which studies a particular redaction of the Veda (see the Petersburg Dict. s. v.) The latter meaning is that applicable to this Sûtra. By 'Parishada*h*' are here intended the Vedic schools, and their writings and teaching. Gautama also says, XVI, 49, Prâtividya*m* yân smaranti smaranti, '(he shall observe the stoppages of the

of the Veda-study may be learnt) from the (teaching and works of other) Vedic schools.

PRASNA I, PATALA 4, KHANDA 12.

1. A Brâhmana declares, 'The daily recitation (of the Veda) is austerity.'

2. In the same (sacred text) it is also declared, 'Whether he recites the daily portion of the Veda standing, or sitting, or lying down, he performs austerity thereby; for the daily recitation is austerity.'

3. Now the Vâgasaneyi-brâhmana declares also, 'The daily recitation is a sacrifice at which the Veda is offered. When it thunders, when lightning flashes or thunderbolts fall, and when the wind blows violently, these sounds take the place of the exclamations Vashat (Vaushat and Svâhâ). Therefore he shall recite the Veda whilst it thunders, whilst lightning flashes and thunderbolts fall, and whilst the wind blows violently, lest the Vashat (should be heard) in vain.'

Veda-study) which they teach in (the writings belonging to) each of the Vedas.'

12. 1. 'It procures as much reward as penance.'—Haradatta. Manu II, 166; Weber, Ind. Stud. X, 113. The phrase occurs frequently in the Brâhmanas, e.g. Taitt. Âr. II, 14, 3.

2. Regarding the proper position at the 'Veda-offering,' or daily recitation, see above, I, 3, 11, 23, and Taitt. Âr. II, 11, 3. Passages similar to the first part of the sentence quoted in this Sûtra occur Taitt. Âr. II, 12, 3, and 15, 3. It ought to be observed, that the Taitt. Âr. in both places has the word 'vragan,' which is also read in the P. and P. U. MSS. The second part is taken apparently from the same work, II, 14, 2.

3. See Satapatha-brâhmana XI, 5, 6, 8, where a passage very similar to that quoted by Âpastamba occurs. Vashat and the other exclamations, which are pronounced by the Hotri-priest, serve as signals for the Adhvaryu to throw the oblations into the fire.

4. The conclusion of the passage from that (Vâ*g*asaneyi-brâhma*n*a is found) in another *S*âkhâ (of the Veda).

5. 'Now, if the wind blows, or if it thunders, or if lightning flashes, or thunderbolts fall, then he shall recite one *Ri*k-verse (in case he studies the *Ri*g-veda), or one Ya*g*us (in case he studies the Ya*g*ur-veda), or one Sâman (in case he studies the Sâma-veda), or (without having regard to his particular Veda, the following Ya*g*us), "Bhû*h* Bhuva*h*, Suva*h*, in faith I offer true devotion." Then, indeed, his daily recitation is accomplished thereby for that day.'

6. If that is done, (if the passage of the Vâ*g*asaneyi-brâhma*n*a is combined with that quoted in Sûtra 5, the former stands) not in contradiction with the decision of the Âryas.

7. For they (who know the law) teach both the continuance and the interruption (of the daily recitation of the Veda). That would be meaningless, if one paid attention to the (passage of the) Vâ*g*asaneyi-brâhma*n*a (alone).

8. For no (worldly) motive for the decision of those Âryas is perceptible; (and hence it must have a religious motive and be founded on a passage of the Veda).

9. (The proper interpretation therefore is, that) the prohibition to study (given above and by the

---

5. 'Some suppose that the words Bhû*h* Bhuva*h* and Suva*h* &c. (are to be used only) if one studies the Brâhma*n*a portion of the Veda, not everywhere.'—Haradatta.

6. Haradatta explains Âryas by vi*s*ish*t*â*h*, 'excellent ones,' i.e. persons who know the law, and he gives Manu as an instance.

8. See above, I, 1, 4, 9 and 10, and notes.

Âryas generally) refers only to the repetition of the sacred texts in order to learn them, not to their application at sacrifices.

10. (But if you ask, why the decision of the Âryas presupposes the existence of a Vedic passage, then I answer): All precepts were (originally) taught in the Brâhma*n*as, (but) these texts have been lost. Their (former existence) may, however, be inferred from usage.

11. But it is not (permissible to infer the former existence of) a (Vedic) passage in cases where pleasure is obtained (by following a rule of the Sm*ri*ti or a custom).

12. He who follows such (usages) becomes fit for hell.

13. Now follow (some rites and) rules that have been declared in the Brâhma*n*as.

14. By way of laudation they are called 'great sacrifices' or 'great sacrificial sessions.'

15. (These rites include): The daily Bali-offering

---

10. How then is their existence known? 'They are inferred from usage.' '"Usage" means the teaching of the law-books and the practice. From that it is inferred that Manu and other (authors of law-books) knew such texts of the Brâhma*n*as. For how could otherwise (*Ri*shis like Manu) teach in their works or practise (such customs) for which no authority is now found? And certainly they were intimately connected with the revealed texts (i.e. saw them).'—Haradatta.

11. Compare above, I, 1, 4, 8–10.

13. The consequence of the introduction of these rules into a Sm*ri*ti work is, that their omission must be expiated by a Smârta penance and not by a *S*rauta one.

14. The commentator observes, that, as these rites are called 'great sacrifices,' by way of laudation only, the particular laws binding on performers of real Soma-sacrifices cannot be transferred to the performers of these ceremonies. Regarding the

to the (seven classes of) beings; the (daily) gift of (food) to men according to one's power;

PRASNA I, PATALA 4, KHANDA 13.

1. The oblation to the gods accompanied by the exclamation Svâhâ, which may consist even of a piece of wood only; the offering to the Manes accompanied by the exclamation Svadhâ, which may consist even of a vessel with water only; the daily recitation.

2. Respect must be shown to those who are superior by caste,

3. And also to (persons of the same caste who are) venerable (on account of learning, virtue, and the like).

4. A man elated (with success) becomes proud, a proud man transgresses the law, but through the transgression of the law hell indeed (becomes his portion).

5. It has not been declared, that orders (may be addressed by the teacher) to a pupil who has returned home.

6. The syllable 'Om' is the door of heaven.

---

term 'great sacrifices,' see also Taitt. Âr. II, 11, 10, 1 seq., and *S*atapatha-brâhma*n*a XI, 5, 6, 1.

13. 1. Taitt. Âr. II, 10, 2 and 3, and *S*atapatha-br. loc. cit. 2. Haradatta observes, that some consider the Devaya*gñ*a, mentioned in the Sûtra, to be different from the Vai*s*vadeva, but that he holds it to be the same. Further he mentions, that some prescribe this Vai*s*vadeva to be performed even if one has nothing to eat.

2. 'Namely, by allowing them to walk in front on the road and by giving them perfumed garlands and the like at festive occasions.' —Haradatta.

5. Haradatta gives as an example the order to fetch water, and adds that a voluntary act on a former pupil's part ought not to be forbidden.

6. Compare also Taitt. Âr. I, 2, 4, and Manu II, 74.

Therefore he who is about to study the Veda, shall begin (his lesson) by (pronouncing) it.

7. If he has spoken anything else (than what refers to the lesson, he shall resume his reading by repeating the word 'Om'). Thus the Veda is separated from profane speech.

8. And at sacrifices the orders (given to the priests) are headed by this word.

9. And in common life, at the occasion of ceremonies performed for the sake of welfare, the sentences shall be headed by this word, as, for instance, '(Om) an auspicious day,' '(Om) welfare,' '(Om) prosperity.'

10. Without a vow of obedience (a pupil) shall not study (nor a teacher teach) a difficult (new book) with the exception of (the texts called) Tri*h*srâva*n*a and Tri*h*sahava*k*ana.

11. Hârîta declares, that the (whole) Veda must be studied under a vow of obedience until there is no doubt (regarding it in the mind of the pupil).

---

9. The example given in the Sûtra is that of the Pu*n*yâhavâ*k*ana, which precedes every G*ri*hya ceremony, and at which the sacrificer requests a number of invited Brâhma*n*as to wish him success. The complete sentences are, The sacrificer: O*m* karma*n*a*h* pu*n*yâham bhavanto bruvantviti, 'Om, wish that the day may be auspicious for the performance of the ceremony.' The Brâhma*n*as: Om pu*n*yâha*m* karma*n*a iti, 'Om, may the day be auspicious for the ceremony.' In the same manner the Brâhma*n*as afterwards wish 'welfare,' svasti, 'prosperity,' v*ri*ddhi, to the sacrificer.

10. Manu II, 112.

11. The meaning of Hârîta is, that the vow of obedience is required for the Tri*h*srâva*n*a and Tri*h*sahava*k*ana, which Âpastamba exempted in the preceding Sûtra. It follows from this rule that the Aṅgas or works explanatory of the Veda need not be studied under a vow of obedience.

12. No obedience is due (to the teacher for teaching) works which do not belong to the Veda.

13. (A student) shall embrace the feet of a person, who teaches him at the request of his (regular teacher), as long as the instruction lasts.

14. Some (declare, that he shall do so) always, (if the substitute is) a worthy person.

15. But obedience (as towards the teacher) is not required (to be shown towards such a person).

16. And (pupils) older (than their teacher need not show him obedience).

17. If (two persons) teach each other mutually (different redactions of) the Veda, obedience (towards each other) is not ordained for them.

18. (For) the (wise) say, 'The Veda-knowledge (of either of them) grows.'

19. *S*vetaketu declares, 'He who desires to study more, after having settled (as a householder), shall dwell two months every year, with collected mind, in the house of his teacher,'

20. (And he adds), 'For by this means I studied a larger part of the Veda than before, (during my studentship.)'

21. That is forbidden by the *S*âstras.

22. For after the student has settled as a householder, he is ordered by the Veda, to perform the daily rites,

---

13. This rule is a supplement to I, 2, 7, 29.

14. '"A worthy person," i.e. on account of his learning or character.'—Haradatta.

16. 'According to some, this rule refers only to the time after the instruction has been completed; according to others, to the time of studentship.'—Haradatta. But see Manu II, 151 seq.

PRASNA I, PATALA 4, KHANDA 14.

1. (That is to say) the Agnihotra, hospitality,

2. And what else of this kind (is ordained).

3. He whom (a student) asks for instruction, shall certainly not refuse it;

4. Provided he does not see in him a fault, (which disqualifies him from being taught).

5. If by chance (through the pupil's stupidity the teaching) is not completed, obedience towards the (teacher is the pupil's only refuge).

6. Towards a mother (grandmother and great-grandmother) and a father (grandfather and great-grandfather) the same obedience must be shown as towards a teacher.

7. The feet of all Gurus must be embraced (every day) by a student who has returned home;

8. And also on meeting them, after returning from a journey.

9. The feet of (elder) brothers and sisters must be embraced, according to the order of their seniority.

10. And respect (must) always (be shown to one's elders and betters), according to the injunction

---

14. 1. The Agnihotra, i.e. certain daily oblations of clarified butter.

3. Manu II, 109–115. 5. Manu II, 218.

6. Manu II, 228, 235.

7. The word Gurus, 'venerable persons,' includes besides the teacher and persons mentioned in the preceding Sûtra, an elder brother, a maternal uncle, and all others who are one's betters or elders. See above, I, 2, 6, 29–35.

8. 'That is to say, whether he himself or "the venerable persons" undertook the journey.'—Haradatta.

9. Manu II, 133. 10. See above, I, 4, 13, 2.

(given above and according to the order of their seniority).

11. He shall salute an officiating priest, a father-in-law, a father's brother, and a mother's brother, (though they may be) younger than he himself, and (when saluting) rise to meet them.

12. Or he may silently embrace their feet.

13. A friendship kept for ten years with fellow-citizens (is a reason for giving a salutation, and so is) a friendship, contracted at school, which has lasted for five years. But a learned Brâhma*n*a (known) for less than three years, must be saluted.

14. If the age (of several persons whom one meets) is exactly known, one must salute the eldest (first).

15. He need not salute a person, who is not a Guru, and who stands in a lower or higher place than he himself.

16. Or he may descend or ascend (to the place where such a person stands) and salute him.

17. But every one (Gurus and others) he shall salute, after having risen (from his seat).

18. If he is impure, he shall not salute (anybody);

19. (Nor shall he salute) a person who is impure.

---

11. Manu II, 130.

12. The commentator adds that the mode of salutation must depend on their learning and virtue.

13. Manu II, 134.

16. This Sûtra, like the preceding, refers to those who are not 'Gurus.'

17. Manu II, 120.

18. 'Impure,' i.e. unfit for associating with others on account of the death of relations or through other causes, see below, I, 5, 15, 7 seq.

20. Nor shall he, being impure, return a salutation.

21. Married women (must be saluted) according to the (respective) ages of their husbands.

22. He shall not salute with his shoes on, or his head wrapped up, or his hands full.

23. In saluting women, a Kshatriya or a Vaisya he shall use a pronoun, not his name.

24. Some (declare, that he shall salute in this manner even) his mother and the wife of his teacher.

25. Know that a Brâhmana of ten years and a Kshatriya of a hundred years stand to each other in the relation of father and son. But between those two the Brâhmana is the father.

26. A younger person or one of equal age he shall ask, about his well-being (employing the word kusala).

27. (He shall ask under the same conditions) a Kshatriya, about his health (employing the word anâmaya);

28. A Vaisya if he has lost anything (employing the word anashta).

---

23. He shall say, 'I salute,' not 'I, N. N., salute.' Manu II, 123.

24. Âpastamba, of course, holds the contrary opinion. Manu II, 216.

25. This verse, which is found with slight variations in most Smritis, contains, according to Haradatta, an instruction given by a teacher to his pupil. Manu II, 135.

26. Of course, in case the person addressed is a Brahman. Manu II, 127. Kullûka quotes under this verse the above and the following Sûtras. But his quotation has only a faint resemblance to our text.

28. That is to say in these terms: 'I hope you have not lost any cattle or other property!'—Haradatta.

29. A *S*ûdra, about his health (employing the word ârogya).

30. He shall not pass a learned Brâhma*n*a without addressing him;

31. Nor an (unprotected) woman in a forest (or any other lonely place).

PRA*S*NA I, PA*T*ALA 5, KHA*N*DA 15.

1. When he shows his respect to Gurus or aged persons or guests, when he offers a burnt-oblation (or other sacrifice), when he murmurs prayers at dinner, when sipping water and during the (daily) recitation of the Veda, his garment (or his sacrificial thread) shall pass over his left shoulder and under his right arm.

2. By sipping (pure) water, that has been collected on the ground, he becomes pure.

3. Or he, whom a pure person causes to sip water, (becomes also pure).

---

31. He shall address a woman in order to re-assure her, and do it in these terms: 'Mother, or sister, what can I do for you? Don't be afraid!' &c.—Haradatta.

15. 1. Taitt. Âr. II, 1, 2 seq.; Manu IV, 58.

2. Pure water is that which a cow will drink. Yâ*gñ*. I, 192; Manu V, 128.

3. The ceremony of 'sipping water' may be performed in two ways; either the 'person sipping' may take the water out of a river, pond, &c., or he may get the water poured into his hand by another person. But, according to Âpastamba, he must not take a pot or gourd in his left hand and pour the water into his right, as some Sm*ri*tis allow. The reason for this rule is, that Âpastamba considers it essential that both hands should be used in conveying the water to the mouth; see also above, I, 1, 4, 21. This agrees with the custom now followed, which is to bend the right hand into the form of a cow's ear, and to touch the right wrist with the left hand while drinking.

4. He shall not sip rain-drops.

5. (He shall not sip water) from a (natural) cleft in the ground.

6. He shall not sip water heated (at the fire) except for a particular reason (as sickness).

7. He who raises his empty hands (in order to scare) birds, (becomes impure and) shall wash (his hands).

8. If he can (find water to sip) he shall not remain impure (even) for a muhûrta.

9. Nor (shall he remain) naked (for a muhûrta if he can help it).

10. Purification (by sipping water) shall not take place whilst he is (standing) in the water.

11. Also, when he has crossed a river, he shall purify himself by sipping water.

12. He shall not place fuel on the fire, without having sprinkled it (with water).

---

4. 'Some think, that this Sûtra is intended to forbid also the drinking of rain-water. Other commentators declare that, according to this Sûtra, it is allowed to use for "sipping" drops of water which fall from a vessel suspended by ropes [because the Sûtra emphatically excludes "rain-drops" only].'—Haradatta.

6. Manu II, 61. 'Because the term "heated by fire" is used, there is no objection to water heated by the rays of the sun. In the same manner the use of "hot" water only is usually forbidden in the Smritis.'—Haradatta.

7. 'Because the phrase "with empty hands" is used, he commits no fault if he raises his hand, holding a stick or a clod. Some declare, that the term "touching water" (rendered by "washing") means "sipping water."'—Haradatta.

11. The translation given above is based on the interpretation of Haradatta, who considers that Âpastamba holds 'crossing a river' to cause impurity. The natural and probably the right interpretation, however, is that rejected by Haradatta, 'But he shall sip water after having come out (of the river or tank).'

12. '"On the fire used for Vedic or Smârta sacrifices or for

13. (If he is seated in company with) other unclean persons on a seat consisting of a confused heap of straw, and does not touch them, he may consider himself pure.

14. (The same rule applies, if he is seated) on grass or wood fixed in the ground.

15. He shall put on a dress, (even if it is clean,) only after having sprinkled it with water.

16. If he has been touched by a dog, he shall bathe, with his clothes on;

17. Or he becomes pure, after having washed that part (of his body) and having touched it with fire and again washed it, as well as his feet, and having sipped water.

18. Unpurified, he shall not approach fire, (so near that he can feel the heat).

19. Some declare, that (he shall not approach nearer) than the length of an arrow.

20. Nor shall he blow on fire with his breath.

21. Nor shall he place fire under his bedstead.

---

household purposes." . . . Some declare, that (the fuel need not be sprinkled with water) if used for the kitchen fire.'—Haradatta.

14. Haradatta's commentary is of little use, and I am not quite certain that my translation is correct.

15. Manu V, 118.

17. This second proceeding is adopted in case the dog has touched the hands or the lower parts of the body, as may be learnt by the comparison of a verse of Manu.

18. Manu IV, 142; Yâ*gñ*. I, 155.

20. Manu IV, 53. Haradatta mentions other explanations of this Sûtra. Some say, that the *S*rauta fire may be kindled by blowing, because that is ordained particularly in the Vâ*g*asaneyaka, but that the domestic fire is not to be treated so. Others again consider the rule absolute, and say, that a hollow reed or bellows must be used for kindling the fire, lest drops of saliva should fall upon it.

21. Manu IV, 54.

22. It is lawful for a Brâhma*n*a to dwell in a village, where there is plenty of fuel and water, (and) where he may perform the rites of purification by himself.

23. When he has washed away the stains of urine and fæces after voiding urine or fæces, the stains of food (after dinner), the stains of the food eaten the day before (from his vessels), and the stains of semen, and has also washed his feet and afterwards has sipped water, he becomes pure.

Prasna I, Patala 5, Khanda 16.

1. He shall not drink water standing or bent forwards.

2. Sitting he shall sip water (for purification) thrice, the water penetrating to his heart.

---

22. The last condition mentioned in the Sûtra indicates, that the place must have a river or tank, not wells only, as the purification by sipping water cannot be performed without help, with water from wells.

23. Manu V, 138.

16. 1. Haradatta takes â*k*am here to mean 'to drink water,' and thinks that it is forbidden to do this standing or in a bent position. Others refer the prohibition to 'sipping water for the sake of purification,' and translate, 'He shall not sip water standing or in a bent position (except in case of necessity),' i.e. if the bank of the river is so high that he cannot reach the water sitting down, and in this case he shall enter it up to his thighs or up to his navel.

2. Manu II, 60 and 62; V, 139; and Yâ*gñ*. I, 20 and 27; Weber, Ind. Stud. X, 165. Haradatta observes, that the further particulars regarding purification by sipping water must be supplied from other Sm*ri*tis. The rule quoted by him is as follows: 'The performer should be sitting in a pure place, not on a seat, except when sipping water after dinner, and should sip thrice from his hand water which is free from bubbles and foam, and which he has attentively regarded, in such a quantity as would cover a Mâsha-

3. He shall wipe his lips three times.

4. Some (declare, that he shall do so) twice.

5. He shall then touch (his lips) once (with the three middle fingers).

6. Some (declare, that he shall do so) twice.

7. Having sprinkled water on his left hand with his right, he shall touch both his feet, and his head and (the following three) organs, the eyes, the nose, and the ears.

8. Then he shall wash (his hands).

9. But if he is going to eat he shall, though pure, twice sip water, twice wipe (his mouth), and once touch (his lips).

10. He shall rub the gums and the inner part of his lips (with his finger or with a piece of wood) and then sip water.

11. He does not become impure by the hair (of his moustaches) getting into his mouth, as long as he does not touch them with his hand.

12. If (in talking), drops (of saliva) are perceived to fall from his mouth, then he shall sip water.

13. Some declare, that if (the saliva falls) on the ground, he need not sip water.

---

bean. The water sipped by a Brahman should reach his heart, that sipped by a Kshatriya the throat, and that sipped by a Vaisya the palate. A *S*ûdra sips once as much as to wet his tongue.'

7. The eyes are to be touched with the thumb and the fourth finger, either at once, or one after the other, the nostrils with the thumb and the second finger, the ears with the thumb and the small finger.

9. Manu V, 138.

11. Haradatta observes that this Sûtra shows, that every other foreign substance brought with the food into the mouth, makes the food 'leavings' and the eater impure. Manu V, 141.

12. Manu V, 141 declares sipping to be unnecessary in this case.

14. On touching during sleep or in sternutation the effluvia of the nose or of the eyes, on touching blood, hair, fire, kine, a Brâhma*n*a, or a woman, and after having walked on the high road, and after having touched an impure (thing or man), and after having put on his lower garment, he shall either bathe or sip or merely touch water (until he considers himself clean).

15. (Or he may touch) moist cowdung, wet herbs, or moist earth.

16. He shall not eat meat which has been cut with a sword (or knife) used for killing.

17. He shall not bite off with his teeth (pieces from) cakes (roots or fruits).

18. He shall not eat in the house of a (relation within six degrees) where a person has died, before the ten days (of impurity) have elapsed.

19. (Nor shall he eat in a house) where a lying-in woman has not (yet) come out (of the lying-in chamber),

20. (Nor in a house) where a corpse lies.

---

14. Manu V, 145.

18. 'The term "ten days" is used in order to indicate the time of impurity generally. In some cases, as that of a Kshatriya, this lasts longer. In other cases, where the impurity lasts thirty-six hours only, (the abstention from dining in such houses is shorter.)'—Haradatta. Manu IV, 217.

19. A lying-in woman is impure, and must not be touched during the first ten days after her confinement. During this time, she exclusively occupies the Sûtikâg*ri*ha or lying-in chamber. Manu IV, 217.

20. Haradatta remarks that in the case of the death of a person who is not a relation, it is customary to place at the distance of 'one hundred bows' a lamp and water-vessel, and to eat (beyond that distance).

21. Food touched by a (Brâhma*n*a or other high-caste person) who is impure, becomes impure, but not unfit for eating.

22. But what has been brought (be it touched or not) by an impure *S*ûdra, must not be eaten,

23. Nor that food in which there is a hair,

24. Or any other unclean substance.

25. (Nor must that food be eaten) which has been touched with an unclean substance (such as garlic),

26. Nor (that in which) an insect living on impure substances (is found),

27. Nor (that in which) excrements or limbs of a mouse (are found),

28. Nor that which has been touched by the foot (even of a pure person),

29. Nor what has been (touched) with the hem of a garment,

30. Nor that which has been looked at by a dog or an Apapâtra,

---

21. 'Food which is simply impure, may be purified by putting it on the fire, sprinkling it with water, touching it with ashes or earth, and praising it.'—Haradatta.

22. Others say, that the food becomes unfit for eating, only, if in bringing it, the *S*ûdra has touched it.—Haradatta.

23. Manu IV, 207; Yâg*ñ*. I, 167. 'But this rule holds good only if the hair had been cooked with the food. If a hair falls into it at dinner, then it is to be purified by an addition of clarified butter, and may be eaten.'—Haradatta.

24. Haradatta quotes a passage from Baudhâyana, which enumerates as 'unclean things' here intended, 'hair, worms or beetles, nail-parings, excrements of rats.' The rule must be understood as the preceding, i.e. in case these things have been cooked with the food.

26. Manu IV, 207; Yâg*ñ*. I, 167, 168. This Sûtra must be read with Sûtra 23 above.

30. Manu IV, 208; Yâg*ñ*. I, 167. Apapâtras are persons whom

31. Nor what has been brought in the hem of a garment, (even though the garment may be clean),

32. Nor what has been brought at night by a female slave.

33. If during his meal,

PRASNA I, PATALA 5, KHANDA 17.

1. A *S*ûdra touches him, (then he shall leave off eating).

2. Nor shall he eat sitting in the same row with unworthy people.

3. Nor shall he eat (sitting in the same row with persons) amongst whom one, whilst they eat, rises and gives his leavings to his pupils or sips water;

4. Nor (shall he eat) where they give him food, reviling him.

---

one must not allow to eat from one's dishes, e.g. *Kand*âlas, Patitas, a woman in her courses or during the ten days of impurity after confinement. See also above, I, 1, 3, 25.

32. Haradatta thinks, that as the Sûtra has the feminine gender, dâsî, it does not matter if a male slave brings the food. But others forbid also this.

17. 1. 'Some say, that this Sûtra indicates that the touch of a *S*ûdra does not defile at any other time but at dinner, whilst others hold that a *S*ûdra's touch defiles always, and that the Sûtra is intended to indicate an excess of impurity, if it happens at dinner-time.'—Haradatta.

2. 'Unworthy people are those who are neither of good family, nor possess learning and virtue.'—Haradatta.

3. According to Haradatta a person who misbehaves thus, is called 'a dinner-thorn.' This point of etiquette is strictly observed in our days also. Manu IV, 212.

4. Manu IV, 212; Yâg*ñ*. I, 167.

5. Nor (shall he eat) what has been smelt at by men or other impure (beings, as cats).

6. He shall not eat in a ship,

7. Nor on a wooden platform.

8. He may eat sitting on ground which has been purified (by the application of cowdung and the like).

9. (If he eats) out of an earthen vessel, he shall eat out of one that has not been used (for cooking).

10. (If he can get) a used vessel (only, he shall eat from it), after having heated it thoroughly.

11. A vessel made of metal becomes pure by being scoured with ashes and the like.

12. A wooden vessel becomes pure by being scraped.

13. At a sacrifice (the vessels must be cleaned) according to the precepts of the Veda.

14. He shall not eat food which has been bought or obtained ready-prepared in the market.

15. Nor (shall he eat) flavoured food (bought in the market) excepting raw meat, honey, and salt.

16. Oil and clarified butter (bought in the market) he may use, after having sprinkled them with water.

17. Prepared food which has stood for a night, must neither be eaten nor drunk.

---

5. 'As the text has avaghrâta, "smelt at," it does not matter if they smell the food from a distance.'—Haradatta.

11. 'It must be understood from other Sm*ri*tis, that brass is to be cleaned with ashes, copper with acids, silver with cowdung, and gold with water.'—Haradatta. Manu V, 114.

12. Manu V, 115.

16. 'Having sprinkled them with water and purified them by boiling; or, according to others, mixing them with so much water as will not spoil them.'—Haradatta.

17. The Sanskrit has two terms for 'eating;' the first 'khâd'

18. Nor (should prepared food) that has turned sour (be used in any way).

19. (The preceding two rules do) not (hold good in regard to) the juice of sugar-cane, roasted rice-grains, porridge prepared with whey, roasted yava, gruel, vegetables, meat, flour, milk and preparations from it, roots and fruits of herbs and trees.

20. (Substances which have turned) sour without being mixed with anything else (are to be avoided).

21. All intoxicating drinks are forbidden.

22. Likewise sheep's milk,

23. Likewise the milk of camels, of does, of animals that give milk while big with young, of those that bear twins, and of (one-hoofed animals),

24. Likewise the milk of a cow (buffalo-cow or she-goat) during the (first) ten days (after their giving birth to young ones),

25. Likewise (food mixed) with herbs which serve for preparing intoxicating liquors,

26. (Likewise) red garlic, onions, and leeks,

---

applies to hard substances, the second 'ad' to soft substances. Manu IV, 211; Yâgñ. I, 167.

18. Manu IV, 211; V, 9; Yâgñ. I, 167.

19. Manu V, 10, 24 and 25.

20. According to Haradatta, Âpastamba returns once more to the question about sour food, in order to teach that dishes prepared with curds and other sour substances may be eaten.

22. Manu V, 8; Yâgñ. I, 170.

23. Manu V, 8, 9; Yâgñ. I, 170. 'Sandhinî, translated by "females that give milk while big with young," means, according to others, "female animals that give milk once a day."'—Haradatta.

24. Manu V, 8.

26. Manu V, 5; Yâgñ. I. 176.

27. Likewise anything else which (those who are learned in the law) forbid.

28. Mushrooms ought not to be eaten; that has been declared in a Brâhma*n*a;

29. (Nor the meat) of one-hoofed animals, of camels, of the Gayal, of village pigs, of *S*arabhas, and of cattle.

30. (But the meat) of milch-cows and oxen may be eaten.

31. The Vâ*g*asaneyaka declares 'bull's flesh is fit for offerings.'

32. Amongst birds that scratch with their feet for food, the (tame) cock (must not be eaten).

33. Amongst birds that feed thrusting forward their beak, the (heron, called) Plava (or *S*aka*t*abila, must not be eaten).

34. Carnivorous (birds are forbidden),

35. Likewise the swan, the Bhâsa, the Brâhma*n*î duck, and the falcon.

36. Common cranes and Sâras-cranes (are not to

---

27. Haradatta observes that Âpastamba, finding the list of forbidden vegetables too long, refers his pupils to the advice of the *S*ish*t*as. The force of this Sûtra is exactly the same as that of I, 3, 11, 38.

28. Yâ*gñ*. I, 171.

29. The camel, Gayal, and *S*arabha are mentioned as 'forbidden animals,' *S*atapatha-br. I, 2, 1, 8; Aitareya-br. II, 1, 8; see also Weber, Ind. Stud. X, 62; Manu V, 11, 18; Yâ*gñ*. I, 172, 176.

32. Yâ*gñ*. I, 176.

33. Manu V, 12; Yâ*gñ*. I, 172.

34. Manu V, 11; Yâ*gñ*. I, 172.

35. Yâ*gñ*. I, 172.

36. Manu V, 12; Yâ*gñ*. I, 172. Other commentators take the whole Sûtra as one compound, and explain it as an exception to Sûtra 34. In that case the translation runs thus: ('Carnivorous birds are forbidden) except the Kru*ñk*a, Krau*ñk*a, Vârdhrâ*n*asa,

be eaten) with the exception of the leather-nosed Lakshma*n*a.

37. Five-toed animals (ought not to be eaten) with the exception of the iguana, the tortoise, the porcupine, the hedgehog, the rhinoceros, the hare, and the Pûtikhasha.

38. Amongst fishes, the *Ket*a ought not to be eaten,

39. Nor the snake-headed fish, nor the alligator, nor those which live on flesh only, nor those which are misshaped (like) mermen.

PRA*S*NA I, PA*T*ALA 6, KHA*ND*A 18.

1. Honey, uncooked (grain), venison, land, roots, fruits, (a promise of) safety, a pasture for cattle, a house, and fodder for a draught-ox may be accepted (even) from an Ugra.

2. Hârîta declares, that even these (presents) are to be accepted only if they have been obtained by a pupil.

---

and Lakshma*n*a.'—Haradatta. This translation is objectionable, because both the Kru*ñk*as, now called Kulam or Kû*ñk*, and the Krau*ñk*a, the red-crested crane, now called Sâras (Cyrus), feed on grain. Kru*ñk*akrau*ñk*a is a Vedic dual and stands for kru*ñk*a-krau*ñk*â or kru*ñk*akrau*ñk*au.

37. Manu V, 18; Yâ*gñ*. I, 177. Pûtikhasha is, according to Haradatta, an animal resembling a hare, and found in the Himâlayas.

39. Haradatta closes this chapter on flesh-eating by quoting Manu V, 56, which declares flesh-eating, drinking spirituous liquor, and promiscuous intercourse to be allowable, but the abstinence therefrom of greater merit. He states that the whole chapter must be understood in this sense.

18. 1. Manu IV, 247. 'Ugra denotes either a bad twice-born man or the offspring of a Vai*s*ya and of a *S*ûdra-woman. Other persons of a similar character must be understood to be included by the term.'—Haradatta.

3. Or they (Brâhmaṇa householders) may accept (from an Ugra) uncooked or (a little) unflavoured boiled food.

4. (Of such food) they shall not take a great quantity (but only so much as suffices to support life).

5. If (in times of distress) he is unable to keep himself, he may eat (food obtained from anybody),

6. After having touched it (once) with gold,

7. Or (having touched it with) fire.

8. He shall not be too eager after (such a way of living). He shall leave it when he has obtained a (lawful) livelihood.

9. (A student of the Brahmanic caste) who has returned home shall not eat (in the house) of people belonging to the three tribes, beginning with the Kshatriya (i. e. of Kshatriyas, Vaisyas, and Sûdras).

10. He may (usually) eat (the food) of a Brâhmaṇa on account of (the giver's) character (as a Brâhmaṇa). It must be avoided for particular reasons only.

---

4. Also this rule seems to belong to Hârîta, on account of its close connection with the preceding two.

8. Haradatta quotes, in support of the last Sûtras, a passage of the *Kh*ândogya Upanishad, I, 10, 1, and one from the *Ri*g-veda, IV, 18, 13, according to which it would be lawful to eat even impure food, as a dog's entrails, under such circumstances. Other commentators explain this and the preceding three Sûtras differently. According to them the translation would run thus: 'If he himself does not find any livelihood (in times of distress, he may dwell even with low-caste people who give him something to eat, and) he may eat (food given by them) paying for it with (some small gift in) gold or with animals.' This second explanation is perhaps preferable.

9. Manu IV, 218, 219, and 223.

11. He shall not eat in a house where (the host) performs a rite which is not a rite of penance, whilst he ought to perform a penance.

12. But when the penance has been performed, he may eat (in that house).

13. According to some (food offered by people) of any caste, who follow the laws prescribed for them, except that of *S*ûdras, may be eaten.

14. (In times of distress) even the food of a *S*ûdra, who lives under one's protection for the sake of spiritual merit, (may be eaten).

15. He may eat it, after having touched it (once) with gold or with fire. He shall not be too eager after (such a way of living). He shall leave it when he obtains a (lawful) livelihood.

16. Food received from a multitude of givers must not be eaten,

17. Nor food offered by a general invitation (to all comers).

18. Food offered by an artisan must not be eaten,

19. Nor (that of men) who live by the use of arms (with the exception of Kshatriyas),

---

11. 'If a Brâhma*n*a who has been ordered to perform a penance, performs a Vai*s*vadeva or other rite without heeding the order of his spiritual teacher, then a student who has returned home ought not to eat in his house, until the enjoined penance has been performed.'—Haradatta.

12. 'The use of the part. perf. pass. "performed" indicates that he must not eat there, whilst the penance is being performed.'—Haradatta.

14. Yâg*ñ*. I, 166. 15. Manu IV, 223.

16. Manu IV, 209. 17. Manu IV, 209; Yâg*ñ*. I, 168.

18. Manu IV, 210, 215; Yâg*ñ*. I, 162–164.

19. Yâg*ñ*. I, 164.

20. Nor (that of men) who live by letting lodgings or land.

21. A (professional) physician is a person whose food must not be eaten,

22. (Also) a usurer,

23. (Also) a Brâhma*n*a who has performed the Dîksha*n*îyesh*t*i (or initiatory ceremony of the Soma-sacrifice) before he has bought the king (Soma).

24. (The food given by a person who has performed the Dîksha*n*îyesh*t*i may be eaten), when the victim sacred to Agni and Soma has been slain.

25. Or after that the omentum of the victim (sacred to Agni and Soma) has been offered.

26. For a Brâhma*n*a declares, 'Or they may eat of the remainder of the animal, after having set apart a portion for the offering.'

27. A eunuch (is a person whose food must not be eaten),

28. (Likewise) the (professional) messenger employed by a king (or others),

29. (Likewise a Brâhma*n*a) who offers substances that are not fit for a sacrifice,

30. (Likewise) a spy,

---

21. Manu IV, 212; Yâg*ñ*. I, 162.

22. Manu IV, 210; Yâg*ñ*. I, 161.

23. 'That is to say, one who has begun, but not finished a Soma-sacrifice.'—Haradatta. Manu IV, 210, and Gopatha-brâhma*n*a III, 19.

25. Aitareya-brâhma*n*a II, 1, 9.

27. Manu IV, 211; Yâg*ñ*. I, 161.

28. The village or town messengers are always men of the lowest castes, such as the Mahârs of Mahârâsh*t*/*h*ra.

29. 'For example, he who offers human blood in a magic rite.'—Haradatta.

30. Haradatta explains *k*ârî, translated by 'spy,' to mean 'a

31. (Also) a person who has become an ascetic without (being authorized thereto by) the rules (of the law),

32. (Also) he who forsakes the sacred fires (without performing the sacrifice necessary on that occasion),

33. Likewise a learned Brâhma*n*a who avoids everybody, or eats the food of anybody, or neglects the (daily) recitation of the Veda, (and) he whose (only living) wife is of the *S*ûdra caste.

PRA*S*NA I, PA*T*ALA 6, KHA*ND*A 19.

1. A drunkard, a madman, a prisoner, he who learns the Veda from his son, a creditor who sits with his debtor (hindering the fulfilment of his duties), a debtor who thus sits (with his creditor, are persons whose food must not be eaten) as long as they are thus engaged or in that state.

2. Who (then) are those whose food may be eaten?

---

secret adherent of the *S*âkta sect' (gû*dh*a*k*ârî, *s*âkta*h*). The existence of this sect in early times has not hitherto been proved.

31. Haradatta gives the *S*âkyas or Bauddhas as an instance. But it is doubtful, whether Âpastamba meant to refer to them, though it seems probable that heretics are intended.

32. Yâg*ñ*. I, 160.

33. 'Who avoids everybody, i.e. who neither invites nor dines with anybody.'—Haradatta.

19. 1. Manu IV, 207; Yâg*ñ*. I, 161, 162. Another commentator explains a*n*ika, translated above 'he who learns the Veda from his son,' by 'a money-lender,' and combines pratyupavish*t*a*h* with this word, i.e. 'a money-lender who sits with his debtor hindering him from fulfilling his duties.' This manner of forcing a debtor to pay, which is also called Â*k*arita (see Manu VIII, 49), is, though illegal, resorted to sometimes even now.

2. 'The object of this Sûtra is to introduce the great variety of opinions quoted below.'—Haradatta.

3. Ka*n*va declares, that it is he who wishes to give.

4. Kautsa declares, that it is he who is holy.

5. Vârshyâya*n*i declares, that it is every giver (of food).

6. For if guilt remains fixed on the man (who committed a crime, then food given by a sinner) may be eaten (because the guilt cannot leave the sinner). But if guilt can leave (the sinner at any time, then food given by the sinner may be eaten because) he becomes pure by the gift (which he makes).

7. Offered food, which is pure, may be eaten, according to Eka, Ku*n*ika, Kâ*n*va, Kutsa, and Pushkarasâdi.

8. Vârshyâya*n*i's opinion is, that (food) given unasked (may be accepted) from anybody.

9. (Food offered) willingly by a holy man may be eaten.

10. Food given unwillingly by a holy man ought not to be eaten.

11. Food offered unasked by any person whatsoever may be eaten,

12. 'But not if it be given after an express previous announcement;' thus says Hârîta.

13. Now they quote also in a Purâ*n*a the following two verses:

---

4. 'Holy' means not only 'following his lawful occupations,' but particularly 'practising austerities, reciting prayers, and offering burnt-oblations.'—Haradatta.

10. Another commentator explains this Sûtra thus: 'He need not eat the food offered by a righteous man, if he himself does not wish to do so.'—Haradatta.

13. See Manu IV, 248 and 249, where these identical verses occur.

'The Lord of creatures has declared, that food offered unasked and brought by the giver himself, may be eaten, though (the giver be) a sinner, provided the gift has not been announced beforehand. The Manes of the ancestors of that man who spurns such food, do not eat (his oblations) for fifteen years, nor does the fire carry his offerings (to the gods).'

14. (Another verse from a Purâna declares): 'The food given by a physician, a hunter, a surgeon, a fowler, an unfaithful wife, or a eunuch must not be eaten.'

15. Now (in confirmation of this) they quote (the following verse): 'The murderer of a Brâhmana learned in the Veda heaps his guilt on his guest, an innocent man on his calumniator, a thief set at liberty on the king, and the petitioner on him who makes false promises.'

Prasna I, Patala 7, Khanda 20.

1. He shall not fulfil his sacred duties merely in order to acquire these worldly objects (as fame, gain, and honour).

2. For when they ought to bring rewards, (duties thus fulfilled) become fruitless.

3. (Worldly benefits) are produced as accessories (to the fulfilment of the law), just as in the case of a mango tree, which is planted in order to obtain fruit, shade and fragrance (are accessory advantages).

---

14. Manu IV, 211, 212.

15. Regarding the liberation of the thief, see Âpastamba I, 9, 25, 4. A similar verse occurs Manu VIII, 317, which has caused the confusion observable in many MSS., as has been stated in the critical notes to the text.

4. But if (worldly advantages) are not produced, (then at least) the sacred duties have been fulfilled.

5. Let him not become irritated at, nor be deceived by the speeches of hypocrites, of rogues, of infidels, and of fools.

6. For Virtue and Sin do not go about and say, 'Here we are;' nor do gods, Gandharvas, or Manes say (to men), 'This is virtue, that is sin.'

7. But that is virtue, the practice of which wise men of the three twice-born castes praise; what they blame, is sin.

8. He shall regulate his course of action according to the conduct which in all countries is unanimously approved by men of the three twice-born castes, who have been properly obedient (to their teachers), who are aged, of subdued senses, neither given to avarice, nor hypocrites.

9. Acting thus he will gain both worlds.

10. Trade is not lawful for a Brâhma*n*a.

11. In times of distress he may trade in lawful merchandise, avoiding the following (kinds), that are forbidden:

12. (Particularly) men, condiments and liquids, colours, perfumes, food, skins, heifers, substances

---

20. 7. The Sûtra is intended to show how the law should be ascertained in difficult cases. Haradatta quotes here the passage of Yâ*gñ*. I, 9, on Parishads, and states that the plural âryâ*h* shows that three or four must be employed to arrive at a decision. See also Manu XII, 108 seq.

8. Manu I, 6.

11. This Sûtra, which specifies only one part of a Vai*s*ya's occupations as permissible for Brâhma*n*as in distress, implies, according to Haradatta, that his other occupations also, as well as those of a Kshatriya, are permissible. Manu IV, 6; X, 82; Yâ*gñ*. III, 35.

12. Manu X, 86–89; Yâ*gñ*. III, 36–39.

used for glueing (such as lac), water, young corn-stalks, substances from which spirituous liquor may be extracted, red and black pepper, corn, flesh, arms, and the hope of rewards for meritorious deeds.

13. Among (the various kinds of) grain he shall especially not sell sesamum or rice (except he have grown them himself).

14. The exchange of the one of these (above-mentioned goods) for the other is likewise unlawful.

15. But food (may be exchanged) for food, and slaves for slaves, and condiments for condiments, and perfumes for perfumes, and learning for learning.

16. Let him traffic with lawful merchandise which he has not bought,

Prasna I, Patala 7, Khanda 21.

1. With Muñga-grass, Balbaga-grass (and articles made of them), roots, and fruits,

2. And with (other kinds of) grass and wood which have not been worked up (into objects of use).

3. He shall not be too eager (after such a livelihood).

4. If he obtains (another lawful) livelihood, he shall leave off (trading).

---

13. The exception stated above, is given by Haradatta on the authority of Manu X, 90; Yâgñ. III, 39.

15. 'From the permission to exchange learning for learning, it may be known that it is not lawful to sell it.'—Haradatta. Manu X, 94.

21. 2. 'Since it is known that Muñga and Balbaga are kinds of grass, it may be inferred from their being especially mentioned (in Sûtra 1) that objects made of them (may be also sold).'—Haradatta.

4. Yâgñ. III, 35.

5. Intercourse with fallen men is not ordained,

6. Nor with Apapâtras.

7. Now (follows the enumeration of) the actions which cause loss of caste (Patanîya).

8. (These are) stealing (gold), crimes whereby one becomes an Abhi*s*asta, homicide, neglect of the Vedas, causing abortion, incestuous connection with relations born from the same womb as one's mother or father, and with the offspring of such persons, drinking spirituous liquor, and intercourse with persons the intercourse with whom is forbidden.

9. That man falls who has connection with a female friend of a female Guru, or with a female friend of a male Guru, or with any married woman.

10. Some (teachers declare), that he does not fall by having connection with any other married female except his teacher's wife.

11. Constant commission of (other) sins (besides those enumerated above) also causes a man to lose his caste.

12. Now follows (the enumeration of) the acts which make men impure (A*s*u*k*ikara).

13. (These are) the cohabitation of Aryan women with *S*ûdras,

14. Eating the flesh of forbidden (creatures),

---

5. Manu XI, 180.

6. Regarding the definition of the word Apapâtra, see above, I, 5, 16, 29.

8. The crimes by which a person becomes Abhi*s*asta are enumerated below, I, 9, 24, 6 seq., where an explanation of the term will be given.

9. Regarding the 'male Gurus' see above. By 'female Gurus' their wives are meant.

10. I.e. he need not perform so heavy a penance.

15. As of a dog, a man, village cocks or pigs, carnivorous animals,

16. Eating the excrements of men,

17. Eating what is left by a *S*ûdra, the cohabitation of Aryans with Apapâtra women.

18. Some declare, that these acts also cause a man to lose his caste.

19. Other acts besides those (enumerated) are causes of impurity.

20. He who learns (that a man has) committed a sin, shall not be the first to make it known to others; but he shall avoid the (sinner), when performing religious ceremonies.

PRA*S*NA I, PA*T*ALA 8, KHA*ND*A 22.

1. He shall employ the means which tend to the acquisition of (the knowledge of) the Âtman, which are attended by the consequent (destruction of the passions, and) which prevent the wandering (of the mind from its object, and fix it on the contemplation of the Âtman).

2. There is no higher (object) than the attainment of (the knowledge of the) Âtman.

3. We shall quote the verses (from the Veda)

---

20. 'That is to say, he is not to invite the sinner to dinners, given at the occasion of religious ceremonies.'—Haradatta.

22. 1. The knowledge of the Vedânta and the means which prepare men for the knowledge of the Âtman, the 'Self, the universal soul,' are placed in this Pa*t*ala at the head of the penances, because they are most efficacious for the removal of all sin. The means are absence of anger &c., which are enumerated I, 8, 23, 6.

2. Haradatta gives in his commentary a lengthy discussion on the Âtman, which corresponds nearly to *S*aṅkara's Introduction to and Commentary on the first Sûtra of Bâdarâya*n*a.

3. According to Haradatta, the following verses are taken from an Upanishad.

which refer to the attainment of (the knowledge of) the Âtman.

4. All living creatures are the dwelling of him who lies enveloped in matter, who is immortal and who is spotless. Those become immortal who worship him who is immovable and lives in a movable dwelling.

5. Despising all that which in this world is called an object (of the senses) a wise man shall strive after the (knowledge of the) Âtman.

6. O pupil, I, who had not recognised in my own self the great self-luminous, universal, (absolutely) free Âtman, which must be obtained without the mediation of anything else, desired (to find) it in others (the senses). (But now as I have obtained the pure knowledge, I do so no more.) Therefore follow thou also this good road that leads to welfare (salvation), and not the one that leads into misfortune (new births).

7. It is he who is the eternal part in all creatures, whose essence is wisdom, who is immortal, unchangeable, destitute of limbs, of voice, of the (subtle) body,

4. The spotless one &c. is the Paramâtman. The spots are merit and demerit which, residing in the Manas, the internal organ of perception, are only falsely attributed to the Âtman, 'the soul.' To become immortal means 'to obtain final liberation.'

5. It seems to me that Haradatta's explanation of the words 'idam idi ha idi ha' is wrong. They ought to be divided thus, 'idamid, iha id, iha loke.' The general sense remains the same, and there is no necessity to assume very curious and otherwise unknown Vedic forms.

6. The verse is addressed by a teacher to his pupil. My translation strictly follows Haradatta's gloss. But his interpretation is open to many doubts. However, I am unable to suggest anything better.

7. The Sûtra contains a further description of the Paramâtman.

(even) of touch, exceedingly pure; he is the universe, he is the highest goal; (he dwells in the middle of the body as) the Vishuvat day is (the middle of a Sattra-sacrifice); he, indeed, is (accessible to all) like a town intersected by many streets.

8. He who meditates on him, and everywhere and always lives according to his (commandments), and who, full of devotion, sees him who is difficult to be seen and subtle, will rejoice in (his) heaven.

PRASNA I, PATALA 8, KHANDA 23.

1. That Brâhmana, who is wise and recognises all creatures to be in the Âtman, who pondering (thereon) does not become bewildered, and who recognises the Âtman in every (created) thing, shines, indeed, in heaven.

2. He, who is intelligence itself and subtler than the thread of the lotus-fibre, pervades the universe, and who, unchangeable and larger than the earth, contains the universe; he, who is different from the knowledge of this world, obtained by the senses and identical with its objects, possesses the highest (form consisting of absolute knowledge). From him, who divides himself, spring all (created) bodies. He is the primary cause, he is eternal, he is unchangeable.

---

8. Haradatta explains the word vishtap, 'heaven,' by 'pain-freed greatness,' apparently misled by a bad etymology. The heaven of the Âtman is, of course, liberation, that state where the individual soul becomes merged in the Brahman or Paramâtman, which is pure essence, intelligence and joy.

23. 2. This Sûtra again contains a description of the Paramâtman. The translation strictly follows the commentary, though the explanation, given in the latter, is open to objections.

3. But the eradication of the faults is brought about in this life by the means (called Yoga). A wise man who has eradicated the (faults) which destroy the creatures, obtains salvation.

4. Now we will enumerate the faults which tend to destroy the creatures.

5. (These are) anger, exultation, grumbling, covetousness, perplexity, doing injury, hypocrisy, lying, gluttony, calumny, envy, lust, secret hatred, neglect to keep the senses in subjection, neglect to concentrate the mind. The eradication of these (faults) takes place through the means of (salvation called) Yoga.

6. Freedom from anger, from exultation, from grumbling, from covetousness, from perplexity, from hypocrisy (and) hurtfulness; truthfulness, moderation in eating, silencing slander, freedom from envy, self-denying liberality, avoiding to accept gifts, uprightness, affability, extinction of the passions, subjection of the senses, peace with all created beings, concentration (of the mind on the contemplation of the Âtman), regulation of one's conduct according to that of the Âryas, peacefulness and contentedness; —these (good qualities) have been settled by the agreement (of the wise) for all (the four) orders; he who, according to the precepts of the sacred law, practises these, enters the universal soul.

PRAS*N*A I, PA*T*ALA 9, KHA*N*D*A 24.

1. He who has killed a Kshatriya shall give a thousand cows (to Brâhma*n*as) for the expiation of his sin.

24. 1. Manu XI, 128; Yâg*ñ*. III, 266. Others explain the phrase vairayâtanârtham, 'for the expiation of his sin,' thus: 'He, who is

2. (He shall give) a hundred cows for a Vaisya,

3. Ten for a Sûdra,

4. And in every one (of these cases) one bull (must be given) in excess (of the number of cows) for the sake of expiation.

5. And if women of the (three castes mentioned have been slain) the same (composition must be paid).

6. He who has slain a man belonging to the two (first-mentioned castes) who has studied the Veda, or had been initiated for the performance of a Soma-sacrifice, becomes an Abhisasta.

7. And (he is called an Abhisasta) who has slain a man belonging merely to the Brâhmana caste (though he has not studied the Veda or been initiated for a Soma-sacrifice),

---

slain by anybody, becomes, in dying, an enemy of his slayer (and thinks), "O that I might slay him in another life," for the removal of this enmity!'—Haradatta. I am strongly inclined to agree with the other commentator, and to translate vairayâtanârtham, 'in order to remove the enmity.' I recognise in this fine a remnant of the law permitting compositions for murder which was in force in ancient Greece and among the Teutonic nations. With the explanation adopted by Haradatta, it is impossible to find a reasonable interpretation for prâyaskittârthah, Sûtra 4. Haradatta, seduced by the parallel passage of Manu, takes it to be identical with vairayâtanârtham. I propose to translate our Sûtra thus: 'He who has killed a Kshatriya shall give a thousand cows (to the relations of the murdered man) in order to remove the enmity.' According to Baudhâyana I, 10. 19. 1 (compare Zeitschr. d. D. Morg. Ges., vol. 41, pp. 672–76; Festgruss an Roth, pp. 44–52), the cows are to be given to the king.

2. Manu XI, 130; Yâgñ. III, 267.

3. Manu XI, 131; Yâgñ. III, 267.

6. Manu XI, 87. Abhisasta means literally 'accused, accursed,' and corresponds in Âpastamba's terminology to the mahâpâtakin of Manu and Yâgñavalkya, instead of which latter word Manu uses it occasionally, e.g. II, 185.

8. Likewise he who has destroyed an embryo of a (Brâhma*n*a, even though its sex be) undistinguishable,

9. Or a woman (of the Brâhma*n*a caste) during her courses.

10. (Now follows) the penance for him (who is an Abhi*s*asta).

11. He (himself) shall erect a hut in the forest, restrain his speech, carry (on his stick) the skull (of the person slain) like a flag, and cover the space from his navel to his knees with a quarter of a piece of hempen cloth.

12. The path for him when he goes to a village, is the space between the tracks (of the wheels).

13. And if he sees another (Ârya), he shall step out of the road (to the distance of two yards).

14. He shall go to the village, carrying a broken tray of metal of an inferior quality.

15. He may go to seven houses only, (crying,) 'Who will give alms to an Abhi*s*asta?'

16. That is (the way in which he must gain) his livelihood.

17. If he does not obtain anything (at the seven houses), he must fast.

18. And (whilst performing this penance) he must tend cows.

19. When they leave and enter the village, that is the second occasion (on which he may enter) the village.

---

9. 'Others interpret âtreyî, "during her courses," by "belonging to the race of Atri."'—Haradatta.

11. Others say that he may carry the skull of any corpse. This Sûtra is to be construed with Sûtra 14, Sûtras 12 and 13 being inserted parenthetically.—Haradatta. Manu XI, 72–78; Yâ*gñ*. III, 243.

20. After having performed (this penance) for twelve years, (he must perform) the ceremony known (by custom), through which he is re-admitted into the society of the good.

21. Or (after having performed the twelve years' penance), he may build a hut on the path of robbers, and live there, trying to take from them the cows of Brâhma*n*as. He is free (from his sin), when thrice he has been defeated by them, or when he has vanquished them.

22. Or he is freed (from his sin), if (after the twelve years' penance) he bathes (with the priests) at the end of a horse-sacrifice.

23. This very same (penance is ordained) for him who, when his duty and love of gain come into conflict, chooses the gain.

24. If he has slain a Guru or a Brâhma*n*a, who has studied the Veda and finished the ceremonies of a Soma-sacrifice, he shall live according to this very same rule until his last breath.

25. He cannot be purified in this life. But his sin is removed (after death).

---

20. 'I.e. after having performed the penance, he shall take grass and offer it to a cow. If the cow approaches and confidingly eats, then one should know that he has performed the penance properly, not otherwise.'—Haradatta. Manu XI, 195 and 196.

21. Manu XI, 81.—Thus Haradatta, better, 'when thrice he has fought with them,' see the Pet. Dict. s. v. râdh.

22. Manu XI, 83; Weber, Ind. Stud. X, 67.

23. 'Or the Sûtra may have reference to unrighteous gain acquired by false testimony and the like.'—Haradatta.

24. 'Guru means "the father and the rest."'—Haradatta.

25. 'His sin is removed after death. Hence the meaning is that his sons or other (relations) may perform the funeral ceremonies and the like. But others think that the first part of the Sûtra forbids this, and that the meaning of pratyâpatti*h* (can be

PRASNA I, PATALA 9, KHANDA 25.

1. He who has had connection with a Guru's wife shall cut off his organ together with the testicles, take them into his joined hands and walk towards the south without stopping, until he falls down dead.

2. Or he may die embracing a heated metal image of a woman.

3. A drinker of spirituous liquor shall drink exceedingly hot liquor so that he dies.

4. A thief shall go to the king with flying hair, carrying a club on his shoulder, and tell him his deed. He (the king) shall give him a blow with that (club). If the thief dies, his sin is expiated.

5. If he is forgiven (by the king), the guilt falls upon him who forgives him,

6. Or he may throw himself into the fire, or perform repeatedly severe austerities,

7. Or he may kill himself by diminishing daily his portion of food,

8. Or he may perform K*rikkh*ra penances (uninterruptedly) for one year.

---

purified) is "connection by being received as a son or other relation."'—Haradatta.

25. 1. Haradatta's explanation of a 'Guru's wife' by 'mother' rests on a comparison of similar passages from other Sm*ri*tis, where a different 'penance' is prescribed for incestuous intercourse with other near relations. Manu XI, 105; Yâg*ñ*. III, 259.

2. Manu XI, 104; Yâg*ñ*. III, 259.

3. Manu XI, 91, 92; Yâg*ñ*. III, 253.

4. I.e. who has stolen the gold of a Brâhma*n*a. Manu VIII, 314, 316; XI, 99–101; Yâg*ñ*. III, 257.

5. Manu VIII, 317. 6. Manu XI, 102.

8. According to Haradatta this Sûtra refers to all kinds of sins,

9. Now they quote also (the following verse):

10. Those who have committed a theft (of gold), drunk spirituous liquor, or had connection with a Guru's wife, but not those who have slain a Brâhma*n*a, shall eat every fourth meal-time a little food, bathe at the times of the three libations (morning, noon, and evening), passing the day standing and the night sitting. After the lapse of three years they throw off their guilt.

11. (A man of any caste) excepting the first, who has slain a man of the first caste, shall go on a battle-field and place himself (between the two hostile armies). There they shall kill him (and thereby he becomes pure).

12. Or such a sinner may tear from his body and make the priest offer as a burnt-offering his hair, skin, flesh, and the rest, and then throw himself into the fire.

13. If a crow, a chameleon, a peacock, a Brâhma*n*î duck, a swan, the vulture called Bhâsa, a frog, an ichneumon, a musk-rat, or a dog has been killed, then the same penance as for a *S*ûdra must be performed.

---

and it must be understood that the K*r*i*kkh*ra penances must be heavy for great crimes, and lighter for smaller faults; see also below, I, 9, 27, 7 and 8.

9. Haradatta states that the verse is taken from a Purâ*n*a.

11. Manu XI, 74; Yâg*ñ*. III, 248.

12. The Mantras given in the commentary, and a parallel passage of Vasish*th*a XX, 25–26, show that this terrible penance is not altogether a mere theory of Âpastamba. Yâg*ñ*. III, 247.

13. 'According to some, the penance must be performed if all these animals together have been slain; according to others, if only one of them has been killed.'—Haradatta. Manu XI, 132, 136; Yâg*ñ*. III, 270–272.

PRASNA I, PATALA 9, KHANDA 26.

1. (The same penance must be performed), if a milch-cow or a full-grown ox (has been slain), without a reason.

2. And for other animals (which have no bones), if an ox-load of them has been killed.

3. He who abuses a person who (on account of his venerability) ought not to be abused, or speaks an untruth (regarding any small matter) must abstain for three days from milk, pungent condiments, and salt.

4. (If the same sins have been committed) by a *S*ûdra, he must fast for seven days.

5. And the same (penances must also be performed) by women, (but not those which follow).

6. He who cuts off a limb of a person for whose murder he would become an Abhi*s*asta (must perform the penance prescribed for killing a *S*ûdra), if the life (of the person injured) has not been endangered.

---

26. 1. 'A reason' for hurting a cow is, according to Haradatta, anger, or the desire to obtain meat.

2. Manu XI, 141; Yâ*gñ*. III, 269. That 'animals without bones,' i.e. insects or mollusks, are intended in the Sûtra is an inference, drawn by Haradatta from the parallel passages of Gautama, Manu, and Yâ*gñ*avalkya.

3. 'A person who ought not to be abused, i.e. a father, a teacher, and the like.'—Haradatta.

5. The same penances, i.e. those prescribed I, 9, 24–I, 9, 26, 4. According to Haradatta this Sûtra is intended to teach that women shall not perform the penances which follow. Others, however, are of opinion that it is given in order to indicate that the preceding Sûtras apply to women by an atide*s*a, and that, according to a Smârta principle, applicable to such cases, it may be inferred, that women are to perform one-half only of the penances prescribed for men.

7. He who has been guilty of conduct unworthy of an Aryan, of calumniating others, of actions contrary to the rule of conduct, of eating or drinking things forbidden, of connection with a woman of the *S*ûdra caste, of an unnatural crime, of performing magic rites with intent (to harm his enemies) or (of hurting others) unintentionally, shall bathe and sprinkle himself with water, reciting the (seven) verses addressed to the Waters, or the verses addressed to Varu*n*a, or (other verses chosen from the Anuvâka, called) Pavitra, in proportion to the frequency with which the crime has been committed.

8. A (student) who has broken the vow of chastity, shall offer to Nir*ri*ti an ass, according to the manner of the Pâkaya*gñ*a-rites.

9. A *S*ûdra shall eat (the remainder) of that (offering).

10. (Now follows) the penance for him who transgresses the rules of studentship.

11. He shall for a year serve his teacher silently, emitting speech only during the daily study (of the Veda, in announcing necessary business to) his teacher or his teacher's wife, and whilst collecting alms.

12. The following (penances) which we are going to proclaim, may be performed for the same sin, and

---

7. The Anuvâka intended is Taitt. Sa*m*h. II, 5, 12.

8. Taitt. Âr. II, 18, and Weber, Ind. Stud. X, 102; Manu XI, 119 seq.; and Yâ*gñ*. III, 280. Regarding the Pâkaya*gñ*a-rites, see Â*s*v. G*ri*. Sû. I, 1, 2, and Max Müller's History of Ancient Sanskrit Literature, p. 203.

12. Regarding the Patanîya-crimes which cause loss of caste, see above, I, 7, 21, 7 seq.

also for other sinful acts, which do not cause loss of caste.

13. He may either offer oblations to Kâma and Manyu (with the following two Mantras), 'Kâma (passion) has done it; Manyu (anger) has done it.' Or he may mutter (these Mantras).

14. Or, after having eaten sesamum or fasted on the days of the full and new moon he may, on the following day bathe, and stopping his breath, repeat the Gâyatrî one thousand times, or he may do so without stopping his breath.

PRASNA I, PATALA 9, KHANDA 27.

1. After having eaten sesamum or having fasted on the full moon day of the month *S*râva*n*a (July–August), he may on the following day bathe in the water of a great river and offer (a burnt-oblation of) one thousand pieces of sacred fuel, whilst reciting the Gâyatrî, or he may mutter (the Gâyatrî) as many times.

2. Or he may perform Ish*t*is and Soma-sacrifices for the sake of purifying himself (from his sins).

3. After having eaten forbidden food, he must fast, until his entrails are empty.

4. That is (generally) attained after seven days.

5. Or he may during winter and during the dewy

13. Weber, Ind. Stud. X, 102. According to the greatness of the crime the number of the burnt-oblations must be increased and the prayers be repeated.

27. 1. 'The oblations of sacred fuel (samidh) are not to be accompanied by the exclamation Svâhâ.'—Haradatta.

2. Ish*t*is are the simplest forms of the *S*rauta-sacrifices, i.e. of those for which three fires are necessary.

3. For some particular kinds of forbidden food the same penance is prescribed, Manu XI, 153–154.

season (November–March) bathe in cold water both morning and evening.

6. Or he may perform a K*rikkh*ra penance, which lasts twelve days.

7. The rule for the K*rikkh*ra penance of twelve days (is the following): For three days he must not eat in the evening, and then for three days not in the morning; for three days he must live on food which has been given unasked, and three days he must not eat anything.

8. If he repeats this for a year, that is called a K*rikkh*ra penance, which lasts for a year.

9. Now follows another penance. He who has committed even a great many sins which do not cause him to fall, becomes free from guilt, if, fasting, he recites the entire *S*âkhâ of his Veda three times consecutively.

10. He who cohabits with a non-Aryan woman, he who lends money at interest, he who drinks (other) spirituous liquors (than Surâ), he who praises everybody in a manner unworthy of a Brâhma*n*a, shall sit on grass, allowing his back to be scorched (by the sun).

11. A Brâhma*n*a removes the sin which he committed by serving one day and night (a man of) the black race, if he bathes for three years, eating at every fourth meal-time.

---

7. The same penance is described, under the name Prâ*g*âpatya k*rikkh*ra, the K*rikkh*ra invented by Pra*g*âpati, Manu XI, 212, and Yâ*gñ*. III, 320.

9. Manu XI, 259.

11. The expression k*r*ish*n*a var*n*a, 'the black race,' is truly Vedic. In the *R*ig-veda it usually denotes the aboriginal races, and sometimes the demons. Others explain the Sûtra thus:

PRASNA I, PATALA 10, KHANDA 28.

1. He who, under any conditions whatsoever, covets (and takes) another man's possessions is a thief; thus (teach) Kautsa and Hârîta as well as Kanva and Pushkarasâdi.

2. Vârshyâyani declares, that there are exceptions to this law, in regard to some possessions.

3. (E.g.) seeds ripening in the pod, food for a draught-ox; (if these are taken), the owners (ought) not (to) forbid it.

4. To take even these things in too great a quantity is sinful.

5. Hârîta declares, that in every case the permission (of the owner must be obtained) first.

6. He shall not go to visit a fallen teacher or blood relation.

7. Nor shall he accept the (means for procuring) enjoyments from such a person.

8. If he meets them accidentally he shall silently embrace (their feet) and pass on.

9. A mother does very many acts for her son, therefore he must constantly serve her, though she be fallen.

10. But (there shall be) no communion (with a fallen mother) in acts performed for the acquisition of spiritual merit.

A Brâhmana removes the sin, which he committed by cohabiting for one night with a female of the Sûdra caste, &c.—Haradatta. The latter explanation has been adopted by Kullûka on Manu XI, 179.

28. 3. The same rule Manu emphatically ascribes to himself, Manu VIII, 339. But see also VIII, 331.

7. Haradatta remarks, that this Sûtra implicitly forbids to accept the heritage of an outcast.

11. Enjoyments taken unrighteously he shall give up; he shall say, 'I and sin (do not dwell together).' Clothing himself with a garment reaching from the navel down to the knee, bathing daily, morn, noon, and evening, eating food which contains neither milk nor pungent condiments, nor salt, he shall not enter a house for twelve years.

12. After that he (may be) purified.

13. Then he may have intercourse with Aryans.

14. This penance may also be employed in the case of the other crimes which cause loss of caste (for which no penance has been ordained above).

15. But the violator of a Guru's bed shall enter a hollow iron image and, having caused a fire to be lit on both sides, he shall burn himself.

16. According to Hârîta, this (last-mentioned penance must) not (be performed).

17. For he who takes his own or another's life becomes an Abhiśasta.

18. He (the violator of a Guru's bed) shall perform to his last breath (the penance) prescribed by that rule (Sûtra 11). He cannot be purified in this world. But (after death) his sin is taken away.

19. He who has unjustly forsaken his wife shall put on an ass's skin, with the hair turned outside, and beg in seven houses, saying, 'Give alms to him who forsook his wife.' That shall be his livelihood for six months.

20. But if a wife forsakes her husband, she shall

11. A similar but easier penance is prescribed, Manu XI, 194.

15. '(This penance, which had been prescribed above, I, 9, 25, 1), is enjoined (once more), in order to show that it is not optional (as might be expected according to Sûtra 14).'—Haradatta.

perform the twelve-night K*rikkh*ra penance for as long a time.

21. He who has killed a Bhrû*n*a (a man learned in the Vedas and Vedâṅgas and skilled in the performance of the rites) shall put on the skin of a dog or of an ass, with the hair turned outside, and take a human skull for his drinking-vessel,

PRA*S*NA I, PA*T*ALA 10, KHA*N*DA 29.

1. And he shall take the foot of a bed instead of a staff and, proclaiming the name of his deed, he shall go about (saying), 'Who (gives) alms to the murderer of a Bhrû*n*a?' Obtaining thus his livelihood in the village, he shall dwell in an empty house or under a tree, (knowing that) he is not allowed to have intercourse with Aryans. According to this rule he shall act until his last breath. He cannot be purified in this world. But (after death) his sin is taken away.

2. He even who slays unintentionally, reaps nevertheless the result of his sin.

3. (His guilt is) greater, (if he slays) intentionally.

4. The same (principle applies) also to other sinful actions,

5. And also to good works.

6. A Brâhma*n*a shall not take a weapon into his hand, though he be only desirous of examining it.

7. In a Purâ*n*a (it has been declared), that he who

29. 5. Haradatta gives, as an example, the case where a warrior saves the property of a traveller from thieves. If the traveller turns out to be a Brâhma*n*a, and the warrior did not know his caste before rescuing his property, his merit will be less than if he had rescued knowingly the property of a Brâhma*n*a.

slays an assailant does not sin, for (in that case) wrath meets wrath.

8. But Abhi*s*astas shall live together in dwellings (outside the village); considering this their lawful (mode of life), they shall sacrifice for each other, teach each other, and marry amongst each other.

9. If they have begot sons, let them say to them: 'Go out from amongst us, for thus the Âryas, (throwing the guilt) upon us, will receive you (amongst their number).

10. For the organs do not become impure together with the man.

11. (The truth of) that may be learned from this (parallel case); a man deficient in limbs begets a son who possesses the full number of limbs.

12. Hârîta declares that this is wrong.

13. A wife is similar to the vessel which contains the curds (for the sacrifice).

14. For if one makes impure milk curdle (by mixing it with whey and water) in a milk-vessel and stirs it, no sacrificial rite can be performed with (the curds produced from) that. Just so no intercourse

---

9. It is impossible to agree with Haradatta's explanation of the words to be addressed by Abhi*s*astas to their children. No Vedic license can excuse the use of the second person plural instead of the third. I propose the following: 'Go out from among us; for thus (leaving the guilt) to us, you will be received (as) Âryas.' It is, however, not improbable that our text is disfigured by several very old corruptions, compare Baudhâyana II, 1, 2, 18.

11. 'In like manner a man who has lost his rights, (can) beget a son, who possesses the rights (of his caste). For the wife is also a cause (of the birth of the son), and she is guiltless.'—Haradatta.

13. The statements now following are those with which Âpastamba agrees. Those contained in Sûtras 8–11 are merely the pûrvapaksha.

can be allowed with the impure seed which comes (from an Abhi*s*asta).

15. Sorcery and curses (employed against a Brâhma*n*a) cause a man to become impure, but not loss of caste.

16. Hârîta declares that they cause loss of caste.

17. But crimes causing impurity must be expiated, (when no particular penance is prescribed,) by performing the penance enjoined for crimes causing loss of caste during twelve months, or twelve half months, or twelve twelve-nights, or twelve se'nnights, or twelve times three days, or twelve days, or seven days, or three days, or one day.

18. Thus acts causing impurity must be expiated according to the manner in which the (sinful) act has been committed (whether intentionally or unintentionally).

PRA*S*NA I, PA*T*ALA 11, KHA*N*DA 30.

1. Some declare, that a student shall bathe after (having acquired) the knowledge of the Veda, (however long or short the time of his studentship may have been).

2. (He may) also (bathe) after having kept the student's vow for forty-eight, (thirty-six or twenty-four) years, (though he may not have mastered the Veda).

3. Some declare, that the student (shall bathe) after (having acquired) the knowledge of the Veda and after (the expiration of) his vow.

---

30. 1. The bath is taken at the end of the studentship, and forms part of the Samâvartana-ceremony. From this rite a student who has completed his course of study derives the name Snâtaka, 'one who has bathed.' See also Weber, Ind. Stud. X, 125.

4. To all those persons who have bathed (in accordance with any of the above rules must be shown) the honour due to a Snâtaka.

5. The reverence (shown to a Snâtaka) brings, however, different rewards according to the degree of devotion or of learning (possessed by the person honoured).

6. Now follow the observances (chiefly to be kept) by a Snâtaka.

7. He shall usually enter the village and leave it by the eastern or the northern gate.

8. During the morning and evening twilights, he shall sit outside the village, and not speak anything (referring to worldly matters).

9. (But an Agnihotrî, who is occupied at home by oblations in the morning and evening, must not go out; for) in the case of a conflict (of duties), that enjoined by the Veda is the more important.

10. He shall avoid all dyed dresses,

11. And all naturally black cloth.

12. He shall wear a dress that is neither shining,

13. Nor despicable, if he is able (to afford it).

14. And in the day-time he shall avoid to wrap up his head, except when voiding excrements.

15. But when voiding excrements, he shall envelop his head and place some (grass or the like) on the ground.

16. He shall not void excrements in the shade (of a tree, where travellers rest).

---

10. The rule to wear white garments is given Yâgñ. I, 131; Manu IV, 35.

13. Manu IV, 34.

15. Manu IV, 49.

17. But he may discharge urine on his own shadow.

18. He shall not void excrements with his shoes on, nor on a ploughed field, nor on a path, nor in water.

19. He shall also avoid to spit into, or to have connection with a woman in water.

20. He shall not void excrements facing the fire, the sun, water, a Brâhma*n*a, cows, or (images of) the gods.

21. He shall avoid to clean his body from excrements with a stone, a clod of earth, or with (boughs of) herbs or trees which he has broken off, whilst they were on the tree and full of sap.

22. If possible, he shall not stretch out his feet towards a fire, water, a Brâhma*n*a, a cow, (images of) the gods, a door, or against the wind.

23. Now they quote also (the following verse):

Prasna I, Patala 11, Kha*nd*a 31.

1. He shall eat facing the east, void fæces facing the south, discharge urine facing the north, and wash his feet turned towards the west.

2. He shall void excrements far from his house, having gone towards the south or south-west.

3. But after sunset he must not void excrements outside the village or far from his house.

4. And as long as he is impure he (shall avoid) to pronounce the names of the gods.

---

18. Manu IV, 45, 46; Yâg*ñ*. I, 137.

19. Manu IV, 56.

20. Manu IV, 48, 52; Yâg*ñ*. I, 134.

22. The prohibition to stretch the feet towards a fire occurs also Manu IV, 53; Yâg*ñ*. I, 137.

31. 2. Manu IV, 151; Yâg*ñ*. I, 16.

5. And he shall not speak evil of the gods or of the king.

6. He shall not touch with his foot a Brâhma*n*a, a cow, nor any other (venerable beings).

7. (Nor shall he touch them) with his hand, except for particular reasons.

8. He shall not mention the blemishes of a cow, of sacrificial presents, or of a girl.

9. And he shall not announce it (to the owner) if a cow does damage (by eating corn or grass in a field).

10. (Nor shall he call attention to it) if a cow is together with her calf, except for a particular reason.

11. And of a cow which is not a milch-cow he shall not say, 'She is not a milch-cow.' He must say, 'This is a cow which will become a milch-cow.'

12. He shall not call 'lucky' that which is lucky. He shall call it 'a mercy, a blessing.'

13. He shall not step over a rope to which a calf (or cow) is tied.

14. He shall not pass between the posts from which a swing is suspended.

15. (In company) he shall not say, 'This person

---

5. Manu IV, 163.

8. 'In the section on transcendental knowledge (I, 8, 23, 5), "speaking evil" has been forbidden, in connection with the means of salvation. And below (Sûtra 25) the (author) will declare that the sins which destroy the creatures are to be avoided. But this precept (is given in order to indicate that) in the case of cows and the rest an extra penance must be performed.'—Haradatta.

12. Manu IV, 139. 13. Manu IV, 38.

14. 'Or according to others, "He shall not pass between pillars supporting an arch."'—Haradatta.

is my enemy.' If he says, 'This person is my enemy,' he will raise for himself an enemy, who will show his hatred.

16. If he sees a rainbow, he must not say to others, 'Here is Indra's bow.'

17. He shall not count (a flock of) birds.

18. He shall avoid to look at the sun when he rises or sets.

19. During the day the sun protects the creatures, during the night the moon. Therefore let him eagerly strive to protect himself on the night of the new moon by purity, continence, and rites adapted for the season.

20. For during that night the sun and the moon dwell together.

21. He shall not enter the village by a by-path. If he enters it thus, he shall mutter this *Ri*k-verse, 'Praise be to Rudra, the lord of the dwelling,' or some other (verse) addressed to Rudra.

22. He shall not (ordinarily) give the residue of his food to a person who is not a Brâhma*n*a. When he gives it (to such a one), he shall clean his teeth and give (the food) after having placed in it (the dirt from his teeth).

---

16. Manu IV, 59.

17. 'Others explain (the Sûtra thus): He shall not announce it to others, if he sees (the souls of) good men falling from heaven on account of the expenditure of their merit, (i.e.) he shall not call attention to shooting-stars.'—Haradatta.

18. Manu IV, 37. 19. Manu IV, 153.

21. Manu IV, 73; Yâg*ñ*. I, 140.

22. Manu IV, 80. 'This prohibition (given in the first part of the Sûtra) refers to *S*ûdras who are not dependents; to dependents the following (exception applies).'—Haradatta.

23. And let him avoid the faults that destroy the creatures, such as anger and the like.

PRASNA I, PATALA 11, KHANDA 32.

1. Let him who teaches, avoid connubial intercourse during the rainy season and in autumn.

2. And if he has had connection (with his wife), he shall not lie with her during the whole night.

3. He shall not teach whilst he is lying on a bed.

4. Nor shall he teach (sitting) on that couch on which he lies (at night with his wife).

5. He shall not show himself adorned with a garland, or anointed with ointments.

6. At night he shall always adorn himself for his wife.

7. Let him not submerge his head together with his body (in bathing),

8. And (let him avoid) to bathe after sunset.

9. Let him avoid to use a seat, clogs, sticks for cleaning the teeth, (and other utensils) made of Palâsa-wood.

10. Let him avoid to praise (himself) before his teacher, saying, 'I have properly bathed or the like.'

11. Let him be awake from midnight.

12. Let him not study (or teach) in the middle of the night; but (he may point out) their duties to his pupils.

13. Or (he may) by himself mentally (repeat the sacred texts).

14. After midnight he may teach.

---

23. See above, I, 8, 23, 4 and 5, and Manu IV, 163.

32. 1. Weber, Ind. Stud. X, 42.

2. Manu IV, 40. 5. Manu IV, 72.

15. When he has risen (at midnight, and taught) during the third watch of the night, let him not lie down again (saying), 'Studying is forbidden.'

16. At his pleasure he may (sleep) leaning (against a post or the like).

17. Or he may mentally repeat (the sacred texts).

18. Let him not visit inferior men (such as Nishâdas), nor countries which are inhabited by them,

19. Nor assemblies and crowds.

20. If he has entered a crowd, he shall leave it, turning his right hand towards the crowd.

21. Nor shall he enter towns frequently.

22. Let him not answer directly a question (that is difficult to decide).

23. Now they quote also (the following verse):

24. (The foolish decision) of a person who decides wrongly destroys his ancestors and his future happiness, it harms his children, cattle, and house. 'Oh Dharmaprahrâda, (this deed belongs) not to Kumâlana!' thus decided Death, weeping, the question (addressed to him by the *Ri*shi).

---

15. I. e. if the following day is a forbidden day, e.g. an Ash*t*amî. See also Manu IV, 99.

18. Manu IV, 60 and 61.

24. Haradatta tells the story to which the second half of the verse alludes, in the following manner: 'A certain *Ri*shi had two pupils, called Dharmaprahrâda and Kumâlana. Once they brought from the forest two great bundles of firewood and threw them negligently into their teacher's house, without looking. One of the bundles struck the teacher's little son so that he died. Then the teacher asked his two pupils, "Which of you two has killed him?" Both answered, "Not I, not I." Hereupon the teacher, being unable to (come to a decision in order to) send away the sinner and to keep the innocent one, called Death, and asked him, "Which of the two has killed the boy?" Then Death, finding himself involved in a difficult law-question, began to weep, and

25. Let him not ascend a carriage yoked with asses; and let him avoid to ascend or to descend from vehicles in difficult places.

26. And (let him avoid) to cross a river swimming.

27. And (let him avoid) ships of doubtful (solidity).

28. He shall avoid cutting grass, crushing clods of earth, and spitting, without a particular reason,

29. And whatever else they forbid.

Prasna II, Patala 1, Khanda 1.

1. After marriage the rites prescribed for a householder and his wife (must be performed).

2. He shall eat at the two (appointed) times, (morning and evening).

---

giving his decision, said, "Oh Dharmaprahrâda, not to Kumâlana (the dative has the sense of the genitive), this sin is none of Kumâlana's!" Instead of declaring, "Dharmaprahrâda, thou hast done this," he said, "The other did not do it." Still from the circumstances of the case it appeared that the meaning of the answer was, "The other has done it." "This was the decision which he gave crying."'—The reading of the text rendered in the translation is, dharmaprahrâda na kumâlanâya.

26. Manu IV, 77. 28. Manu IV, 70 and 71.

1. 1. According to Haradatta, this rule is intended to refute the opinion of those who hold that the sacred household-fire may be kept, and the prescribed offerings therein may be performed, either from the time of the marriage, or after the division of the family estate. He also states that the use of the dual *gri*hamedhino*h* indicates that husband and wife must perform the rites conjointly. Manu III, 67.

2. Haradatta thinks that this Sûtra is intended to prevent householders from having more than two meals a day, and to keep them from gluttony. Others are of opinion that its object is to keep householders from excessive fasting, and to make them perform the Prâ*n*âgnihotra at either meal. At the Prâ*n*âgnihotra the sacrificer eats five mouthfuls invoking successively, whilst he

3. And he shall not eat to repletion.

4. And both (the householder and his wife) shall fast on (the days of) the new and full moon.

5. To eat once (on those days in the morning), that also is called fasting.

6. And they may eat (at that meal) until they are quite satisfied.

7. And on (the anniversary of) that (wedding)-day they may eat that food of which they are fond.

8. And (on the night of that day) they shall sleep on the ground (on a raised heap of earth).

9. And they shall avoid connubial intercourse.

10. And on the day after (that day) a Sthâlîpâka must be offered.

11. The manner in which that offering must be

---

eats, the five vital airs. At the first mouthful he says, 'To Prâ*n*a svâhâ;' at the second, 'To Apâna svâhâ,' &c.

5. Â*s*v. G*ri*. Sû. I, 10, 2.

7. Haradatta holds that the words 'on that day' do not refer to the days of the new and full moon, the Parvan-days, mentioned in Sûtra 4. His reasons are, first, that the permission to eat food, of which the householder may be particularly fond, has already been given in Sûtra 6, by the term *tri*pti*h*, 'satisfaction'; and, secondly, that the singular 'on this day' does not agree with the plural 'on the Parvan-days.' Hence he comes to the conclusion that the words 'on that day' must refer to the wedding-day, mentioned in Sûtra 1, as well as to its anniversary. Haradatta is, probably, right in his explanation, though the reasons adduced here are very weak. A stronger reason for detaching this Sûtra from Sûtra 4 will be brought forward below, under Sûtra 11. Mahâdeva, the commentator of the Hira*n*yake*s*idharma, adopts the view rejected by Haradatta.

8. Â*s*v. G*ri*. Sû. I, 3, 10.

10. A Sthâlîpâka is an offering at which rice cooked in a pot, sthâlî, is offered in the fire. A full description of this kind of sacrifice occurs, Â*s*v. G*ri*. Sû. I, 10, 1 seq.

11. The Pârva*n*a Sthâlîpâka has been described by Âpastamba

performed has been declared by (the description of the Sthâlîpâka) to be performed on the days of the new and full moon (the Pârva*n*a).

12. And they declare (that this rite which is known) amongst the people (must be performed) every (year).

13. At every (burnt-offering), when he wishes to place the fire on the altar (called Stha*nd*ila), let him draw on that (altar) three lines from west to east and three lines from south to north, and sprinkle (the altar) with water, turning the palm of the hand downwards, and let him then make the fire burn brightly by adding (fuel).

14. He shall pour out (the remainder of) this water used for sprinkling, to the north or to the east (of the altar), and take other (water into the vessel).

15. The water-vessels in the house shall never be empty; that is the duty to be observed by the householder and his wife.

---

in the G*ri*hya-sûtra, III, 7. Again, Haradatta returns to the question whether the words on that day (Sûtra 7) refer to the Parvan-days, or the marriage-day and its anniversaries. He now adds, in favour of the latter view, that the word Pârva*n*ena, 'by the rite to be performed on Parvan-days,' by which the Sthâlîpâka on Parvan-days is intended, clearly proves the impossibility to refer the preceding rules to the Parvan-days. He adds that some, nevertheless, adopt the explanation rejected by himself.

12. They, i.e. the *S*ish*t*as, those learned in the law. 'Another commentator says, the rite which will be taught (in the following Sûtra), and which is known from the usage of the learned, is constant, i.e. must be performed in every case. That it is what the "learned" declare.'—Haradatta. The latter explanation of the Sûtra is adopted by Mahâdeva.

13. Â*s*v. G*ri*. Sû. I, 3, 1–3.

15. Haradatta states that the object of the repetition of the words 'the householder and his wife' is to show that they

16. Let him not have connubial intercourse (with his wife) in the day-time.

17. But let him have connection with his wife at the proper time, according to the rules (of the law).

18. Let him have connubial intercourse in the interval also, if his wife (desires it, observing the restrictions imposed by the law).

19. (The duty of) connubial intercourse (follows from) the passage of a Brâhma*n*a, ('Let us dwell together until a son be born.')

20. But during intercourse he shall be dressed in a particular dress kept for this purpose.

21. And during intercourse only they shall lie together,

22. Afterwards separate.

23. Then they both shall bathe;

PRA*S*NA II, PA*T*ALA 1, KHA*N*DA 2.

1. Or they shall remove the stains with earth or water, sip water, and sprinkle the body with water.

2. Men of all castes, if they fulfil their (assigned) duties, enjoy (in heaven) the highest, imperishable bliss.

3. Afterwards when (a man who has fulfilled his duties) returns to this world, he obtains, by virtue of

---

themselves must fill the water-vessels, and not employ others for this purpose. He adds that, according to another commentator, the object of the repetition is to show that Sûtras 13 and 14 apply not only to householders, but also to students, and that hence students, when they offer the daily oblations of sacred fuel (above, I, 1, 4, 14 seq.), should also perform the rites taught in the preceding Sûtras.

17. See Manu III, 46–48; Yâg*ñ*. I, 79 80.

18. Manu III, 45; Yâg*ñ*. I, 81.

19. See Taittirîya Sa*m*hitâ II, 5, 1, 5.

a remainder of merit, birth in a distinguished family, beauty of form, beauty of complexion, strength, aptitude for learning, wisdom, wealth, and the gift of fulfilling the laws of his (caste and order). Therefore in both worlds he dwells in happiness, (rolling) like a wheel (from the one to the other).

4. As the seed of herbs (and) trees, (sown) in good and well-cultivated soil, gives manifold returns of fruit (even so it is with men who have received the various sacraments).

5. The increase of the results of sins has been explained hereby.

6. Thus after having undergone a long punishment in the next world, a person who has stolen (the gold of a Brâhma*n*a) or killed a (Brâhma*n*a) is born again, in case he was a Brâhma*n*a as a *K*â*nd*âla, in case he was a Kshatriya as a Paulkasa, in case he was a Vai*s*ya as a Vai*n*a.

7. In the same manner other (sinners) who have become outcasts in consequence of their sinful actions are born again, on account of (these) sins, losing their caste, in the wombs (of various animals).

8. As it is sinful to touch a *K*â*nd*âla, (so it is also sinful) to speak to him or to look at him. The penance for these (offences will be declared).

9. (The penance) for touching him is to bathe, submerging the whole body; for speaking to him to speak to a Brâhma*n*a; for looking at him to look at the lights (of heaven).

---

2. 6. Manu XII, 55; Yâg*ñ*. III, 206, 207. A Paulkasa is said to be the offspring of a Nishâda and a Kshatriya woman. See the Pet. Dict. s. v. A Vai*n*a is a rope-dancer, or equilibrist.

7. Manu XII, 52.

PRASNA II, PATALA 2, KHANDA 3.

1. Pure men of the first three castes shall prepare the food (of a householder which is used) at the Vaisvadeva ceremony.

2. The (cook) shall not speak, nor cough, nor sneeze, while his face is turned towards the food.

3. He shall purify himself by touching water if he has touched his hair, his limbs, or his garment.

4. Or *S*ûdras may prepare the food, under the superintendence of men of the first three castes.

5. For them is prescribed the same rule of sipping water (as for their masters).

6. Besides, the (*S*ûdra cooks) daily shall cause to be cut the hair of their heads, their beards, the hair on their bodies, and their nails.

7. And they shall bathe, keeping their clothes on.

8. Or they may trim (their hair and nails) on the eighth day (of each half-month), or on the days of the full and new moon.

9. He (the householder himself) shall place on the fire that food which has been prepared (by *S*ûdras) without supervision, and shall sprinkle it with water. Such food also they state to be fit for the gods.

10. When the food is ready, (the cook) shall place

---

3. 1. 'The food which is used at the Vai*s*vadeva, i.e. the food prepared for the meals of the householder and of his wife.'—Haradatta.

5. This Sûtra is a *G*ñâpaka, as it indicates that Âpastamba also recognises the different rules which are usually prescribed in the Sm*ri*tis for Brâhma*n*as, Kshatriyas, Vai*s*yas, and *S*ûdras. See above, I, 5, 16, 2.

7. Usually in bathing both Âryas and *S*ûdras wear no dress except the lango*t*î.

himself before his master and announce it to him (saying), 'It is ready.'

11. The answer (of the master) shall be, 'That well-prepared food is the means to obtain splendour; may it never fail!'

12. The burnt-oblations and Bali-offerings made with the food which the husband and his wife are to eat, bring (as their reward) prosperity, (and the enjoyment of) heaven.

13. Whilst learning the sacred formulas (to be recited during the performance) of those (burnt-oblations and Bali-offerings, a householder) shall sleep on the ground, abstain from connubial intercourse and from eating pungent condiments and salt, during twelve days.

14. (When he studies the Mantras) for the last (Bali offered to the goblins), he shall fast for one (day and) night.

15. For each Bali-offering the ground must be prepared separately. (The performer) sweeps (the ground) with his (right) hand, sprinkles it with water, turning the palm downwards, throws down (the offering), and afterwards sprinkles water around it.

---

11. Manu II, 54.

12. Balis are portions of food which are thrown before the door, or on the floor of the house. See below, Sûtra 16 seq.

13. Others explain this Sûtra thus: 'After having used for the first time these sacred formulas (which are to be recited in offering the burnt-oblation and the Balis, the householder and his wife) shall sleep,' &c.

14. Regarding the use of ekarâtra in the sense of 'a (day and a) night,' see above. The 'last' Bali-offering is that described below, II, 2, 4, 5.

15. 'They say that the word "afterwards" is used in order to indicate that perfumes, garlands, and other (Upa*k*âras) must be offered between (the last two acts).'—Haradatta.

16. (At the Vaisvadeva sacrifice) he shall offer the oblations with his hand, (throwing them) into the kitchen-fire or into the sacred (Grihya)-fire, and reciting (each time one of) the first six Mantras (prescribed in the Nârâyanî Upanishad).

17. He shall sprinkle water all around both times (before and after the oblations), as (has been declared) above.

18. In like manner water is sprinkled around once only after the performance of those Bali-offerings that are performed in one place.

19. (If a seasoning) has been prepared, (the Bali-offering should consist of rice) mixed with that seasoning.

20. With the seventh and eighth Mantras (Balis

---

16. It is a disputed point with the commentators whether every Brâhmana may offer the Vaisvadeva in the common kitchen-fire, or those persons only who do not keep a sacred domestic fire. The six Mantras, which are given Taitt. Âr. X, 67, 1, are: 1. Agnaye svâhâ, 'to Agni svâhâ'; 2. Somâya svâhâ, 'to Soma svâhâ'; 3. Visvebhyo devebhyah svâhâ, 'to all the gods svâhâ'; 4. Dhruvâya bhûmaya svâhâ, 'to Dhruva Bhûma svâhâ'; 5. Dhruvakshitaye svâhâ, 'to Dhruvakshiti svâhâ'; 6. Akyutakshitaye svâhâ, 'to Akyutakshiti svâhâ.' Haradatta adds that some add a seventh formula, addressed to Agni svishtakrit, 'to the fire which causes the proper performance of the sacrifice,' while others leave out the second Mantra and give that addressed to Agni svishtakrit the sixth place. This latter is the order given in the Calcutta edition of the Taittirîya Âranyaka.

17. 'Above, i.e. Grihya-sûtra, I, 2, 3, 8.'—Haradatta. The Mantras recited are: 1. at the first sprinkling, Adite 'numanyasva, 'Aditi permit'; Anumate 'numanyasva, 'Anumati permit'; Sarasvaty anumanyasva, 'Sarasvatî permit'; Deva Savitah prasuva, 'Divine Savitri permit'; 2. at the second sprinkling, the same as above, anvamamsthâh and prâsâvîh, 'thou hast permitted,' being substituted for anumanyasva and prasuva.

18. This Sûtra is a restriction of Sûtra 15.

20. The first six offerings constitute the Devayagña or Vaisva-

must be offered to Dharma and Adharma) behind the fire, and must be placed the one to the north of the other.

21. With the ninth (Mantra a Bali offered to the waters must be placed) near the water-vessel (in which the water for domestic purposes is kept).

22. With the tenth and eleventh (Mantras, Balis, offered to the herbs and trees and to Rakshodeva-*g*ana, must be placed) in the centre of the house, and the one to the east of the other.

23. With the following four (Mantras, Balis must be placed) in the north-eastern part of the house (and the one to the east of the other).

PRA*S*NA II, PA*T*ALA 2, KHA*N*DA 4.

1. Near the bed (a Bali must be offered) with (a Mantra) addressed to Kâma (Cupid).

2. On the door-sill (a Bali must be placed) with (a Mantra) addressed to Antariksha (the air).

3. With (the Mantra) that follows (in the Upanishad, he offers a Bali) near the door.

---

deva, which is offered in the fire. Now follow the Bali-offerings, which are merely placed on the ground. 'Behind the fire' means 'to the east of the fire'; for the sacrificer must face the east.

21. The Mantra is, Adbhya*h* svâhâ, 'to the Waters svâhâ.'

22. The Mantras are, Oshadhivanaspatibhya*h* svâhâ, 'to the herbs and trees svâhâ'; Rakshodeva*g*anebhya*h* svâhâ, 'to the Râkshasas and the servants of the gods svâhâ.'

23. These four Balis are sacred to the G*ri*hâs, to the Avasânas, to the Avasânapatis, and to all creatures.

4. 2. 'Others explain dehalî, "the door-sill," to mean "the door-case."'—Haradatta.

3. 'Others explain apidhâna, "the panels of the door," to mean "the bolt of the door."'—Haradatta. The offering is made to Nâma, 'the name, or essence of things.'

4. With the following (ten Mantras, addressed to Earth, Air, Heaven, Sun, Moon, the Constellations, Indra, B*ri*haspati, Pra*g*âpati, and Brahman, he offers ten Balis, each following one to the east of the preceding one), in (the part of the house called) the seat of Brahman.

5. He shall offer to the south (of the Balis offered before, a Bali) with a Mantra addressed to the Manes; his sacrificial cord shall be suspended over the right shoulder, and the (palm of his right hand shall be turned upwards and) inclined to the right.

6. To the north (of the Bali given to the Manes, a Bali shall be offered) to Rudra, in the same manner as to the (other) gods.

7. The sprinkling with water (which precedes and follows the oblation) of these two (Balis, takes place) separately, on account of the difference of the rule (for each case).

---

4. Haradatta gives two explanations of the word Brahmasadana, 'the seat of Brahman.' According to some, it is an architectural term, designating the centre of the house; according to others, it denotes the place where, at the time of the burnt-oblations, the Brahman or superintending priest is seated, i.e. a spot to the south of the sacred fire.

5. Balis and water for the Manes are placed or poured into the palm of the hand and thrown out between the thumb and forefinger. That part of the palm is, therefore, sometimes called 'the tîrtha sacred to the Manes.' See Manu II, 39.

6. 'That is to say, the sacrificial cord shall not be suspended over the right shoulder, nor shall the Bali be thrown out between the thumb and forefinger.'—Haradatta.

7. In sprinkling around an offering to the gods, the sacrificer turns his right hand towards the oblation and pours out the water, beginning in the south and ending in the east. In sprinkling around an offering to the Manes, exactly the opposite order is to be followed.

8. At night only he shall offer (the Bali to the goblins), throwing it into the air and reciting the last (Mantra).

9. He who devoutly offers those (above-described Balis and Homas), according to the rules, (obtains) eternal bliss in heaven and prosperity.

10. And (after the Balis have been performed, a portion of the food) must first be given as alms.

11. He shall give food to his guests first,

12. And to infants, old or sick people, female (relations, and) pregnant women.

13. The master (of the house) and his wife shall not refuse a man who asks for food at the time (when the Vaisvadeva offering has been performed).

14. If there is no food, earth, water, grass, and a kind word, indeed, never fail in the house of a good man. Thus (say those who know the law).

---

8. At night, i.e. before the evening meal. The Mantra is, 'To those beings which, being servants of Vituda, roam about day and night, desiring a Bali-offering, I offer this Bali, desirous of prosperity. May the Lord of prosperity grant me prosperity, svâhâ.' Haradatta adds, that according to another commentator, no other Bali but this is to be offered in the evening, and that some modify the Mantra for each occasion, offering the Bali in the morning to 'the Bhûtas that roam about during the day,' and in the evening 'to the night-walkers.' Compare for the whole section Manu III, 90–92; Yâgñ. I, 102–104.

10. Manu III, 94 seq.

11. Manu III, 115; Yâgñ. I, 105.

12. Manu III, 114; Yâgñ. I, 105.

14. Manu III, 101; Yâgñ. I, 107. As read in the text, the first line of the verse has one syllable in excess. This irregularity would disappear if *trinâ*, the Vedic form of the nom. acc. plural, were read for *trinâni*, and it seems to me not improbable that *trinâni* is a correction made by a Pandit who valued grammatical correctness higher than correctness of metre.

15. Endless worlds are the portion (of those householders and wives) who act thus.

16. To a Brâhma*n*a who has not studied the Veda, a seat, water, and food must be given. But (the giver) shall not rise (to do him honour).

17. But if (such a man) is worthy of a salutation (for other reasons), he shall rise to salute him.

18. Nor (shall a Brâhma*n*a rise to receive) a Kshatriya or Vai*s*ya (though they may be learned).

19. If a *S*ûdra comes as a guest (to a Brâhma*n*a), he shall give him some work to do. He may feed him, after (that has been performed).

20. Or the slaves (of the Brâhma*n*a householder) shall fetch (rice) from the royal stores, and honour the *S*ûdra as a guest.

21. (A householder) must always wear his garment over (his left shoulder and under his right arm).

22. Or he may use a cord only, slung over his left shoulder and passed under his right arm, instead of the garment.

23. He shall sweep together (the crumbs) on the place where he has eaten, and take them away. He shall sprinkle water on that place, turning the palm downwards, and remove the stains (of food from the cooking-vessels with a stick), wash them with water, and take their contents to a clean place to the north (of the house, offering them) to Rudra. In this manner his house will become prosperous.

---

16. Manu III, 99.

18. Manu III, 110–112; Yâ*gñ*. I, 107.

19. Manu loc. cit.

20. 'Hence it is known that the king ought to keep stores of rice and the like in every village, in order to show hospitality to *S*ûdra guests.'—Haradatta.

24. It is declared in the Smritis that a Brâhmana alone should be chosen as teacher (or spiritual guide).

25. In times of distress a Brâhmana may study under a Kshatriya or Vaisya.

26. And (during his pupilship) he must walk behind (such a teacher).

27. Afterwards the Brâhmana shall take precedence before (his Kshatriya or Vaisya teacher).

PRASNA II, PATALA 2, KHANDA 5.

1. On the day on which, beginning the study of the whole sacred science, the Upanishads (and the rest, he performs the Upâkarma in the morning), he shall not study (at night).

2. And he shall not leave his teacher at once after having studied (the Veda and having returned home).

---

24. Manu II, 241, 242. From here down to II, 3, 6, 2, Âpastamba again treats of the duties of students and teachers, a subject which appears to have in his eyes a greater importance than any other. The rules given now apply chiefly to householders. It would seem that they have been inserted in this particular place, because the reception of a former teacher is to be described II, 3, 5, 4-11, and that of a 'learned guest' II, 3, 6, 3 seq.

5. 1. This rule refers to the Upâkarma, to be performed yearly by householders. In our days, too, the custom is observed, and the whole Brahminical community change on this occasion their Genvîs or sacrificial cords in the month of Srâvana. The adherents of the various Sâkhâs of the Vedas, however, perform the ceremony on different days. According to Haradatta, the Upanishads are named, in order to show that they are of the highest importance. See also Satapatha-brâhmana X, 3, 5, 12.

2. Others consider that this Sûtra refers to the annual Upâkarma of the householder. In that case the translation would be, 'And after having performed the Upâkarma,' &c. Probably Âpastamba means to give a general rule, applicable both to householders and to students who have returned home.

3. If he is in a hurry to go, he shall perform the daily recitation of the Veda in the presence of his teacher, and then go at his pleasure. In this manner good fortune will attend both of them.

4. If the (former) teacher visits him after he has returned home, he shall go out to meet him, embrace his (feet), and he shall not wash himself (after that act), showing disgust. He then shall let him pass first into the house, fetch (the materials necessary for a hospitable reception), and honour him according to the rule.

5. If (his former teacher is) present, he himself shall use a seat, a bed, food, and garments inferior to, and lower (than those offered to the teacher).

6. Standing (with his body bent), he shall place his left hand (under the water-vessel, and bending with his other hand its mouth downwards), he shall offer to his teacher water for sipping.

7. And (he shall offer water for sipping in this manner) to other guests also who possess all (good qualities) together.

8. He shall imitate (his teacher) in rising, sitting, walking about, and smiling.

---

4. 'Though he may suspect that the teacher had been defiled by the touch of a *K*â*nd*âla or the like, still he shall not show disgust nor wash himself.'—Haradatta. Regarding the rule of receiving guests, see below, II, 4, 8, 6 seq.

6. According to Haradatta, the repetition of the word â*k*âryam, 'the teacher,' in this Sûtra, indicates that the rule holds good not only when the teacher comes as a guest to his former pupil, but on every occasion when he receives water for sipping.

7. 'He is called samudeta, "possessed of all (good qualities) together," who is endowed with (good) birth, disposition, behaviour, (great) learning, and a (venerable) age.'—Haradatta.

8. The word syât is to be understood from Sûtra 5.

9. In the presence (of his teacher) he shall not void excrements, discharge wind, speak aloud, laugh, spit, clean his teeth, blow his nose, frown, clap his hands, nor snap his fingers.

10. Nor shall he tenderly embrace or address caressing words to his wife or children.

11. He shall not contradict his teacher,

12. Nor any of his betters.

13. (He shall not) blame or revile any creature.

14. (He shall not revile one branch of) sacred learning by (invidiously comparing it with) another.

15. If he is not well versed in a (branch of) sacred learning (which he studied formerly), he shall again go to the (same) teacher and master it, observing the (same) rules as (during his first studentship).

16. The restrictions (to be kept) by the teacher from the beginning of the course of teaching to its end are, to avoid cutting the hair on the body, partaking of meat or of oblations to the Manes, and connection (with a woman).

17. Or (he may have conjugal intercourse) with his wife at the proper season.

18. He shall be attentive in instructing his pupils in the sacred learning, in such a manner that they

13. Haradatta states that 'speaking evil' is forbidden here once more in order that it should be particularly avoided.

14. 'For example, he shall not say, "The *Ri*g-veda is sweet to the ear, the other Vedas grate on the ear," or "the Taittirîya-veda is a *S*âkhâ consisting of leavings," or "the Brâhma*n*a proclaimed by Yâ*gñ*avalkya is of modern origin."'—Haradatta. The second sentence refers to the story that Yâ*gñ*avalkya vomited the Black Ya*g*ur-veda, and his fellow-students, becoming partridges, picked it up. Regarding the third sentence, see Vârttika on Pâ*n*ini IV, 3, 105, and Max Müller's History of Ancient Sanskrit Literature, p. 363.

16. Weber, Ind. Stud. X, 42.

master it, and in observing the restrictions (imposed upon householders during their teaching). He who acts thus, gains heavenly bliss for himself, his descendants and ancestors.

19. He who entirely avoids with mind, word, nose, eye, and ear the sensual objects (such as are) enjoyed by the touch, the organ, or the stomach, gains immortality.

Prasna II, Patala 3, Khanda 6.

1. If he has any doubts regarding the caste and conduct of a person who has come to him in order to fulfil his duty (of learning the Veda), he shall kindle a fire (with the ceremonies prescribed for kindling the sacrificial fire) and ask him about his caste and conduct.

2. If he declares himself to be (of) good (family and conduct, the teacher elect) shall say, 'Agni who sees, Vâyu who hears, Âditya who brings to light, vouch for his goodness; may it be well with this person! He is free from sin.' Then he shall begin to teach him.

3. A guest comes to the house resembling a burning fire.

---

6. 1. The person desirous to study addresses his teacher elect with the following Mantra: Bhagavan maitre*n*a *k*akshushâ pa*s*ya *s*ivena manasânug*ri*hâ*n*a prasîda mâm adhyâpaya, 'venerable Sir, look on me with a friendly eye, receive me with a favourable mind, be kind and teach me.' The teacher elect then asks: Ki*m*gotro 'si saumya, kimâ*k*âra*h*, 'friend, of what family art thou? what is thy rule of conduct?'

3. The object of this Sûtra is to show the absolute necessity of feeding a guest. For, if offended, he might burn the house with the flames of his anger.

4. He is called a *S*rotriya who, observing the law (of studentship), has learned one recension of the Veda (which may be current in his family).

5. He is called a guest (who, being a *S*rotriya), approaches solely for the fulfilment of his religious duties, and with no other object, a householder who lives intent on the fulfilment of his duties.

6. The reward for honouring (such a guest) is immunity from misfortunes, and heavenly bliss.

7. He shall go to meet such (a guest), honour him according to his age (by the formulas of salutation prescribed), and cause a seat to be given to him.

8. Some declare that, if possible, the seat should have many feet.

9. The (householder himself) shall wash the feet of that (guest); according to some, two *S*ûdras shall do it.

10. One of them shall be employed in pouring water (over the guest, the other in washing his feet).

11. Some declare that the water for the (guest) shall be brought in an earthen vessel.

---

4. The object of this Sûtra is to complete the definition of the term 'guest' to be given in the following Sûtra. In my translation I have followed Haradatta's gloss. The literal sense of Âpastamba's words is, 'He who, observing the law, has studied one recension of each (of the four) Vedas, becomes a *S*rotriya.' Haradatta says this definition would be contrary to the current acceptation of the term. That argument proves, however, nothing for Âpastamba's times.

5. Manu III, 102, 103; Yâ*gñ*. I, 111.

6. Yâ*gñ*. I, 109; Manu III, 101.

8. Haradatta states that this is also Âpastamba's opinion.

11. According to Haradatta, Âpastamba is of opinion that it should be brought in a pot made of metal.

12. But (a guest) who has not yet returned home from his teacher shall not be a cause for fetching water.

13. In case a (student comes, the host) shall repeat the Veda (together with him) for a longer time (than with other guests).

14. He shall converse kindly (with his guest), and gladden him with milk or other (drinks), with eatables, or at least with water.

15. He shall offer to his guest a room, a bed, a mattress, a pillow with a cover, and ointment, and what else (may be necessary).

16. (If the dinner has been finished before the arrival of the guest), he shall call his cook and give him rice or yava for (preparing a fresh meal for) the guest.

17. (If dinner is ready at the arrival of the guest), he himself shall portion out the food and look at it, saying (to himself), 'Is this (portion) greater, or this?'

18. He shall say, 'Take out a larger (portion for the guest).'

19. A guest who is at enmity (with his host) shall not eat his food, nor (shall he eat the food of a host) who hates him or accuses him of a crime, or of one who is suspected of a crime.

20. For it is declared in the Veda that he (who eats the food of such a person) eats his guilt.

---

12. I.e. it is unnecessary to offer water for washing the feet to a student.

15. 'Ointment, (i.e.) oil or clarified butter for anointing the feet.'—Haradatta. Manu III, 107.

16. Manu III, 108.

19. Manu IV, 213; Yâgñ. I, 162.

PRASNA II, PATALA 3, KHANDA 7.

1. This reception of guests is an everlasting (*S*rauta)-sacrifice offered by the householder to Pra*g*âpati.

2. The fire in the stomach of the guest (represents) the Âhavanîya, (the sacred fire) in the house of the host represents the Gârhapatya, the fire at which the food for the guest is cooked (represents) the fire used for cooking the sacrificial viands (the Dakshi*n*âgni).

3. He who eats before his guest consumes the food, the prosperity, the issue, the cattle, the merit which his family acquired by sacrifices and charitable works.

4. Food (offered to guests) which is mixed with milk procures the reward of an Agnish*t*oma-sacrifice, food mixed with clarified butter procures the reward of an Ukthya, food mixed with honey the reward of an Atirâtra, food accompanied by meat the reward of a Dvâda*s*âha, (food and) water numerous offspring and long life.

5. It is declared in the Veda, 'Both welcome and indifferent guests procure heaven (for their host).'

---

7. 1. 'Prâ*g*âpatya may mean either "created by Pra*g*âpati" or "sacred to Pra*g*âpati."'—Haradatta.

2. In the first Sûtra the reception of guests had been compared to an everlasting Vedic sacrifice. This analogy is traced further in detail in this Sûtra. One of the chief characteristics of a Vedic sacrifice is the vitâna, or the use of three sacred fires. Hence Âpastamba shows that three fires also are used in offering hospitality to guests.

4. Regarding the Agnish*t*oma and the other sacrifices mentioned, see Aitareya-brâhma*n*a III, 8; IV, 1; IV, 4.

6. When he gives food in the morning, at noon, and in the evening, (these gifts) are the Savanas (of that sacrifice offered to Pragâpati).

7. When he rises after his guest has risen (to depart), that act represents the Udavasânîyâ ishti (of a Vedic sacrifice).

8. When he addresses (the guest) kindly, that kind address (represents) the Dakshinâ.

9. When he follows (his departing guest, his steps represent) the steps of Vishnu.

10. When he returns (after having accompanied his guest), that (act represents) the Avabhritha, (the final bath performed after the completion of a sacrifice.)

11. Thus (a Brâhmana shall treat) a Brâhmana, (and a Kshatriya and a Vaisya their caste-fellows.)

12. If a guest comes to a king, he shall make (his Purohita) honour him more than himself.

13. If a guest comes to an Agnihotrin, he himself

---

6. The morning, midday, and evening offerings offered at the great Vedic sacrifices are called Savanas. The object of this Sûtra is to prescribe the hospitable reception of guests at all times of the day, and to further describe the similarity of a guest-offering to a Vedic sacrifice.

7. Regarding the Udavasânîyâ ishti, see Aitareya-brâhmana VIII, 5. It is the 'concluding ishti.'

8. Dakshinâ is the reward given to priests who officiate at a sacrifice.

9. 'The steps of Vishnu' are three steps which the sacrificer has to make between the Vedi and the Âhavanîya-fire. See Pet. Dict. s. v.

12. 'A guest,' i.e. such a one as described above, II, 3, 6, 4 and 5.

13. An Agnihotrin is a Brâhmana who offers certain daily burnt-offerings called Agnihotra. The translation of the last clause renders tarpayantu, the reading of the Atharva-veda.

shall go to meet him and say to him: 'O faithful fulfiller of thy vows, where didst thou stay (last night)?' (Then he offers water, saying): 'O faithful fulfiller of thy vows, here is water.' (Next he offers milk or the like, saying): 'O faithful fulfiller of thy vows, may (these fluids) refresh (thee).'

14. (If the guest stays at the time of the Agnihotra, he shall make him sit down to the north of the fire and) murmur in a low voice, before offering the oblations: 'O faithful fulfiller of thy vows, may it be as thy heart desires;' 'O faithful fulfiller of thy vows, may it be as thy will is;' 'O faithful fulfiller of thy vows, may it be as thy wish is;' 'O faithful fulfiller of thy vows, may it be as thy desire is.'

15. If a guest comes, after the fires have been placed (on the altar), but before the oblations have been offered, (the host) himself shall approach him and say to him: 'O faithful fulfiller of thy vows, give me permission; I wish to sacrifice.' Then he shall sacrifice, after having received permission. A Brâhma*n*a declares that he commits a sin if he sacrifices without permission.

16. He who entertains guests for one night obtains earthly happiness, a second night gains the middle air, a third heavenly bliss, a fourth the world of unsurpassable bliss; many nights procure endless worlds. That has been declared in the Veda.

17. If an unlearned person who pretends to be

---

14. According to some, all these sentences must be pronounced; according to Haradatta, one only, which may be selected optionally.

15. Haradatta states that the Brâhma*n*a mentioned in the text is the Âtharva*n*a-brâhma*n*a. See Atharva-veda XV, 11–12.

(worthy of the appellation) 'guest' comes to him, he shall give him a seat, water, and food, (thinking) 'I give it to a learned Brâhma*n*a.' Thus (the merit) of his (gift) becomes (as) great (as if a learned Brâhma*n*a had received it).

PRA*S*NA II, PA*T*ALA 4, KHA*N*DA 8.

1. On the second and following days of the guest's stay, the host shall not rise or descend (from his couch) in order to salute his (guest), if he has been saluted before (on the first day).

2. He shall eat after his guests.

3. He shall not consume all the flavoured liquids in the house, so as to leave nothing for guests.

4. He shall not cause sweetmeats to be prepared for his own sake.

5. (A guest) who can repeat the (whole) Veda (together with the supplementary books) is worthy to receive a cow and the Madhuparka,

6. (And also) the teacher, an officiating priest, a Snâtaka, and a just king (though not learned in the Veda).

7. A cow and the Madhuparka (shall be offered) to the teacher, to an officiating priest, to a father-in-law, and to a king, if they come after a year has elapsed (since their former visit).

---

8. 2. Manu III, 117; Yâg*ñ*. I, 105.

3. Flavoured liquids, i.e. milk, whey, &c.

4. Manu III, 106.

5. Manu III, 119 and 120; Yâg*ñ*. I, 110; Weber, Ind. Stud. X, 125. A guest is also called goghna, 'cow-killer,' because formerly a cow used to be killed on the arrival of a distinguished guest. The rite is described by Â*s*valâyana G*ri*hya-sûtra I, 24, 31-33.

8. The Madhuparka shall consist of curds mixed with honey, or of milk mixed with honey.

9. On failure (of these substances) water (mixed with honey may be used).

10. The Veda has six Aṅgas (auxiliary works).

11. (The six auxiliary works are) the Kalpa (teaching the ritual) of the Veda, the treatises on grammar, astronomy, etymology, phonetics, and metrics.

12. (If any one should contend that) the term Veda (on account of its etymology, implying that which teaches duty or whereby one obtains spiritual merit) applies to the complete collection of (works which contain) rules for rites to be performed on the authority of precepts, (that, consequently, the Kalpa-sûtras form part of the Veda, and that thereby) the number (fixed above) for those (Aṅgas) is proved to be wrong,

13. (Then we answer), All those who are learned in Mîmâ*m*sâ are agreed that (the terms Veda, Brâhma*n*a, and the like, which are applied to) the principal (works), do not include the Aṅgas (the Kalpa-sûtras and the rest).

14. If he remembers at any time during dinner, that he has refused a guest, he shall at once leave off eating and fast on that day,

---

8. Â*s*valâyana G*ri*hya-sûtra I, 24, 5 and 6.

10. This Sûtra explains the term vedâdhyâya, '(a guest) who can repeat the (whole) Veda,' which occurs above, Sûtra 5.—Haradatta. See Max Müller's History of Ancient Sanskrit Literature, p. 111.

12. This Sûtra and the following one are directed against those who consider the Kalpa-sûtras to be a part of the Veda, the revealed texts. See also Max Müller's History of Ancient Sanskrit Literature, p. 95 seq.

PRASNA II, PATALA 4, KHANDA 9.

1. And on the following day (he shall search for him[1], feast him to his heart's content, and accompany him (on his departure).

2. (If the guest) possesses a carriage, (he shall accompany him) as far as that.

3. Any other (guest he must accompany), until permission to return is given.

4. If (the guest) forgets (to give leave to depart), the (host) may return on reaching the boundary of his village.

5. To all (those who come for food) at (the end of) the Vaisvadeva he shall give a portion, even to dogs and *Kand*âlas.

6. Some declare that he shall not give anything to unworthy people (such as *Kand*âlas).

7. A person who has been initiated shall not eat the leavings of women or of an uninitiated person.

8. All gifts are to be preceded by (pouring out) water.

9. (But gifts offered to priests) at sacrifices (are to be given) in the manner prescribed by the Veda.

10. The division of the food must be made in such a manner that those who receive daily portions (slaves) do not suffer by it.

---

9. 1. Yâ*gñ*. I, 113.

7. After a long discussion on the object of this Sûtra, Haradatta comes to the conclusion that it is given 'against the improper custom to dine out of the same vessel with one's wife and uninitiated children, which prevails in some countries.'

8. 'Consequently a gift of food also.' The custom is to pour water, usually with the spoon called Darvî (Pallî), into the extended palm of the recipient's right hand.

11. At his pleasure, he may stint himself, his wife, or his children, but by no means a slave who does his work.

12. And he must not stint himself so much that he becomes unable to perform his duties.

13. Now they quote also (the following two verses):

'Eight mouthfuls are the meal of an ascetic, sixteen that of a hermit living in the woods, thirty-two that of a householder, and an unlimited quantity that of a student. An Agnihotrin, a draught-ox, and a student, those three can do their work only if they eat; without eating (much), they cannot do it.'

PRASNA II, PATALA 5, KHANDA 10.

1. The reasons for (which) begging (is permissible are), (the desire to collect the fee for) the teacher, (the celebration of) a wedding, (or of) a *S*rauta-sacrifice, the desire to keep one's father and mother, and the (impending) interruption of ceremonies performed by a worthy man.

2. (The person asked for alms) must examine the qualities (of the petitioner) and give according to his power.

3. But if persons ask for alms for the sake of sensual gratification, that is improper; he shall not take heed of that.

4. The lawful occupations of a Brâhma*n*a are,

---

13. Manu VI, 28; Yâg*ñ*. III, 55.

10. 1. Manu IV, 251; XI, 1 seq.; Yâg*ñ*. I, 216. By the term arhat, 'a worthy person,' a Brâhma*n*a is here designated who has studied the Veda and performs an Agnihotra.

4. Manu I, 88; X, 75; Yâg*ñ*. I, 118.

studying, teaching, sacrificing for himself, officiating as priest for others, giving alms, receiving alms, inheriting, and gleaning corn in the fields;

5. And (he may live by taking) other things which belong to nobody.

6. (The lawful occupations) of a Kshatriya are the same, with the exception of teaching, officiating as priest, and receiving alms. (But) governing and fighting must be added.

7. (The lawful occupations) of a Vaisya are the same as those of a Kshatriya, with the exception of governing and fighting. (But in his case) agriculture, the tending of cattle, and trade must be added.

8. He (shall) not choose (for the performance of a Srauta-sacrifice) a priest who is unlearned in the Veda, nor one who haggles (about his fee).

9. (A priest) shall not officiate for a person unlearned in the Veda.

10. In war (Kshatriyas) shall act in such a manner as those order, who are learned in that (art of war).

11. The Âryas forbid the slaughter of those who have laid down their arms, of those who (beg for mercy) with flying hair or joined hands, and of fugitives.

12. The spiritual guide shall order those who,

---

5. I.e. wild roots and fruits.

6. Manu I, 89; X, 77, 79; Yâgñ. I, 118, 119.

7. Manu I, 90; X, 78, 79; Yâgñ. loc. cit.

11. Manu VII, 91 seq.; Yâgñ. I, 325.

12. Haradatta explains the words Sâstrair adhigatânâm, 'who whilst participating, according to the sacred law, (in the rights of their caste,)' by 'who have been sanctified according to the law by the sacraments, such as the Garbhâdhâna, and are entitled (to the rights and occupations of their caste).'

(whilst) participating according to sacred law (in the rights of their caste), have gone astray through the weakness of their senses, to perform penances proportionate to (the greatness of) their sins, according to the precepts (of the Sm*ri*ti).

13. If (such persons) transgress their (Â*k*ârya's) order, he shall take them before the king.

14. The king shall (send them) to his domestic priest, who should be learned in the law and the science of governing.

15. He shall order (them to perform the proper penances if they are) Brâhma*n*as.

16. He shall reduce them (to reason) by forcible means, excepting corporal punishment and servitude.

PRA*S*NA II, PA*T*ALA 5, KHA*ND*A 11.

1. In the cases of (men of) other castes, the king, after having examined their actions, may punish them even by death.

2. And the king shall not punish on suspicion.

3. But having carefully investigated (the case) by means of questions (addressed to witnesses) and even of ordeals, the king may proceed to punish.

4. A king who acts thus, gains both (this and the next) world.

5. The road belongs to the king except if he meets a Brâhma*n*a.

---

16. Probably this Sûtra is meant to give a general rule, and to exempt Brâhma*n*as in every case from corporal punishment and servitude. Manu VIII, 379–380.

11. 3. See also below, II, 11, 29, 6.

5. Manu II, 139; Yâ*gñ*. I, 117. According to Haradatta this Sûtra is given, though the precedence among the various castes has been already settled, in order to show that common Kshatriyas must make way for an anointed king.

6. But if he meets a Brâhma*n*a, the road belongs to the latter.

7. All must make way for a (laden) vehicle, for a person who carries a burden, for a sick man, for a woman and others (such as old men and infants).

8. And (way must be made), by the other castes, for those men who are superior by caste.

9. For their own welfare all men must make way for fools, outcasts, drunkards, and madmen.

10. In successive births men of the lower castes are born in the next higher one, if they have fulfilled their duties.

11. In successive births men of the higher castes are born in the next lower one, if they neglect their duties.

12. If he has a wife who (is willing and able) to perform (her share of) the religious duties and who bears sons, he shall not take a second.

13. If a wife is deficient in one of these two (qualities), he shall take another, (but) before he kindles the fires (of the Agnihotra).

14. For a wife who assists at the kindling of the fires, becomes connected with those religious rites of which that (fire-kindling) forms a part.

---

6. Manu II, 138; Yâ*gñ*. I, 117.

10. Manu X, 64, 65; Yâ*gñ*. I, 96.

12. Manu IX, 95; Yâ*gñ*. I, 76.

13. Manu IX, 80, 81; Yâ*gñ*. I, 73.

14. A wife who assists at the kindling of the fires for any sacrificial rite, becomes connected with that rite like any priest, and in that rite no other woman can take her place. Hence in the case of an Agnihotra, which lasts during the performer's lifetime, or at least as long as he is a householder, the performer cannot take another principal wife after he once has begun his sacrifice. If the wife of an Agnihotrin dies, he must marry again, and also kindle his fires afresh. Manu V, 167, 168; Yâ*gñ*. I, 89.

15. He shall not give his daughter to a man belonging to the same family (Gotra),

16. Nor to one related (within six degrees) on the mother's or (the father's) side.

17. At the wedding called Brâhma, he shall give away (his daughter) for bearing children and performing the rites that must be performed together (by a husband and his wife), after having enquired regarding (the bridegroom's) family, character, learning, and health, and after having given (to the bride) ornaments according to his power.

18. At the wedding called Ârsha, the bridegroom shall present to the father of the bride a bull and a cow.

19. At the wedding called Daiva, (the father) shall give her to an officiating priest, who is performing a *S*rauta-sacrifice.

---

15. The term Gotra corresponds to the Latin Gens. It may be of two kinds, Vaidika for Brâhma*n*as and Laukika, 'worldly,' for men of other castes. In the first case it denotes 'persons descended from the same *Ri*shi;' in the second, 'persons distinguished by the same family name, or known to be descended from the same ancestor.' In our days Brâhma*n*as also have Laukika Gotras, which form subdivisions of the very large Vedic Gotras. Regarding the Vaidika Gotras, see Max Müller's History of Ancient Sanskrit Literature, pp. 379–390, and particularly p. 387. Manu III, 5; Yâ*gñ*. I, 33; Weber, Ind. Stud. X, 75 seq.

16. The term yonisambandha, 'related (within six degrees),' corresponds to the more common Sapi*nd*a of Manu, Yâ*gñ*avalkya, and others; see the definitions given below, II, 6, 15, 2. In Âpastamba's terminology Sapi*nd*a has probably a more restricted sense. It seems very doubtful whether Haradatta's explanation of *k*a, translated by 'or,' is correct, and whether his interpolation of 'the father's' ought to be admitted. Probably Sûtra 15 refers to the father's side, and Sûtra 16 to the mother's side.

17. Manu III, 27; Yâ*gñ*. I, 58.

18. Manu III, 29; Yâ*gñ*. I, 59.

19. Manu III, 28; Yâ*gñ*. I, 59.

20. If a maiden and a lover unite themselves through love, that is called the Gândharva-rite.

PRASNA II, PATALA 5, KHANDA 12.

1. If the suitor pays money (for his bride) according to his ability, and marries her (afterwards), that (marriage is called) the Âsura-rite.

2. If the (bridegroom and his friends) take away (the bride), after having overcome (by force) her father (or relations), that is called the Râkshasa-rite.

3. The first three amongst these (marriage-rites are considered) praiseworthy; each preceding one better than the one following.

4. The quality of the offspring is according to the quality of the marriage-rite.

5. He shall not step on a spot which has been touched by the hand of a Brâhmana, without having sprinkled it with water.

6. He shall not pass between a fire and a Brâhmana,

7. Nor between Brâhmanas.

8. Or he may pass between them after having received permission to do so.

9. He shall not carry fire and water at the same time.

---

20. Manu III, 32; Yâgñ. I, 61.

12. 1. Manu III, 31; Yâgñ. I, 61. It must be understood that, at this rite, a regular sale of the bride must take place. If a suitor merely gives presents to the bride, that is not an Âsura-marriage.

2. Manu III, 33; Yâgñ. I, 61. Haradatta points out that the other law-books enumerate two additional marriage-rites, the Prâgâpatya or Kâya and the Paisâka. But Vasishtha I, 29-35, like Âpastamba, gives six rites only.

3. Manu III, 24, 25; Yâgñ. I, 58-60.

4. I. e. from praiseworthy marriages virtuous children are born, and from blamable marriages bad ones. Manu III, 42.

10. He shall not carry fires (burning in) separate (places) to one (spot).

11. If, whilst he walks, fire is being carried towards him, he shall not walk around it with his right hand turned towards it, except after it has been placed on the ground.

12. He shall not join his hands on his back.

13. If the sun sets whilst he sleeps, he shall sit up, fasting and silent, for that night. On the following morning he shall bathe and then raise his voice (in prayer).

14. If the sun rises whilst he is asleep, he shall stand during that day fasting and silent.

15. Some declare that he shall restrain his breath until he is tired.

16. And (he shall restrain his breath until he is tired) if he has had a bad dream,

17. Or if he desires to accomplish some object,

18. Or if he has transgressed some other rule.

19. (If he is) doubtful (whether) the result (of an action will be good or evil), he shall not do it.

20. (He shall follow) the same principle (if he is in doubt whether he ought) to study or not.

21. He shall not talk of a doubtful matter as if it were clear.

22. In the case of a person who slept at sunset, of

---

10. Another commentator says, 'He shall not throw (brands taken from) one fire into another fire.'—Haradatta.

11. The Sûtra implies that under other circumstances he must show this respect to a fire.

13. Manu II, 220.

18. Manu XI, 200.

21. See above, I, 11, 32, 22.

22. These sinners are enumerated in nearly the same order,

one who slept at sunrise, of one who has black nails, or black teeth, of one who married a younger sister before the elder one was married, of one who married an elder sister whose younger sister had been married already, (of a younger brother who has kindled the sacred Grihya-fire before his elder brother,) of one whose younger brother has kindled the sacred fire first, (of a younger brother who offers a Soma-sacrifice before his elder brother,) of an elder brother whose younger brother offered a Soma-sacrifice first, of an elder brother who marries or receives his portion of the inheritance after his younger brother, and of a younger brother who takes a wife or receives his portion of the inheritance before his elder brother,—penances ordained for crimes causing impurity, a heavier one for each succeeding case, must be performed.

23. Some declare, that after having performed that penance, he shall remove its cause.

Prasna II, Patala 6, Khanda 13.

1. Sons begotten by a man who approaches in the proper season a woman of equal caste, who has

---

Taittirîya-brâhmana III, 2, 8, 11 and 12, and Âp. Srauta-sûtra IX, 12, 11. See also Manu XI, 44-49. Regarding the crimes causing impurity, see above, I, 7, 21, 12-19.

23. 'Its cause, i.e. the black nails, &c. According to another Smriti, one shall not put away a wife or extinguish a fire, for the taking or kindling of which the penance had to be performed.'—Haradatta. But see Vasishtha XX, 7 seq.

13. 1. 'Sâstravihitâ (translated by "who has been married to him legally") means either "married according to the rites prescribed in the Sâstras," or "possessed of the qualities (which have been described) by (the rule of) the Sâstras, He shall not give his daughter to a man of the same Gotra," and in similar (passages).'—Haradatta. See also Colebrooke, Digest, Book V, Text cxcix.

not belonged to another man, and who has been married legally, have a right to (follow) the occupations (of their castes),

2. And to (inherit the) estate,

3. If they do not sin against either (of their parents).

4. If a man approaches a woman who had been married before, or was not legally married to him, or belongs to a different caste, they both commit a sin.

5. Through their (sin) their son also becomes sinful.

6. A Brâhma*n*a (says), 'The son belongs to the begetter.'

7. Now they quote also (the following Gâthâ from the Veda): '(Having considered myself) formerly a father, I shall not now allow (any longer) my wives (to be approached by other men), since they have declared that a son belongs to the begetter in the world of Yama. The giver of the seed carries off the son after death in Yama's world; therefore they guard

---

3. Another (commentator) says, 'Neither of the parents shall pass them over at (the distribution of) the heritage. Both (parents) must leave their property to them.'—Haradatta. The text of the Sûtra admits of either explanation.

6. See also Manu IX, 32 seq., where the same difference of opinion occurs.

7. According to Haradatta this Gâthâ gives the sentiments of a husband who neglected to watch his wives, and who had heard from those learned in the law that the sons of his unfaithful wives would in the next world belong to their natural fathers, and that he would not derive any spiritual benefit from their oblations. He adds that this verse does not refer to or prevent the appointment of a eunuch's wife or of a childless widow to a relation. He also quotes a passage from the *S*rauta-sûtra I, 9, 7, in which the dvipitâ, 'the son of two fathers,' is mentioned. But Haradatta's view cannot be reconciled with the statements made below, II, 10, 27,

their wives, fearing the seed of strangers. Carefully watch over (the procreation of) your children, lest stranger seed be sown on your soil. In the next world the son belongs to the begetter, an (imprudent) husband makes the (begetting of) children vain (for himself).'

8. Transgression of the law and violence are found amongst the ancient (sages).

9. They committed no sin on account of the greatness of their lustre.

10. A man of later times who seeing their (deeds) follows them, falls.

11. The gift (or acceptance of a child) and the right to sell (or buy) a child are not recognised.

12. It is declared in the Veda that at the time of marriage a gift, for (the fulfilment of) his wishes, should be made (by the bridegroom) to the father

---

2–7, where the Niyoga is plainly forbidden. Baudhâyana, who (II, 2, 3, 34) quotes the same Gâthâ, reads in the first line the vocative '*g*anaka' instead of the nominative '*g*anaka*h*,' and in the fifth line 'pare bî*g*âni' instead of 'parabî*g*âni.' The commentator Govindasvâmin adds that the verses are addressed by the *Ri*shi Aupa*g*aṅghani to king *G*anaka of Videha. The translation of the first line must therefore run thus: 'O *G*anaka, now I am jealous of my wives, (though I was) not so formerly,' &c. Baudhâyana's readings are probably the older ones, and Govindasvâmin's explanation the right one. See also Colebrooke, Digest, Book V, Text ccli.

11. Haradatta thinks that, as most other Sm*ri*tis enumerate the adopted son, and 'the son bought' in their lists of substitutes for lawful sons of the body, Âpastamba's rule can refer only to the gift or sale of an eldest son, or to the gift or sale of a child effected by a woman. Though it is possible that he may be right in his interpretation, it remains a remarkable fact that Âpastamba does not mention the 'twelve kinds of sons,' which are known to other Sm*ri*tis.

12. This Sûtra seems to be directed against Vasish*th*a I, 36.

of the bride, in order to fulfil the law. 'Therefore he should give a hundred (cows) besides a chariot; that (gift) he should make bootless (by returning it to the giver).' In reference to those (marriage-rites), the word 'sale' (which occurs in some Smritis is only used as) a metaphorical expression; for the union (of the husband and wife) is effected through the law.

13. After having gladdened the eldest son by some (choice portion of his) wealth,

PRASNA II, PATALA 6, KHANDA 14.

1. He should, during his lifetime, divide his wealth equally amongst his sons, excepting the eunuch, the mad man, and the outcast.

2. On failure of sons the nearest Sapinda (takes the inheritance).

---

14. 1. The last Sûtra of Khanda 13 and the first of Khanda 14 are quoted by Colebrooke, Digest, Book V, Text xlii, and Mitâksharâ, Chap. I, Sect. iii, Par. 6. Colebrooke translates gîvan, 'during his lifetime,' by 'who makes a partition during his lifetime.' I think that this is not quite correct, and that Âpastamba intends to exhort householders to make a division during their lifetime, as later they ought to become ascetics or hermits. Haradatta introduces into his commentary on this Sûtra the whole chapter on the division of a father's estate amongst his sons, supplementing Âpastamba's short rule by the texts of other lawyers. No doubt, Âpastamba means to lay down, in these and the following Sûtras, only the leading principles of the law of inheritance, and he intends that the remaining particulars should be supplied from the law of custom or other Smritis.

2. Haradatta gives in his commentary a full summary of the rules on the succession of remoter relations. One point only deserves special mention. He declares that it is the opinion of Âpastamba, that widows cannot inherit. In this he is probably right, as Âpastamba does not mention them, and the use of the

3. On failure of them the spiritual teacher (inherits); on failure of the spiritual teacher a pupil shall take (the deceased's wealth), and use it for religious works for the (deceased's) benefit, or (he himself may enjoy it);

4. Or the daughter (may take the inheritance).

5. On failure of all (relations) let the king take the inheritance.

6. Some declare, that the eldest son alone inherits.

7. In some countries gold, (or) black cattle, (or) black produce of the earth is the share of the eldest.

8. The chariot and the furniture in the house are the father's (share).

---

masculine singular '*sapindah*' in the text precludes the possibility of including them under that collective term. It seems to me certain, that Âpastamba, like Baudhâyana, considered women, especially widows, unfit to inherit.

4. 'Some say "on failure of sons," others that the rule refers to the preceding Sûtra (i.e. that the daughter inherits on failure of pupils only).'—Haradatta. The latter seems to be the correct interpretation.

5. 'Because the word "all" is used, (the king shall take the estate) only on failure of Bandhus and Sagotras, i.e. gentiles within twelve degrees.'—Haradatta.

6. 'The other sons shall live under his protection.'—Haradatta. Colebrooke, Mitâksharâ, Chap. I, Sect. iii, Par. 6.

7. '"Black produce of the earth," i.e. black grain, or according to others black iron.'—Haradatta. Compare for this and the following Sûtras Colebrooke, Mitâksharâ, Chap. I, Sect. iii, Par. 6, and Digest, Book V, Text xlviii.

8. The translation given above agrees with what I now recognise to be Haradatta's explanation, and with Colebrooke, Mitâksharâ, Chap. I, Sect. iii, Par. 6. Both the P. U. and Mr. U. MSS. of the U*gg*valâ read ratha*h* pitura*ms*o g*ri*he yatparibhâ*nd*am upakara*n*am pî*th*âdi tadapi, 'the chariot (is) the father's share; the furniture which (is) in the house, that also.' To this reading Mahâdeva's U*gg*valâ on the Hira*n*yake*s*i Sûtra points likewise, which gives pitur anta*h*. The N. U. MS. of the U*gg*valâ, according to which

9. According to some, the share of the wife consists of her ornaments, and the wealth (which she may have received) from her relations.

10. That (preference of the eldest son) is forbidden by the *S*âstras.

11. For it is declared in the Veda, without (marking) a difference (in the treatment of the sons): Manu divided his wealth amongst his sons.

12. Now the Veda declares also in conformity with (the rule in favour of the eldest son) alone: They distinguish the eldest by (a larger share of) the heritage.

I made the translation given in the Appendix to West and Bühler's Digest (1st edition), leaves out the word a*m*sa*h*, and therefore makes it necessary to combine this Sûtra with the preceding one, and to translate, 'The father's chariot and the furniture in the house (are) also (the share of the eldest).' This latter translation agrees nearly with that given by Colebrooke, Digest, Book V, Text xlviii, where this and the preceding Sûtra have been joined; but the chariot is not mentioned. A further variation in the interpretation of this Sûtra occurs in Colebrooke's Digest, Book V, Text lxxxix, and Mitâksharâ, loc. cit., where the words 'the furniture in the house' are joined with Sûtra 9, and the furniture is declared to be the wife's share. Considering that Sûtra 9 is again quoted in Colebrooke's Digest, Book V, Text cccclxxii, and is not joined with the latter part of Sûtra 8, it is not too much to say that *G*agannâtha has not shown any greater accuracy than his brethren usually do.

9. The Mitâksharâ, loc. cit., apparently takes the words 'according to some' as referring only to property received from relations. I follow Haradatta. The former interpretation is, however, admissible, if the Sûtra is split into two.

10. The *S*âstras are, according to Haradatta, the Vedas.

11. Taittirîyâ Sa*m*hitâ III, 1, 9, 4.

12. 'Athâpi (now also) means "and certainly." They distinguish, they set apart the eldest son by wealth: this has been declared in the Veda in conformity with (the rule regarding) one (heir, Sûtra 6). He denies (Sûtra 13) that a passage also, which

13. (But to this plea in favour of the eldest I answer): Now those who are acquainted with the interpretation of the law declare a statement of facts not to be a rule, as for instance (the following): 'Therefore amongst cattle, goats and sheep walk together;' (or the following), 'Therefore the face of a learned Brâhma*n*a (a Snâtaka) is, as it were, resplendent;' (or), 'A Brâhma*n*a who has studied the Vedas (a *S*rotriya) and a he-goat evince the strongest sexual desires.'

14. Therefore all (sons) who are virtuous inherit.

15. But him who expends money unrighteously, he shall disinherit, though he be the eldest son.

16. No division takes place between husband and wife.

---

agrees with the statement that the eldest son alone inherits, is found in the Veda.'—Haradatta. See Taittirîyâ Sa*m*hitâ II, 5, 2, 7.

13. Those who are acquainted with the interpretation of the law are the Mîmâ*m*sakas. The translation of the second Vedic passage is by no means certain, as the root ribh, translated by 'to be resplendent,' usually means 'to give a sound.' Haradatta thinks that Âpastamba means to show that the passage 'Manu divided his wealth among his sons' is likewise merely a statement of facts, and cannot be considered a rule. This is probably erroneous, as Sûtras 10 and 11 distinctly state, that the practice to allow the eldest alone to inherit, is forbidden by the above-mentioned passage of the Veda.

15. Compare for this Sûtra and the following one Colebrooke's Digest, Book V, Text cccxv. The translation of pratipâdayati, 'expends,' by 'gains,' which is also proposed by *G*agannâtha, is against Âpastamba's usage, see II, 5, 11, 17, and below, II, 8, 20, 19.

16. According to Haradatta, this Sûtra gives the reason why, in Sûtra 1, no share has been set apart for the wife. Compare Colebrooke's Digest, Book V, Text lxxxix, for this Sûtra and the following two.

17. For, from the time of marriage, they are united in religious ceremonies,

18. Likewise also as regards the rewards for works by which spiritual merit is acquired,

19. And with respect to the acquisition of property.

20. For they declare that it is not a theft if a wife expends money on occasions (of necessity) during her husband's absence.

Prasna II, Patala 6, Khanda 15.

1. By this (discussion) the law of custom, which is observed in (particular) countries or families, has been disposed of.

2. On account of the blood relations of his mother and (on account of those) of his father within six degrees, or, as far as the relationship is traceable, he shall bathe if they die, excepting children that have not completed their first year.

3. On account of the death of the latter the parents alone bathe,

4. And those who bury them.

5. If a wife or one of the chief Gurus (a father or Âkârya) die, besides, fasting (is ordained from the time at which they die) up to the same time (on the following day).

---

20. See below, II, 11, 29, 3.

15. 1. Customs are to be followed only if they are not opposed to the teaching of the Vedas and Smritis.

2. Manu V, 60; Yâgñ. I, 53; Manu V, 60; Manu V, 58; Yâgñ. III, 3.

4. Manu V, 69 and 70.

5. Manu V, 80.

6. (In that case) they shall also show the (following) signs of mourning :

7. Dishevelling their hair and covering themselves with dust (they go outside the village), and, clothed with one garment, their faces turned to the south, stepping into the river they throw up water for the dead once, and then, ascending (the bank), they sit down.

8. This (they repeat) thrice.

9. They pour out water consecrated in such a manner that the dead will know it (to be given to them). Then they return to the village without looking back, and perform those rites for the dead which (pious) women declare to be necessary.

10. Some declare, that these same (observances) shall also be kept in the case (of the death) of other (Sapi*nd*as).

11. At all religious ceremonies, he shall feed Brâhma*n*as who are pure and who have (studied and remember) the Veda.

12. He shall distribute his gifts at the proper places, at the proper times, at the occasion of purificatory rites, and to proper recipients.

13. That food must not be eaten of which (no portion) is offered in the fire, and of which no portion is first given (to guests).

7–9. Yâ*gñ*. III, 5, 7 seq. The Mantra to be spoken in throwing the water is, 'I give this water to you N. N. of the family of N. N.' The water ought to be mixed with sesamum. According to Haradatta those who know the correct interpretation, declare that the word 'women' denotes in this Sûtra 'the Sm*ri*tis.' But I fear these learned interpreters will find few adherents among those who pay attention to the last Sûtra of this work.

11. Manu III, 128. 12. Manu III, 98.

14. No food mixed with pungent condiments or salt can be offered as a burnt-offering.

15. Nor (can food) mixed with bad food (be used for a burnt-oblation).

16. If (he is obliged to offer) a burnt-offering of food unfit for that purpose, he shall take hot ashes from the northern part of his fire and offer the food in that. That oblation is no oblation in the fire.

17. A female shall not offer any burnt-oblation,

18. Nor a child, that has not been initiated.

19. Infants do not become impure before they receive the sacrament called Annaprâ*s*ana (the first feeding).

20. Some (declare, that they cannot become impure) until they have completed their first year,

21. Or, as long as they cannot distinguish the points of the horizon.

22. The best (opinion is, that they cannot be defiled) until the initiation has been performed.

23. For at that (time a child) according to the rules of the Veda obtains the right (to perform the various religious ceremonies).

---

14. 'That (substance) is called kshâra, "of pungent or alkaline taste," the eating of which makes the saliva flow.'—Haradatta.

15. Avarânna, 'bad food,' is explained by 'kulittha and the like.' Kulittha, a kind of vetch, is considered low food, and eaten by the lower castes only. The meaning of the Sûtra, therefore, is, 'If anybody has been forced by poverty to mix his rice or *D*âl with kulittha or similar bad food, he cannot offer a burnt-oblation at the Vai*s*vadeva ceremony with that. He must observe the rule, given in the following Sûtra.

17. Manu V, 155; XI, 36.

18. Manu II, 171.

24. That ceremony is the limit (from which the capacity to fulfil the law begins).

25. And the Sm*ri*ti (agrees with this opinion).

PRA*S*NA II, PA*T*ALA 7, KHA*ND*A 16.

1. Formerly men and gods lived together in this world. Then the gods in reward of their sacrifices went to heaven, but men were left behind. Those men who perform sacrifices in the same manner as the gods did, dwell (after death) with the gods and Brahman in heaven. Now (seeing men left behind), Manu revealed this ceremony, which is designated by the word *S*râddha (a funeral-oblation).

2. And (thus this rite has been revealed) for the salvation of mankind.

3. At that (rite) the Manes (of one's father, grandfather, and great-grandfather) are the deities (to whom the sacrifice is offered). But the Brâhma*n*as, (who are fed,) represent the Âhavanîya-fire.

4. That rite must be performed in each month.

---

25. Haradatta quotes Gautama II, 1–3, on this point, and is apparently of opinion that Âpastamba alludes to the same passage. But he is probably wrong, as all Sm*ri*tis are agreed on the point mentioned by Âpastamba.

16. 1. 'Intending to give the rules regarding the monthly *S*râddha, he premises this explanatory statement in order to praise that sacrifice.'—Haradatta.

2. The reading 'ni*h*s*reyasâ *k*a' apparently has given great trouble to the commentators. Their explanations are, however, grammatically impossible. The right one is to take ni*hs*reyasâ as a Vedic instrumental, for ni*hs*reyasena, which may designate the 'reason.' If the dative is read, the sense remains the same.

3. 'The comparison of the Brâhma*n*as with the Âhavanîya indicates that to feed Brâhma*n*as is the chief act at a *S*râddha.'—Haradatta.

4. Manu III, 122, 123; Yâ*gñ*. I, 217.

5. The afternoon of (a day of) the latter half is preferable (for it).

6. The last days of the latter half (of the month) likewise are (preferable to the first days).

7. (A funeral-oblation) offered on any day of the latter half of the month gladdens the Manes. But it procures different rewards for the sacrificer according to the time observed.

8. If it be performed on the first day of the half-month, the issue (of the sacrificer) will chiefly consist of females.

9. (Performed on the second day it procures) children who are free from thievish propensities.

10. (If it is performed) on the third day children will be born to him who will fulfil the various vows for studying (portions of the Veda).

11. (The sacrificer who performs it) on the fourth day becomes rich in small domestic animals.

12. (If he performs it) on the fifth day, sons (will be born to him). He will have numerous and distinguished offspring, and he will not die childless.

13. (If he performs it) on the sixth day, he will become a great traveller and gambler.

14. (The reward of a funeral-oblation performed) on the seventh day is success in agriculture.

15. (If he performs it) on the eighth day (its reward is) prosperity

16. (If he performs it) on the ninth day (its reward consists in) one-hoofed animals.

---

5. Manu III, 255, 278.

7. Manu III, 277; Yâgñ. I, 264, 265.

12. The translation follows the corrected reading given in the Addenda to the Critical Notes.

17. (If he performs it) on the tenth day (its reward is) success in trade.

18. (If he performs it) on the eleventh day (its reward is) black iron, tin, and lead.

19. (If he performs a funeral-oblation) on the twelfth day, he will become rich in cattle.

20. (If he performs it) on the thirteenth day, he will have many sons (and) many friends, (and) his offspring will be beautiful. But his (sons) will die young.

21. (If he performs it) on the fourteenth day (its reward is) success in battle.

22. (If he performs it) on the fifteenth day (its reward is) prosperity.

23. The substances (to be offered) at these (sacrifices) are sesamum, mâsha, rice, yava, water, roots, and fruits.

24. But, if food mixed with fat (is offered), the satisfaction of the Manes is greater, and (lasts) a longer time,

25. Likewise, if money, lawfully acquired, is given to worthy (persons).

26. Beef satisfies (the Manes) for a year,

---

20. Others read the last part of the Sûtra, ayuvamârinas-tu bhavanti, 'they will not die young.'—Haradatta. If the two halves of the Sûtra are joined and Dar*s*anîyâpatyoyuvamâri*n*a*h* is read, the Sandhi may be dissolved in either manner.

21. Manu III, 276, and Yâ*gñ*. I, 263, declare the fourteenth day to be unfit for a *S*râddha, and the latter adds that *S*râddhas for men killed in battle may be offered on that day. This latter statement explains why Âpastamba declares its reward to be 'success in battle.' The nature of the reward shows that on that day Kshatriyas, not Brâhma*n*as, should offer their *S*râddhas.

23. Manu III, 267; Yâ*gñ*. I, 257.

26. Manu III, 271.

27. Buffalo's (meat) for a longer (time) than that.

28. By this (permission of the use of buffalo's meat) it has been declared that the meat of (other) tame and wild animals is fit to be offered.

PRASNA II, PATALA 7, KHANDA 17.

1. (If) rhinoceros' meat (is given to Brâhma*n*as seated) on (seats covered with) the skin of a rhinoceros, (the Manes are satisfied) for a very long time.

2. (The same effect is obtained) by (offering the) flesh (of the fish called) *S*atabali,

3. And by (offering the) meat of the (crane called) Vârdhrâ*n*asa.

4. Pure, with composed mind and full of ardour, he shall feed Brâhma*n*as who know the Vedas, and who are not connected with him by marriage, blood relationship, by the relationship of sacrificial priest and sacrificer, or by the relationship of (teacher and) pupil.

5. If strangers are deficient in the (requisite) good qualities, even a full brother who possesses them, may be fed (at a *S*râddha).

6. (The admissibility of) pupils (and the rest) has been declared hereby.

7. Now they quote also (in regard to this matter the following verse):

8. The food eaten (at a sacrifice) by persons related to the giver is, indeed, a gift offered to the goblins. It reaches neither the Manes nor the

---

17. 1. Manu III, 272; Yâg*ñ*. I, 259.

2. Manu V, 16, where Rohita is explained by *S*atabali.

4. Manu III, 128-138, and 149, 188; Yâg*ñ*. I, 225.

8. See Manu III, 141, where this Trish*t*ubh has been turned into an Anush*t*ubh.

gods. Losing its power (to procure heaven), it errs about in this world as a cow that has lost its calf runs into a strange stable.

9. The meaning (of the verse) is, that gifts which are eaten (and offered) mutually by relations, (and thus go) from one house to the other, perish in this world.

10. If the good qualities (of several persons who might be invited) are equal, old men and (amongst these) poor ones, who wish to come, have the preference.

11. On the day before (the ceremony) the (first) invitation (must be issued).

12. On the following day the second invitation takes place.

13. (On the same day also takes place) the third invitation (which consists in the call to dinner).

14. Some declare, that every act at a funeral-sacrifice must be repeated three times.

15. As (the acts are performed) the first time, so they must be repeated) the second and the third times.

16. When all (the three oblations) have been

---

11. Manu III, 187; Yâ*g*ñ. I, 225. According to Haradatta the formula of invitation is, *S*va*h* *s*râddham bhavitâ, tatrâhavanîyârthe bhavadbhi*h* prasâda*h* kartavya iti, 'to-morrow a *S*râddha will take place. Do me the favour to take at that the place of the Âhavanîya-fire.'

12. The formula is, Adya *s*râddham, 'to-day the *S*râddha takes place.'

13. The call to dinner is, Siddham âgamyatâm, 'the food is ready; come.'

16. Âpastamba G*ri*hya-sûtra VIII, 21, 9. 'He shall eat it pronouncing the Mantra, "Prâ*n*e nivish*t*osm*ri*ta*m* *g*uhomi."' Taitt. Âr. X, 34, 1.

offered, he shall take a portion of the food of all (three), and shall eat a small mouthful of the remainder in the manner described (in the G*ri*hya-sûtra).

17. But the custom of the Northerners is to pour into the hands of the Brâhma*n*as, when they are seated on their seats, (water which has been taken from the water-vessel.)

18. (At the time of the burnt-offering which is offered at the beginning of the dinner) he addresses the Brâhma*n*as with this Mantra: 'Let it be taken out, and let it be offered in the fire.'

19. (They shall give their permission with this Mantra): 'Let it be taken out at thy pleasure, let it be offered in the fire at thy pleasure.' Having received this permission, he shall take out (some of the prepared food) and offer it.

20. They blame it, if dogs and Apapâtras are allowed to see the performance of a funeral-sacrifice.

21. The following persons defile the company if they are invited to a funeral-sacrifice, viz. a leper, a bald man, the violator of another man's bed, the son of a Brâhma*n*a who follows the profession of a Kshatriya, and the son of (a Brâhma*n*a who by marrying first a *S*ûdra wife had himself become) a *S*ûdra, born from a Brâhma*n*a woman.

---

17. The North of India begins to the north of the river *S*arâvatî. The rule alluded to is given by Yâg*ñ*. I, 226, 229; Manu III, 210.

18. Yâg*ñ*. I, 235. 20. Manu III, 239.

21. Manu III, 152–166, and particularly 153 and 154; Yâg*ñ*. I, 222–224. Haradatta's explanation of the word '*S*ûdra' by 'a Brâhma*n*a who has become a *S*ûdra' is probably right, because the son of a real *S*ûdra and of a Brâhma*n*a female is a *K*a*nd*âla, and has been disposed of by the preceding Sûtra.

22. The following persons sanctify the company if they eat at a funeral-sacrifice, viz. one who has studied the three verses of the Veda containing the word 'Madhu,' each three times; one who has studied the part of the Veda containing the word 'Supar*n*a' three times; a Tri*n*â*k*iketa; one who has studied the Mantras required for the four sacrifices (called A*s*vamedha, Purushamedha, Sarvamedha, and Pit*ri*-medha); one who keeps five fires; one who knows the Sâman called *G*yesh*th*a; one who fulfils the duty of daily study; the son of one who has studied and is able to teach the whole Veda with its Aṅgas, and a *S*rotriya.

23. He shall not perform (any part of) a funeral-sacrifice at night.

24. After having begun (a funeral-sacrifice), he shall not eat until he has finished it.

25. (He shall not perform a funeral-sacrifice at

22. Compare Manu III, 185, 186; Yâ*gñ*. I, 219–221. The three verses to be known by a Trimadhu are, Madhu vâtâ *ri*tâyate, &c., which occur both in the Taitt. Sa*m*h. and in the Taitt. Âr. The explanation of Trisupar*n*a is not certain. Haradatta thinks that it may mean either a person who knows the three verses *K*atushkapardâ yuvati*h* supe*s*â, &c., Taittirîya-brâhma*n*a I, 2, 1, 27, &c., or one who knows the three Anuvâkas from the Taittirîya Âra*n*yaka X, 48–50, beginning, Brahmametu mâm, &c. The word 'Tri*n*â*k*iketa' has three explanations:—*a*. A person who knows the Nâ*k*iketa-fire according to the Taittirîyaka, Ka*th*avallî, and the *S*atapatha, i.e. has studied the portions on the Nâ*k*iketa-fire in these three books. *b*. A person who has thrice kindled the Nâ*k*iketa-fire. *c*. A person who has studied the Anuvâka, called Vira*g*as. *K*aturmedha may also mean 'one who has performed the four sacrifices' enumerated above.

23. Manu III, 280.

24. 'The *S*râddha is stated to begin with the first invitation to the Brahmans.'—Haradatta.

25. 'The Northerners do not generally receive this Sûtra, and

night), except if an eclipse of the moon takes place.

PRASNA II, PATALA 8, KHANDA 18.

1. He shall avoid butter, butter-milk, oil-cake, honey, meat.

2. And black grain (such as kulittha), food given by Sûdras, or by other persons, whose food is not considered fit to be eaten.

3. And food unfit for oblations, speaking an untruth, anger, and (acts or words) by which he might excite anger. He who desires a (good) memory, fame, wisdom, heavenly bliss, and prosperity, shall avoid these twelve (things and acts);

4. Wearing a dress that reaches from the navel to the knees, bathing morning, noon, and evening, living on food that has not been cooked at a fire, never seeking the shade, standing (during the day), and sitting (during the night), he shall keep this vow for one year. They declare, that (its merit) is equal to that of a studentship continued for forty-eight years.

5. (Now follows) the daily funeral-oblation.

6. Outside the village pure (men shall) prepare (the food for that rite) in a pure place.

---

therefore former commentators have not explained it.'—Haradatta.

18. 1. Sûtras 1–4 contain rules for a vow to be kept for the special objects mentioned in Sûtras 3 and 4 for one year only. Haradatta (on Sûtra 4) says that another commentator thinks that Sûtras 1–3 prescribe one vow, and Sûtra 4 another, and that the latter applies both to householders and students. A passage from Baudhâyana is quoted in support of this latter view.

5. Manu III, 82 seq.

6. The term 'pure (men)' is used in order to indicate that they must be so particularly, because, by II, 2, 3, 1, purity has already been prescribed for cooks.

7. New vessels are used for that,

8. In which the food is prepared, and out of which it is eaten.

9. And those (vessels) he shall present to the (Brâhma*n*as) who have been fed.

10. And he shall feed (Brâhma*n*as) possessed of all (good qualities).

11. And he shall not give the residue (of that funeral-dinner) to one who is inferior to them in good qualities.

12. Thus (he shall act every day) during a year.

13. The last of these (funeral-oblations) he shall perform, offering a red goat.

14. And let him cause an altar to be built, concealed (by a covering and outside the village).

15. Let him feed the Brâhma*n*as on the northern half of that.

16. They declare, that (then) he sees both the Brâhma*n*as who eat and the Manes sitting on the altar.

17. After that he may offer (a funeral-sacrifice once a month) or stop altogether.

18. For (by appearing on the altar) the Manes signify that they are satisfied by the funeral-offering.

19. Under the constellation Tishya he who desires prosperity,

---

7. For the unusual meaning of dravya, 'vessel,' compare the term sîtâdravyâ*n*i, 'implements of husbandry,' Manu IX, 293, and the Petersburg Dict. s. v.

13. The red goat is mentioned as particularly fit for a *S*râddha, Yâ*gñ*. I, 259, and Manu III, 272.

PRASNA II, PATALA 8, KHANDA 19.

1. Shall cause to be prepared powder of white mustard-seeds, cause his hands, feet, ears, and mouth to be rubbed with that, and shall eat (the remainder). If the wind does not blow too violently, he shall eat sitting, silent and his face turned towards the south, on a seat (facing the) same (direction)—the first alternative is the skin of a he-goat.

2. But they declare, that the life of the mother of that person who eats at this ceremony, his face turned in that direction, will be shortened.

3. A vessel of brass, the centre of which is gilt, is best (for this occasion).

4. And nobody else shall eat out of that vessel.

5. He shall make a lump of as much (food) as he can swallow (at once).

6. (And he shall) not scatter anything (on the ground).

7. He shall not let go the vessel (with his left hand);

8. Or he may let it go.

---

19. 1. The ceremony which is here described, may also be performed daily. If the reading prâsya is adopted, the translation must run thus: 'and he shall scatter (the remainder of the powder). If the wind,' &c.

2. 'Therefore those whose mothers are alive should not perform this ceremony.'—Haradatta.

4. If the masculine bhoktavya*h* is used instead of bhoktavyam, the participle must be construed with *k*amasa*h*.

5. The verbum finitum, which according to the Sanskrit text ought to be taken with the participle sa*m*nayan, is grasîta, Sûtra 9.

8. 'Why is this second alternative mentioned, as (the first Sûtra) suffices? True. But according to the maxim that "restrictions are made on account of the continuance of an action once begun," the meaning of this second Sûtra is that he shall

9. He shall swallow the whole mouthful at once, introducing it, together with the thumb, (into the mouth.)

10. He shall make no noise with his mouth (whilst eating).

11. And he shall not shake his right hand (whilst eating).

12. After he (has eaten and) sipped water, he shall raise his hands, until the water has run off (and they have become dry).

13. After that he shall touch fire.

14. And (during this ceremony) he shall not eat in the day-time anything but roots and fruit.

15. And let him avoid Sthâlîpâka-offerings, and food offered to the Manes or to the Gods.

16. He shall eat wearing his upper garment over his left shoulder and under his right arm.

17. At the (monthly) *S*râddha which must necessarily be performed, he must use (food) mixed with fat.

18. The first (and preferable) alternative (is to employ) clarified butter and meat.

19. On failure (of these), oil of sesamum, vegetables, and (similar materials may be used).

20. And under the asterism Maghâ he shall feed the Brâhma*n*as more (than at other times) with (food mixed with) clarified butter, according to the rule of the *S*râddha.

---

continue to the end to handle the vessel (in that manner in which) he has handled it when eating for the first time.'—Haradatta.

16. Haradatta remarks that some allow, according to II, 2, 4, 22, the sacred thread to be substituted, and others think that both the thread and the garment should be worn over the left shoulder and under the right arm.

PRASNA II, PATALA 8, KHANDA 20.

1. At every monthly *S*râddha he shall use, in whatever manner he may be able, one dro*n*a of sesamum.

2. And he shall feed Brâhma*n*as endowed with all (good qualities), and they shall not give the fragments (of the food) to a person who does not possess the same good qualities (as the Brâhma*n*as).

3. He who desires prosperity shall fast in the half of the year when the sun goes to the north, under the constellation Tishya, in the first half of the month, for (a day and) a night at least, prepare a Sthâlîpâka-offering, offer burnt-oblations to Kubera (the god of riches), feed a Brâhma*n*a with that (food prepared for the Sthâlîpâka) mixed with clarified butter, and make him wish prosperity with (a Mantra) implying prosperity.

4. This (rite he shall repeat) daily until the next Tishya(-day).

5. On the second (Tishya-day and during the second month he shall feed) two (Brâhma*n*as).

6. On the third (Tishya-day and during the third month he shall feed) three (Brâhma*n*as).

7. In this manner (the Tishya-rite is to be performed) for a year, with a (monthly) increase (of the number of Brâhma*n*as fed).

---

20. 1. A dro*n*a equals 128 seers or *s*eras. The latter is variously reckoned at 1–3 lbs.

3. The reason why the constellation Tishya has been chosen for this rite seems to be that Tishya has another name, Pushya, i.e. 'prosperous.' This sacrifice is to begin on the Tishya-day of the month called Taisha or Pausha (December–January), and to continue for one year.

8. (Thus) he obtains great prosperity.

9. But the fasting takes place on the first (Tishya-day) only.

10. He shall avoid to eat those things which have lost their strength (as butter-milk, curds, and whey).

11. He shall avoid to tread on ashes or husks of grain.

12. To wash one foot with the other, or to place one foot on the other,

13. And to swing his feet,

14. And to place one leg crosswise over the knee (of the other),

15. And to make his nails

16. Or to make (his finger-joints) crack without a (good) reason,

17. And all other (acts) which they blame.

18. And let him acquire money in all ways that are lawful.

19. And let him spend money on worthy (persons or objects).

20. And let him not give anything to an unworthy (person), of whom he does not stand in fear.

21. And let him conciliate men (by gifts or kindness).

22. And he may enjoy the pleasures which are not forbidden by the holy law.

23. (Acting) thus he conquers both worlds.

---

11. Manu IV, 78.

16. 'Good reasons for cracking the joints are fatigue or rheumatism.'—Haradatta.

19. Manu XI, 6, and passim.

PRASNA II, PATALA 9, KHANDA 21.

1. There are four orders, viz. the order of householders, the order of students, the order of ascetics, and the order of hermits in the woods.

2. If he lives in all these four according to the rules (of the law), without allowing himself to be disturbed (by anything), he will obtain salvation.

3. The duty to live in the teacher's house after the initiation is common to all of them.

4. Not to abandon sacred learning (is a duty common) to all.

5. Having learnt the rites (that are to be performed in each order), he may perform what he wishes.

6. Worshipping until death (and living) according to the rule of a (temporary) student, a (professed) student may leave his body in the house of his teacher.

7. Now (follow the rules) regarding the ascetic (Samnyâsin).

8. Only after (having fulfilled) the duties of that (order of students) he shall go forth (as an ascetic), remaining chaste.

---

21. 1. 'Though four (orders) are enumerated, he uses the word "four," lest, in the absence of a distinct rule of the venerable teacher, one order only, that of the householder, should be allowed, as has been taught in other Smritis.'—Haradatta. Manu VI, 87.

2. Manu VI, 88.

3. Manu II, 247–249, and above.

8. The meaning of the Sûtra is, that the studentship is a necessary preliminary for the Samnyâsin. If a man considers himself sufficiently purified by his life in that order, he may become a Samnyâsin immediately after its completion. Otherwise he may first become a householder, or a hermit, and enter the last

9. For him (the Sa*m*nyâsin) they prescribe (the following rules):

10. He shall live without a fire, without a house, without pleasures, without protection. Remaining silent and uttering speech only on the occasion of the daily recitation of the Veda, begging so much food only in the village as will sustain his life, he shall wander about neither caring for this world nor for heaven.

11. It is ordained that he shall wear clothes thrown away (by others as useless).

12. Some declare that he shall go naked.

13. Abandoning truth and falsehood, pleasure and pain, the Vedas, this world and the next, he shall seek the Âtman.

14. (Some say that) he obtains salvation if he knows (the Âtman).

15. (But) that (opinion) is opposed to the *S*âstras.

16. (For) if salvation were obtained by the knowledge of the Âtman alone, then he ought not to feel any pain even in this (world).

17. Thereby that which follows has been declared.

---

order, when his passions are entirely extinct. See also Manu VI, 36; Yâ*gñ*. III, 56-57.

10. Manu VI, 33, 42-45; Yâ*gñ*. III, 58 seq.

12. 'Another (commentator) says, "Some declare that he is free from all injunctions and prohibitions, i.e. he need neither perform nor avoid any (particular actions)."'—Haradatta.

13. 'He shall seek, i.e. worship, the Âtman or Self, which has been described in the section on transcendental knowledge (I, 8).'—Haradatta.

15. Haradatta apparently takes the word *S*âstras to mean 'Dharma*s*âstras.

17. 'That which follows' are the Yogas, which must be employed in order to cause the annihilation of pain, after the knowledge of the Âtman or Self has been obtained.

18. Now (follow the rules regarding) the hermit living in the woods.

19. Only after (completing) that (studentship) he shall go forth, remaining chaste.

20. For him they give (the following rules):

21. He shall keep one fire only, have no house, enjoy no pleasures, have no protector, observe silence, uttering speech on the occasion of the daily recitation of the Veda only.

PRASNA II, PATALA 9, KHANDA 22.

1. A dress of materials procured in the woods (skins or bark) is ordained for him.

2. Then he shall wander about, sustaining his life by roots, fruits, leaves, and grass.

3. In the end (he shall live on) what has become detached spontaneously.

4. Next he shall live on water, (then) on air, then on ether.

5. Each following one of these modes of subsistence is distinguished by a (greater) reward.

6. Now some (teachers) enjoin for the hermit the

---

21. 'But which is that one fire? Certainly not the Grihya-fire, because he must remain chaste. Therefore the meaning intended is, "He shall offer a Samidh morn and evening in the common fire, just as formerly, (during his studentship)." Another commentator says, "Gautama declares that he shall kindle a fire according to the rule of the Srâmanaka Sûtra. The Srâmanaka Sûtra is the Vaikhânasa Sûtra. Having kindled a fire in the manner prescribed there, he shall sacrifice in it every morning and every evening."'—Haradatta. See also Manu VI, 4; Yâgñ. III, 45.

22. 1. Manu VI, 6. 2. Manu VI, 5, 21; Yâgñ. III, 46.

4. 'Then he shall live on ether, i. e. eat nothing at all.'—Haradatta. Manu VI, 31; Yâgñ. III, 55.

successive performance (of the acts prescribed for the several orders).

7. After having finished the study of the Veda, having taken a wife and kindled the sacred fires, he shall begin the rites, which end with the Soma-sacrifices, (performing) as many as are prescribed in the revealed texts.

8. (Afterwards) he shall build a dwelling, and dwell outside the village with his wife, his children, and his fires,

9. Or (he may live) alone.

10. He shall support himself by gleaning corn.

11. And after that he shall not any longer take presents.

12. And he shall sacrifice (only) after having bathed (in the following manner):

13. He shall enter the water slowly, and bathe without beating it (with his hand), his face turned towards the sun.

14. This rule of bathing is valid for all (castes and orders).

15. Some enjoin (that he shall prepare) two sets of utensils for cooking and eating, (and) of choppers, hatchets, sickles, and mallets.

---

6. 'The word atha, "now," introduces a different opinion. Above, it has been declared that the life in the woods (may be begun) after the studentship only. But some teachers enjoin just for that hermit a successive performance of the acts.

8. Manu VI, 3 seq.; Yâg*ñ*. III, 45.

10. Haradatta thinks that this rule refers both to the hermit who lives with his family and to him who lives alone. Others refer it to the latter only.

15. According to Haradatta, the word kâ*g*a appears to designate 'a mallet;' in the passage from the Râmâya*n*a quoted in the Petersburg Dict. the commentator explains it by pe*t*aka, 'basket.'

16. He shall take one of each pair (of instruments), give the others (to his wife), and (then) go into the forest.

17. After that time (he shall perform) the burnt-oblations, (sustain) his life, (feed) his guests, and (prepare) his clothes with materials produced in the forest.

18. Rice must be used for those sacrifices for which cakes mixed with meat (are employed by the householder).

19. And all (the Mantras), as well as the daily portion of the Veda, (must be recited) inaudibly.

20. He shall not make the inhabitants of the forest hear (his recitation).

21. (He shall have) a house for his fire (only).

22. He himself (shall live) in the open air.

23. His couch and seat must not be covered (with mats).

24. If he obtains fresh grain, he shall throw away the old (store).

Prasna II, Patala 9, Khanda 23.

1. If he desires (to perform) very great austerities, he (shall not make a hoard of grain, but) collect food every day only, morning and evening, in his vessel.

2. Afterwards he shall wander about, sustaining his life with roots, fruits, leaves, and grass (which he

---

17. Yâgñ. III, 46.

20. This Sûtra explains the word upâmsu, 'inaudibly.'

24. Manu VI, 15; Yâgñ. III, 47.

23. 1. The following rules apply to a solitary hermit.

2. These Sûtras are repeated in order to show that, according to the opinion of those who allow hermits to live with their families, the end should be the same.

collects). Finally (he shall content himself with) what has become detached spontaneously. Then he shall live on water, then on air, (and finally) upon ether. Each succeeding mode of subsistence procures greater rewards.

3. Now they quote (the following) two verses from a Purâ*n*a:

4. Those eighty thousand sages who desired offspring passed to the south by Aryaman's road and obtained burial-grounds.

5. Those eighty thousand sages who desired no offspring passed by Aryaman's road to the north and obtained immortality.

6. Thus are praised those who keep the vow of chastity.

7. Now they accomplish also their wishes merely by conceiving them,

8. For instance, (the desire to procure) rain, to bestow children, second-sight, to move quick as thought, and other (desires) of this description.

9. Therefore on account of (passages) of the revealed texts, and on account of the visible results, some declare these orders (of men keeping the vow of chastity to be) the most excellent.

10. But (to this we answer): It is the firm opinion of those who are well versed in the threefold sacred learning, that the Vedas are the highest authority.

---

3. 'The "orders" have been described. Now, giving conflicting opinions, he discusses which of them is the most important.'—Haradatta.

4. This verse and the next are intended to disparage the order of householders. Haradatta explains 'burial-grounds' by 'new births which lead to new deaths;' but see below, Sûtra 10. See also Yâ*gñ*. III, 186–187.

They consider that the (rites) which are ordered there to be performed with rice, yava, animals, clarified butter, milk, potsherds, (in conjunction) with a wife, (and accompanied) by loud or muttered (Mantras), must be performed, and that (hence) a rule of conduct which is opposed to these (rites) is of no authority.

11. But by the term burial-ground (in the text above given) it is intended to ordain the last rites for those who have performed many sacrifices, (and not to mean that dead householders become demons and haunt burial-grounds.)

12. The revealed texts declare that after (the burial follows) a reward without end, which is designated by the term 'heavenly bliss.'

Prasna II, Patala 9, Khanda 24.

1. Now the Veda declares also one's offspring to be immortality (in this verse): 'In thy offspring thou art born again, that, mortal, is thy immortality.'

2. Now it can also be perceived by the senses that the (father) has been reproduced separately (in the son); for the likeness (of a father and of a son) is even visible, only (their) bodies are different.

3. 'These (sons) who live, fulfilling the rites taught (in the Veda), increase the fame and heavenly bliss of their departed ancestors.'

4. 'In this manner each succeeding (generation increases the fame and heavenly bliss) of the preceding ones.'

---

11. The Sûtra is intended to remove the blame thrown on the order of householders by the verse quoted. Haradatta seems to have forgotten his former explanation of *S*maśânâni.

5. 'They (the ancestors) live in heaven until the (next) general destruction of created things.'

6. At the new creation (of, the world) they become the seed. That has been declared in the Bhavishyatpurâ*n*a.

7. Now Pra*g*âpati also says,

8. 'Those dwell with us who fulfil the following (duties): the study of the three Vedas, the studentship, the procreation of children, faith, religious austerities, sacrifices, and the giving of gifts. He who praises other (duties), becomes dust and perishes.'

9. Those among these (sons) who commit sin, perish alone, just as the leaf of a tree (which has been attacked by worms falls without injuring its branch or tree). They do not hurt their ancestors.

10. (For) the (ancestor) has no connection with the acts committed (by his descendant) in this world, nor with their results in the next.

11. (The truth of) that may be known by the following (reason):

12. This creation (is the work) of Pra*g*âpati and of the sages.

13. The bodies of those (sages) who stay there (in heaven) on account of their merits appear visibly most excellent and brilliant (as, for instance, the constellation of the seven *Ri*shis).

14. But even though some (ascetic), whilst still

---

24. 6. 'They become the seed,' i.e. 'The Pra*g*âpatis.'

8. 'Other (duties), i.e. the order of ascetics and the like.'—Haradatta.

13. As the *Ri*shis have not lost heaven through the sins of their sons, the dogma according to which ancestors lose heaven through the sins of their sons, must be false.

14. Âpastamba's own opinion is apparently against pure asceticism.

in the body, may gain heaven through a portion of (the merit acquired by his former) works or through austerities, and though he may accomplish (his objects) by his mere wish, still this is no reason to place one order before the other.

PRASNA II, PATALA 10, KHANDA 25.

1. The general and special duties of all castes have been explained. But we will now declare those of a king in particular.

2. He shall cause to be built a town and a palace, the gates of both of which (must look) towards the south.

3. The palace (shall stand) in the heart of the town.

4. In front of that (there shall be) a hall. That is called the hall of invitation.

5. (At a little distance) from the town to the south, (he shall cause to be built) an assembly-house with doors on the south and on the north sides, so that one can see what passes inside and outside.

6. In all (these three places) fires shall burn constantly.

7. And oblations must be offered in these fires daily, just as at the daily sacrifice of a householder.

8. In the hall he shall put up his guests, at least those who are learned in the Vedas.

---

25. 3. 'In the heart of the town, i.e. in that town which is surrounded by all the walls.'—Haradatta. Compare Manu VII, 76.

6. According to Haradatta, the fires are to be common, not consecrated ones.

7. Manu VII, 78; Yâgñ. I, 313.

8. Manu VII, 82 seq.

9. Rooms, a couch, food and drink should be given to them according to their good qualities.

10. Let him not live better than his Gurus or ministers.

11. And in his realm no (Brâhma*n*a) should suffer hunger, sickness, cold, or heat, be it through want, or intentionally.

12. In the midst of the assembly-house, (the superintendent of the house) shall raise a play-table and sprinkle it with water, turning his hand downwards, and place on it dice in even numbers, made of Vibhîtaka (wood), as many as are wanted.

13. Men of the first three castes, who are pure and truthful, may be allowed to play there.

14. Assaults of arms, dancing, singing, music, and the like (performances) shall be held only (in the houses) of the king's servants.

15. That king only takes care of the welfare of his subjects in whose dominions, be it in villages or forests, there is no danger from thieves.

---

10. 'The Gurus are the father and other (venerable relations).'—Haradatta.

11. Manu VII, 134. 'Or intentionally; with reference to that the following example may be given. If anybody is to be made to pay his debts or taxes, then he is to be exposed to cold or heat, or to be made to fast (until he pays). The king shall punish (every one) who acts thus.'—Haradatta.

13. 'Having played there, they shall give a fixed sum to the gambling-house keeper and go away. The latter shall, every day or every month or every year, give that gain to the king. And the king shall punish those who play elsewhere or quarrel in the assembly-house.'—Haradatta.

14. 'At festivals and the like occasions (these performances) take place also elsewhere, that is the custom.'—Haradatta.

15. Manu VII, 143, and passim; Yâg*ñ*. I, 335.

PRASNA II, PATALA 10, KHANDA 26.

1. A (king) who, without detriment to his servants, gives land and money to Brâhma*n*as according to their deserts gains endless worlds.

2. They say (that) a king, who is slain in attempting to recover the property of Brâhma*n*as, (performs) a sacrifice where his body takes the place of the sacrificial post, and at which an unlimited fee is given.

3. Hereby have been declared (the rewards of) other heroes, who fall fighting for a (worthy) cause.

4. He shall appoint men of the first three castes, who are pure and truthful, over villages and towns for the protection of the people.

5. Their servants shall possess the same qualities.

6. They must protect a town from thieves in every direction to the distance of one yo*g*ana.

7. (They must protect the country to the distance of) one kro*s*a from each village.

8. They must be made to repay what is stolen within these (boundaries).

---

26. 1. Manu VII, 83, 84, 88; Yâ*gñ*. I, 314.

2. According to Haradatta the king's body represents the post (yûpa), his soul the sacrificial animal, the recovered property the reward for the priests or fee.

3. Manu VII, 89; Yâ*gñ*. I, 323, 324.

4. Manu VII, 115–124; Yâ*gñ*. I, 321.

6. Yâ*gñ*. II, 271–272. A yo*g*ana is a distance of 4 kro*s*a, kos.

7. A kro*s*a, kos, or gâu, literally 'the lowing of a cow,' is variously reckoned at 1½–4 miles.

8. Yâ*gñ*. I, 272. This law is, with certain modifications, still in force. See Bombay Regulations, XII, 27 par.

9. The (king) shall make them collect the lawful taxes (*s*ulka).

10. A learned Brâhma*n*a is free from taxes,

11. And the women of all castes,

12. And male children before the marks (of puberty appear),

13. And those who live (with a teacher) in order to study,

14. And those who perform austerities, being intent on fulfilling the sacred law,

15. And a *S*ûdra who lives by washing the feet,

16. Also blind, dumb, deaf, and diseased persons (as long as their infirmities last),

17. And those to whom the acquisition of property is forbidden (as Sannyâsins).

18. A young man who, decked with ornaments, enters unintentionally (a place where) a married woman or a (marriageable) damsel (sits), must be reprimanded.

---

9. According to Haradatta, who quotes Gautama in his commentary, the *s*ulka is the $\frac{1}{20}$th part of a merchant's gains. On account of the Sûtras immediately following, it is, however, more probable that the term is here used as a synonym of 'kara,' and includes all taxes. 'Lawful' taxes are, of course, those sanctioned by custom and approved of by the Sm*ri*tis.

10. Manu VII, 133.

11. Haradatta thinks that the rule applies to women of the Anuloma, the pure castes, only.

14. 'Why does he say "intent on fulfilling the holy law?" Those shall not be free from taxes who perform austerities in order to make their magic charms efficacious.'—Haradatta.

18. The ornaments would indicate that he was bent on mischief. Compare above, I, 11, 32, 6.

19. But if he does it intentionally with a bad purpose, he must be fined.

20. If he has actually committed adultery, his organ shall be cut off together with the testicles.

21. But (if he has had intercourse) with a (marriageable) girl, his property shall be confiscated and he shall be banished.

22. Afterwards the king must support (such women and damsels),

23. And protect them from defilement.

24. If they agree to undergo the (prescribed) penance, he shall make them over to their (lawful) guardians.

Prasna II, Patala 10, Khanda 27.

1. If (adulteresses) have performed (the prescribed penance), they are to be treated as before (their fault). For the connection (of husband and wife) takes place through the law.

2. (A husband) shall not make over his (wife), who occupies the position of a 'gentilis,' to others (than to his 'gentiles'), in order to cause children to be begot for himself.

---

19. 'The punishment must be proportionate to his property and the greatness of his offence. The term "with a bad purpose" is added, because he who has been sent by his teacher (to such a place) should not be punished.'—Haradatta. Manu VIII, 354; Yâgñ. II, 284.

24. 'I.e. a married woman to her husband or father-in-law, an unmarried damsel to her father or to her brother.'—Haradatta.

27. 2. This Sûtra refers to the begetting of a Kshetraga son, and gives the usual rule, that only the Sagotras in the order of the grade of relationship, a brother-in-law, a Sapinda, &c., shall be employed for this purpose.

3. For they declare, that a bride is given to the family (of her husband, and not to the husband alone).

4. That is (at present) forbidden on account of the weakness of (men's) senses.

5. The hand (of a gentilis is considered in law to be) that of a stranger, and so is (that of any other person except the husband).

6. If the (marriage vow) is transgressed, both (husband and wife) certainly go to hell.

7. The reward (in the next world) resulting from obeying the restrictions of the law is preferable to offspring obtained in this manner (by means of Niyoga).

8. A man of one of the first three castes (who commits adultery) with a woman of the *S*ûdra caste shall be banished.

9. A *S*ûdra (who commits adultery) with a woman of one of the first three castes shall suffer capital punishment.

10. And he shall emaciate a woman who has committed adultery with a (*S*ûdra, by making her undergo penances and fasts, in case she had no child).

11. They declare, that (a Brâhma*n*a) who has

---

4. 'For now-a-days the senses of men are weak, and therefore the peculiar (law formerly) in force regarding gentiles is so no longer, lest husbands should be set aside under the pretended sanction of the *S*âstras.'—Haradatta.

9. Manu VIII, 374; Yâ*gñ*. II, 286. According to Haradatta, this refers to a *S*ûdra servant who seduces a woman committed to his charge. In other cases the punishment prescribed, II, 10, 26, 10, is to take effect. The same opinion is expressed by Gautama.

11. This refers to the wife of a *S*rotriya, as Haradatta states according to Gautama. The penance is three years' chastity.

once committed adultery with a married woman of equal class, shall perform one fourth of the penance prescribed for an outcast.

12. In like manner for every repetition (of the crime), one-fourth of the penance (must be added).

13. (If the offence be committed) for the fourth time, the whole (penance of twelve years must be performed).

14. The tongue of a *S*ûdra who speaks evil of a virtuous person, belonging to one of the first three castes, shall be cut out.

15. A *S*ûdra who assumes a position equal (to that of a member of one of the first three castes), in conversation, on the road, on a couch, in sitting (and on similar occasions), shall be flogged.

16. In case (a *S*ûdra) commits homicide or theft, appropriates land (or commits similar heinous crimes), his property shall be confiscated and he himself shall suffer capital punishment.

17. But if these (offences be committed) by a Brâhma*n*a, he shall be made blind (by tying a cloth over his eyes).

18. He shall keep in secret confinement him who violates the rules (of his caste or order), or any other sinner, until (he promises) amendment.

19. If he does not amend, he shall be banished.

20. A spiritual teacher, an officiating priest, a

15. In conversation, i.e. addressing Âryas familiarly, with tvam, 'thou,' &c.

17. Haradatta states expressly that the eyes of a Brâhma*n*a must not be put out by any sharp instrument. He should be kept blindfold all his life.

20. 'The intercession is to take effect in this manner: that mutilation is commuted to a fine, a fine to a flogging, a flogging to a reprimand.'—Haradatta.

Snâtaka, and a prince shall be able to protect (a criminal from punishment by their intercession), except in case of a capital offence.

Prasna II, Patala 11, Khanda 28.

1. If a person who has taken (a lease of) land (for cultivation) does not exert himself, and hence (the land) bears no crop, he shall, if he is rich, be made to pay (to the owner of the land the value of the crop) that ought to have grown.

2. A servant in tillage who abandons his work shall be flogged.

3. The same (punishment shall be awarded) to a herdsman (who leaves his work);

4. And the flock (entrusted) to him shall be taken away (and be given to some other herdsman).

5. If cattle, leaving their stable, eat (the crops of other persons, then the owner of the crops, or the king's servants), may make them lean (by impounding them); (but) he shall not exceed (in such punishment).

---

28. 1. This Sûtra shows that the system of leasing land against a certain share of the crops, which now prevails generally in Native States, and is not uncommon in private contracts on British territory, was in force in Âpastamba's times.

2. See Colebrooke, Digest, Book III, Text lxviii, for this Sûtra and the following two. Another commentator, quoted by Haradatta, connects this Sûtra with the preceding, and refers it to a poor lessee of land, who cannot pay the value of the crop which was lost through his negligence. A third explanation refers the Sûtra to a cultivator who neglects to till his land. *G*agannâtha's authorities, the *K*intâma*n*i and Ratnâkara, agree with Haradatta's first explanation.

5. Manu VIII, 240; Yâg*ñ*. II, 159-161.

6. If (a herdsman) who has taken cattle under his care, allows them to perish, or loses (them by theft, through his negligence), he shall replace them (or pay their value) to the owners.

7. If (the king's forester) sees cattle that have been sent into the forest through negligence (without a herdsman), he shall lead them back to the village and make them over to the owners.

8. If the same negligence (occur) again, he shall once impound them (and afterwards give them back).

9. (If the same fault be committed again) after that (second time), he shall not take care (of them).

10. He who has taken unintentionally the property of another shall be reprimanded, in case (the property be) fuel, water, roots, flowers, fruits, perfumes, fodder, or vegetables.

11. (If he takes the above-mentioned kinds of property) intentionally, his garment shall be taken away.

12. He who takes intentionally food when he is in danger of his life shall not be punished.

13. If the king does not punish a punishable offence, the guilt falls upon him.

Prasna II, Patala 11, Khanda 29.

1. He who instigates to, he who assists in, and he who commits (an act, these three) share its rewards in heaven and its punishments in hell.

2. He amongst these who contributes most to

6. Manu VIII, 232; Yâgñ. II, 164.

13. Manu VIII, 18, 308; Yâgñ. I, 336.

the accomplishment (of the act obtains) a greater share of the result.

3. Both the wife and the husband have power over (their) common property.

4. By their permission, others also may act for their good (in this and the next world, even by spending money).

5. Men of learning and pure descent, who are aged, clever in reasoning, and careful in fulfilling the duties (of their caste and order, shall be the judges) in lawsuits.

6. In doubtful cases (they shall give their decision) after having ascertained (the truth) by inference, ordeals, and the like (means).

7. A person who is possessed of good qualities (may be called as a witness, and) shall answer the questions put to him according to the truth on an auspicious day, in the morning, before a kindled fire, standing near (a jar full of) water, in the presence of the king, and with the consent of all (of both parties and of the assessors), after having been exhorted (by the judge) to be fair to both sides.

8. If (he is found out speaking) an untruth, the king shall punish him.

---

29. 3. 'Though this is so, still the wife cannot spend (money) without the permission of her husband, but the husband can do (so without the consent of his wife). That may be known by Sûtra II, 6, 14, 11, "They do not declare it to be a theft if the wife spends money for a good reason during the absence of her husband."'—Haradatta.

4. 'Others, i.e. the sons and the rest.'—Haradatta.

5. Yâ*gñ*. II, 2.

6. 'And the like, i.e. by cross-examination, &c.'—Haradatta.

7. Manu VIII, 87 seq.; Yâ*gñ*. II, 68–75.

8. Manu VIII, 119 seq.

9. Besides, in that case, after death, hell (will be his punishment).

10. If he speaks the truth, (his reward will be) heaven and the approbation of all created beings.

11. The knowledge which *S*ûdras and women possess is the completion (of all study).

12. They declare, that (this knowledge) is a supplement of the Atharva-veda.

13. It is difficult to learn the sacred law from (the letter of) the Vedas (only); but by following the indications it is easily accomplished.

14. The indications for these (doubtful cases are), 'He shall regulate his course of action according to the conduct which is unanimously recognised in all countries by men of the three twice-born castes, who have been properly obedient (to their teachers), who are aged, of subdued senses, neither given to avarice, nor hypocrites. Acting thus he will gain both worlds.'

15. Some declare, that the remaining duties (which have not been taught here) must be learnt from women and men of all castes.

---

9. Manu VIII, 89 seq.

10. Manu VIII, 81 seq.

11. Manu II, 223. The meaning of the Sûtra is, that men ought not to study solely or at first such *S*âstras as women or *S*ûdras also learn, but that at first they must study the Veda. See Manu II, 168. The knowledge which women and *S*ûdras possess is dancing, music, and other branches of the Artha*s*âstra.

14. See above, I, 7, 20, 8 and 9.

GAUTAMA,

INSTITUTES OF THE SACRED LAW.

GAUTAMA,

INSTITUTES OF THE SACRED LAW.

CHAPTER I.

1. THE Veda is the source of the sacred law,

2. And the tradition and practice of those who know the (Veda).

3. Transgression of the law and violence are observed (in the case) of (those) great (men); but both are without force (as precedents) on account of the weakness of the men of later ages.

4. If (authorities) of equal force are conflicting, (either may be followed at) pleasure.

5. The initiation of a Brâhma*n*a (shall ordinarily take place) in his eighth year;

I. 1–2. Âpastamba I, 1, 1, 1–2.

3. Âpastamba II, 6, 13, 8–10. Instances of transgressions of the law are the adultery of Kataka and Bharadvâ*g*a, Vasish*th*a's marriage with the *K*â*n*d*âlî Akshamâlâ, Râma *G*âmadagnya's murder of his mother. Haradatta explains the term 'avara,' translated by 'men of later ages,' to mean 'men like ourselves' (asmadâdi). In his comment on the parallel passage of Âpastamba he renders it by idânîntana, 'belonging to our times;' and in his notes on Âpastamba I, 2, 5, 4, he substitutes arvâ*k*îna kaliyugavartin, 'men of modern times living in the Kaliyuga.' The last explanation seems to me the most accurate, if it is distinctly kept in mind that in the times of Gautama the Kaliyuga was not a definite period of calculated duration, but the Iron Age of sin as opposed to the happier times when justice still dwelt on earth.

6. (It may also be performed) in the ninth or fifth (years) for the fulfilment of (some particular) wish.

7. The number of years (is to be calculated) from conception.

8. That (initiation) is the second birth.

9. The (person) from whom he receives that (sacrament is called) the Â*k*ârya (teacher).

10. And (the same title is also bestowed) in consequence of the teaching of the Veda.

11. (The initiation) of a Kshatriya (shall ordinarily take place) in the eleventh (year after conception), and that of a Vai*s*ya in the twelfth.

12. Up to the sixteenth year the time for the Sâvitrî of a Brâhma*n*a has not passed,

13. Nor (for the initiation) of a Kshatriya up to the twentieth (year).

14. (And the limit for that) of a Vai*s*ya (extends) two years beyond (the latter term).

15. The girdles (worn by students) shall be strings of Mu*ñg*a grass, a bow-string, or a (wool) thread, according to the order (of the castes).

16. (Their upper garments shall be) skins of black-bucks, spotted deer, (or) he-goats.

---

6. Âpastamba I, 1, 1, 20–21.
7. Âpastamba I, 1, 1, 19. 8. Âpastamba I, 1, 1, 17–18.
9. Âpastamba I, 1, 1, 14. 10. Manu II, 140; Yâ*gñ*avalkya I, 34.
11. Âpastamba I, 1, 1, 19.
12. Âpastamba I, 1, 1, 27. Sâvitrî, literally the *Ri*k sacred to Savit*ri*, is here used as an equivalent for upanayana, initiation, because one of the chief objects of the ceremony is to impart to the neophyte the Mantra sacred to Savit*ri*, Rig-veda III, 62, 10.
13–14. Âpastamba I, 1, 1, 27.
15. Âpastamba I, 1, 2, 33–36. 16. Âpastamba I, 1, 3, 3–6.

17. Hempen or linen cloth, the (inner) bark (of trees), and woollen blankets (may be worn as lower garments by students) of all (castes),

18. And undyed cotton cloth.

19. Some (declare that it) even (may be dyed) red.

20. (In that case the garment) of a Brâhma*n*a (shall be dyed with a red dye) produced from a tree,

21. (And those of students) of the other two (castes shall be) dyed with madder or turmeric.

22. The staff (carried by a student) of the Brâhma*n*a (caste shall be) made of Bilva or Palâ*s*a wood.

23. Staves made of A*s*vattha or Pîlu wood (are fit) for (students of) the remaining (two castes).

24. Or (a staff cut from a tree) that is fit to be used at a sacrifice (may be carried by students) of all (castes).

25. (The staves must be) unblemished, bent (at the top) like a sacrificial post, and covered by their bark.

26. They shall reach the crown of the head, the forehead, (or) the tip of the nose (according to the caste of the wearer).

---

17. Haradatta explains *k*îra, the inner bark of a tree, by 'made of Ku*s*a grass and the like.' Regarding dresses made of Ku*s*a grass, see the Petersburg Dict. s.v. Ku*s*a*k*îra. *K*îra may also mean 'rags,' such as were worn by Sannyâsins (see below, III, 19) and Bauddha ascetics.

19–21. Âpastamba I, 1, 2, 41—I, 1, 3, 2.

22. Âpastamba I, 1, 2, 38.

24. 'Because the term "fit to be used at a sacrifice" is employed, the Vibhîtaka and the like (unclean trees) are excluded.'—Haradatta. Regarding the Vibhîtaka, see Report of Tour in Ka*s*mîr, Journal Bombay Br. Roy. As. Soc. XXXIV A, p. 8.

25. Manu II, 47. 'Unblemished means uninjured by worms and the like.'—Haradatta.

26. Manu II, 46.

27. (It is) optional (for students) to shave (their heads), to wear the hair tied in a braid, (or) to keep (merely) a lock on the crown of the head tied in a braid (shaving the other portions of the head).

28. If he becomes impure while holding things in his hands, he shall (purify himself) by sipping water without laying (them on the ground).

---

27. Âpastamba I, 1, 2, 31-32. The above translation follows the reading of my MSS. mu*nd*aga*t*ilasikhâ*g*a*t*â vâ, which seems more in accordance with the Sûtra style. It must, however, be understood that the arrangement of the hair is not regulated by the individual choice of the student, but by the custom of his family, school, or country. In the commentary, as given by one of my MSS., it is stated the custom of shaving the whole head prevailed among the *Kh*andogas. Max Müller, History of Ancient Sanskrit Literature, p. 53; Weber, Indische Studien, X, 95.

28. The above translation agrees with Professor Stenzler's text and Manu V, 143. But according to Haradatta the meaning of the Sûtra is not so simple. His explanation is as follows: 'If while holding things in his hands he becomes impure, i.e. he is defiled by urine, fæces, leavings of food, and the like (impurities) which are causes for sipping water, then he shall sip water after placing those things on the ground. This refers to uncooked food, intended to be eaten. And thus Vasish*th*a (III, 4, 3, Benares edition) declares: "If he who is occupied with eatables touches any impure substance, then he shall place that thing on the ground, sip water, and afterwards again use it." But the following text of another Sm*ri*ti, "A substance becomes pure by being sprinkled with water after having been placed on the ground," refers to cooked food, such as boiled rice and the like. Or (the above Sûtra may mean), "If he becomes impure while holding things in his hands, then he shall sip water without laying them on the ground." And thus Manu (V, 143) says: "He who carries in any manner anything in his hands and is touched by an impure substance shall cleanse himself by sipping water without laying his burden down." This rule refers to things not destined to be eaten, such as garments. And in the (above) Sûtra the words, "He who becomes impure shall sip water," must be taken as one sentence, and (the whole), "If while holding things in his hands he becomes impure,

29. (As regards) the purification of things, (objects) made of metal must be scoured, those made of clay should be thoroughly heated by fire, those made of wood must be planed, and (cloth) made of thread should be washed.

30. (Objects made of) stone, jewels, shells, (or) mother-of-pearl (must be treated) like those made of metal.

31. (Objects made of) bone and mud (must be treated) like wood.

---

he shall sip water without laying (them) down," must be taken as a second.'

Though it may be doubted if the yogavibhâga, or 'division of the construction,' proposed by Haradatta, is admissible, still it seems to me not improbable that Gautama intended his Sûtra to be taken in two different ways. For, if according to the ancient custom it is written without an Avagraha and without separating the words joined by Sandhi, dravyahasta u*kkh*ish*t*onidhâyâ*k*âmet, the latter group may either stand for u*kkh*ish*t*o nidhâya â*k*âmet or for u*kkh*ish*t*o anidhâya â*k*âmet. As the Sûtrakâras aim before all things at brevity, the Sûtra may have to be read both ways. If that had to be done, the correct translation would be: 'If while holding things in his hands, he becomes impure, he shall (purify himself by) sipping water, either laying (his burden) down (or) not laying it down, (as the case may require.)'

29. Âpastamba I, 5, 17, 10–12; Manu V, 115, 122.

30. Manu V, 111–112.

31. 'Bone, i. e. ivory and the like. Mud, i. e. (the mud floor of) a house and the like. The purification of these two is the same as that of wood, i. e. by scraping (or planing). How is it proper that, since the author has declared (Sûtra 29) that objects made of wood shall be purified by planing, the expression "like wood" should be substituted (in this Sûtra)? (The answer is that), as the author uses the expression "like wood," when he ought to have said "like objects made of wood," he indicates thereby that the manner of purification is the same for the material as for the object made thereof.'—Haradatta. The

32. And scattering (earth taken from a pure spot is another method of purifying defiled) earth.

33. Ropes, chips (of bamboo), and leather (must be treated) like garments.

34. Or (objects) that have been defiled very much may be thrown away.

35. Turning his face to the east or to the north, he shall purify himself from personal defilement.

36. Seated in a pure place, placing his right arm between his knees, arranging his dress (or his

Sûtra is, therefore, a so-called *Gñ*âpaka, intended to reveal the existence of a general rule or paribhâshâ which has not been given explicitly.

32. 'Scattering over, i.e. heaping on (earth) after bringing it from another spot is an additional method of purifying earth. With regard to this matter Vasish*th*a (III, 57) says: "Earth is purified by these four (methods, viz.) by digging, burning, scraping, being trodden on by cows, and, fifthly, by being smeared with cowdung."'—Haradatta.

What Haradatta and probably Gautama mean, is that the mud floors of houses, verandahs, and spots of ground selected for sitting on, if defiled, should be scraped, and that afterwards fresh earth should be scattered over the spot thus cleansed. See, however, Manu V, 125, who recommends earth for the purification of other things also. The Sûtra may also be interpreted so as to agree with his rule.

33. 'Chips (vidala), i.e. something made of chips of ratan-cane or bamboo, or, according to others, something made of feathers.'—Haradatta.

34. 'The word "or" is used in order to exclude the alternative (i.e. the methods of purification described above).'—Haradatta. For the explanation of the expression 'very much' Haradatta refers to Vasish*th*a III, 58, with which Manu V, 123 may be compared.

35. 'The alternative (position) depends on the pleasure of the performer.'—Haradatta.

36. My MSS. more conveniently make five Sûtras of Professor Stenzler's one Sûtra. The divisions have been marked in the translation by semicolons.

a. 'How many times? Three times or four times; the alter-

sacrificial cord) in the manner required for a sacrifice to the gods, he shall, after washing his hands up to the wrist, three or four times, silently, sip water that reaches his heart; twice wipe (his lips); sprinkle his feet and (his head); touch the cavities in the head (severally) with (certain fingers of his) right hand; (and finally) place (all the fingers) on the crown of his head and (on the navel).

37. After sleeping, dining, and sneezing (he shall) again (sip water though he may have done so before).

38. (Remnants of food) adhering to the teeth (do not make the eater impure as little) as his teeth, except if he touches them with his tongue.

39. Some (declare, that such remnants do not defile) before they fall (from their place).

40. If they do become detached, he should know that he is purified by merely swallowing them, as (in the case of) saliva.

---

native depends upon the pleasure of the performer. Another (commentator says): When, according to a special rule of the Vedas the sipping must be accompanied by the recitation of sacred texts, then the act shall be repeated four times, else three times.'—Haradatta.

b. The custom of touching the lips twice is noted as the opinion of some, by Âpastamba I, 5, 16, 4.

c. '"Sprinkle his feet and." On account of the word "and" he shall sprinkle his head also.'—Haradatta.

d. '"Touch the cavities," &c. Here the word "and" indicates that each organ is to be touched separately.'—Haradatta. Regarding the manner of touching, see Âpastamba I, 5, 16, 5 and 7 note.

e. '"(And finally) place," &c. Because the word "and" is used, he shall touch the navel and the head with all the fingers.'—Haradatta. Regarding the whole Â*k*amanakalpa, see Âpastamba I, 5, 16, 1 seq.

37. Manu V, 145.

38. Manu V, 141.

39. Vasish*th*a III, 41.

40. 'As the author ought to have said, "If they become de-

41. Drops (of saliva) falling from the mouth do not cause impurity, except if they fall on a limb of the body.

42. Purification (from defilement) by unclean substances (has been effected) when the stains and the (bad) smell have been removed.

43. That (should be done) by first (using) water and (afterwards) earth,

44. When urine, fæces, or semen fall on a (limb) and when (a limb) is stained (by food) during meals (water should be sipped).

45. And in case the Veda ordains (a particular manner of purification, it must be performed according to the precept).

46. Taking hold with (his right) hand of the left

---

tached, he is purified by merely swallowing them," the addition of the words "he should know" and "as in the case of saliva" is intended to indicate that in the case of saliva, too, he becomes pure by swallowing it, and that purification by sipping need not be considered necessary.'—Haradatta. This Sûtra consists of the second half of a verse, quoted by Baudhâyana I, 5, 8, 25, and Vasishtha III, 41.

41. Âpastamba I, 5, 16, 12.

42. In explanation of the term amedhya, 'unclean substances,' Haradatta quotes Manu V, 135.

43. Manu V, 134; see also Âpastamba I, 5, 16, 15.

44. Âpastamba I, 5, 16, 14.

45. 'If the Veda ordains any particular manner of purification for any particular purpose, that alone must be adopted. Thus the sacrificial vessels called *k*amasa, which have been stained by remnants of offerings, must be washed with water on the heap of earth called mâr*g*âlîya.'—Haradatta.

46. This and the following rules refer chiefly to the teaching of the Sâvitrî, which forms part of the initiation. According to Gobhila G*ri*hya-sûtra II, 10, 38, the complete sentence addressed to the teacher is, 'Venerable Sir, recite! May the worshipful one teach me the Sâvitrî.'

hand (of his teacher), but leaving the thumb free, (the pupil) shall address his teacher, (saying): 'Venerable Sir, recite!'

47. He shall fix his eyes and his mind on the (teacher).

48. He shall touch with Kusa grass the (seat of the) vital airs.

49. He shall thrice restrain his breath for (the space of) fifteen moments;

50. And he shall seat himself on (blades of Kusa grass) the tops of which are turned toward the east.

51. The five Vyâhritis must (each) be preceded by (the syllable) Om and end with Satya.

52. (Every) morning the feet of the teacher must be embraced (by the pupil),

53. And both at the beginning and at the end of a lesson in the Veda.

54. After having received permission, the pupil

---

47. Âpastamba I, 2, 5, 23; I, 2, 6, 20; Manu II, 192.

48. 'The (seat of the) vital airs are the organs of sense located in the head. The pupil shall touch these, his own (organs of sense) located in the head, in the order prescribed for the Âkamana (see Âpastamba I, 5, 16, 7 note).'—Haradatta. See also Manu II, 75.

49. 'Passing one's hand along the side of the knee, one will fill the space of one Trutikâ. That is one moment (mâtrâ).'—Haradatta. Manu II, 75.

50. Manu II, 75.

51. 'In the Vyâhriti-sâmans (see Burnell, Ârsheya-br., Index s.v.) five Vyâhritis are mentioned, viz. Bhûh, Bhuvah, Svah, Satyam, Purushah. Each of these is to be preceded by the syllable Om. But they are to end with Purushah, which (in the above enumeration) occupies the fourth place.'—Haradatta. See also Manu II, 75 seq.

52–53. Âpastamba I, 2, 5, 18–20.

54. Âpastamba I, 2, 6, 24; Manu II, 193. '"Turning his face towards the east or towards the north." This alternative depends upon (the nature of) the business.'—Haradatta.

shall sit down to the right (of his teacher), turning his face towards the east or towards the north,

55. And the Sâvitrî must be recited;

56. (All these acts must be performed) at the beginning of the instruction in the Veda.

57. The syllable Om (must precede the recitation of) other (parts of the Veda) also.

58. If (any one) passes between (the teacher and the pupil) the worship (of the teacher must be performed) once more.

59. If a dog, an ichneumon, a snake, a frog, (or) a cat (pass between the teacher and the pupil) a three days' fast and a journey (are necessary).

---

55. Manu II, 77.

56. 'All those acts beginning with the touching of the organs of sense with Kusa grass and ending with the recitation of the Sâvitrî, which have been prescribed (Sûtras 48–57), must be performed before the pupil begins to study the Veda with his teacher, but should not be repeated daily. After the initiation follows the study of the Sâvitrî. The touching of the organs of sense and the other (acts mentioned) form part of this (study). But the rules prescribed in the three Sûtras, the first of which is Sûtra 52, and the rule to direct the eye and mind towards the teacher (Sûtra 47), must be constantly kept in mind. This decision is confirmed by the rules of other Smritis and of the Grihya-sûtras.'—Haradatta.

57. Âpastamba I, 4, 13, 6–7.

58. 'The worship of the teacher (upasadana) consists in the performance of the acts prescribed in Sûtras 46–57, with the exception of the study of the Sâvitrî and the acts belonging to that. The meaning of the Sûtra is that, though the worship of the teacher may have already been performed in the morning of that day, it must, nevertheless, be repeated for the reason stated.'—Haradatta.

59. 'A journey (vipravâsa) means residence in some other place than the teacher's house.'—Haradatta. The commentator adds that the somewhat different rule, given by Manu IV, 126, may be reconciled with the above, by referring the former to the study for the sake of remembering texts recited by the teacher (dhâranâdhyayana), and the latter to the first instruction in the sacred texts.

60. (In case the same event happens) with other (animals, the pupil) must thrice restrain his breath and eat clarified butter,

61. And (the same expiation must be performed), if (unwittingly) a lesson in the Veda has been given on the site of a burial-ground.

CHAPTER II.

1. Before initiation (a child) may follow its inclinations in behaviour, speech, and eating. (It shall) not partake of offerings. (It shall remain) chaste. It may void urine and fæces according to its convenience.

---

60. 'This penance must be performed by the pupil, not by the teacher. Others declare that both shall perform it.'—Haradatta.

61. See also Âpastamba I, 3, 9, 6–8. The last clauses of this and all succeeding chapters are repeated in order to indicate that the chapter is finished.

II. 1. In concluding the explanation of this Sûtra, Haradatta states that its last clause is intended to give an instance of the freedom of behaviour permitted to a child. In his opinion Gautama indicates thereby that a person who, before initiation, drinks spirituous liquor, commits murder or other mortal sins, becomes an outcast, and is liable to perform the penances prescribed for initiated sinners. In support of this view he quotes a passage, taken from an unnamed Smṛiti, according to which the parents or other relatives of children between five and eleven years are to perform penances vicariously for the latter, while children between eleven and fifteen years are declared to be liable to half the penances prescribed for initiated adults. Hence he infers that though the above text of Gautama speaks of uninitiated persons in general, its provisions really apply to children under five years of age only. Though it would seem that some of Gautama's rules refer to half-grown persons rather than to infants or very young boys, it is impossible to assume that Gautama meant to give full licence of behaviour, speech, and eating to Brâhmaṇas who were not

2. No rule of (purification by) sipping water is prescribed for it. But (the stains of impure substances) shall be removed by wiping, by washing, or by sprinkling water.

3. (Other persons) cannot be defiled by the touch of such (a child).

4. But one must not employ a (child) to perform oblations in the fire or Bali-offerings;

5. Nor must one make it recite Vedic texts, except in pronouncing Svadhâ.

6. The restrictive rules, (which will be enumerated hereafter, must be obeyed) after initiation,

7. And (for a student the duty of) chastity, which has been prescribed (above for a child is likewise obligatory),

8. (Also) to offer (daily) sacred fuel in the fire, and to beg, to speak the truth, (and) to bathe (daily).

---

initiated before their sixteenth year, or to Kshatriyas and Vaisyas up to the age of twenty and twenty-two. It seems more likely that, as Haradatta thinks, his rules are meant in the first instance for infants and very young children only, and that he intended the special cases of half-grown or nearly grown up boys to be dealt with according to the custom of the family or of the country.

2. Haradatta points out that the Sûtra does not forbid uninitiated persons to sip water, but that it merely denies the applicability of the rules (kalpa) given above, I, 36. Uninitiated persons may, therefore, sip water in the manner practised by women and *S*ûdras.

4. Âpastamba II, 6, 15, 18; Manu XI, 36.

5. 'The expression "pronouncing Svadhâ" includes by implication the performance of all funeral rites.'—Haradatta.

7. Âpastamba I, 1, 2, 26.

8. Âpastamba I, 1, 4, 14-17; I, 1, 3, 25; I, 1, 2, 28-30; Manu II, 176.

9. Some (declare, that the duty) to bathe (exists) after (the performance of) the Godâna (only).

10. And the morning and evening devotions (Sandhyâ must be performed) outside (the village).

11. Silent he shall stand during the former, and sit during the latter, from (the time when one) light (is still visible) until (the other) light (appears).

12. He shall not look at the sun.

13. He shall avoid honey, meat, perfumes, garlands, sleep in the day-time, ointments, collyrium, a carriage, shoes, a parasol, love, anger, covetousness, perplexity, garrulity, playing musical instruments, bathing (for pleasure), cleaning the teeth, elation, dancing, singing, calumny, (and) terror,

14. (And) in the presence of his Gurus, covering his throat, crossing his legs, leaning (against a wall or the like, and) stretching out his feet,

15. (As well as) spitting, laughing, yawning, cracking the joints of the fingers,

---

9. Regarding the sacrament called Godâna, see Gobhila Gr*i*hya-sûtra I, 9, 26.

10. Âpastamba I, 11, 30, 8.

11. 'From (the time when one) light (is still visible,' &c.), i. e. in the morning from the time when the stars are still visible until the sun rises, and in the evening from the time when the sun still stands above the horizon until the stars appear. Haradatta observes that, as Manu II, 102 prescribes the recitation of the Gâyatrî during the morning and evening devotions, either his or Gautama's rule may be followed. He adds that another commentator refers the injunction to keep silence to conversations on worldly matters only. He himself has adopted this view in his commentary on Âpastamba I, 11, 30, 8.

12. Âpastamba I, 11, 31, 18.

13. Âpastamba I, 1, 2, 23–28; I, 1, 3, 11–14, 20–24; I, 2, 7, 5.

14. Âpastamba I, 2, 6, 3, 14, 17–18. The term Guru includes, besides the teacher, the parents and other venerable persons.

15. Âpastamba I, 2, 7, 6–7; II, 2, 5, 9. Haradatta observes

16. To gaze at and to touch women, if there is danger of a breach of chastity,

17. Gambling, low service, to take things not offered, to injure animate beings,

18. To pronounce the names of the teacher, of the (teacher's) sons and wives, and of a person who has performed the Dîkshanîyeshti of a Soma-sacrifice,

19. To make bitter speeches.

20. A Brâhmana (shall) always (abstain from) spirituous liquor.

21. (A student) shall occupy a seat and a couch lower (than those of his teacher), shall rise before (him) and retire to rest after (him).

22. He shall keep his tongue, his arms, and his stomach in subjection.

23. (If it is absolutely necessary to pronounce)

---

that this Sûtra again contains a general rule, and does not merely refer to the presence of Gurus.

16. Âpastamba I, 2, 7, 3, 8-10.

17. Âpastamba I, 1, 3, 12. '"Low service," i.e. service by wiping off urine, fæces, and the like. . . . That is not even to be performed for the teacher. Or the expression may mean that he shall not serve a teacher deficient in learning and virtue. The same opinion is expressed by Âpastamba I, 1, 1, 11.'—Haradatta.

18. Manu II, 199. 19. Âpastamba I, 2, 7, 24.

20. 'A Brâhmana shall avoid it always, i.e. even as a householder; Kshatriyas and Vaisyas need do it only as long as they are students. But in their case, too, they forbid the use of liquor distilled from bruised rice, under all circumstances.'—Haradatta.

21. Âpastamba I, 1, 2, 21; I, 1, 4, 22, 28.

22. Âpastamba I, 1, 3, 13. 'Keeping his arms in subjection means that he shall not (without a cause) break clods of earth and the like. Keeping his stomach in subjection, i.e. eating with moderation.'—Haradatta.

23. 'He shall indicate it by another synonymous word,

his teacher's name and family-name, he ought to indicate it by (using) a synonymous term.

24. (He must speak) in the same (respectful) manner of a man who is (generally) revered and of his betters.

25. (If the teacher speaks to him), he shall answer after having risen from his couch or seat (in case he was lying down or sitting).

26. At the command (of his teacher) he shall approach, though the (teacher) may not be visible.

27. And if he sees his teacher standing or sitting in a lower place or to the leeward or to the windward, he shall rise (and change his position).

28. If (his teacher) is walking, he shall walk after him, informing him of the work (which he is going to do and) telling (him what he has done).

29. He shall study after having been called (by the teacher, and not request the latter to begin the lesson).

---

e.g. instead of saying, "Haradatta (given by Hara)," he shall say, "the venerable Bhavarâta (given by Bhava)."'—Haradatta.

25. Âpastamba I, 2, 6, 5–7.

26. He must not think that, as the teacher cannot see him, he need not obey the summons.

27. Âpastamba I, 2, 6, 15, 23.

28. 'Work (karma) means performance. The meaning is that the pupil shall announce to his teacher the performance of all he is going to do. But what is useful for the teacher, as fetching water and the like, he shall inform him of the performance of that, i.e. knowing himself (without being told) that such work is necessary at a particular time (and acting on this knowledge). Any other explanation of this Sûtra does not please me.'—Haradatta. See also Âpastamba I, 2, 6, 8. My MSS. divide this Sûtra into two, beginning the second with 'Informing' &c. Haradatta's final remark, quoted above, seems to indicate that the division was intended by him.

29. Âpastamba I, 2, 5, 26.

30. He shall be intent on (doing) what is pleasing and serviceable (to the teacher);

31. And (he shall behave) towards (the teacher's) wives and sons just as (towards the teacher),

32. But not eat their leavings, attend them while bathing, assist them at their toilet, wash their feet, shampoo them nor embrace their feet.

33. On returning from a journey he shall embrace the feet of the wives of his teacher.

34. Some declare, that (a pupil) who has attained his majority is not (to act thus) towards young (wives of his teacher).

35. Alms may be accepted from men of all castes, excepting Abhi*s*astas and outcasts.

36. (In begging) the word 'Lady' must be pronounced in the beginning, in the middle, or at the end (of the request), according to the order of the castes.

37. (He may beg in the houses) of the teacher, of blood relations, (or) of Gurus, and in his own, if he obtains no (alms) elsewhere.

---

30. Âpastamba I, 1, 4, 23.

31. Âpastamba I, 2, 7, 27, 30; Manu II, 207–212.

34. 'One who has attained his majority, i.e. one who has completed his sixteenth year and is (already) a youth.'—Haradatta.

35. Haradatta explains abhi*s*asta by upapâtakin, 'one who has committed a minor offence,' apparently forgetting Âpastamba I, 7, 21, 7. See also Âpastamba I, 1, 3, 25.

36. Âpastamba I, 1, 3, 28–30, where the formulas have been given in the notes. Haradatta remarks that the *G*aimini G*ri*hya-sûtra forbids the lengthening or drawling pronunciation of the syllables kshâ*m* and hi in begging. Baudhâyana I, 2, 3, 16 likewise forbids it. In the text read var*n*ânupûrvye*n*a.

37. Manu II, 184. It is just possible that the translation ought to be 'in the houses of his teacher's blood relations,' instead of 'in the houses of his teacher (and) of blood relations.'

38. Among these he shall avoid each preceding one (more carefully than those named later).

39. Having announced to the teacher (what he has received) and having received his permission, the (student) may eat (the collected food).

40. If (the teacher) is not present, (he shall seek the permission to eat) from his (teacher's) wives or sons, from fellow-students or virtuous (strangers).

41. Having placed water by his side, (he shall eat) in silence, contented, (and) without greed.

42. (As a rule) a pupil shall not be punished corporally.

43. If no (other course) is possible, (he may be corrected) with a thin rope or a thin cane.

44. If (the teacher) strikes him with any other (instrument), he shall be punished by the king.

45. He shall remain a student for twelve years in order (to study) one (recension of the Veda),

46. Or, if (he studies) all (the Vedas) twelve years for each,

47. Or during (as long a period as he requires for) learning (them).

48. On completion of the instruction the teacher must be offered a fee.

---

38. The meaning of the Sûtra is, that if a student does not obtain anything from strangers, he shall first go to his own family, next to the houses of Gurus, i.e. paternal and maternal uncles and other venerable relatives, then to his other blood relations, i.e. Sapi*nd*as, and in case of extreme necessity only apply to the teacher's wife.

39. Âpastamba I, 1, 3, 31-32.

40. Âpastamba I, 1, 3, 33-34. 41. Manu II, 53-54.

42. Âpastamba I, 2, 8, 29; Macnaghten, Mitâksharâ IV, 1, 9.

43. Manu VIII, 299. 45-47. Âpastamba I, 1, 2, 12-16.

48. Âpastamba I, 2, 7, 19.

49. After (the pupil) has paid (that) and has been dismissed, he may, at his pleasure, bathe (as is customary on completion of the studentship).

50. The teacher is chief among all Gurus.

51. Some (say) that the mother (holds that place).

CHAPTER III.

1. Some (declare, that) he (who has studied the Veda) may make his choice (which) among the orders (he is going to enter).

2. (The four orders are, that of) the student, (that of) the householder, (that of) the ascetic (bhikshu), (and that of) the hermit in the woods (vaikhânasa).

---

49. Âpastamba I, 2, 8, 30. 50. Manu II, 225–237.

III. 1. Other Smritikâras maintain that a Brâhmana must pass through all the four orders. Compare Âpastamba II, 9, 21, 5; Manu VI, 34–38; and the long discussion on the comparative excellence of the orders of householders and of ascetics. Âpastamba II, 9, 23, 3—II, 9, 24, 14.

2. 'Though the order of studentship has already been described above, still in the following chapter the rules for a professed (naishthika) student will be given (and it had therefore again to be mentioned). Bhikshu has generally been translated by ascetic (sannyâsin). Vaikhânasa, literally, he who lives according to the rule promulgated by Vikhanas, means hermit. For that (sage) has chiefly taught that order. In all other Sâstras (the order of) hermits is the third, and (the order of) ascetics the fourth. Here a different arrangement is adopted. The reason of the displacement of the hermit is that the author considers the first-named three orders preferable. Hence if a man chooses to pass through all four, the sequence is that prescribed in other Sâstras.'—Haradatta. In making these statements the commentator has apparently forgotten that Âpastamba (II, 9, 21, 1) agrees exactly with Gautama. It is, however, very probable that Haradatta has given correctly the reason why the hermit is placed last by our author and by Âpastamba.

3. The householder is the source of these, because the others do not produce offspring.

4. Among them a (professed) student (must follow the rules) given (in the preceding chapters).

5. He shall remain obedient to his teacher until (his) end.

6. In (the time) remaining after (he has attended to) the business of his Guru, he shall recite (the Veda).

7. If the Guru dies, he shall serve his son,

8. (Or) if there is no (son of the teacher), an older fellow-student, or the fire.

9. He who lives thus, gains the heaven of Brahman, and (of him it is said that) he has subdued his organs (of sense and action).

10. And these (restrictions imposed on students must also be observed by men) of other (orders, provided they are) not opposed (to their particular duties).

11. An ascetic shall not possess (any) store.

12. (He must be) chaste,

13. He must not change his residence during the rainy season.

---

3. Manu VI, 87. 4. Âpastamba I, 1, 4, 29.

5. Âpastamba II, 9, 21, 6.

6. According to Haradatta the term Guru here includes the father. But see the next Sûtra, where Guru can only mean the teacher.

10. Âpastamba II, 9, 21, 3-4. My MSS. have uttareshâm, 'of the later named,' instead of itareshâm, 'of the other' (orders), both in the Sûtra and in subsequent quotations of the same.

11. Âpastamba II, 9, 21, 8-10; Manu VI, 41-43; Colebrooke, Mitâksharâ II, 8, 7.

13. This rule shows that the Vasso of the Bauddhas and *G*ainas is also derived from a Brahmanical source; see also Baudhâyana II, 6, 11, 20.

14. He shall enter a village (only) in order to beg.

15. He shall beg late (after people have finished their meals), without returning (twice),

16. Abandoning (all) desire (for sweet food).

17. He shall restrain his speech, his eyes, (and) his actions.

18. He shall wear a cloth to cover his nakedness.

19. Some (declare, that he shall wear) an old rag, after having washed it.

20. He shall not take parts of plants and trees, except such as have become detached (spontaneously).

21. Out of season he shall not dwell a second night in (the same) village.

22. He may either shave or wear a lock on the crown of the head.

23. He shall avoid the destruction of seeds.

24. (He shall be) indifferent towards (all) creatures, (whether they do him) an injury or a kindness.

25. He shall not undertake (anything for his temporal or spiritual welfare).

---

15. Manu VI, 55-56.

19. Âpastamba II, 9, 21, 11.

20. 'He shall not appropriate, i. e. take parts of these, i.e. fruits, leaves, and the like, which have not been detached, i. e. have not fallen off. But he may take what has become detached spontaneously.'—Haradatta.

21. Out of season, i. e. except in the rainy season, during which, according to Sûtra 13, an ascetic must not wander about.

23. 'He shall avoid, i. e. neither himself nor by the agency of others cause the destruction, i. e. the pounding by means of a pestle or the like, of seeds, i. e. raw rice and the like. Hence he shall accept as alms cooked food only, not rice and the like.'—Haradatta.

26. A hermit (shall live) in the forest subsisting on roots and fruits, practising austerities.

27. Kindling the fire according to the (rule of the) Srâma*n*aka (Sûtra, he shall offer oblations in the morning and evening).

28. He shall eat wild-growing (vegetables only).

29. He shall worship gods, manes, men, goblins, and *Ri*shis.

30. He shall receive hospitably (men of) all (castes) except those (with whom intercourse is) forbidden.

31. He may even use the flesh of animals killed by carnivorous beasts.

32. He shall not step on ploughed (land),

33. And he shall not enter a village.

34. He shall wear (his hair in) braids, and dress in (garments made of) bark and skins.

35. He shall not eat anything that has been hoarded for more than a year.

---

26. Âpastamba II, 9, 21, 18—II, 9, 23, 2. 'Austerities (tapas) means emaciating his body.'—Haradatta.

27. 'He shall offer oblations in the morning and evening,' (these words), though not expressed, are understood.

29. I. e. he shall perform the five Mahâyag*ñ*as, just like a householder, only using wild-growing fruits, roots, &c., for the oblations.

31. 'They declare, that baishka means the flesh of an animal, slain by a tiger or the like. He may use even that. The word "even" implies blame. Hence this is a rule for times of distress, and it must be understood that such food is to be eaten only on failure of roots and fruits and the like.'—Haradatta. The commentator adds that the flesh of forbidden animals must be avoided.

34. According to Haradatta the lower garment shall be made of *k*îra, which he again explains as cloth made of Ku*s*a grass and the like, and the upper of a skin.

35. Haradatta reads atisa*m*vatsaram, not atisâ*m*vatsaram, as in

36. But the venerable teacher (prescribes) one order only, because the order of householders is explicitly prescribed (in the Vedas).

CHAPTER IV.

1. A householder shall take a wife (of) equal (caste), who has not belonged to another man and is younger (than himself).

2. A marriage (may be contracted) between persons who have not the same Pravaras,

3. (And) who are not related within six degrees on the father's side,

4. Or on the side of the begetter,

Professor Stenzler's edition, though he notices the latter reading. Manu VI, 15.

36. 'The duties of a householder, the Agnihotra, and the like, are frequently prescribed and praised in all Vedas, Dharmaśâstras, and Itihâsas. As, therefore, the order of householders is explicitly prescribed, this alone is the order (obligatory on all men). But the other orders are prescribed only for those unfit for the (duties of a householder). That is the opinion of many teachers.'—Haradatta. Haradatta's explanation of âkâryâh, which he takes to mean 'many teachers,' seems to me inadmissible. Eke, 'some (teachers),' is used in that sense, and âkâryâh cannot possibly be a synonymous term. Further on (IV, 23) Haradatta himself admits that by âkâryâh one teacher is meant. It must be translated 'the venerable teacher,' because the Hindus are very fond of the use of the pluralis majestatis. I have no doubt that Gautama means his own teacher, whom, of course, etiquette forbids him to name. See also R. Garbe, Uebersetzung des Vaitâna-sûtra, I, 3.

IV. 1. Âpastamba II, 6, 13, 1; Manu III, 4, 12; Yâgñ. I, 52.

2. Regarding the Pravaras, see Max Müller's History of Ancient Sanskrit Literature, p. 386. Âpastamba II, 5, 11, 15.

3. Âpastamba II, 5, 11, 16; Manu III, 5; Yâgñ. I, 52.

4. This rule refers to the case where a husband has made over his wife to another man and the bridegroom stands in the relation of a son to the husband of his mother and to his natural father (dvipitâ). See Yâgñ. I, 68.

5. (Nor) within four degrees on the mother's side.

6. (If the father) gives (his daughter) dressed (in two garments) and decked with ornaments to a person possessing (sacred) learning, of virtuous conduct, who has relatives and a (good) disposition, (that is a) Brâhma (wedding).

7. At the Prâ*g*âpatya (wedding) the marriage-formula is, 'Fulfil ye the law conjointly.'

8. At the Ârsha (wedding the bridegroom) shall present a cow and a bull to him who has (authority over) the maiden.

9. (If the bride) is given, decked with ornaments, to a priest at the altar, that is a Daiva wedding.

10. The spontaneous union with a willing (maiden is called) a Gândharva wedding.

11. If those who have (authority over) a female are propitiated by money, (that is) an Âsura wedding.

12. (If the bride) is taken by force, (that is) a Râkshasa wedding.

13. If (a man) embraces a female deprived of consciousness, (that is) a Pai*s*â*k*a wedding.

14. The first four (rites) are lawful;

15. Some say, (the first) six.

---

5. Yâ*gñ*. I, 53.

6. Âpastamba II, 5, 11, 17. 'Virtuous conduct (*k*âritra), i.e. the performance of the acts prescribed (in the Vedas and Sm*ri*tis), ... good disposition (*s*îla), i.e. faith in the ordinances of the law.'—Haradatta.

7. Manu III, 30; Yâ*gñ*. I, 60.

8. Âpastamba II, 5, 11, 18.

9. Âpastamba II, 5, 11, 19.

10. Âpastamba II, 5, 11, 20.

11. Âpastamba II, 5, 12, 1.

12. Âpastamba II, 5, 12, 2.

13. Manu III, 34; Yâ*gñ*. I, 61.

14. Manu III, 24, 39.

15. Manu III, 23.

16. (Children) born in the regular order of wives of the next, second or third lower castes (become) Savar*n*as, Ambash*th*as, Ugras, Nishâdas, Daushyantas or Pâra*s*avas.

17. (Children born) in the inverted order (of wives of higher castes become) Sûtas, Mâgadhas, Âyogavas, Kshatt*ri*s, Vaidehakas or *K*a*nd*âlas.

18. Some declare, that a woman of the Brâhma*n*a caste has born successively to (husbands of) the (four) castes, sons (who are) Brâhma*n*as, Sûtas, Mâgadhas or *K*a*nd*âlas;

19. (And that) a woman of the Kshatriya caste (has born) to the same, Mûrdhâvasiktas, Kshatriyas, Dhîvaras, Pulkasas;

20. Further, a woman of the Vai*s*ya caste to the same, Bh*rig*yaka*nth*as, Mâhishyas, Vai*s*yas, and Vaidehas;

21. (And) a woman of the *S*ûdra caste to the same, Pâra*s*avas, Yavanas, Kara*n*as, and *S*ûdras.

---

16. I.e. from a Brâhma*n*a and a Kshatriyâ springs a Savar*n*a, from a Brâhma*n*a and a Vai*s*yâ a Nishâda, from a Brâhma*n*a and a *S*ûdrâ a Pâra*s*ava, from a Kshatriya and a Vai*s*yâ an Ambash*th*a, and from a Kshatriya and a *S*ûdrâ a Daushyanta, from a Vai*s*ya and a *S*ûdrâ an Ugra. Compare for this and the following five Sûtras Manu X, 6–18; Yâ*gñ*. I, 91–95.

17. I.e. from a Kshatriya and a Brâhma*n*î springs a Sûta, from a Vai*s*ya and a Kshatriyâ a Mâgadha, from a *S*ûdra and a Vai*s*yâ an Âyogava, from a Vai*s*ya and a Brâhma*n*î a Kshatt*ri*, from a *S*ûdra and a Kshatriyâ a Vaidehaka, from a *S*ûdra and a Brâhma*n*î a *K*a*nd*âla.

18. The words 'Some declare' stand only at the end of Sûtra 21. But Haradatta rightly declares that they refer to all the four Sûtras. The proof for the correctness of his interpretation lies in the use of the form a*g*î*g*anat, which refers to each of the Sûtras. The four Sûtras are, however, probably spurious, as Sûtra 28 refers back to Sûtra 17 by calling the *K*a*nd*âla 'the last (named).'

22. In the seventh (generation men obtain) a change of caste, either being raised to a higher one or being degraded to a lower one.

23. The venerable teacher declares (that this happens) in the fifth (generation).

24. And (the same rule applies) to those born (from parents of different classes that are) intermediate between (two of the castes originally) created (by Brahman).

25. But those born in the inverse order (from fathers of a lower and mothers of a higher caste stand) outside (the pale of) the sacred law,

---

22. Âpastamba II, 5, 11, 10–11. 'That is as follows: If a Savar*n*â female, born of the Kshatriya wife of a Brâhma*n*a, is married to a Brâhma*n*a, and her female descendants down to the seventh likewise, then the offspring which that seventh female descendant bears to her Brâhma*n*a husband is equal in caste to a Brâhma*n*a. In like manner, if a Savar*n*a male, the son of a Brâhma*n*a and of his Kshatriya wife, again marries a Kshatriya wife and his male descendants down to the seventh likewise, then the offspring of that seventh male descendant is equal in caste to a Kshatriya. The same principle must be applied to the offspring of Kshatriyas and wives of the Vai*s*ya caste as well as to Vai*s*yas and wives of the *S*ûdra caste.'—Haradatta.

23. '(The venerable) teacher opines that the change of caste takes place in the fifth generation. They declare that the plural may be used to denote one teacher. This Sûtra refers to (cases of extraordinary merit acquired through) virtuous conduct and study of the Veda.'—Haradatta. It is clear that in this case Haradatta, too, has seen that the word â*k*âryâ*h* has another force than the more common eke; see above, note to III, 36.

24. 'That is as follows: If the daughter of a Savar*n*a, born of a wife of the Ambash*th*a caste, is married again to a Savar*n*a, and her female descendants down to the seventh likewise, then the offspring of that seventh female descendant, begotten by a Savar*n*a husband, is equal in caste to a Savar*n*a.'—Haradatta. Regarding the birth of the four castes from Brahman, see Rig-veda X, 90, 12.

25. Manu X, 41, 67–68.

26. As well as (those born in the regular order) from a female of the *S*ûdra caste.

27. But he whom a *S*ûdra (begets) on a female of unequal caste shall be treated like an outcast.

28. The last (named, the *K*a*nd*âla), is the foulest.

29. Virtuous sons (born of wives of equal caste) and wedded according to approved rites sanctify (their father's family).

30. (A son born of a wife married) according to the Ârsha rite (saves) three ancestors (from hell),

31. (A son born of a wife married) according to the Daiva rite ten,

32. (A son born of a wife married) according to the Prâ*g*âpatya rite, also ten.

33. (But) the son of a wife married according to the Brâhma rite (saves) ten ancestors, ten descendants, and himself.

Chapter V.

1. (A householder) shall approach (his wife) in the proper season,

2. Or (he may do so) at any time except on the forbidden (days).

---

26. Manu X, 68.

27. '"Shall be treated like an outcast," i.e. one must avoid to look at him, &c., just as in the case of an outcast.'—Haradatta.

28. Manu X, 51-56.

30. Manu III, 38; Yâ*gñ*. I, 59.

31. Manu III, 38; Yâ*gñ*. I, 59.

32. Manu III, 38; Yâ*gñ*. I, 60.

33. Manu III, 37; Yâ*gñ*. I, 58.

V. 1. Âpastamba II, 1, 1, 17.

2. Âpastamba II, 1, 1, 18.

3. He shall worship gods, manes, men, goblins, (and) *Ri*shis.

4. Every day he shall recite privately (a portion of the Veda),

5. And the (daily) libation of water to the manes (is obligatory on him).

6. Other (rites than these he may perform) according to his ability.

7. The (sacred) fire (must be kindled) on his marriage or on the division of the family estate.

8. The domestic (ceremonies must be performed) with (the aid of) that (fire).

9. (Also) the sacrifices to the gods, manes, (and) men, and the private recitation (and) the Bali-offerings.

---

3. Âpastamba I, 4, 12, 15; I, 4, 13, 1; Manu III, 69–72; IV, 29, 21; Yâg*ñ*. I, 99, 102–104.

4. Manu III, 81; Yâg*ñ*. I, 104.

5. Manu III, 82; Yâg*ñ*. I, 104. 'The word "and" indicates that water must be offered to the gods and *Ri*shis also.'—Haradatta.

6. '(Rites) other than those prescribed in Sûtras 3–5 he may perform according to his energy, i.e. according to his ability. But those he should zealously perform. As the oblations to the gods and the other (Mahâyag*ñ*as) are mentioned before the kindling of the domestic fire, they must be performed by a person who has not yet kindled the domestic fire with the aid of the common (kitchen)-fire.'—Haradatta.

7. As long as the family remains united, its head offers the oblations for all its members.

8. 'The domestic rites, i.e. the Pu*m*savana and the rest. . . . Now with the aid of which fire must a man, who has not yet kindled the domestic fire, perform the Pu*m*savana, &c.? Some answer that he shall use a common fire. But the opinion of the teacher (Gautama) is that he shall use the sacred fire which has been kindled on that occasion.'—Haradatta.

9. Haradatta states that the Mahâyag*ñ*as are again enumerated in order to show that a person who has kindled the sacred fire

10. The oblations (which are thrown) into the (sacred) fire (at the Vaisvadeva-sacrifice are offered) to Agni, to Dhanvantari, to all the gods, to Pragâpati, (and to Agni) Svishtakrit;

11. And (Bali-offerings must be given) to the deities presiding over the (eight) points of the horizon, in their respective places,

12. At the doors (of the house) to the Maruts,

13. To the deities of the dwelling inside (the house),

---

shall use this for them, not a common fire. He also states that a passage of Usanas, according to which some teachers prescribe the performance of the daily recitation near the sacred fire, shows that this rite too has a connection with the sacred fire.

10. Âpastamba II, 2, 3, 16, where, however, as in all other works, the order of the offerings differs. Haradatta adds that the word 'oblations' is used in the Sûtra in order to indicate that the word svâhâ must be pronounced at the end of each Mantra, and that the expression 'in the fire' indicates that the Bali-offerings described in the following Sûtra must be thrown on the ground.

11. Compare Âpastamba II, 2, 3, 20—II, 2, 4, 8; Manu III, 87–90, where, as elsewhere, the order of the offerings differs. According to Haradatta the deities intended are, Indra, Agni, Yama, Nirriti, Varuna, Vâyu, Soma, and Îsâna. The first offering must be placed to the east, the next to the south-east, south, &c.

12. At all the doors, as many as there are, a Bali must be offered with the Mantra, 'To the Maruts, svâhâ.'—Haradatta.

13. 'As he says "inside" (pravisya, literally "entering") he must stand outside while offering the Balis at the doors. . . . At this occasion some require the following Mantra, "To the deities of the dwelling, svâhâ," because that is found in the Âsvalâyana (Grihya-sûtra I, 2, 4). Others consider it necessary to mention the deities by name, and to present as many offerings as there are deities, while pronouncing the required words.'—Haradatta. The commentator then goes on to quote a passage from Usanas, which he considers applicable, because it contains the names of the Grihadevatâs. I doubt, however, if the 'others' are right, and still more if, in case they should be right, it would be advisable to supply the names of the Grihadevatâs from Usanas.

14. To Brahman in the centre (of the house),

15. To the Waters near the water-pot,

16. To the Ether in the air,

17. And to the Beings walking about at night in the evening.

18. A gift of food shall be preceded by a libation of water and (it shall be presented) after (the recipient) has been made to say, 'May welfare attend thee,'

19. And the same (rule applies) to all gifts presented for the sake of spiritual merit.

20. The reward of a gift (offered) to a person who is not a Brâhma*n*a is equal (to the value of the gift), those (of presents given) to a Brâhma*n*a twofold, to a *S*rotriya thousandfold, to one who knows the whole Veda (vedapâraga) endless.

21. Presents of money (must be given) outside the Vedi to persons begging for their Gurus, (or) in order to defray the expenses of their wedding, (or

---

14. 'Because the word "and" occurs in Sûtra 11 after the word "to the deities presiding over the points of the horizon" a Bali-offering must be presented to the deities mentioned by the author in Sûtra 10, viz. to the earth, wind, Pragâpati, and to all the gods, after a Bali has been offered to Brahman.'—Haradatta.

16. 'The Bali presented to Âkâ*s*a, "the ether," must be thrown up into the air, as Manu says, III, 90.'—Haradatta.

17. 'Because of the word "and," he must, also, present Balis to the deities mentioned above.'—Haradatta. The commentator means to say that in the evening not only the 'Beings walking about at night' (nakta*mk*ara) are to receive a portion, but all the other deities too, and that the Balikarma must be offered twice a day.

18–19. Âpastamba II, 4, 9, 8.

20. According to Haradatta the term *S*rotriya here denotes one who has studied one Veda, (but see also Âpastamba II, 3, 6, 4; II, 4, 8, 5.) Vedapâraga is a man who has studied one Veda, together with the Angas, Kalpa-sûtras, and Upanishads.

21. Âpastamba II, 5, 10, 1–2. 'Now he promulgates a Sûtra

to procure) medicine for the sick, to those who are without means of subsistence, to those who are going to offer a sacrifice, to those engaged in study, to travellers, (and) to those who have performed the Visvagit-sacrifice.

22. Prepared food (must be given) to other beggars.

23. For an unlawful purpose he shall not give (anything), though he may have promised it.

24. An untruth spoken by people under the influence of anger, excessive joy, fear, pain (or) greed, by infants, very old men, persons labouring under a delusion, those being under the influence of drink (or) by mad men does not cause (the speaker) to fall.

25. Before (a householder eats) he shall feed his guests, the infants, the sick people, the pregnant women, the females under his protection, the very aged men, and those of low condition (who may be in his house).

---

which refers to those cases where one must necessarily make gifts, and where one incurs guilt by a refusal. . . . As the expression "outside the Vedi" is used, presents must be given to others also "inside the Vedi" (i.e. fees to priests, &c.)'—Haradatta.

22. Âpastamba II, 2, 4, 14.

23. Âpastamba II, 5, 10, 3; Colebrooke II, Digest IV, 47; Mayûkha IX, 5. 'As he says "for an unlawful purpose," what has been promised must in other cases necessarily be given.'—Haradatta.

24. Colebrooke II, Digest IV, 56. '"Does not cause (the speaker) to fall," i.e. produces no guilt. Hence such persons need not even give a promised present.'—Haradatta.

25. Âpastamba II, 2, 4, 11–13; II, 4, 9, 10; Manu III, 116. 'Females under his protection (suvâsinyah), i.e. daughters and sisters . . . , those of low condition (gaghanyâh), i.e. servants, slaves, and the like. . . . The term "men of low condition" is made a separate word in the text in order to show that they come after the others.'—Haradatta.

26. But (when) his teacher, parents (or intimate) friends (visit his house), he shall proceed to the preparation of the dinner after asking them (for orders).

27. When an officiating priest, his teacher, his father-in-law, paternal or maternal uncles visit (him), a Madhuparka (or honey-mixture must be offered to them).

28. (If they have been once honoured in this manner, the ceremony need be) repeated (only) after a year.

29. (But) on (the occasion of) a sacrifice and of the wedding (a Madhuparka must be offered, though) less than a year (has passed since the last visit of the persons thus honoured).

30. And to a king who is a *S*rotriya (a Madhuparka must be offered as often as he comes),

31. (But to a king) who is not a *S*rotriya a seat and water.

32. But for a *S*rotriya he shall cause to be prepared a foot-bath, an Arghya, and food of a superior quality,

---

26. Manu III, 113.

27. Âpastamba II, 4, 8, 5–9.

30. 'And to a king a Madhuparka must be offered on his arrival. If he is a *S*rotriya (this must be done) on each visit.'—Haradatta.

31. 'A king who is not a *S*rotriya shall be honoured with a seat and water, not with a Madhuparka.'—Haradatta.

32. Âpastamba II, 3, 6, 7–10, 14–15. 'This Sûtra may be optionally taken as referring to a Brâhma*n*a, because the word *S*rotriya is repeated. For a *S*rotriya who has come as a guest, a foot-bath, i. e. water for washing the feet, an Arghya, i. e. water mixed with Dûrvâ grass, flowers, &c., and food of a superior quality, i. e. milk and rice; cakes and the like shall be particularly prepared, if the host is able to afford it.'—Haradatta.

33. Or his usual food distinguished by a (particularly careful) preparation.

34. To a (Brâhma*n*a) who is not learned in the Vedas, (but) of good conduct, food of a middling (quality) shall be given,

35. To one who is the reverse (of virtuous) grass, water, and earth,

36. (Or) at least a welcome.

37. Honour (must be shown to a guest, and the host must) not dine better (than his guest).

38. A couch, a seat, (and) a lodging (of the) same (quality as the host uses must be given) to (a guest) of equal condition and to one's betters; they must be accompanied (on departure) and respectfully attended to (during their stay).

39. (The host shall show similar) though less (attention) to (a guest) who is inferior (to himself).

---

33. 'But if (the host is) not able (to afford dainties), he shall prepare that same food which is daily used in his house, distinguished in the preparation, i. e. by adding pepper and the like condiments, by frying it, and so forth.'—Haradatta.

34. Âpastamba II, 2, 4, 16; II, 3, 6, 12. Haradatta points out that in this case nothing but a simple dinner shall be given.

36. Âpastamba II, 2, 4, 14. 'On failure of grass and the rest, a welcome, i. e. (the host shall say), "Thou art tired, sit down here."'—Haradatta.

37. Manu III, 106–107. 'This Sûtra refers solely to such a guest, as is described below, Sûtra 40.'—Haradatta.

38. 'Accompanying, i. e. walking after him; respectfully attending to, i. e. sitting with him and so forth. As it is not possible that these two acts can be performed by the host in the same manner as for himself, the meaning of the Sûtra must be taken to be merely that they are to be performed.'—Haradatta.

39. Haradatta says that some explain this Sûtra to mean, '(The host shall show the same attention) even to a man who is a little inferior (to himself in learning, &c.),' but that he disapproves of their opinion.

40. He is called a guest who, belonging to a different village (and) intending to stay for one night only, arrives when the sun's beams pass over the trees.

41. According (to his caste a guest) must be asked about his well-being (ku*s*ala), about his being free from hurt (anâmaya), or about his health (ârogya).

42. The last (formula must also be used in addressing) a *S*ûdra.

43. A man of a lower caste (is) not (to be considered) a guest by a Brâhma*n*a, except if he has approached on (the occasion of) a sacrifice.

44. But a Kshatriya must be fed after the Brâhma*n*a (guests).

45. (Men of) other (castes he shall feed) with his servants for mercy's sake.

CHAPTER VI.

1. (To salute) every day on meeting (by) an embrace of the feet,

2. And (particularly) on return from a journey,

3. (Is prescribed in the case) of parents, of their blood relations, of elder (brothers), of persons venera-

---

40. Âpastamba II, 3, 6, 5. Haradatta states, that by 'the time when the sun's rays pass over the trees,' either the middle of the day or the late afternoon may be meant.

41. Âpastamba I, 4, 14, 26–29.

43. Âpastamba II, 2, 4, 18–19.

VI. 1. Âpastamba I, 4, 14, 7–9; I, 2, 5, 18; I, 2, 8, 17–18.

3. 'Their blood relations, i.e. paternal and maternal uncles and the rest; elders, i.e. elder brothers; persons venerable on account of their learning, i.e. the teacher who has initiated him (â*k*ârya), the teacher who has instructed him (upâdhyâya), and the rest.'—Haradatta.

ble on account of their learning, and of the Gurus of the latter.

4. On meeting (several persons, to whom such a salutation is due), together, the most venerable (must be saluted first).

5. On meeting persons who understand (the rule of returning salutes) one shall salute (them) pronouncing one's name, and (saying), 'I N. N. (ho! salute thee).'

6. Some (declare that) there is no restrictive rule for salutations between man and wife.

---

4. Âpastamba I, 2, 6, 29; I, 2, 8, 19. 'On meeting his mother and other persons whose feet must be embraced, he shall first embrace the highest, i.e. the most excellent, afterwards the others. Who the most excellent is has been declared above, II, 50–51.

5. Âpastamba I, 2, 5, 12–15. Professor Stenzler reads *agña*-samavâye, while my copies and their commentary show that *gña*samavâye has to be read. Besides, it seems impossible to make any sense out of the former reading without assuming that the construction is strongly elliptical. 'On meeting, i.e. on coming together with him who knows the rule of returning a salute, he shall utter, i.e. loudly pronounce his name, i.e. the name which he has received on the tenth day (after his birth), and which is to be employed in saluting, and speak the word "I" as well as the word "this." They declare that instead of the word "this," which here is explicitly prescribed, the word "I am" must be used. Some salute thus, "I Haradatta by name;" others, "I Haradatta*s*arman;" and the common usage is to say, "I Haradatta-*s*arman by name." Thus the salutation must be made. Salutation means saluting. The affix a*k* is added to causatives and the rest. With reference to this matter the rule for returning salutes has been described by Manu II, 126. . . . As (in the above Sûtra) the expression "on meeting persons knowing" is used, those who are unacquainted with the manner of returning a salute must not be saluted in this manner. How is it then to be done? It is described by Manu III, 123.'—Haradatta.

6. 'As Gautama says, "Some declare," the restrictive rule must, in his opinion, be followed.'—Haradatta.

7. (The feet of) other female (relations) than the mother, a paternal uncle's wife and (elder) sisters (need) not (be embraced, nor need they be saluted) except on return from a journey.

8. The feet of wives of brothers and of the mother-in-law (need) not be embraced (on any occasion).

9. But (on the arrival of an) officiating priest, a father-in-law, paternal and maternal uncles who are younger (than oneself), one must rise; they need not be saluted (as prescribed above, Sûtra 5).

10. In like manner (any) other aged fellow-citizen, even a *S*ûdra of eighty years and more, (must be honoured) by one young enough to be his son,

11. (And) an Ârya, though (he be) younger, by a *S*ûdra;

12. And he shall avoid (to pronounce) the name of that (person who is worthy of a salutation).

13. And an official who (is) not (able to) recite (the Veda shall avoid to pronounce the name) of the king.

---

7. Manu II, 132; Âpastamba I, 4, 14, 6, 9.

9. Âpastamba I, 4, 14, 11.

10. 'Old (pûrva), i. e. of greater age. . . . A *S*ûdra even, who answers this description, must be honoured by rising, not, however, be saluted by one young enough to be his son, i. e. by a Brâhma*n*a who is very much younger. The *S*ûdra is mentioned as an instance of a man of inferior caste. Hence a *S*ûdra must (under these circumstances) be honoured by rising, not be saluted by men of the three higher castes, a Vai*s*ya by those of the two higher castes, and a Kshatriya by a Brâhma*n*a.'—Haradatta.

11. 'An Ârya, i. e. a man of the three twice-born castes, though he be inferior, i. e. younger, must be honoured by rising, not be saluted by a *S*ûdra. The *S*ûdra is mentioned in order to give an instance of (a man of) inferior caste.'—Haradatta.

12. 'An inferior shall avoid to take his name, i.e. that of a superior.'—Haradatta.

14. A contemporary who is born on the same day (shall be addressed with the terms) bho*h* or bhavan (your honour),

15. (Likewise) a fellow-citizen who is ten years older (than oneself),

16. (Also) an artist who is five years (older),

17. And a *S*rotriya belonging to one's own Vedic school who is three years older,

18. (Further), Brâhma*n*as destitute of learning and those who follow the occupations of Kshatriyas or Vai*s*yas,

19. And (a contemporary) who has performed the Dîksha*n*îyesh*t*i of a Soma-sacrifice before he buys (the Soma).

20. Wealth, relations, occupation, birth, learning, and age must be honoured; (but) each later named

---

14. Haradatta says that samânehani, 'on the same day,' means 'in the same year.' He is probably right in thinking that the expression must not be interpreted too strictly. But his assertion that aha*h* means also 'year' cannot be proved by his quotation from the Nigha*nt*uka, abde sa*m*vatsaram ahar*g*aram.

15. 'A person aged by ten years, i. e. at least ten years older, who lives in the same town as oneself, is to be addressed as bho*h*, bhavan, though he may be deficient in good qualities.'—Haradatta.

16. 'The words "years older" must be understood. He who lives by the fine arts (kalâ), i. e. the knowledge of music, painting, leaf-cutting, and the like, and is at least five years older than oneself, must be addressed as bho*h* or bhavan.'—Haradatta.

17. Haradatta notes that Âpastamba I, 4, 14, 13 gives a somewhat different rule.

18. Haradatta adds that a person destitute of learning, be he ever so old, may still be treated as an equal, and addressed as bho*h*, bhavan, by a more learned man.

20. Manu II, 136. 'As wealth and the rest cannot be directly honoured, the persons possessing them are to be honoured. . . . . Respect (mâna) means honour shown by saluting and the like.'—Haradatta.

(quality) is more important (than the preceding ones).

21. But sacred learning is more important than all (other good qualities),

22. Because that is the root of the sacred law,

23. And because the Veda (expressly declarés it).

24. Way must be made for a man seated in a carriage, for one who is in his tenth (decade), for one requiring consideration, for a woman, for a Snâtaka, and for a king.

25. But a king (must make way) for a *S*rotriya.

Chapter VII.

1. The rule for (times of) distress (is) that a Brâhma*n*a may study under a teacher who is not a Brâhma*n*a.

2. (A student is bound) to walk behind and to obey (his non-Brahmanical teacher).

3. (But) when (the course of study) has been finished, the Brâhma*n*a (pupil is more) venerable (than his teacher).

4. (In times of distress it is permissible) to offer

---

21. Manu II, 154.

23. Haradatta says that a passage to this effect occurs in the *Kh*ândogya-brâhma*n*a. He also refers to Manu II, 151.

24. Âpastamba II, 5, 11, 5, 7-9. 'A person requiring consideration, i. e. one afflicted by disease. A woman, i. e. a bride or a pregnant woman. A Snâtaka, i. e. a person who has bathed after completing his studies and after having kept the vow of studentship.'—Haradatta.

25. Âpastamba II, 5, 11, 6.

VII. 1. Âpastamba II, 2, 4, 25.

2. Âpastamba II, 2, 4, 26. 3. Âpastamba II, 2, 4, 27.

4. Haradatta quotes Manu X, 103 in support of the above explanation, and adds that another commentator interprets the

sacrifices for (men of) all (castes), to teach (them), and to accept (presents from them).

5. Each preceding (mode of living is) preferable (to those named later).

6. On failure of the (occupations lawful for a Brâhma*n*a) he may live by the occupations of a Kshatriya.

7. On failure of those, he may live by the occupations of a Vai*s*ya.

8. (Goods) that may not be sold by a (Brâhma*n*a are),

9. Perfumes, substances (used for) flavouring (food), prepared food, sesamum, hempen and linen cloth, skins,

10. Garments dyed red or washed,

11. Milk and preparations from it,

12. Roots, fruits, flowers, medicines, honey, flesh, grass, water, poison,

---

Sûtra to mean, that in times of distress men of all castes may support themselves by sacrificing for others, teaching, and the acceptance of gifts, though in ordinary times these modes of living are reserved for Brâhma*n*as.

5. The use of the masculine in the text, 'pûrva*h* pûrvo guru*h*,' may, I think, be explained by the fact that the compound in the preceding Sûtra ends with a noun of the masculine gender.

6. Manu X, 81; Yâ*g*ñ. III, 35. 7. Âpastamba I, 7, 20, 11.

9. Âpastamba I, 7, 20, 12–13. 'Substances used for flavouring (rasa), i. e. oil, sugar, clarified butter, salt, and the like.'—Haradatta. From Sûtra 19 it is clear that 'rasa' does not simply mean 'liquids.'

10. My MSS. read nir*n*ikte for nikte, and nir*n*iktam is explained by 'washed by a washerman or the like person.' It is possible to translate Professor Stenzler's reading in accordance with Manu X, 87, 'pairs of (i. e. upper and lower) garments dyed red.'

11. 'Preparations from it, i. e. sour milk and the like.'—Haradatta.

13. Nor animals for slaughter,

14. Nor, under any circumstances, human beings, heifers, female calves, cows big with young.

15. Some (declare, that the traffic in) land, rice, barley, goats, sheep, horses, bulls, milch-cows, and draught-oxen (is) likewise (forbidden).

16. But (it is permissible) to barter,

17. One kind of substances used for flavouring others,

18. And animals (for animals).

19. Salt and prepared food (must) not (be bartered),

20. Nor sesamum.

21. But for present use an equal (quantity of) uncooked (food may be exchanged) for cooked (food).

22. But if no (other course is) possible (a Brâhma*n*a) may support himself in any way except by (following the occupations) of a *S*ûdra.

23. Some (permit) even this in case his life is in danger.

24. But to mix with that (caste) and forbidden food must be avoided (even in times of distress).

---

14. 'Under any circumstances (nityam, literally "always") means even when they are not sold for slaughter. Another (commentator) says, that, as the expression "under any circumstances" is used here, the prohibition regarding the above-mentioned things, i.e. sesamum and the like, does not hold good under all circumstances, and that hence self-grown sesamum and other grain may be sold, see Manu X, 90.'—Haradatta.

15. Manu X, 88. Haradatta explains 'land' by 'houses.'

16–21. Âpastamba I, 7, 20, 14–15.

19. 'The sale of salt and prepared food has been forbidden by Sûtra 9, but their barter has been permitted (by Sûtra 17).'—Haradatta.

22. Regarding the *S*ûdra's occupations, see below, X, 57–60.

24. 'Restriction (niyama), i. e. avoiding. That Brâhma*n*a

25. If his life is threatened, even a Brâhma*n*a may use arms.

26. (In times of distress) a Kshatriya (may follow) the occupations of a Vai*s*ya.

Chapter VIII.

1. A king and a Brâhma*n*a, deeply versed in the Vedas, these two, uphold the moral order in the world.

2. On them depends the existence of the fourfold human race, of internally conscious beings, of those which move on feet and on wings, and of those which creep,

---

even who lives the life of a *S*ûdra must not mix with that *S*ûdra caste, i.e. he must not sit among *S*ûdras and so forth.'—Haradatta.

25. Âpastamba I, 10, 29, 7; Manu VIII, 348.

26. Haradatta adds, that in accordance with the principle exemplified by the rule of this Sûtra a Vai*s*ya may follow in times of distress the occupations of a *S*ûdra.

VIII. 1. *S*atapatha-brâhma*n*a V, 4, 4, 5; Weber, Ind. Stud. X, 29. Haradatta explains vrata, 'moral order,' by karmâ*n*i, 'the rites and occupations,' and loka, 'world,' by râsh*t*ra, 'kingdom.' Ultimately my translation and his explanation come to the same thing. He adds that the king upholds order by punishing, and a learned Brâhma*n*a by teaching. Regarding the excellence of these two, see also Manu IV, 135.

2. 'Internally conscious beings, i.e. trees and the like, which are immovable, but grow and decay. For such possess internal consciousness only, no corresponding external faculty of acting.... The existence of these, i.e. of men and the rest, depends upon, i.e. is subordinate to the king and to a Brâhma*n*a deeply versed in the Vedas. How is that? As regards the Brâhma*n*a, an offering which has been properly thrown into the fire reaches the sun; from the sun comes rain; from rain food is produced and thereon live the creatures. By this reasoning he is shown to

3. (As well as) the protection of offspring, the prevention of the confusion (of the castes and) the sacred law.

4. He is (called) deeply versed in the Vedas,

5. Who is acquainted with the (ways of the) world, the Vedas (and their) Aṅgas (auxiliary sciences),

6. Who is skilled in disputations (and), in (reciting) legends and the Purâ*n*a,

7. Who looks to these (alone), and lives according to these,

8. Who has been sanctified by the forty sacraments (sa*m*skâra),

9. Who is constantly engaged in the three occupations (prescribed for all twice-born men),

10. Or in the six (occupations prescribed specially for a Brâhma*n*a),

11. (And) who is well versed in the duties of

---

be the cause of their existence. But the king is (also) the cause of their existence; for he punishes robbers and the like.'—Haradatta.

3. Haradatta takes prasûtiraksha*n*am, 'the protection of their offspring,' as a copulative compound, and explains it by 'their prosperity (abhiv*ri*ddhi) and their protection.' But a samâhâra-dvandva is here out of place.

4. Macnaghten, Mitâksharâ I, 2, 27. 'By the word loka, "the world," are intended the laws of countries and the like, which may be learnt from the practice of the world.'—Haradatta. Regarding the Aṅgas, see Âpastamba II, 4, 8, 10.

8. Regarding the forty sacraments, see below, Sûtras 14–20.

9. Regarding the three occupations, common to all twice-born men, see below, X, 1.

10. See below, X, 2.

11. The Sâmayâ*k*ârika or Smârta duties are those taught in the Dharma-sûtras and Sm*ri*tis, see Âpastamba I, 1, 1, 1, and Max Müller's History of Ancient Sanskrit Literature, p. 101.

daily life settled by the agreement (of those who know the law).

12. (Such a Brâhma*n*a) must be allowed by the king immunity from (the following) six (kinds of opprobrious treatment):

13. (I. e.) he must not be subjected to corporal punishment, he must not be imprisoned, he must not be fined, he must not be exiled, he must not be reviled, nor be excluded.

14. The Garbhâdhâna (or ceremony to cause conception), the Pu*m*savana (or ceremony to cause the birth of a male child), the Sîmantonnayana (or arranging the parting of the pregnant wife's hair), the *G*âtakarman (or ceremony on the birth of the child), the ceremony of naming the child, the first feeding, the *K*aula (or tonsure of the head of the child), the initiation,

15. The four vows (undertaken) for the study of the Veda,

16. The bath (on completion of the studentship),

---

12. See Weber, Ind. Stud. X, 41, 60, 66; Macnaghten, Mitâksharâ I, 2, 27.

14. Regarding the Sa*m*skâras mentioned in this Sûtra, see Â*s*valâyana G*ri*hya-sûtra I, 13-23; *S*âṅkhâyana G*ri*hya-sûtra I, 19—II, 5; Pâraskara G*ri*hya-sûtra I, 13—II, 2.

15. The four vows, as Haradatta states, are, according to Â*s*valâyana, the Mahânâmnîvrata, the Mahâvrata, the Upanishadvrata, and the Godâna; see Â*s*valâyana *S*rauta-sûtra VIII, 14, where the first three are described in detail, and G*ri*hya-sûtra I, 22, 3, with the commentary thereon. Other G*ri*hya-sûtras give more and different names, see H. Oldenberg, *S*âṅkhâyana G*ri*hya-sûtra II, 11-12 (S. B. E., vol. xxix), and Gobhila G*ri*hya-sûtra III, 1, 28—III, 2, 62.

16. Haradatta explains snâna, 'the bath,' by samâvartana, 'the ceremony on completion of the studentship.' Regarding the five sacrifices, usually called the great sacrifices, see above, VII, 9 seq.

the taking of a help-mate for the fulfilment of the religious duties, the performance of the five sacrifices to gods, manes, men, goblins, and Brahman,

17. And (the performance) of the following (sacrifices):

18. The seven kinds of Pâkayag*ñ*as (or small sacrifices), viz. the Ash*t*akâ, the Pârva*n*a (Sthâlîpâka, offered on the new and full moon days), the funeral oblations, the *S*râva*n*î, the Âgrahâya*n*î, the *K*aitrî, and the Âsvayu*g*î;

19. The seven kinds of Haviryag*ñ*as, viz. the Agnyâdheya, the Agnihotra, the Dar*s*apaur*n*amâsas, the Âgraya*n*a, the *K*âturmâsyas, the Nirû*dh*apa*s*ubandha, and the Sautrâma*n*î;

20. The seven kinds of Soma-sacrifices, viz. the Agnish*t*oma, the Atyagnish*t*oma, the Ukthya, the Sho*d*a*s*in, the Atirâtra, and the Aptoryâma;

21. These are the forty sacraments.

22. Now (follow) the eight good qualities of the soul,

---

18. The various Pâkayag*ñ*as, named here, are fully described by Â*s*valâyana G*ri*hya-sûtra II, 1, 1—II, 10, 8; Gobhila III, 10 seq.; Pâraskara III, 3 seq. See also Max Müller, History of Ancient Sanskrit Literature, p. 203. The Ash*t*akâs are sacrifices offered on the eighth day of the dark halves of the winter months, and of those of the dewy season, i.e. Kârttika, Mârga*s*iras, Pausha, and Mâgha. The *S*râva*n*î is offered on the full moon day of the month of *S*râva*n*a, the Âgrahâya*n*î on the fourteenth, or on the full moon day of Mârga*s*iras, the *K*aitrî on the full moon day of the *K*aitra, and the Â*s*vayu*g*î on the full moon day of the month Â*s*vayu*g*a or Â*s*vina.

19–20. The Haviryag*ñ*as and Soma-sacrifices are described in the Brâhma*n*as and *S*rauta-sûtras. Havis denotes any kind of food used for oblations, such as clarified butter, milk, rice, meat, &c.

22. Âpastamba I, 8, 23, 6.

23. (Viz.) compassion on all creatures, forbearance, freedom from anger, purity, quietism, auspiciousness, freedom from avarice, and freedom from covetousness.

24. He who is sanctified by these forty sacraments, but whose soul is destitute of the eight good qualities, will not be united with Brahman, nor does he reach his heaven.

25. But he, forsooth, who is sanctified by a few only of these forty sacraments, and whose soul is endowed with the eight excellent qualities, will be united with Brahman, and will dwell in his heaven.

Chapter IX.

1. Such (a man) shall bathe, after (having fulfilled) the law (regarding studentship), take unto him a wife, and, fulfilling the duties of a householder which have been declared above, in addition obey the following ordinances :

---

23. Haradatta explains maṅgalya, 'auspiciousness, to mean 'always doing what is praised (by good men) and avoiding what is blamed by them.' Anâyâsa, 'quietism,' means, according to him, 'avoiding to undertake that which causes pain to oneself, even though it be a duty.'

IX. 1. Âpastamba I, 11, 30, 1-4. Haradatta says that the expression sa, 'such (a man),' refers to the king and to the Brâhma*n*a deeply versed in the Vedas, who have been described in the preceding chapter. My MSS. insert between this and the following one another Sûtra, which has been left out in Professor Stenzler's edition. It seems to me that it is absolutely required, and I therefore insert it here, together with Haradatta's comment, according to my best copy, P.

Gautama: '(And) a Snâtaka (i.e, a person who has completed his studentship, but has not yet taken a wife, shall act thus).' Haradatta: 'It must be understood that the word "and" has been left

2. (He shall be) always pure (and) sweet-smelling (and) bathe frequently.

3. If he possesses wealth, he shall not be dressed in old or dirty clothes;

4. Nor shall he wear dyed or sumptuous garments, nor such as have been worn (before) by others,

5. Nor a garland and shoes (that have been worn by others).

6. (He may wear a cast-off garment) which has been washed, if he is unable (to afford a new one).

7. He shall not allow his beard to grow without a (sufficient) reason.

---

out. (The meaning is): "And a Snâtaka shall obey the following ordinances." If this Sûtra were not given, those ordinances would have to be obeyed after marriage only; and if the preceding Sûtra (1) had not been given, before marriage only, because the term Snâtaka is usually employed in that (sense) only. For this reason both (Sûtras) have been given. Hence, though a man may not enter another order, he shall, after taking the bath (on completion of his studentship), obey these ordinances during his whole life. As here (Sûtra 1) the word sa, "such a man," is used, a Kshatriya and a Brâhma*n*a only must necessarily obey the rules prescribed for a Snâtaka and perform a penance for breaking them; and the penance for breaking the rules prescribed for a Snâtaka is fasting. This is (the object of the insertion of the word sa, "such (a man)." But, if a Vai*s*ya follows them, (his reward will be) prosperity; if he breaks them, he need not perform a penance. With respect to this matter another Sm*ri*ti says: "The penance which is prescribed for a breach of the Snâtaka laws, must be performed by a Kshatriya and a Brâhma*n*a alone, never by (men of) the other (caste)."'

2. Manu IV, 35.

3-4. Âpastamba I, 11, 30, 10-13. 5. Manu IV, 66.

6. According to Haradatta the same rule applies to garlands and shoes.

7. Manu IV, 35. 'The expression "his beard" includes by implication the nails and the rest. . . . . As he says "without a sufficient reason," he shall allow his beard to grow during the preg-

8. He shall not carry water and fire at the same time.

9. He shall not drink out of his joined hands.

10. He shall not sip water standing, nor (shall he sip) water drawn up (from a well),

11. Nor (water) that is offered by a *S*ûdra or an impure man, or that has been taken up with one hand.

12. Facing or within sight of wind, fire, Brâhma*n*as, the sun, water, (images of the) gods, and cows he shall not eject urine or fæces or other impurities.

13. He shall not stretch out his feet towards those divine beings.

14. He shall not remove urine or fæces with leaves, clods of earth, or stones.

15. He shall not stand upon ashes, hair, nail (parings), husks (of grain), pot-sherds, or impure substances.

16. He shall not converse with barbarians, impure or wicked men.

---

nancy of his wife and on other occasions. With respect to this matter they quote the following verse: "In the sixth year and in the sixteenth year, likewise in the year of his marriage and during the pregnancy of his wife, he shall avoid the use of a razor."'—Haradatta.

8. Âpastamba II, 5, 12, 9. 9. Manu IV, 63.

10. Âpastamba I, 5, 16, 1.

11. Âpastamba I, 4, 21; I, 5, 15, 3.

12. Âpastamba I, 11, 30, 18-20.

13. Âpastamba I, 11, 30, 22.

14. Âpastamba I, 11, 30, 21. Haradatta remarks that some explain losh*th*a, 'a clod of earth,' by kapâla, 'a pot-sherd.'

15. Âpastamba II, 8, 20, 11-12. Kapâla, 'pot-sherds,' may also mean 'skull-bones.'

16. Manu IV, 57. Haradatta says that only a conversation,

17. If he has conversed (with such persons), he shall meditate on virtuous (men);

18. Or he may speak with a Brâhma*n*a.

19. He shall call (a cow that is) not a milch-cow, a cow that will become a milch-cow.

20. (An event) that is not lucky (he shall call) lucky.

21. (In speaking of) a skull (he shall use the word) bhagâla instead of kapâla,

22. (And in speaking of) a rainbow, ma*n*idhanus (the jewelled bow) instead of indradhanus (Indra's bow).

23. Let him not announce it to others, if a cow suckles (her calf),

24. Nor let him prevent her (from doing it).

25. After conjugal intercourse he shall at once clean himself.

26. Let him not recite the daily portion of the Veda (lying) on that couch (on which he lies with his wife).

---

properly so called, is forbidden, not to ask barbarians &c. about the road and similar matters.

18. Compare the analogous case, mentioned Âpastamba I, 3, 9, 13.

19. Âpastamba I, 11, 31, 11.

22. Âpastamba I, 11, 31, 16.

23. Âpastamba I, 11, 31, 10. Haradatta remarks that the prohibition does not extend to those cases where the Vedic ritual requires the fact to be pointed out. He is, of course, right in making this statement, as an express injunction of the *S*ruti always overrides the rules of the Sm*ri*ti.

24. Haradatta adds that this and the preceding Sûtras include by implication the cases where a cow does damage in a field; see Âpastamba I, 11, 31, 9.

25. Âpastamba II, 1, 1, 21—II, 1, 2, 1.

26. Âpastamba I, 11, 32, 3.

27. And when he has studied during the third watch of the night, he shall not again retire to rest.

28. Let him not have intercourse with his wife when she is ill,

29. Nor during her courses;

30. Nor let him embrace her (during that period).

31. Nor an unmarried female.

32. He shall avoid to blow the fire with his mouth, to contend with words, to show himself covered with perfumed ointments or wearing garlands, to scratch himself with any impure (implement), to take his meals with his wife, to look at (a woman) who is anointing herself, to enter (his village) by a back-gate, to wash one foot with the other, to eat food deposited on a chair, to cross a river swimming, to ascend trees and dangerous (places), or to descend therefrom, and to imperil his life (in any other manner).

33. Let him not ascend a ship (of) doubtful (solidity).

34. He shall protect himself by all (possible) means.

35. In the day-time he shall not wrap up his head while walking about;

36. But at night he shall cover it,

37. And while voiding urine and fæces.

---

27. Âpastamba I, 11, 32, 15.

29-30. Manu IV, 40.

32. Âpastamba I, 5, 15, 20; I, 11, 32, 5; Manu IV, 43; Âpastamba I, 11, 31, 21; Manu IV, 74; Âpastamba I, 11, 32, 26; I, 11, 32, 25.

33. Âpastamba I, 11, 32, 27.

35. Âpastamba I, 11, 30, 14. Haradatta adds that he may wrap up his head while sitting down and in walking when the sun or rain annoys him.

38. (Let him) not (ease nature) without (first) covering the ground (with grass or the like),

39. Nor close to his dwelling,

40. Nor on ashes, on cow-dung, in a ploughed field, in the shade (of a tree), on a road, in beautiful (spots).

41. Let him eject both urine and fæces, facing the north in the day-time,

42. And in the twilight,

43. But at night, facing the south.

44. Let him avoid to use a seat, clogs, a stick for cleaning the teeth (and other implements) made of Palâ*s*a-wood.

45. With shoes on (his feet), he shall not eat, sit down, salute, or worship (the gods).

46. Let him not pass idly (any part of the day, be it) morning, midday, or evening; (but) according to his ability (he shall make each useful) by the acquisition of spiritual merit or of wealth, and by taking his pleasure.

47. But among those (three aims of human life) he shall chiefly attend to the acquisition of spiritual merit.

---

38. Âpastamba I, 11, 30, 15. 39. Âpastamba I, 11, 31, 2.
40. Âpastamba I, 11, 30, 16–18. 41. Âpastamba I, 11, 31, 1.
43. Âpastamba I, 11, 31, 3. 44. Âpastamba I, 11, 32, 9.
45. Âpastamba I, 4, 14, 22.

46. Colebrooke, Mitâksharâ II, 1, 22. 'He shall use the morning, according to his ability, for acts tending to the acquisition of spiritual merit, such as reciting the Vedas; the middle part of the day for the acquisition of wealth; and the evening for scenting himself, adorning himself with garlands and the like acts giving pleasure.'—Haradatta.

47. Âpastamba I, 7, 20, 1–4.

48. Let him not look at a naked woman wedded to another man.

49. Let him not draw a seat towards himself with his foot.

50. He shall keep his organ, his stomach, his hands, his feet, his tongue, and his eyes under due restraint.

51. Let him avoid to cut, to break, to scratch, and to crush (anything), or to make (his joints) crack, without a (sufficient) reason.

52. Let him not step over a rope (to which) a calf (is tied).

53. Let him not be a stay-at-home.

54. Let him not go to (perform) a sacrifice without being chosen (to officiate as priest).

55. But at his pleasure (he may go) to see it.

56. Let him not eat food (that he has placed) in his lap,

57. Nor what has been brought at night by a servant.

58. He shall not eat (substances) from which the fat has been extracted, such as milk from which the cream has separated, butter, oil-cake, buttermilk, and the like.

---

48. Manu IV, 53.

50. Âpastamba II, 2, 5, 19; Manu IV, 175, 177.

51. Âpastamba I, 11, 32, 28; II, 8, 20, 16.

52. Âpastamba I, 11, 31, 13. Haradatta remarks that the word 'calf' is used to designate any animal of the bovine species.

56. Manu IV, 63. 57. Âpastamba I, 5, 16, 32.

58. Âpastamba II, 8, 18, 1; II, 8, 20, 10. Haradatta adds that this rule has been inserted here instead of in the chapter on forbidden food in order to indicate that its breach must be expiated by the penance prescribed for a breach of the Snâtaka's vow, not by that prescribed for eating forbidden food.

59. But he shall take his meals in the morning and in the evening, blessing his food, not grumbling at it.

60. He shall never sleep naked at night;

61. Nor shall he bathe (naked);

62. And he shall perform whatever (else) aged (Brâhma*n*as), of subdued senses, who have been properly obedient (to their teachers), who are free from deceit, covetousness, and error, and who know the Vedas, declare (to be right).

63. In order to acquire wealth and for the sake of security he may go to a ruling (king),

64. (But) to no other (being) except the gods, his Gurus, and righteous (Brâhma*n*as).

65. He shall seek to dwell in a place where firewood, water, fodder, Ku*s*a grass, (materials for making) garlands and roads exist in abundance, which is chiefly inhabited by Âryans, which is rich in industrious (men), and which is governed by a righteous (ruler).

66. He shall pass excellent (beings and things),

---

59. Âpastamba II, 1, 1, 2; II, 2, 3, 11.

60. Manu IV, 75. 61. Manu IV, 61.

62. Âpastamba I, 11, 32, 29; I, 7, 20, 8. Haradatta adds that the plural is used in the above Sûtra in order to indicate that many Brâhma*n*as must be unanimous regarding the practices to be followed.

63. Manu IV, 33; X, 113. 'For the sake of these objects he may go to a ruler, i.e. a king, without cringing, because the preposition adhi is used (in the text, and) adhi denotes mastership (Pâ*n*ini I, 4, 97). The meaning that he shall go (as becomes) an independent man.'—Haradatta.

65. Âpastamba I, 5, 15, 22; I, 11, 32, 18. Âryans, i.e. Brâhma*n*as, Kshatriyas, and Vai*s*yas.

66. Manu IV, 39. 'A cow, a Brâhma*n*a, a well-known tree,

auspicious (objects), temples of the gods, cross-roads, and the like with his right turned towards them.

67. The rule for times of distress (is, that) he shall mentally perform all (that is required by the rule of) conduct.

68. He shall always speak the truth.

69. He shall conduct himself (as becomes) an Âryan.

70. He shall instruct virtuous (men only).

71. He shall follow the rules of purification taught (in the *S*âstras).

72. He shall take pleasure in the (study of the) Veda.

73. He shall never hurt (any being), he shall be gentle, (yet) firm, ever restrain his senses, and be liberal.

74. A Snâtaka who conducts himself in this manner will liberate his parents, his ancestors, and descendants from evil, and never fall from Brahman's heaven.

---

and the like are called excellent (beings or things). An auspicious (object), i.e. a filled jar and the like.'—Haradatta.

67. Haradatta observes that this rule refers to cases where, being in a hurry, one cannot show one's reverence in the manner described in the preceding Sûtra.

68. Manu IV, 138, 175, 236.

70. Manu IV, 80–81.

71. Purification is here again mentioned in order (to indicate that Snâtaka must pay) particular attention to it.

72. Manu IV, 147–149. 73. Manu IV, 2, 238, 246.

74. Manu II, 260.

CHAPTER X.

1. (The lawful occupations common) to (all) twice-born men are studying the (Veda), offering sacrifices (for their own sake), and giving (alms).

2. Teaching, performing sacrifices for others, and receiving alms (are) the additional (occupations) of a Brâhmana.

3. But the former (three) are obligatory (on him).

4. Instruction in the Veda (may be given) without the above-mentioned (vows and ceremonies) in case a teacher, blood relations, friends or Gurus (receive it), and in case (the Veda) is exchanged for money or learning.

X. 1. Twice-born men, i. e. Brâhmanas, Kshatriyas, and Vaisyas. Haradatta says that some believe the term 'twice-born' to have been used in order to indicate that the three occupations may be lawfully followed after the second birth, i.e. the initiation only. But he declares that alms may be given even by an uninitiated Âryan, while studying the Veda and sacrificing are specially forbidden to him.

2. Âpastamba II, 5, 10, 4.

3. Manu X, 76. 'The former, i.e. the three beginning with studying (Sûtra 1), must necessarily be followed. If he neglects them, he commits sin; if he follows them, he will be exalted. But the other occupations, teaching, &c., shall be followed if there is occasion for them. No sin is committed by neglecting them, nor any greatness gained by following them. They are merely means of livelihood.'—Haradatta.

4. Âpastamba I, 4, 13, 15–18. The expression 'above-mentioned' refers to the whole of the rules regarding a pupil's conduct given above, I, 52—II, 51. It is difficult to understand what is intended by 'the exchange of the Veda for wealth or money,' if it is not the bhritakâdhyâpana or teaching for money which Manu III, 156 blames so severely. It seems to me unlikely that Gautama means simply to sanction this practice. It is more probable that his rule refers to the case of Brâhmans in distress, who avail themselves of the permission given above, VII, 4.

5. Agriculture and trade (are) also (lawful for a Brâhma*n*a) provided he does not do the work himself,

6. Likewise lending money at interest.

7. To protect all created beings is the additional (occupation) of a king,

8. And to inflict lawful punishments.

9. He shall support (those) *S*rotriyas, (who are) Brâhma*n*as,

10. And people unable to work, (even if they are) not Brâhma*n*as,

11. And those who are free from taxes,

12. And (needy) temporary students.

13. And (to take) measures for ensuring victory (is another duty of a king),

14. Especially when danger (from foes threatens the kingdom);

5–6. These rules which allow Brâhma*n*as to be gentlemen farmers and sleeping partners in mercantile or banking firms, managed by Vai*s*yas, do not occur in other Sm*ri*tis. But they agree with the practice followed at present in many parts of India, and the praise bestowed in Vedic works on those who present land to Brâhma*n*as as well as the numerous ancient land grants show that from early times many Brâhma*n*as were holders of land, which, as a rule, was cultivated by *S*ûdras.

7–8. Âpastamba II, 5, 10, 6; Manu VII, 27.

9. Âpastamba II, 10, 25, 11; Manu VII, 135.

11. Haradatta takes this Sûtra differently. He says: 'The immunity from taxes which has been granted to Brâhma*n*as and others by former kings he shall maintain in the same manner as formerly.' But I think that 'akara' must be taken as a Bahuvrîhi compound, and is used to designate widows, orphans, ascetics, &c.; see Âpastamba II, 10, 26, 10–17.

12. Haradatta observes that others explain upakurvâ*n*a, 'temporary students,' opposed to naish*th*ika, 'permanent students,' to mean 'men who benefit the people,' i.e. physicians and the like.

13. Manu VII, 103–110, 160–200; X, 119.

15. And (to learn) the management of chariots and the use of the bow (is a further duty of the king),

16. As well as to stand firm in battle and not to turn back.

17. No sin (is committed) by injuring or slaying (foes) in battle,

18. Excepting those who have lost their horses, charioteers, or arms, those who join their hands (in supplication), those who flee with flying hair, those who sit down with averted faces, those who have climbed (in flight) on eminences or trees, messengers, and those who declare themselves to be cows or Brâhma*n*as.

19. If another Kshatriya is supported by (the king), he shall follow the same occupations as his (master).

20. The victor shall receive the booty gained in battle.

21. But chariots and animals used for riding (belong) to the king,

22. And a preferential share, except when the booty has been gained in single combat.

23. But the king shall equitably divide (all) other (spoils).

24. Cultivators (must) pay to the king a tax

---

16. Manu VII, 87-89; X, 119; Yâ*gñ*avalkya I, 233.

17-18. Âpastamba II, 5, 10, 11. Persons who declare themselves to be cows or Brâhma*n*as become inviolable on account of the sacred character of the beings they personate. Historical instances are narrated where conquered kings were forced to appear before their victors, holding grass in their mouths or dancing like peacocks in order to save their lives.

20. Manu VII, 96. 22-23. Manu VII, 97.

24. Manu VII, 130. The amount depends on the nature of the soil and the manner of cultivation.

(amounting to) one-tenth, one-eighth, or one-sixth (of the produce).

25. Some declare, that (there is a tax) also on cattle and gold, (viz.) one-fiftieth (of the stock).

26. In the case of merchandise one-twentieth (must be paid by the seller) as duty,

27. (And) of roots, fruits, flowers, medicinal herbs, honey, meat, grass, and firewood one-sixtieth.

28. For it is the duty (of the king) to protect the (tax-payers).

29. But to (the collection of) these (taxes) he shall always pay particular attention.

30. He shall live on the surplus.

31. Each artisan shall monthly do one (day's) work (for the king).

32. Hereby (the taxes payable by) those who

---

25. Manu VII, 130. The above translation follows Haradatta's explanation, while Sir W. Jones' rendering of Manu gives a different meaning to the identical words.

26. Manu VII, 127. 27. Manu X, 120.

28. Manu VII, 128.

29. Manu VII, 128, 139.

30. Haradatta takes this Sûtra differently. He says, 'Adhika, "additional," means the money which is paid on account of (the additional occupations) which have been explained above (Sûtra 7 seq.) "To protect all created beings," &c. Thereon shall he live, he himself, his servants, his elephants, horses, and his other (animals).' If this explanation is adopted, the Sûtra ought to be translated thus, 'He shall live on (the taxes paid for his) additional (occupations).' It seems, however, more probable that Gautama means to say that the king shall live on the surplus which remains after providing for the external and internal security of the kingdom, and that his object is to forbid the application of the whole revenue to the personal expenses of the ruler.

31. Manu VII, 131.

32. Haradatta says that wood-carriers, dancers, and the like are intended.

support themselves by personal labour have been explained,

33. And (those payable by) owners of ships and carts.

34. He must feed these (persons while they work for him).

35. The merchants shall (each) give (every month one) article of merchandise for less than the market value.

36. Those who find lost (property) the owner of which is not (known), shall announce it to the king.

37. The king shall cause it to be proclaimed (by the public crier), and (if the owner does not appear) hold it in his custody for a year.

38. Afterwards one-fourth (of the value goes) to the finder (and) the remainder to the king.

39. A (man becomes) owner by inheritance, purchase, partition, seizure, or finding.

40. Acceptance is for a Brâhma*n*a an additional (mode of acquisition);

41. Conquest for a Kshatriya;

42. Gain (by labour) for a Vai*s*ya or *S*ûdra.

43. Treasure-trove is the property of the king,

36–38. Manu VIII, 30–36; Yâ*gñ*avalkya II, 33, 173; Macnaghten, Mitâksharâ V, 1, 6.

39. Manu X, 115; Mayûkha IV, 1, 2; Colebrooke, Mitâksharâ I, 1, 8; III, Digest IV, 22. 'Partition, i.e. the division (of the estate) between brothers and other (coparceners); seizure, i.e. the appropriation before (others) of forest trees and other things which have no owner; finding, i.e. the appropriation of lost property the owner of which is unknown, such as treasure-trove.'—Haradatta.

43. Manu VIII, 38; Yâ*gñ*avalkya II, 34; Macnaghten, Mitâksharâ V, 1, 10.

44. Excepting (such as is found) by a Brâhma*n*a who lives according to (the law).

45. Some declare, that a finder of a non-Brâhmanical caste even, who announces (his find to the king), shall obtain one-sixth (of the value).

46. Having recovered property stolen by thieves, he shall return it to the owner;

47. Or (if the stolen property is not recovered) he shall pay (its value) out of his treasury.

48. The property of infants must be protected until they attain their majority or complete their studentship.

49. The additional (occupations) of a Vai*s*ya are, agriculture, trade, tending cattle, and lending money at interest.

50. The *S*ûdra (belongs to) the fourth caste, which has one birth (only).

---

44. Manu VIII, 37; Yâg*ñ*avalkya II, 34; Macnaghten loc. cit.

46. Manu VIII, 40; Yâg*ñ*avalkya II, 36; Macnaghten, Mitâksharâ V, 1, 14.

47. Âpastamba II, 10, 26, 8; Macnaghten loc. cit.

48. Manu VIII, 27.

49. Âpastamba II, 5, 10, 7.

50. Âpastamba I, 1, 1, 6; Manu X, 4. Between this Sûtra and the next, my MSS. insert an additional one, not found in Professor Stenzler's edition, *S*ûdrasyâpi nishekapu*m*savanasîmantonnayanag*â*takarmanâmakara*n*opanishkrama*n*ânnaprâ*s*ana*k*aulânyamantrakâ*n*i yathâkâlam upadish*t*âni*t*i, 'for the *S*ûdra also the Nisheka (or impregnation), the Pu*m*savana (or rite for securing male offspring), the Sîmantonnayana (or arranging the parting of a pregnant wife), the *G*âtakarman (or ceremony on the birth of the child), the name-giving, the first walk in the open air, the first feeding, and the *K*aula (or tonsure of the child's head) are prescribed to be performed at the proper periods, but without the recitation of sacred texts.' But I am inclined to consider it spurious: first, because there is no proper commentary; secondly, because the enumeration of the Sa*m*skâras given here does not agree with

51. For him also (are prescribed) truthfulness, meekness, and purity.

52. Some (declare), that instead of sipping water, he shall wash his hands and feet.

53. (He shall also offer) the funeral oblations,

54. Maintain those depending upon him,

55. Live with his wife (only),

56. And serve the higher (castes).

57. From them he shall seek to obtain his livelihood.

58. (He shall use their) cast-off shoes, umbrellas, garments, and mats (for sitting on),

59. (And) eat the remnants of their food;

60. And (he may) live by (practising) mechanical arts;

61. And the Ârya under whose protection he places himself, must support him even if he (becomes) unable to work.

62. And a man of higher caste (who is his master and has fallen into distress must be maintained) by him.

63. His hoard shall serve this purpose.

64. If permission has been given to him, he

---

that given above, VIII, 14; and thirdly, because, according to the practice of Gautama, this Sûtra should begin with 'tasyâpi' instead of with '*S*ûdrasyâpi,' and the 'tasyâpi' in the next would become superfluous. The rule agrees however with Manu X, 63, 127.

51. Manu IX, 335.

53. Manu X, 127–128.

55. 'Another commentator explains the Sûtra to mean that he shall live with his wife only, and never enter another order (i.e. never become a student, hermit, or ascetic).'—Haradatta.

56. Âpastamba, I, 1, 1, 7–8; Manu X, 121–123.

57. Manu X, 124.

58–59. Manu X, 125.

60. Manu X, 99.

may use the exclamation nama*h* (adoration) as his Mantra.

65. Some (declare), that he himself may offer the Pâkaya*gñ*as.

66. And all men must serve those who belong to higher castes.

67. If Âryans and non-Âryans interchange their occupations and conduct (the one taking that of the other, there is) equality (between them).

Chapter XI.

1. The king is master of all, with the exception of Brâhma*n*as.

2. (He shall be) holy in acts and speech,

3. Fully instructed in the threefold (sacred science) and in logic,

4. Pure, of subdued senses, surrounded by com-

---

65. Manu X, 127. Regarding the Pâkaya*gñ*as, see above, VIII, 18.

67. 'There is equality between them, i.e. the one need not serve the other. A *S*ûdra need not serve even a Brâhma*n*a, (much less) any other (twice-born man) who lives the life of a non-Âryan (*S*ûdra). A *S*ûdra, even, who conducts himself like an Âryan must not be despised by men of other castes, who follow the occupations of non-Âryans, on account of his inferior birth.'—Haradatta.

XI. 1. Macnaghten, Mitâksharâ I, 1, 27; Manu IX, 313–322; Weber, Ind. Stud. X, 29, 60.

2. Manu VII, 26. 'Holy in acts,' i.e. constantly acting in conformity with the *S*âstras; 'holy in speech,' i.e. when administering justice he shall not speak partially.

3. Manu VII, 43; Yâ*gñ*avalkya I, 310. Haradatta thinks that the term 'the threefold sacred science includes the fourth Veda also, because it consists chiefly of *Rik*as and Ya*g*us formulas.'

4. Manu VII, 30–31; Yâ*gñ*avalkya I, 354; Âpastamba II, 11, 27, 18. 'Of subdued senses, i.e. free from the (seven) vices

panions possessing excellent qualities and by the means (for upholding his rule).

5. He shall be impartial towards his subjects;

6. And he shall do (what is) good for them.

7. All, excepting Brâhmanas, shall worship him who is seated on a higher seat, (while they themselves sit on a) lower (one).

8. The (Brâhmanas), also, shall honour him.

9. He shall protect the castes and orders in accordance with justice;

10. And those who leave (the path of) duty, he shall lead back (to it).

11. For it is declared (in the Veda) that he obtains a share of the spiritual merit (gained by his subjects).

12. And he shall select as his domestic priest (purohita) a Brâhmana who is learned (in the Vedas), of noble family, eloquent, handsome, of (a suitable) age, and of a virtuous disposition, who lives righteously and who is austere.

(common among kings), i.e. sensuality, gambling, hunting, drinking, &c.'—Haradatta. The means (upâya) are those mentioned by Yâgñavalkya I, 345–346.

5. Manu VII, 80; Yâgñavalkya I, 333.

6. 'And he shall do what is good, i.e. dig tanks, build embankments and bridges &c. for them, i.e. his subjects.'—Haradatta.

7. '(On a) lower (one), i.e. on the ground only.'—Haradatta. This is still the custom in native courts, where, however, Brâhmanas, as a rule, must also sit on the floor.

8. 'Honour him,' i.e. worship him by invoking blessings on him and the like.

9. Manu VII, 35. 10. Yâgñavalkya I, 360.

11. Manu VIII, 304; Yâgñavalkya I, 334.

12. Manu VII, 78; Yâgñavalkya I, 312. Haradatta explains vâksampanna, 'eloquent,' by 'one who knows Sanskrit.' According to the same, 'the (suitable) age' is the prime of life, when men

13. With his assistance he shall fulfil his religious duties.

14. For it is declared (in the Veda): 'Kshatriyas, who are assisted by Brâhma*n*as, prosper and do not fall into distress.'

15. He shall, also, take heed of that which astrologers and interpreters of omens tell (him).

16. For some (declare), that the acquisition of wealth and security depend also upon that.

17. He shall perform in the fire of the hall the rites ensuring prosperity which are connected with expiations (*s*ânti), festivals, a prosperous march, long life, and auspiciousness; as well as those that are intended to cause enmity, to subdue (enemies), to destroy (them) by incantations, and to cause their misfortune.

18. Officiating priests (shall perform) the other (sacrifices) according to the precepts (of the Veda).

---

are neither too young nor too old. 'Austere' is interpreted to mean 'not given to sensual enjoyments.'

13. Manu VII, 78. 14. *S*atapatha-brâhma*n*a IV, 1, 4, 4–6.

17. Âpastamba II, 10, 25, 4, 7. *S*ântis, 'expiations,' are rites intended to avert an impending misfortune which is announced by an evil omen. 'Festivals' are, according to Haradatta, wedding-days and the like; 'rites connected with auspiciousness' are, according to the same, rites on entering a new dwelling and the like. Haradatta further remarks that, though, according to the text, the king must perform these rites, he is, in reality, only to give the necessary orders, and to furnish the means for their performance, while the Purohita is to officiate as priest. He adds, that another commentator asserts that 'the Purohita,' not 'the king,' must be taken as the subject of the sentence.

18. Manu VII, 78–79; Yâ*gñ*avalkya I, 313. Haradatta says that by the 'other' sacrifices, both G*ri*hya and *S*rauta rites are meant. I think that the latter are chiefly intended, as the Sa*m*skâras are included under the rites of festive days, mentioned in the preceding Sûtra.

19. His administration of justice (shall be regulated by) the Veda, the Institutes of the Sacred Law, the Aṅgas, and the Purâ*n*a.

20. The laws of countries, castes, and families, which are not opposed to the (sacred) records, (have) also authority.

21. Cultivators, traders, herdsmen, money-lenders, and artisans (have authority to lay down rules) for their respective classes.

22. Having learned the (state of) affairs from those who (in each class) have authority (to speak he shall give) the legal decision.

23. Reasoning is a means for arriving at the truth.

24. Coming to a conclusion through that, he shall decide properly.

25. If (the evidence) is conflicting, he shall learn (the truth) from (Brâhma*n*as) who are well versed in

---

19. The Aṅgas, i.e. the six auxiliary branches of learning mentioned above, VIII, 5. My best copy inserts 'the Upavedas' after the Aṅgas. But the words upavedâ*h* and dharma*s*âstrâ*n*i, 'the institutes of law,' are probably interpolations. For the latter are already included by the term Aṅga, as part of the Kalpa.

20. Âpastamba II, 6, 15, 1; Manu VII, 203; VIII, 41, 46; Yâ*gñ*avalkya I, 342. 'The (sacred) records, i.e. the Vedas and the rest.'—Haradatta.

22. 'Having learned, i.e. having heard and considered, from them, i.e. from men of those classes, according to their authority, i.e. from those who in each class are authorised to give decisions, the (state of) affairs, i.e. the peculiar customs, the legal decision must be given in accordance with that which they declare to be the rule in their community.'—Haradatta.

23. Manu VIII, 44; XII, 105–106; Macnaghten, Mitâksharâ II, 8, 8. Haradatta remarks, that this Sûtra refers to the case where the spokesmen of a guild may be suspected of partiality.

25. Manu XII, 108–113. According to Haradatta this Sûtra refers to particularly difficult cases.

the threefold sacred lore, and give his decision (accordingly).

26. For, (if he acts) thus, blessings will attend him (in this world and the next).

27. It has been declared in the Veda: 'Brâhma*n*as, united with Kshatriyas, uphold gods, manes, and men.'

28. They declare, that (the word) da*nd*a (rule or punishment) is derived from (the verb) damayati (he restrains); therefore he shall restrain those who do not restrain themselves.

29. (Men of) the (several) castes and orders who always live according to their duty enjoy after death the rewards of their works, and by virtue of a remnant of their (merit) they are born again in excellent countries, castes, and families, (endowed) with beauty, long life, learning in the Vedas, (virtuous) conduct, wealth, happiness, and wisdom.

30. Those who act in a contrary manner perish, being born again in various (evil conditions).

31. The advice of the spiritual teacher and the punishment (inflicted by the king) guard them.

32. Therefore a king and a spiritual teacher must not be reviled.

CHAPTER XII.

1. A *S*ûdra who intentionally reviles twice-born men by criminal abuse, or criminally assaults them with blows, shall be deprived of the limb with which he offends.

---

26. Âpastamba II, 5, 11, 4. 29. Âpastamba II, 5, 11, 10.

30. Âpastamba II, 5, 11, 11. 'Perish, i. e. fall from one misfortune into the other.'—Haradatta.

31. Âpastamba II, 5, 10, 12–16. 32. Manu VII, 8.

XII. 1. Âpastamba II, 10, 27, 14; Manu VIII, 270, 279–283;

2. If he has criminal intercourse with an Âryan woman, his organ shall be cut off, and all his property be confiscated.

3. If (the woman had) a protector, he shall be executed after (having undergone the punishments prescribed above).

4. Now if he listens intentionally to (a recitation of) the Veda, his ears shall be filled with (molten) tin or lac.

5. If he recites (Vedic texts), his tongue shall be cut out.

6. If he remembers them, his body shall be split in twain.

7. If he assumes a position equal (to that of twice-born men) in sitting, in lying down, in conversation or on the road, he shall undergo (corporal) punishment.

8. A Kshatriya (shall be fined) one hundred (Kârshâpa*n*as) if he abuses a Brâhma*n*a,

9. In case of an assault, twice as much.

Yâ*gñ*avalkya II, 215. Haradatta adds that an abusive word or a blow given in jest must not be punished in the manner prescribed above, as the word 'pârushya' presupposes criminal intent.

2. Âpastamba II, 10, 26, 20; Mayûkha XIX, 7, where, however, ârya has been altered to â*k*ârya. Haradatta adds that the two punishments are cumulative in the case of a Brâhma*n*î only. If the offence is committed with a Kshatriyâ, the offender is liable to the first only; if he sins with a Vai*s*yâ, to the second.

3. Âpastamba II, 10, 27, 9; Manu VIII, 359; Yâ*gñ*avalkya II, 286.

7. Âpastamba II, 10, 27, 15; Manu VIII, 281.—The translation follows Haradatta, who is guided by the parallel passages. But for the latter, one would translate 'he shall be fined.'

8. Manu VIII, 267; Yâ*gñ*avalkya III, 204–207. Manu VIII, 136 states one Kârshâpa*n*a or copper Pa*n*a contains 80 Raktikâs, which would correspond to 97·60 grammes of the metrical system.

10. A Vaisya (who abuses a Brâhmana, shall pay) one and a half (times as much as a Kshatriya).

11. But a Brâhmana (who abuses) a Kshatriya (shall pay) fifty (Kârshâpanas),

12. One half of that (amount if he abuses) a Vaisya,

13. (And if he abuses) a Sûdra, nothing.

14. A Kshatriya and a Vaisya (who abuse one another shall pay the same fines) as a Brâhmana and a Kshatriya.

15. (The value of) property which a Sûdra unrighteously acquires by theft, must be repaid eightfold.

16. For each of the other castes (the fines must be) doubled.

17. If a learned man offends, the punishment shall be very much increased.

18. If fruits, green corn, and vegetables are appropriated in small amounts, (the fine is) five Krishnalas (of copper).

---

10. Manu VIII, 267. 11. Manu VIII, 268.

12. Manu VIII, 268.

13. Manu VIII, 268. Haradatta adds that, as a Brâhmana is declared to pay nothing for abusing a Sûdra, a Kshatriya and a Vaisya are liable to be fined for that offence, and that according to Usanas a Kshatriya shall pay twenty-four Panas, and a Vaisya thirty-six.

14. I.e. a Vaisya shall pay one hundred Panas for abusing a Kshatriya, and a Kshatriya fifty for abusing a Vaisya.

15. Manu VIII, 337.

16. Manu VIII, 337–338. I.e. a Vaisya is to pay sixteen times the value of the stolen property, a Kshatriya thirty-two times, and a Brâhmana sixty-four times.

17. Manu VIII, 338.

18. Manu VIII, 330. Krishnala is another name for Raktikâ,

19. If damage is done by cattle, the responsibility falls on the owner.

20. But if (the cattle) were attended by a herdsman, (it falls) on the latter.

21. (If the damage was done) in an unenclosed field near the road, (the responsibility falls) on the herdsman and on the owner of the field.

22. Five Mâshas (are the fine to be paid) for (damage done by) a cow,

23. Six for a camel or a donkey,

24. Ten for a horse or a buffalo,

25. Two for each goat or sheep.

26. If all is destroyed, (the value of) the whole crop (must be paid and a fine in addition).

27. If (a man) always neglects the prescribed (duties) and does that which is forbidden, his property beyond (the amount required for) raiment and food shall be taken from him (until he amends).

28. He may take, as his own, grass for a cow, and fuel for his fire, as well as the flowers of creepers and trees and their fruit, if they be unenclosed.

29. The legal interest for money lent (is at the rate of) five Mâshas a month for twenty (Kârshâpa*n*as).

---

used also by Yâg*ñ*avalkya I, 362. It equals 0·122 grammes of the metrical system, Prinsep, Useful Tables, p. 97.

20–21. Manu VIII, 240; Yâg*ñ*avalkya II, 162.

22–26. Manu VIII, 241; Yâg*ñ*avalkya II, 159–161; Colebrooke III, Digest IV, 40. Haradatta, relying on U*s*anas everywhere, reckons twenty Mâshas to the Kârshâpa*n*a.

27. Âpastamba II, 11, 27, 18.

28. Âpastamba I, 10, 28, 3; Colebrooke III, Digest IV, 22.

29. Manu VIII, 140; Yâg*ñ*avalkya II, 37; Colebrooke I, Digest 25. Haradatta states that a Kârshâpa*n*a contains twenty

30. Some (declare, that this rate should not be paid) longer than a year.

31. If (the loan) remains outstanding for a long time, the principal may be doubled (after which interest ceases).

32. A loan secured by a pledge that is used (by the creditor) bears no interest;

33. Nor money tendered, nor (a debt due by a debtor) who is forcibly prevented (from paying).

34. (Special forms of interest are) compound interest, periodical interest,

35. Stipulated interest, corporal interest, daily interest, and the use of a pledge.

Mâshas. Thus the monthly interest for 400 Mâshas being five Mâshas, the rate is 1¼ per cent for the month, or 15 per cent per annum.

30. Colebrooke I, Digest 40; Manu VIII, 153.

31. Manu VIII, 151; Colebrooke I, Digest 59.

32. Manu VIII, 143; Colebrooke I, Digest 79.

33. Colebrooke I, Digest 79. 'Likewise the debt of a debtor who, being desirous to pay, is imprisoned by the king or others in a prison or the like, and who is thus unable to pay, does not increase from that day.'—Haradatta.

34. For this and the next Sûtra, see also Colebrooke I, Digest 35–45, in the notes on which latter text the various explanations of these terms, found here, have been fully discussed. 'If a large or a small interest is taken on condition that the loan is to be repaid on a certain date, and that, in case of non-payment, it is to be trebled or quadrupled, that is called periodical interest.'—Haradatta.

35. 'Where the lender and the borrower, having regard to the country, the time, the object, and the condition (of the borrower), agree between themselves (on a certain rate), e. g. of ten per cent per mensem, that is called stipulated interest. Corporal interest is that which is payable by bodily labour. Thus B*ri*haspati says, "Corporal interest is that connected with work." But Vyâsa explains it thus, "Corporal interest is that which arises from the work (or use) of a (pledged female quadruped) to be

36. The interest on products of animals, on wool, on the produce of a field, and on beasts of burden (shall) not (increase) more than the fivefold (value of the object lent).

37. The property of (a person who is) neither an idiot nor a minor, having been used by strangers before his eyes for ten years, (belongs) to him who uses it,

38. (But) not (if it is used) by *S*rotriyas, ascetics, or royal officials.

39. Animals, land, and females are not lost (to the owner) by (another's) possession.

---

milked, or of (a male) to carry burdens." Kâtyâyana explains the daily interest (lit. the interest resembling the growth of the lock on the head), "That which is taken daily is called daily interest." . . . E.g. for a Prastha of grain lent a handful of grain is taken daily.'—Haradatta.

36. Colebrooke I, Digest 62. Haradatta mentions also another explanation of the Sûtra: 'Another (commentator) says, "If products of animals and the rest have been bought, and the price is not paid at once, that may increase fivefold by the addition of interest, but not to a greater sum."'

37. Manu VIII, 147–148; Yâ*gñ*avalkya II, 24.

38. Haradatta adds that in the case of a *S*rotriya and of an ascetic, the owner may allow the use of his property for a long time, desiring to acquire merit by doing so, and that fear may prevent him from opposing the king's servants. Hence prolonged possession by such persons does not necessitate the conclusion that the owner had given up his rights. As ascetics cannot possess any property, the Sûtra must refer to their occupying an empty house which has an owner.

39. Manu VIII, 149; Yâ*gñ*avalkya II, 25. The translation given above agrees with an explanation of the Sûtra which Haradatta mentions, but rejects. He himself prefers the following: 'Animals, i.e. quadrupeds; land, i.e. a field, a garden, and the like; females, i.e. female slaves and the like. No long possession of animals and the rest is necessary in order to acquire the rights of ownership over them. Even after a short period they become the

40. The heirs shall pay the debts (of a deceased person).

41. Money due by a surety, a commercial debt, a fee (due to the parents of the bride), debts contracted for spirituous liquor or in gambling, and a fine shall not involve the sons (of the debtor).

42. An (open) deposit, a sealed deposit, an object lent for use, an object bought (but not paid), and a pledge, being lost without the fault of the holder, (shall not involve) any blameless person.

43. A man who has stolen (gold) shall approach the king, with flying hair, holding a club in his hand, and proclaim his deed.

---

property of the possessor. For how (would it be possible that) a person, who himself wants buttermilk and the like, should allow a cow which he himself has bought, and which gives daily a Dro*n*a of milk, to be milked in the house of another person?' &c. &c.

40. Manu VIII, 162; Yâg*ñ*avalkya II, 51.

41. Manu VIII, 159–160; Yâg*ñ*avalkya II, 47, 54; Colebrooke I, Digest 202. Taking into account the parallel passages of Manu and Yâg*ñ*avalkya, Haradatta very properly restricts this rule to a bail for the personal appearance of an offender. In explanation of the expression 'a commercial debt' he gives the following instance: 'If a person has borrowed money from somebody on the condition that he is to repay the principal together with the gain thereon, and if he dies in a foreign country, while travelling in order to trade, then that money shall not be repaid by the son.' The instance explaining the term 'fee' (*s*ulka) is as follows: 'If a person has promised a fee (to the parents of a woman) and dies after the wedding, then that fee does not involve his son, i.e. need not be paid by him.' The word *s*ulka is, however, ambiguous, and may also mean 'a tax or toll.'

42. Manu VIII, 189; Yâg*ñ*avalkya II, 59, 66; Colebrooke II, Digest I, 29. Haradatta declares the meaning to be, that in case the bailee was guilty of no negligence and took the same care of the deposits &c. as of his own property, neither he nor his heirs need make good the value of those which were lost or destroyed.

43. Âpastamba I, 9, 25, 4.

44. Whether he be slain or be pardoned, he is purified (of his guilt).

45. If the king does not strike, the guilt falls on him.

46. Corporal punishment (must) not (be resorted to in the case) of a Brâhma*n*a.

47. Preventing (a repetition of) the deed, publicly proclaiming his crime, banishment, and branding (are the punishments to which a Brâhma*n*a may be subjected).

48. That (king) who does not do his duty (by inflicting punishment) becomes liable to perform a penance.

49. (A man who) knowingly (becomes) the servant (of a thief shall be treated) like a thief,

50. Likewise he who (knowingly) receives (goods) from (a thief or) an unrighteous man.

51. The award of the punishment (must be regulated) by a consideration (of the status) of the criminal, of his (bodily) strength, of (the nature of) the crime, and whether the offence has been repeated.

52. Or a pardon (may be given) in accordance with the opinion of an assemblage of persons learned in the Vedas.

---

45. Âpastamba I, 9, 25, 5.

46. Manu VIII, 124; Macnaghten, Mitâksharâ III, 4, 9.

47. Manu IX, 239, 241; Âpastamba II, 10, 27, 8, 17-19; Macnaghten loc. cit. Karmaviyoga, 'preventing (a repetition of) the deed,' may also mean 'suspension from (his priestly) functions.'

48. Âpastamba II, 11, 28, 13.

49-50. Manu IX, 278; Yâg*ñ*avalkya II, 276.

51. Manu VII, 16; VIII, 126; Yâg*ñ*avalkya I, 367.

CHAPTER XIII.

1. In disputed cases the truth shall be established by means of witnesses.

2. The (latter) shall be many, faultless as regards the performance of their duties, worthy to be trusted by the king, and free from affection for, or hatred against either (party).

3. (They may be) *S*ûdras even.

4. But a Brâhma*n*a must not be forced (to give evidence) at the word of a non-Brâhma*n*a, except if he is mentioned (in the plaint).

5 (Witnesses) shall not speak singly or without being asked,

6. And if, (being asked,) they do not answer, they are guilty of a crime.

7. Heaven is their reward, if they speak the

XIII. 1. Manu VIII, 45; Yâg*ñ*avalkya II, 22.

2. Âpastamba II, 11, 29, 7. 'Many means at least three.'—Haradatta.

3. Manu VIII, 63. I.e. *S*ûdras endowed with the qualities mentioned above.

4. Manu VIII, 65. 'A Brâhma*n*a means here a *S*rotriya. If a man other than a Brâhma*n*a says: "This Brâhma*n*a is a witness of this fact," then the (*S*rotriya) shall not be forced to become, i.e. not be taken as a witness, provided he has not been mentioned, i.e. he has not been entered in the written plaint (as one of the witnesses). But if he has been entered in the plaint, he certainly becomes a witness.'—Haradatta.

5. Manu VIII, 79; Macnaghten, Mitâksharâ VI, 1, 21. In the Mitâksharâ the Sûtra is read nâsamavetâ*h* p*r*ish*t*â*h* prabrûyu*h*, 'witnesses need not answer if they are examined singly.' Mitrami*s*ra in the Vîramitrodaya says that Haradatta's reading of the text is the same, and that his explanation does not agree with it.

6. Manu VIII, 107; Yâg*ñ*avalkya II, 76–77.

7. Âpastamba II, 11, 29, 9–10.

truth; in the contrary case hell (will be their portion).

8. (Persons) not mentioned (in the plaint), must also give evidence.

9. No objection (can be raised against witnesses) in a case of (criminal) hurt,

10. Nor if they have spoken inadvertently.

11. If the sacred law or the rules (referring to worldly matters) are violated, the guilt (falls) on the witnesses, the assessors, the king, and on the offender.

12. Some (declare, that the witnesses) shall be charged on oath to speak the truth.

13. In the case of others than Brâhma*n*as that (oath shall be sworn) in the presence of the gods, of the king, and of Brâhma*n*as.

14. By false evidence concerning small cattle a witness kills ten,

15. (By false evidence) regarding cows, horses, men, or land, in each succeeding case ten times as many (as in the one mentioned before),

---

9. Manu VIII, 72; Yâg*ñ*avalkya II, 72.

10. 'Negligence, i.e. inadvertence. If anything has been spoken at random by a witness in a conversation referring to something else (than the case), no blame must be thrown on him for that reason.'—Haradatta.

11. Manu VIII, 18. The translation follows Haradatta. Perhaps it would, however, be as well to take dharmatantra, 'the sacred law and the rules referring to worldly matters,' as a Tatpurusha, and to translate, 'If there is a miscarriage of justice, the guilt,' &c.

12–13. Âpastamba II, 11, 29, 7.

14–22. Manu VIII, 98–100. 'By speaking an untruth regarding them, the witness kills ten. Ten what? Even ten (of that kind) regarding which he has lied. His guilt is as great as if he actually killed ten of them, and the punishment (is the same). Equal penances must also be prescribed for both cases.'—Haradatta.

16. Or (by false evidence) regarding land the whole (human race).

17. Hell (is the punishment) for a theft of land.

18. (By false evidence) concerning water (he incurs) the same (guilt) as (for an untruth) about land,

19. Likewise (by false evidence) regarding (criminal) intercourse.

20. (By false evidence) regarding honey or clarified butter (he incurs) the same (guilt) as (by an untruth) about small cattle,

21. (By false evidence) about clothes, gold, grain, and the Veda, the same as (by an untruth) about kine,

22. (And by false evidence) regarding a carriage (or a beast of burden) the same as (by an untruth) about horses.

23. A witness must be reprimanded and punished for speaking an untruth.

24. No guilt is incurred by giving false evidence, in case the life (of a man) depends thereon.

25. But (this rule does) not (hold good) if the life of a very wicked (man depends on the evidence of a witness).

26. The king, or the judge, or a Brâhma*n*a learned in the *S*âstras (shall examine the witnesses).

27. (The litigant) shall humbly go to seek the judge.

---

23. Manu VIII, 119-123; Yâ*gñ*avalkya II, 81. 'Yâpya*h* (literally "must be turned out") means "must be reprimanded" in the presence of the whole audience, lest anybody have intercourse with him.'—Haradatta.

24-25. Manu VIII, 104-105; Yâ*gñ*avalkya II, 83.

26. Manu VIII, 8-9, 79; Yâ*gñ*avalkya II, 1, 3, 73.

27. Manu VIII, 43. The meaning of the Sûtra is that the

28. If (the defendant) is unable to answer (the plaint) at once, (the judge) may wait for a year.

29. But (in an action) concerning kine, draught-oxen, women, or the procreation (of offspring), the defendant (shall answer) immediately,

30. Likewise in a case that will suffer by delay.

31. To speak the truth before the judge is more important than all (other) duties.

Chapter XIV.

1. The Sapi*nd*as become impure by the death (of a relative) during ten (days and) nights, except those who officiate as priests, who have performed the Dîksha*n*îyesh*t*i (or initiatory ceremony of a *S*rauta sacrifice), and those who are students.

2. (The impurity) of a Kshatriya lasts for eleven (days and) nights,

3. (That) of a Vai*s*ya twelve (days and) nights,

4. (Or), according to some, half a month,

5. (And that) of a *S*ûdra a whole month.

6. If during (a period of impurity) another (death) happens, the (relatives) shall be pure after (the lapse of) the remainder of that (first period).

---

judge shall not promote litigation, and incite people to institute suits. If litigants do not humbly appear before him, he is not to send for them.

28. See also Nârada I, 38, 41.

29. Yâ*g*ñavalkya II, 12. Haradatta explains pra*g*anana, 'the procreation (of offspring),' to mean 'marriage.'

XIV. 1. Manu V, 59, 83, 93; Yâ*g*ñavalkya III, 18, 28; see also Âpastamba I, 5, 16, 18. Regarding the meaning of the term Sapi*nd*a, see below, Sûtra 13. This Sûtra refers, of course, to Brâhma*n*as only.

2-3. Manu V, 83; Yâ*g*ñavalkya III, 22.

5. Manu and Yâ*g*ñavalkya l. l. cit. 6. Manu V, 79.

7. (But) if one night (only of the period of impurity) remains (and another death happens, they shall become pure) after (the lapse of) two (days and nights).

8. (If the second death happens) on the morning (after the completion of the period of impurity, they shall be purified) after three (days and nights).

9. (The relatives) of those who are slain for the sake of cows and Brâhma*n*as (become pure) immediately after the burial,

10. And (those of men destroyed) by the anger of the king,

11. (Further, those of men killed) in battle,

12. Likewise (those) of men who voluntarily (die) by starving themselves to death, by weapons, fire, poison, or water, by hanging themselves, or by jumping (from a precipice).

13. Sapi*nd*a-relationship ceases with the fifth or the seventh (ancestor).

14. (The rules regarding impurity caused by the

9. Yâg*ñ*avalkya III, 27. The Sûtra may, however, also be translated 'the relatives of those who have been killed by a cow, or by a Brâhma*n*a, &c.,' as the latter case, too, is mentioned by Yâg*ñ*avalkya III, 21. The word anvaksham, translated by 'immediately after burial,' is explained by Haradatta as follows: 'The corpse is seen, i.e. is visible, so long; the meaning is that they will be pure after having bathed at the end of the burial.'

10. Yâg*ñ*avalkya III, 21.

12. Manu V, 89; Yâg*ñ*avalkya III, 21.

13. Âpastamba II, 6, 15, 2. Haradatta states that the Sapi*nd*a-relationship extends to four degrees in the case of the son of an appointed daughter (see below, XXVIII, 18), while it includes the relatives within six degrees in the case of a legitimate son of the body. In either case the term refers to Sagotra-sap *nd*as, or Sapi*nd*as who bear the same family name only. The case of the Bhinnagotra-sapi*nd*as will be discussed below, Sûtra 20.

14-16. Manu V, 62; Yâg*ñ*avalkya III, 18-19.

death of a relative apply) to the birth (of a child) also.

15. (In) that (case the impurity falls) on the parents,

16. Or on the mother (alone).

17. (The impurity) for a miscarriage (lasts for a number of days and) nights equal to (the number of) months from conception,

18. Or three days.

19. And if he hears (of the death of a Sapi*nd*a) after (the lapse of) ten (days and nights, the impurity lasts for) one night together with the preceding and following days,

20. Likewise when a relative who is not a Sapi*nd*a, a relative by marriage, or a fellow-student (has died).

21. For a man who studies the same recension of the Veda (the impurity lasts) one day,

---

17. Manu V, 66; Yâ*gñ*avalkya III, 20. 19. Manu V, 75–77.

20. Manu V, 81. Haradatta explains asapi*nd*a, 'a kinsman who is not a Sapi*nd*a,' by Samânodaka, i.e. 'a kinsman bearing the same family name, but more than six degrees removed,' and yonisambandha, 'a relative by marriage,' by 'the maternal grandfather, a maternal aunt's sons, and their sons, &c., the fathers of wives and the rest.' The latter term, for which 'a person related through a female' would be a more exact rendering than the one given above, includes, therefore, those persons who, according to the terminology of Manu and Yâ*gñ*avalkya, are called Bhinnagotrasapi*nd*as, Bândhavas, or Bandhus (see Colebrooke, Mitâksharâ II, 53; II, 6). Gautama's terminology agrees in this respect with that of Âpastamba, see note on II, 5, 11, 16.

21. Haradatta explains sabrahma*k*ârin by suh*ri*t, 'a friend.' But the term which elsewhere means 'a fellow-student' cannot have that sense in our Sûtra, as the fellow-student (sahâdhyâyin) has been mentioned already. The translation given above is supported by the manner in which it is used in the ancient land-grants, where expressions like bahv*rik*asabrahma*k*ârin are of common occurrence.

22. Likewise for a *S*rotriya who dwells in the same house.

23. On touching (i.e. on carrying out) a corpse from an interested motive, the impurity lasts for ten days.

24. (The duration of the impurity) of a Vai*s*ya and of a *S*ûdra (in the same case) has been declared (by Sûtras 3–5).

25. Or (it shall last for these two) as many nights as there are seasons (in the year);

26. And (the same rule may be made applicable) to the two higher (castes).

27. Or (the impurity lasts) three days.

28. And if the teacher, his son or wife, a person for whom (a Brâhma*n*a) sacrifices or a pupil (has been carried out, the duration of the impurity is) the same.

---

22. Manu V, 81.

23. 'The word upaspar*s*ana (literally touching) does not denote here simple touching. For below, Sûtra 30, bathing with the clothes on, will be prescribed for that. What does upaspar*s*ana then mean? It means carrying out a corpse. For that an impurity lasting ten days falls on the performer, provided that the carrying out be done for an object, i.e with the intention of gaining a fee or the like, not for the sake of doing one's duty. The word impurity is here repeated in order to indicate that the impurity, here intended, differs from that described above. Hence the rules given below, Sûtra 37, which prescribe sleeping and sitting on the ground and so forth, do not apply. (The word impurity) indicates (here) merely that (the performer of the act) must not be touched, and has no right (to perform sacred ceremonies).'—Haradatta.

25. Haradatta states that Gautama does not simply say 'six days,' because five seasons only are to be reckoned in the case of a Vai*s*ya, and six in the case of a *S*ûdra.

28. Haradatta asserts that m*ri*teshu, 'have died,' must be understood. But as both the preceding and the following Sûtras refer to

29. And if a man of lower caste carries out (the corpse of) one of higher caste, or a man of higher caste (carries out the body of) one of lower caste, (the duration of) the impurity in these (cases) is determined by (the caste of) the dead man.

30. On touching an outcast, a *Kand*âla, a woman impure on account of her confinement, a woman in her courses, or a corpse, and on touching persons who have touched them, he shall purify himself by bathing dressed in his clothes,

31. Likewise if he has followed a corpse (that was being carried out),

32. And (if he has come into contact) with a dog.

33. Some (declare), that (the limb) which (a dog) may touch (must be washed).

34. The Sapi*nd*as shall offer (libations of) water for (a deceased relative) whose *K*aula-karman (or tonsure) has been performed,

35. As well as for the wives and daughters of such (a person).

36. Some (declare, that it must be done in the case) of married female relatives (also).

---

the carrying out of corpses, it is impossible to agree with him. It seems to me that Gautama's rule means, that, if a man has carried out the corpse of a teacher, &c., he becomes impure for ten, eleven, or twelve days, or for three days only. See also Manu V, 91, 103; Yâ*gñ*avalkya III, 15.

30. Âpastamba II, 2, 2, 8–9; Manu V, 85; Yâ*gñ*avalkya III, 30.

31. Manu V, 103; Yâ*gñ*avalkya III, 26.

32–33. Âpastamba I, 5, 15, 16–17.

34. Âpastamba II, 6, 15, 9; Manu V, 70. Haradatta observes that most G*ri*hya-sûtras prescribe the performance of the *K*aula-karman in the third year.

36. Yâ*gñ*avalkya III, 4.

37. (During the period of impurity) all (the mourners) shall sleep and sit on the ground and remain chaste.

38. They shall not clean (themselves);

39. Nor shall they eat meat until (the funeral oblation) has been offered.

40. On the first, third, fifth, seventh, and ninth (days after the death) water (mixed with sesamum) must be offered.

41. And the garments (worn during that ceremony) must be changed,

42. But on the last (day they must be given) to men of the lowest castes.

43. The parents (shall offer water for a son who dies) after he has teethed.

44. If infants, (relatives) who live in a distant country, those who have renounced domestic life, and those who are not Sapi*nd*as, (die), the purification is instantaneous.

45. Kings (remain always pure), lest their business be impeded,

46. And a Brâhma*n*a, lest his daily study of the Veda be interrupted.

---

37. Manu V, 73; Yâ*gñ*avalkya III, 16.

39. Manu V, 73.

43. Manu V, 70.

44. Yâ*gñ*avalkya III, 23. Haradatta remarks that the rule refers to those Sapi*nd*as residing in foreign countries only, of whose death one may hear a year after their decease, and to remoter relations of whose death one hears after the lapse of ten days; see Manu V, 75-76.

45. Manu V, 93-94; Yâ*gñ*avalkya III, 27. Haradatta adds that the plural 'kings' is used in order to include all rulers and governors, and such persons as the king wishes to be pure.

46. Yâ*gñ*avalkya III, 28.

CHAPTER XV.

1. Now (follow the rules regarding) funeral oblations (*S*râddha).

2. He shall offer (them) to the Manes on the day of the new moon,

3. Or in the dark half (of the month) after the fourth (lunar day),

4. Or on any day (of the dark half) according to (the results he may) desire;

5. Or if (particularly appropriate) materials or (particularly holy) Brâhma*n*as are at hand, or (the sacrificer is) near a (particularly sacred) place, no restriction as to time (need be observed):

6. Let him select as good food as he can afford, and have it prepared as well as possible.

7. He shall feed an uneven number (of Brâhma*n*as), at least nine,

8. Or as many as he is able (to entertain).

9. (Let him feed such as are) *S*rotriyas and

XV. 1. 'The word "now" indicates that a new topic begins.'—Haradatta. The rules now following refer in the first instance to the Pârva*n*a or monthly *S*râddha, but most of them serve also as general rules for all the numerous varieties of funeral sacrifices.

2. Manu III, 122; Yâg*ñ*avalkya I, 217.

3. Âpastamba II, 7, 16, 6. 4. Âpastamba II, 7, 16, 6 22.

5. Some of the most famous among the places where the performance of a *S*râddha is particularly efficacious and meritorious are Gayâ in Bihâr, Pushkara or Pokhar near A*g*mîr, the Kurukshetra near Dehli, Nâsika on the Godâvarî. Pilgrims or persons passing through such places may and must perform a *S*râddha on any day of the month.

7. Yâg*ñ*avalkya I, 227. 8. See also below, Sûtra 21.

9. Âpastamba II, 7, 17, 4. Haradatta explains vâk, 'eloquence,' by 'ability to speak Sanskrit,' rûpa, 'beauty,' by 'the proper number of limbs,' and vaya*h*sampanna, 'of (suitable) age,' by 'not too young.'

endowed with eloquence and beauty, of a (suitable) age, and of a virtuous disposition.

10. It is preferable to give (food at a *S*râddha) to young (men in the prime of life).

11. Some (declare, that the age of the guests shall be) proportionate to (that of) the Manes.

12. And he shall not try to contract a friendship by an (invitation to a *S*râddha).

13. On failure of sons (the deceased person's) Sapi*nd*as, the Sapi*nd*as of his mother, or his pupils shall offer (the funeral oblations),

14. On failure of these an officiating priest or the teacher.

15. The Manes are satisfied for a month by gifts of sesamum, Mâsha-beans, rice, barley, and water,

For (three) years by fish and the flesh of common deer, spotted deer, hares, turtles, boars, and sheep,

For twelve years by cow's milk and messes made of milk,

For a very long time by the flesh of (the crane called) Vârdhrî*n*asa, by Ocymum sanctum (sacred Basil), and by the flesh of goats, (especially) of a red (he-goat), and of a rhinoceros, (if these dishes are) mixed with honey.

16. Let him not feed a thief, a eunuch, an outcast, an atheist, a person who lives like an atheist,

---

11. I.e. in honour of the father a young man is to be invited, in honour of the grandfather an old man, and in honour of the great-grandfather a very old man.

12. Âpastamba II, 7, 17, 4, 8; Manu III, 140.

15. Âpastamba II, 7, 16, 23—II, 7, 17, 3; II, 8, 18, 13.

16. Âpastamba II, 7, 17, 21. 'A destroyer of the sacred fire (vîrahan), i.e. one who extinguishes intentionally the (domestic) fire

the destroyer of the sacred fire, (the husband of) a younger sister married before the elder, the husband of an elder sister whose youngest sister was married first, a person who sacrifices for women or for a multitude of men, a man who tends goats, who has given up the fire-worship, who drinks spirituous liquor, whose conduct is blamable, who is a false witness, who lives as a door-keeper;

17. Who lives with another man's wife, and the (husband) who allows that (must not be invited);

18. (Nor shall he feed) a man who eats the food of a person born from adulterous intercourse, a seller of Soma, an incendiary, a poisoner, a man who during studentship has broken the vow of chastity, who is the servant of a guild, who has intercourse with females who must not be touched, who delights in doing hurt, a younger brother married before the elder brother, an elder brother married after his younger brother, an elder brother whose

out of hatred against his wife, and for the like reasons.'—Haradatta. He also remarks that some read agredidhishu instead of agredidhishû, and he proposes to explain the former, on the authority of Vyâghra and of the Naigha*nt*ukas, as 'a Brâhma*n*a whose wife has been wedded before to another man.'

17. My MSS. make two Sûtras out of Professor Stenzler's one, and read upapati*h* | yasya *k*a sa*h*. The sense remains the same, but the latter version of the text is, I think, the correct one.

18. Haradatta says that ku*nd*â*s*in may also mean 'he who eats out of a vessel called ku*nd*a,' as the people have in some countries the habit of preparing their food and afterwards eating out of the ku*nd*a. Haradatta explains tyaktâtman, 'one who despairs of himself,' by 'one who has made an attempt on his own life, and has tried to hang himself, and the like.' He remarks that some explain durvâla, 'a bald man,' by nirvesh*t*ita*s*epha. He who neglects the recitation of the sacred texts, i.e. of those texts which, like the Gâyatrî, ought to be recited.

junior has kindled the sacred fire first, a younger brother who has done that, a person who despairs of himself, a bald man, a man who has deformed nails, or black teeth, who suffers from white leprosy, the son of a twice-married woman, a gambler, a man who neglects the recitation (of the sacred texts), a servant of the king, any one who uses false weights and measures, whose only wife is a *S*ûdra female, who neglects the daily study, who suffers from spotted leprosy, a usurer, a person who lives by trade or handicrafts, by the use of the bow, by playing musical instruments, or, by beating time, by dancing, and by singing;

19. Nor, (sons) who have enforced a division of the family estate against the wish of their father.

20. Some (allow) pupils and kinsmen (to be invited).

21. Let him feed upwards of three (or) one (guest) endowed with (particularly) excellent qualities.

22. If he enters the bed of a *S*ûdra female immediately after partaking of a funeral repast, his ancestors will lie for a month in her ordure.

23. Therefore he shall remain chaste on that day.

---

19. Below, XXVIII, 2, it will be prescribed that the division of the family estate may take place during the lifetime of the father with his consent. From this Sûtra it would appear that sons could enforce a division of the ancestral estate against his will, as Yâ*gñ*avalkya also allows (see Colebrooke, Mitâksharâ I, 6, 5–11), and that this practice, though legal, was held to be contra bonos mores.

20. Âpastamba II, 7, 17, 5–6.

21. According to Haradatta, this Sûtra is intended as a modification of Sûtra 8.

22. Manu III, 250. 23. Manu III, 188.

24. If (a funeral offering) is looked at by dogs, *Kand*âlas, or outcasts, it is blemished.

25. Therefore he shall offer it in an enclosed (place),

26. Or he shall scatter grains of sesamum over it,

27. Or a man who sanctifies the company shall remove the blemish.

28. Persons who sanctify the company are, any one who knows the six Aṅgas, who sings the *G*yeshtha-sâmans, who knows the three texts regarding the Nâ*k*iketa-fire, who knows the text which contains thrice the word Madhu, who knows the text which thrice contains the word Supar*n*a, who keeps five fires, a Snâtaka, any one who knows the Mantras and Brâhma*n*as, who knows the sacred law, and in whose family the study and teaching of the Veda are hereditary.

29. (The same rule applies) to sacrifices offered to gods and men.

30. Some (forbid the invitation of) bald men and the rest to a funeral repast only.

Chapter XVI.

1. The annual (term for studying the Veda) begins on the full moon of the month *S*râva*n*a (July–August); or let him perform the Upâkarman on

---

24. Âpastamba II, 7, 17, 20. 28. Âpastamba II, 7, 17, 22. 29–30. Manu III, 132–137, 148–149.

XVI. 1. Âpastamba I, 3, 9, 1. The Upâkarman is the ceremony which is annually performed at the beginning of the course of study, and it is obligatory on householders also; see Âpastamba II, 2, 5, 1. *Kh*andâ*m*si, 'the Vedic texts,' i.e. the Mantras and Brâhma*n*as. The Aṅgas may be studied out of term; see Âpastamba I, 3, 9, 3 note.

(the full moon of) Bhâdrapada (August–September) and study the Vedic texts,

2. During four months and a half, or during five months, or as long as the sun moves towards the south.

3. Let him remain chaste, let him not shave, nor eat flesh (during that period);

4. Or (this) restrictive rule may (be observed) during two months.

5. He shall not recite the Veda, if the wind whirls up the dust in the day-time,

6. Nor if it is audible at night,

7. Nor if the sound of a Vâ*n*a, of a large or a small drum, the noise of a chariot, and the wail of a person in pain (are heard),

8. Nor if the barking of many dogs and jackals, or the braying of many donkeys (is heard),

9. Nor if (the sky appears flaming) red, a rainbow (is seen), or hoar-frost (lies on the ground),

10. Nor if clouds rise out of season.

11. (Let him not study) when he feels the necessity to void urine or excrements,

12. Nor at midnight, in the twilight, and (while standing) in the water,

13. Nor while rain falls.

---

2. Âpastamba I, 3, 9, 2–3.

3. This Sûtra and the following one refer to a teacher or to a householder who again goes through the Veda; see Âpastamba II, 2, 5, 15, 16.

5–6. Âpastamba I, 3, 11, 8.

7–8. Âpastamba I, 3, 10, 19. A Vâ*n*a is stated to be a kind of lute, or harp, with a hundred strings.

9. Âpastamba I, 3, 11, 25, 31.

10. Âpastamba I, 3, 11, 31.

11. Manu IV, 109.

12. Âpastamba I, 3, 11, 15, 17; Manu IV, 109.

13. Manu IV, 103.

14. Some (declare, that the recitation of the Veda must be interrupted only) when (the rain) is dripping from the edge of the roof.

15. (Nor shall he study) when the teachers (of the gods and Âsuras, i.e. the planets Jupiter and Venus) are surrounded by a halo,

16. Nor (when this happens) to the two (great) lights (the sun and the moon),

17. (Nor) while he is in fear, riding in a carriage or on beasts of burden, or lying down, nor while his feet are raised,

18. (Nor) in a burial-ground, at the extremity of a village, on a high-road, nor during impurity,

19. Nor while a foul smell (is perceptible), while a corpse or a *Kand*âla (is) in (the village), nor in the neighbourhood of a *S*ûdra,

20. Nor while (he suffers from) sour eructations.

21. The *Ri*g-veda and the Ya*g*ur-veda (shall not be studied) while the sound of the Sâmans (is heard).

22. The fall of a thunderbolt, an earthquake, an eclipse, and (the fall of) meteors (are reasons for discontinuing the reading of the Veda) until the same time (next day),

23. Likewise when it thunders and rains and

---

15. 'Another (commentator says): "Parivesha*n*a, being surrounded by a halo, means bringing food." . . . (The Sûtra means, therefore), He shall not study while his teacher eats.'—Haradatta.

16. Âpastamba I, 3, 11, 31.

17. Âpastamba I, 3, 9, 27; I, 3, 11, 12; Manu IV, 112; Yâ*gñ*avalkya I, 150.

18. Âpastamba I, 3, 9, 4, 6; I, 3, 10, 2, 4; I, 3, 11, 9.

19. Âpastamba I, 3, 10, 24; I, 3, 9, 6, 14–15.

20. Âpastamba I, 3, 10, 25. 21. Âpastamba I, 3, 10, 19.

22. Âpastamba I, 3, 11, 30.

23. Âpastamba I, 3, 11, 29; Manu IV, 29.

when lightning (flashes out of season) after the fires have become visible (in the twilight).

24. (If these phenomena appear) during the (rainy) season, (the reading must be interrupted) for a day (or a night),

25. And if lightning (is observed) during the night, (the recitation of the Veda shall be interrupted) until the third watch.

26. If (lightning) flashes during the third part of the day or later, (the Veda must not be read) during the entire (following night).

27. (According to the opinion) of some, a fiery meteor (has the same effect) as lightning,

28. Likewise thunder (which is heard) during the last part of the day,

29. (Or) also in the twilight.

---

24. Âpastamba I, 3, 9, 22. The above translation follows the reading of my MSS., which differ very much from Professor Stenzler's edition. According to them the commentary on the latter part of Sûtra 23 and on Sûtra 24 runs as follows: . . . pratyekam âkâlikâ anadhyâyahetava*h* । apartâv idam । *ri*tâv âha ॥

AHA *RI*TAU ॥ 24 ॥

Varshartâv ete yadi bhaveyu*h* sandhyâyâ*m* tadaharmâtram anâdhyâya*h* । prâta*sk*et । sâya*m* tu râtrâv anadhyâya ityarthasiddhatvâd anuktam ॥ . . . 'are each reasons for discontinuing the recitation until the same time next day. This (rule) refers to other times than the rainy season. He now declares (the rule) for the rainy season:

24. "During the (rainy) season for a day."

'If these (phenomena) happen in the twilight during the rainy season, the interruption of the study lasts for that day only, provided (they happen) in the morning. But if they happen in the evening, study is forbidden during the night. As this is clear from the context, it has not been declared specially.'—Haradatta. I suspect that Professor Stenzler's reading apartau is a correction, made by an ingenious Pandit, of an old varia lectio 'ahartau' for aha *ri*tau, which is found in one of my MSS. (C) also.

25. Âpastamba I, 3, 9, 21.

30. (If thunder is heard) before midnight, (the study of the Veda must be interrupted) during the whole night.

31. (If it is heard) during the (early part of the) day, (the interruption must continue) as long as the sun shines,

32. Likewise if the king of the country has died.

33. If one (pupil) has gone on a journey (and) another (stays) with (the teacher, the study of the Veda shall be interrupted until the absentee returns).

34. When an attack (is made on the village), or a fire (breaks out), when one Veda has been completed, after (an attack of) vomiting, when he has partaken of a funeral repast or of a dinner on the occasion of a sacrifice offered to men, (the study of the Veda shall be interrupted) for a day and a night,

35. Likewise on the day of the new moon.

36. (On the latter occasion it may also be interrupted) for two days.

37. (The Veda shall not be studied for a day and a night) on the full moon days of the months Kârttika, Phâlgu*n*a, and Âshâ*dh*a.

---

30. Âpastamba I, 3, 9, 23.

33. Âpastamba I, 3, 11, 11. Haradatta adds that others enjoin a stoppage of the Veda-study from the hour of the departure until the same hour on the following day, while another commentator gives the following explanation: 'All, indeed, the teacher and the rest, shall, on that day, not even recite the Veda in order to remember it.'

34. Âpastamba I, 3, 9, 25; I, 3, 10, 22, 28–30; I, 3, 11, 6, 30; Manu IV, 118. Haradatta is in doubt whether 'a sacrifice offered in honour of men' means a Sa*m*skâra, or a sacrifice to gods, like Kumâra, who formerly were men; see Âpastamba I, 3, 11, 3.

36. Âpastamba I, 3, 9, 28.

37. Âpastamba I, 3, 10, 1.

38. On the three Ash*t*akâs (the Veda shall not be studied) for three (days and) nights.

39. Some (declare, that the rule applies) to the last Ash*t*akâ (only).

40. (On the occasion of) the annual (Upâkarman and Utsarga the reading shall be interrupted) on the day (of the ceremony) and those preceding and following it.

41. All (teachers declare, that the reading shall be interrupted for three days) when rain, thunder, and lightning (are observed) simultaneously,

42. When the rain is very heavy, (the reading shall be interrupted as long as it lasts).

43. On a festive day (the reading shall be stopped) after the (morning) meal,

44. And he who has begun to study (after the Upâkarman shall not read) at night for four Muhûrtas.

45. Some (declare, that the recitation of the Veda is) always (forbidden) in a town.

46. While he is impure (he shall) not even (recite the Veda) mentally.

---

38. Âpastamba I, 3, 10, 2. Regarding the meaning of the word Ash*t*akâ, see above, VIII, 18 note.

40. Âpastamba I, 3, 10, 2. 41. Âpastamba I, 3, 11, 27.

42. Âpastamba I, 3, 11, 28.

43. Haradatta explains 'a festive day' to mean the day of the initiation and the like, but see Âpastamba I, 3, 11, 20.

44. Haradatta explains this Sûtra as equivalent to Âpastamba I, 3, 9, 1. He adds that another commentator reads prâdhîtasya *k*a as a separate Sûtra, interpreting it to mean, 'And a person who has performed the Upâkarman (shall not study after dinner),' and refers the words 'at night for four Muhûrtas' to the prohibition to read on the evening of the thirteenth day of the dark half of the month.

45. Manu IV, 116. 46. Âpastamba I, 3, 11, 25.

47. (The study) of those who offer a funeral sacrifice (must be interrupted) until the same time next day,

48. Even if uncooked grain is offered at the funeral sacrifice.

49. And (those rules regarding the stoppage of the reading must be observed), which they teach in the several schools.

CHAPTER XVII.

1. A Brâhma*n*a may eat the food given by twice-born men, who are praised for (the faithful performance of their) duties,

2. And he may accept (other gifts from them).

3. Fire-wood, water, grass, roots, fruits, honey, (a promise of) safety, food brought unsolicited, a couch, a seat, shelter, a carriage, milk, sour milk, (roasted) grain, small fish, millet, a garland, venison, and vegetables, (spontaneously offered by a man) of any (caste) must not be refused,

4. Nor anything else that may be required for providing for (the worship of the) Manes and gods, for Gurus and dependents.

5. If the means for sustaining life cannot (be procured) otherwise, (they may be accepted) from a *S*ûdra.

6. A herdsman, a husbandman, an acquaintance

47. Âpastamba ibidem. 49. Âpastamba I, 3, 11, 38.

XVII. 1. Âpastamba I, 6, 18, 13.

3. Âpastamba I, 6, 18, 1; I, 6, 19, 13; Manu IV, 247-250.

4. Manu IV, 251. Gurus, i.e. parents and other venerable persons.

5. Âpastamba I, 6, 18, 14.

6. Manu IV, 253; Yâg*ñ*avalkya I, 166.

of the family, a barber, and a servant are persons whose food may be eaten,

7. And a trader, who is not (at the same time) an artisan.

8. (A householder) shall not eat every day (the food of strangers).

9. Food into which a hair or an insect has fallen (must not be eaten),

10. (Nor) what has been touched by a woman during her courses, by a black bird, or with the foot,

11. (Nor) what has been looked at by the murderer of a learned Brâhma*n*a,

12. (Nor) what has been smelt at by a cow,

13. (Nor) what is naturally bad,

14. Nor (food) that (has turned) sour by itself, excepting sour milk,

15. (Nor) what has been cooked twice,

16. (Nor) what (has become) stale (by being

---

7. E.g. a man who sells pots, but does not make them.

8. Manu III, 104; Yâ*g*ñavalkya I, 112.

9. Âpastamba I, 5, 16, 23, 26.

10. Âpastamba I, 5, 16, 27, 30. Haradatta explains 'a black bird' by 'a crow,' and no doubt the crow, as the *K*â*nd*âla among birds, is intended in the first instance.

11. Manu IV, 208; Yâ*g*ñavalkya I, 167.

12. Manu IV, 209; Yâ*g*ñavalkya I, 168.

13. 'What has been given in a contemptuous manner by the host, or what is not pleasing to the eater, that is called bhâvadush*t*a, "naturally bad."'—Haradatta. The second seems to be the right explanation, as food falling under the first is mentioned below, Sûtra 21.

14. Âpastamba I, 5, 17, 18, 20.

15. Haradatta states that this rule does not refer to dishes the preparation of which requires a double cooking, but to those which ordinarily are cooked once only.

16. Âpastamba I, 5, 17, 17. Haradatta says that food prepared

kept), except vegetables, food that requires mastication, fatty and oily substances, meat and honey.

17. (Food given) by a person who has been cast off (by his parents), by a woman of bad character, an Abhiśasta, a hermaphrodite, a police-officer, a carpenter, a miser, a jailer, a surgeon, one who hunts without using the bow, a man who eats the leavings (of others), by a multitude (of men), and by an enemy (must not be eaten),

18. Nor what is given by such men who defile the company at a funeral dinner, as have been enumerated before bald men;

19. (A dinner) which is prepared for no (holy) purpose or where (the guests) sip water or rise against the rule,

20. Or where (one's) equals are honoured in a different manner, and persons who are not (one's)

---

for the morning meal and kept until supper is also called paryushita, 'stale.'

17. For this and the following Sûtras, see Âpastamba I, 6, 18, 16–I, 6, 19, 1; Manu IV, 205–217; Yâgñavalkya I, 161–165. An Abhiśasta is a person who is wrongly or falsely accused of a heinous crime, see Âpastamba I, 9, 24, 6–9. Haradatta adduces the explanation 'hermaphrodite' for anapadeśya as the opinion of others. He himself thinks that it means 'a person not worthy to be described or named.' 'One who hunts without using the bow' is a poacher who snares animals. Snaring animals is a favourite occupation of the non-Aryan tribes, such as Vâghrîs, Bhils, and Kolis.

18. See above, XV, 15–18, where 'bald men' occupy the fourteenth place in Sûtra 18.

19. Âpastamba I, 5, 17, 3; Manu IV, 212. That is called 'food (prepared) for no (sacred) purpose' which a man cooks only for himself, not for guests and the rest, see Âpastamba II, 4, 8, 4; Manu V, 7.

20. Âpastamba I, 5, 17, 2.

equals are honoured in the same manner (as oneself, must not be eaten),

21. Nor (food that is given) in a disrespectful manner.

22. And the milk which a cow gives during the first ten days after calving (must not be drunk),

23. Nor (that) of goats and buffalo-cows (under the same conditions).

24. (The milk) of sheep, camels, and of one-hoofed animals must not be drunk under any circumstances,

25. Nor (that) of animals from whose udders the milk flows spontaneously, of those that bring forth twins, and of those giving milk while big with young,

26. Nor the milk of a cow whose calf is dead or separated from her.

27. And five-toed animals (must) not (be eaten) excepting the hedgehog, the hare, the porcupine, the iguana, the rhinoceros, and the tortoise,

28. Nor animals which have a double row of teeth, those which are covered with an excessive quantity of hair, those which have no hair, one-hoofed animals, sparrows, the (heron called) Plava, Brahma*n*î ducks, and swans,

---

21. Âpastamba I, 5, 17, 4.

22–23. Âpastamba I, 5, 17, 24.

24. Âpastamba I, 5, 17, 23. 25. Âpastamba I, 5, 17, 23.

26. Manu V, 8; Yâg*ñ*avalkya I, 170.

27. Âpastamba I, 5, 17, 37.

28. Âpastamba I, 5, 17, 29, 33, 35. Haradatta gives as an example of 'animals covered with an excessive quantity of hair' the Yak or Bos grunniens, and of 'those that have no hair' snakes and the like.

29. (Nor) crows, herons, vultures, and falcons, (birds) born in the water, (birds) with red feet and beaks, tame cocks and pigs,

30. (Nor) milch-cows and draught-oxen,

31. Nor the flesh of animals whose milk-teeth have not fallen out, which are diseased, nor the meat of those (which have been killed) for no (sacred) purpose,

32. Nor young sprouts, mushrooms, garlic, and substances exuding (from trees),

33. Nor red (juices) which issue from incisions.

34. Woodpeckers, egrets, ibis, parrots, cormorants, peewits, and flying foxes, (as well as birds) flying at night, (ought not to be eaten).

35. Birds that feed striking with their beaks, or scratching with their feet, and are not web-footed may be eaten,

36. And fishes that are not misshapen,

---

29. Âpastamba I, 5, 17, 29, 32, 34, 35; Yâ*gñ*avalkya I, 173.

30. Âpastamba I, 5, 17, 29–30.

31. Aitareya-brâhma*n*a VII, 14. For the explanation of v*ri*thâmâ*m*sa, 'the flesh (of animals killed) for no (sacred) purpose,' Haradatta refers back to Sûtra 19, but see also the Petersburg Dict. s. v. v*ri*thâ.

32. Âpastamba I, 5, 17, 26, 28; Manu V, 5, 6, 19.

34. Manu V, 12; Yâ*gñ*avalkya I, 173. Haradatta explains mândhâla by vâgvada, which seems to be the same as the bird vâgguda (Manu XII, 64). Mândhâla is not found in our dictionaries, but it apparently is a vicarious form for mânthâla, which occurs in the Vâ*g*asaneyi-sa*m*hitâ, and is said to be the name of a kind of mouse or rat. It seems to me that the large herbivorous bat, usually called the flying fox (in Gu*g*arâtî vâgud or vâgul) is really meant, which, by an inaccurate observer, might be described both as a bird and as a kind of rat. See also Vasish*th*a XIV, 48.

35. Âpastamba I, 5, 17, 32–33.

36. Âpastamba I, 5, 17, 38–39.

37. And (animals) that must be slain for (the fulfilment of) the sacred law.

38. Let him eat (the flesh of animals) killed by beasts of prey, after having washed it, if no blemish is visible, and if it is declared to be fit for use by the word (of a Brâhma*n*a).

Chapter XVIII.

1. A wife is not independent with respect to (the fulfilment of) the sacred law.

2. Let her not violate her duty towards her husband.

3. Let her restrain her tongue, eyes, and (organs of) action.

4. A woman whose husband is dead and who desires offspring (may bear a son) to her brother-in-law.

---

37. I.e. animals offered at *S*râddhas and *S*rauta-sacrifices, though under other circumstances forbidden, may be eaten both by the priests and other Brâhma*n*as.

38. Haradatta takes vyâla, 'beasts of prey,' to mean sporting dogs, which no doubt are also intended.

XVIII. 1. Manu V, 155. This Sûtra refers in the first instance to the inability of wives to offer on their own account *S*rauta or G*ri*hya-sacrifices, or to perform vows and religious ceremonies prescribed in the Purâ*n*as, without the permission of their husbands. As the word strî means both wife and woman, its ulterior meaning is, that women in general are never independent; see Manu V, 148; IX, 3; Yâ*gñ*avalkya I, 85.

2. Âpastamba II, 10, 27, 6; Manu IX, 102.

3. Manu V, 166; Yâ*gñ*avalkya I, 87.

4. Âpastamba II, 10, 27, 2–3; Manu IX, 59–60; Yâ*gñ*avalkya I, 68. Apati, 'she whose husband is dead,' means literally, 'she who has no husband.' But as the case of a woman whose husband has gone abroad, is discussed below, it follows that the former translation alone is admissible. It must, of course, be understood that the widow has no children.

5. Let her obtain the permission of her Gurus, and let her have intercourse during the proper season only.

6. (On failure of a brother-in-law she may obtain offspring) by (cohabiting with) a Sapi*nd*a, a Sagotra, a Samânapravara, or one who belongs to the same caste.

7. Some (declare, that she shall cohabit) with nobody but a brother-in-law.

8. (She shall) not (bear) more than two (sons).

9. The child belongs to him who begat it,

10. Except if an agreement (to the contrary has been made).

11. (And the child begotten at) a living husband's (request) on his wife (belongs to the husband).

12. (But if it was begotten) by a stranger (it belongs) to the latter,

13. Or to both (the natural father and the husband of the mother).

14. But being reared by the husband, (it belongs to him.)

---

5. The Gurus are here the husband's relatives, under whose protection the widow lives.

6. Regarding the term Sapi*nd*a, see above, XIV, 13; a Sagotra is a relative bearing the same family name (laukika gotra) removed seven to thirteen degrees, or still further. A Samânapravara is one who is descended from the same *Ri*shi (vaidika gotra).

8. Colebrooke V, Digest 265. Haradatta explains atidvitîya, 'not more than two (sons),' to mean 'not more than one son' (prathamam apatyam atîtya dvitîyam na *g*anayed iti). But see Manu IX, 61.

9. Âpastamba II, 6, 13, 6–7. 10. Manu IX, 52.

11. Manu IX, 145. Such a son is called Kshetra*g*a, see below, XXVIII, 32.

12. Manu IX, 144.

13. Yâ*gñ*avalkya II, 127. Such a son is called dvipit*ri* or dvyâmushyâya*n*a.

15. (A wife must) wait for six years, if her husband has disappeared. If he is heard of, she shall go to him.

16. But if (the husband) has renounced domestic life, (his wife must refrain) from intercourse (with other men).

17. (The wife) of a Brâhma*n*a (who has gone to a foreign country) for the purpose of studying (must wait) twelve years.

18. And in like manner if an elder brother (has gone to a foreign country) his younger brother (must wait twelve years) before he takes a wife or kindles the domestic fire.

19. Some (declare, that he shall wait) six years.

20. A (marriageable) maiden (who is not given in marriage) shall allow three monthly periods to pass, and afterwards unite herself, of her own will, to a blameless man, giving up the ornaments received from her father (or her family).

21. A girl should be given in marriage before (she attains the age of) puberty.

22. He who neglects it, commits sin.

---

15. Manu IX, 76. 'When the husband has disappeared, i.e. has gone to a foreign country, his wife, though childless, shall wait for six years. After (the lapse of) that (period) she may, if she desires it, produce a child (by cohabiting with a Sapi*nd*a), after having been authorised thereto by her Gurus. If the husband is heard of, i.e. that he dwells in such and such a country, she shall go to him.'—Haradatta. Kshapa*n*a, 'waiting,' is ambiguous, and may also mean being continent or emaciating herself.

17. I.e. before she goes to live with a Sapi*nd*a, or tries to follow her husband, in case his residence is known.

20. Manu IX, 90–92; Yâ*gñ*avalkya I, 64.

21. Manu IX, 88.

22. Manu IX, 4; Yâ*gñ*avalkya I, 64. 'He who,' i.e. the father or guardian.

23. Some (declare, that a girl shall be given in marriage) before she wears clothes.

24. In order to defray the expenses of a wedding, and when engaged in a rite (enjoined by) the sacred law, he may take money (by fraud or force) from a *S*ûdra,

25. Or from a man rich in small cattle, who neglects his religious duties, though he does not belong to the *S*ûdra caste,

26. Or from the owner of a hundred cows, who does not kindle the sacred fire,

27. Or from the owner of a thousand cows, who does not drink Soma.

28. And when he has not eaten (at the time of six meals he may take) at the time of the seventh meal (as much as will sustain life), not (such a quantity as will serve) to make a hoard,

29. Even from men who do not neglect their duties.

30. If he is examined by the king (regarding his deed), he shall confess (it and his condition).

31. For if he possesses sacred learning and a good character, he must be maintained by the (king).

---

24. Manu XI, 11, 13. Haradatta explains dharmatantra, 'a rite prescribed by the sacred law,' here, as well as Sûtra 32, by 'the means,' i.e. a sacrificial animal and the like required by one who is engaged in performing a sacred duty, i.e. a Pa*s*ubandha-sacrifice and the like.

25. Manu XI, 12. 26–27. Manu XI, 14.

28. Manu XI, 16; Yâ*gñ*avalkya III, 43.

30. Manu XI, 17; Yâ*gñ*avalkya III, 43–44.

31. Manu XI, 21–22. Haradatta adds that a Brâhma*n*a who acts thus, must, of course, not be punished.

32. If the sacred law is violated and the (king) does not do (his duty), he commits sin.

Chapter XIX.

1. The law of castes and of orders has been declared.

2. Now, indeed, man (in) this (world) is polluted by a vile action, such as sacrificing for men unworthy to offer a sacrifice, eating forbidden food, speaking what ought not to be spoken, neglecting what is prescribed, practising what is forbidden.

3. They are in doubt if he shall perform a penance for such (a deed) or if he shall not do it.

4. (Some) declare, that he shall not do it,

---

32. Haradatta refers this Sûtra to the case where a sacrificial animal or other requisites for a sacrifice are stolen from a Brâhma*n*a. It seems, however, more probable that it refers to the duty of the king to prevent, by all means in his power, a violation of the sacred duty to perform *S*rauta-sacrifices, and that it is intended to prescribe that he is to assist a man who is engaged in them and too poor to finish them.

XIX. 1. Haradatta thinks that the object of this Sûtra is to assert that in the following chapter the laws given above for castes and orders must be kept in mind. Thus penances like offering a Punastoma are not intended for *S*ûdras, who have no business with Vedic rites, but other penances are. He also states that another commentator believes that the Sûtra is meant to indicate that the following rules refer not merely to those men who belong to castes and orders, but to the Pratilomas also, who have been declared to stand outside the pale of the sacred law. Haradatta's opinion appears to be preferable.

2. 'Ayam purusha*h*, "man (in) this (world)," indicates the universal soul which is dwelling in the body. Yâpya, "vile," i.e. despicable (kutsita).'—Haradatta.

3. 'They, i.e. the theologians (brahmavâdina*h*).'—Haradatta.

5. Because the deed does not perish.

6. The most excellent (opinion is), that he shall perform (a penance).

7. For it is declared in the Veda, that he who has offered a Punastoma (may) again come to (partake of) the libations of Soma,

8. Likewise he who has offered a Vrâtyastoma.

9. (The Veda says) further: 'He who offers a horse-sacrifice, conquers all sin, he destroys the guilt of the murder of a Brâhma*n*a;

10. Moreover: 'He shall make an Abhi*s*asta perform an Agnish*t*ut sacrifice.'

11. Reciting the Veda, austerity, a sacrifice, fasting, giving gifts are the means for expiating such a (blamable act).

12. The purificatory (texts are), the Upanishads, the Vedântas, the Sa*m*hitâ-text of all the Vedas, the (Anuvâkas called) Madhu, the (hymn of)

---

5. I.e. the guilt (adharma) contracted by the deed is not effaced before it has produced its result in the shape of punishment in hell and in other births, see also Manu XI, 45.

6. 'Apara, "most excellent," means that which nothing surpasses, i.e. the settled doctrine.'—Haradatta.

7. The Punastoma is one of the *S*rauta-sacrifices belonging to the class called Ekâha. Regarding its efficacy, see also Lâ*t*yâyana *S*rauta-sûtra IX, 4, 5.

8. The Vrâtyastoma is another Ekâha-sacrifice. Regarding its efficacy, see Yâ*gñ*avalkya I, 38; Lâ*t*yâyana *S*rautra-sûtra VIII, 6, 29.

9. *S*atapatha-brâhma*n*a XIII, 3, 1, 1.

10. The Agnish*t*ut is an Ekâha-sacrifice. Regarding its efficacy, see Manu XI, 75.

11. Manu XI, 46, 228; Âpastamba I, 9, 26, 12—I, 9, 27, 11.

12. 'Those parts of the Âra*n*yakas which are not (Upanishads) are called Vedântas. In all the Vedas (*kh*andas), i.e. in all *S*âkhâs (pravaka*k*ana), the Sa*m*hitâ-text, not the Pada-text, nor the Krama-text. Another commentator says, "One Sa*m*hitâ is to be made

Aghamarsha*n*a, the Atharva*s*iras, the (Anuvâkas called the) Rudras, the Purusha-hymn, the two Sâmans (called) Râ*g*ana and Rauhi*n*eya, the B*ri*hat (Sâman) and the Rathantara, the Purushagati (Sâman), the Mahânâmnîs, the Mahâvairâ*g*a (Sâman), the Mahâdivâkîrtya (Sâman), any of the *G*yesh*th*a Sâmans, the Bahishpavamâna (Sâman), the Kûshmâ*nd*as, the Pâvamânîs, and the Sâvitrî.

13. To live on milk alone, to eat vegetables only, to eat fruits only, (to live on) barley-gruel prepared of a handful of grain, to eat gold, to eat clarified butter, and to drink Soma (are modes of living) which purify.

14. All mountains, all rivers, holy lakes, places of pilgrimage, the dwellings of *Ri*shis, cow-pens, and temples of the gods (are) places (which destroy sin).

---

with all the metres, i.e. the Gâyatrî and the rest, and to be recited according to the manner of the Prâtaranuvâka."'—Haradatta. According to the same authority, the Madhus are found Taittirîya Âra*n*yaka X, 38, the hymn of Aghamarsha*n*a Rig-veda X, 190, the Rudras Taittirîya-sa*m*hitâ IV, 5, 1–11, and in the corresponding eleven chapters of all other Ya*g*us-*s*âkhâs, the Purushasûkta Rig-veda X, 90, the Kûshmâ*nd*as Taittirîya Âra*n*yaka X, 3–5, the Pâvamânîs Rig-veda IX, while by Atharva*s*iras the Upanishad, known by that name, is meant. As regards the Sâmans mentioned in the Sûtra it suffices to refer to Professor Benfey's Index, Ind. Stud. III, 199, and to Dr. Burnell's Index of the Ârsheya-brâhma*n*a.

13. According to Haradatta the word iti, which appears in the text at the end of the enumeration, is intended to include other similar kinds of food, as 'the five products of the cow.' Eating gold means eating small particles of gold which have been thrown into clarified butter and the like.

14. The word iti used in the text is, according to Haradatta, again to be taken in the sense of 'and so forth.' The translation of parishkanda, 'a temple,' not parishkandha, as Professor Stenzler

15. Continence, speaking the truth, bathing morning, noon, and evening, standing in wet clothes, sleeping on the ground, and fasting (are the various kinds of) austerity.

16. Gold, a cow, a dress, a horse, land, sesamum, clarified butter, and food are the gifts (which destroy sin).

17. A year, six months, four (months), three (months), two (months), one (month), twenty-four days, twelve days, six days, three days, a day and a night are the periods (for penances).

18. These (acts) may be optionally performed when no (particular penance) has been prescribed,

19. (Viz.) for great sins difficult (penances), and for trivial faults easy ones.

20. The K*rikkh*ra and the Atik*rikkh*ra, (as well as) the *K*ândrâya*n*a, are penances for all (offences).

Chapter XX.

1. Let him cast off a father who assassinates a king, who sacrifices for *S*ûdras, who sacrifices for

---

reads, is based on Haradatta's explanation. Etymologically it seems to mean 'a place for circumambulation,' and to denote the platform on which the temples usually stand, and which is used for the Pradakshi*n*a ceremony.

15. The word iti in the text is explained as in the preceding Sûtras.

18. These (acts), i.e. the recitation of the Veda and so forth, which have been enumerated above, Sûtras 11-16.

20. Regarding these penances, see chapters XXVI and XXVII. Haradatta again takes the word iti, which occurs in the text, to include other difficult penances.

XX. 1. Haradatta remarks that the father is mentioned here, in order to indicate that other less venerable relatives must certainly

his own sake (accepting) money from *S*ûdras, who divulges the Veda (to persons not authorised to study it), who kills a learned Brâhma*n*a, who dwells with men of the lowest castes, or (cohabits) with a female of one of the lowest castes.

2. Having assembled the (sinner's) spiritual Gurus and the relatives by marriage, (the sons and other kinsmen) shall perform (for him) all the funeral rites, the first of which is the libation of water,

3. And (afterwards) they shall overturn his water-vessel (in the following manner):

4. A slave or a hired servant shall fetch an impure vessel from a dust-heap, fill it (with water taken) from the pot of a female slave and, his face turned towards the south, upset it with his foot, pronouncing (the sinner's) name (and saying): 'I deprive N. N. of water.'

5. All (the kinsmen) shall touch him (the slave) passing their sacrificial cords over the right shoulder and under the left arm, and untying the locks on their heads.

6. The spiritual Gurus and the relatives by marriage shall look on.

7. Having bathed, they (all shall) enter the village.

8. He who afterwards unintentionally speaks to

---

also be abandoned. He also states that bhrû*n*ahan, 'he who slays a learned Brâhma*n*a,' includes sinners who have committed other mortal sins (mahâpâtaka), see XXI, 1.

2. Manu XI, 183–185; Yâg*ñ*avalkya III, 295. The spiritual Gurus, i.e. the teacher who initiated him (â*k*ârya) and those who instructed him in the Veda (upâdhyâya).

8. Manu XI, 185.

the (outcast sinner) shall stand, during one night, reciting the Sâvitrî.

9. If he intentionally (converses with the outcast, he must perform the same penance) for three nights.

10. But if an (outcast sinner) is purified by (performing) a penance, (his kinsmen) shall, after he has become pure, fill a golden vessel (with water) from a very holy lake or a river, and make him bathe in water (taken) from that (vessel).

11. Then they shall give him that vessel and he, after taking it, shall mutter (the following Mantras): 'Cleansed is the sky, cleansed is the earth, cleansed and auspicious is the middle sphere; I here take that which is brilliant.'

12. Let him offer clarified butter, (reciting) these Ya*g*us formulas, the Pâvamânîs, the Taratsamandîs, and the Kûshmâ*nd*as.

13. Let him present gold or a cow to a Brâhma*n*a,

14. And to his teacher.

15. But he, whose penance lasts for his (whole) lifetime, will be purified after death.

16. Let (his kinsmen) perform for him all the funeral rites, the first of which is the libation of water.

17. This same (ceremony of bathing in) water

---

10. Manu XI, 187–188; Yâ*gñ*avalkya III, 296.

11. As appears from Gobhila G*ri*hya-sûtra III, 4, 16, the noun to be understood is apâm a*ñg*ali*h*, 'a handful of water.'

12. Haradatta refers the term Pâvamânîs here to Taittirîya-brâhma*n*a I, 4, 8. The Taratsamandîs are found Rig-veda IX, 58.

17. '"Water (consecrated) for the sake of purification" means

consecrated for the sake of purification (must be performed) in the case of all minor offences (upapâtakas).

Chapter XXI.

1. The murderer of a Brâhmana, he who drinks spirituous liquor, the violator of a Guru's bed, he who has connection with the female relatives of his mother and of his father (within six degrees) or with sisters and their female offspring, he who steals (the gold of a Brâhmana), an atheist, he who constantly repeats blamable acts, he who does not cast off persons guilty of a crime causing loss of caste, and he who forsakes blameless (relatives), become outcasts,

2. Likewise those who instigate others to acts causing loss of caste,

3. And he who for a (whole) year associates with outcasts.

4. To be an outcast means to be deprived of the right to follow the lawful occupations of twice-born men,

5. And to be deprived after death of the rewards of meritorious deeds.

---

water consecrated by the formulas, "Cleansed is the earth," &c.'—Haradatta.

XXI. 1. Âpastamba I, 7, 21, 7–9, 11; I, 9, 24, 6–9; Manu XI, 35; Yâgñavalkya III, 227. Guru, i.e. a father or spiritual teacher. The term yonisambandha, 'sisters and their female offspring,' seems to be used here in a sense different from that which it has III, 3; XIV, 20; and XIX, 20. It may possibly include also daughters-in-law.

2. Âpastamba II, 11, 29, 1.

3. Manu IX, 181; Yâgñavalkya III, 261.

6. Some call (this condition) hell.

7. Manu (declares, that) the first three (crimes, named above) cannot be expiated.

8. Some (declare, that a man) does not become an outcast (by having connection) with female (relatives), except (when he violates) a Guru's bed.

9. A woman becomes an outcast by procuring abortion, by connection with a (man of) lower (caste) and (the like heinous crimes).

10. Giving false evidence, calumnies which will reach (the ears of) the king, an untrue accusation brought against a Guru (are acts) equal to mortal sins (mahâpâtaka).

11. (The guilt of a) minor offence (upapâtaka) rests on those who (have been declared to) defile the company (at a funeral dinner and have been named above) before the bald man, on killers of kine, those who forget the Veda, those who pronounce Vedic texts for the (last-mentioned sinners), students

---

7. Âpastamba I, 9, 24, 24–25; I, 9, 25, 1–3; Manu XI, 90–92, 104–105. The 'penances' prescribed are equal to a sentence of death.

8. Âpastamba I, 7, 21, 10.

9. Yâgñavalkya III, 298. 'On account of the word "and," by slaying a Brâhmana and similar crimes also. Another (commentator) says, "A woman who serves the slayer of a learned Brâhmana or a man of lower caste, i. e. becomes his wife, loses her caste. On account of the word 'and' the same happens in case she kills a Brâhmana or commits a similarly heinous crime. The slayer of a Brâhmana is mentioned in order to include (all) outcasts."'—Haradatta.

10. Manu XI, 56–57; Yâgñavalkya III, 228–229.

11. Manu XI, 60–67; Yâgñavalkya III, 234–242; Âpastamba I, 7, 21, 12–17, 19. The persons who defile the company are enumerated above, XV, 16–18.

who break the vow of chastity, and those who allow the time for the initiation to pass.

12. An officiating priest must be forsaken, if he is ignorant (of the rules of the sacrifice), a teacher, if he does not impart instruction, and (both) if they commit crimes causing loss of caste.

13. He who forsakes (them) under any other circumstances, becomes an outcast.

14. Some declare, that he, also, who receives (a person who has unjustly forsaken his priest or teacher, becomes an outcast).

15. The mother and the father must not be treated improperly under any circumstances.

16. But (the sons) shall not take their property.

17. By accusing a Brâhma*n*a of a crime (the accuser commits) a sin equal (to that of the accused).

18. If (the accused is) innocent, (the accuser's guilt is) twice (as great as that of the crime which he imputed to the other).

19. And he who, though able to rescue a weak man from injury, (does) not (do it, incurs as much guilt as he who injures the other).

20. He who in anger raises (his hand or a weapon)

---

12. Âpastamba I, 2, 4, 26; I, 2, 7, 26; I, 2, 8, 27. Haradatta asserts that, as the desertion of sinners has been prescribed above, XX, 1, the expression patanîyasevâyâm must here mean 'if they associate with outcasts.' The former rule refers, however, to blood relations only, and our Sûtra may be intended to extend it to spiritual relations.

15. Âpastamba I, 10, 28, 9–10. The meaning is that parents, though they have become outcasts, must be provided with the necessaries of life.

16. Haradatta adds that their property goes to the king.

17. Âpastamba I, 7, 21, 20. 18. Yâg*ñ*avalkya III, 285.

20–21. Manu XI, 207; Yâg*ñ*avalkya III, 293. According to

against a Brâhma*n*a, will be banished from heaven for a hundred years.

21. If he strikes, (he will lose heaven) for a thousand (years).

22. If blood flows, (he will lose heaven) for a number of years equal to (that of the particles of) dust which the spilt (blood) binds together.

CHAPTER XXII.

1. (Now follows the description of the) penances.

2. He who has (intentionally) slain a Brâhma*n*a shall emaciate himself, and thrice throw himself into a fire,

3. Or he may become in battle a target for armed men,

4. Or, remaining chaste, he may, during twelve years, enter the village (only) for the purpose of begging, carrying the foot of a bedstead and a skull in his hand and proclaiming his deed.

5. If he meets an Ârya, he shall step out of the road.

Haradatta the word asvargyam, 'will be banished from or lose heaven,' may either mean that a hundred years' residence in heaven will be deducted from the rewards for his meritorious deeds, or that he will reside in hell for the period specified.

22. Manu XI, 208; Yâ*gñ*avalkya III, 293.

XXII. 1. The text of the Sûtra consists of the single word 'penance' in the singular, which, being the adhikâra or heading, must be taken with each of the following Sûtras down to the end of chapter XXIII.

2. Manu XI, 74. 3. Âpastamba I, 9, 25, 11.

4. Âpastamba I, 9, 24, 11–20. Haradatta says, 'the foot of a bedstead' (kha*t*vâṅga) is known in the case of the Pâ*s*upatas, and indicates thereby that he interprets the term to mean 'a club shaped like the foot of a bedstead,' which the Pâ*s*upatas wear.

5. Âpastamba I, 9, 24, 13.

6. Standing by day, sitting at night, and bathing in the morning, at noon, and in the evening, he may be purified (after twelve years),

7. Or by saving the life of a Brâhma*n*a,

8. Or if he is, at least, thrice vanquished in (trying to recover) the property (of a Brâhma*n*a) stolen (by robbers),

9. Or by bathing (with the priests) at (the end of) a horse-sacrifice,

10. Or at (the end of) any other (Vedic) sacrifice, provided that an Agnish*t*ut (sacrifice) forms part of it.

11. (The same penances must be performed) even if he has attempted the life of a Brâhma*n*a, but failed to kill him,

12. Likewise if he has killed a female (of the Brâhma*n*a caste) who had bathed after temporary uncleanness,

13. Also for (destroying) the embryo of a Brâhma*n*a, though (its sex) may be not distinguishable.

14. For (intentionally) killing a Kshatriya the normal vow of continence (must be kept) for six

---

6. Âpastamba I, 9, 25, 10.

7. Manu XI, 80; Yâ*gñ*avalkya III, 244-245.

8. Âpastamba I, 9, 25, 21. 9. Âpastamba I, 9, 25, 22.

10. Haradatta names the Pa*ñk*arâtra sacrifice as an instance of a *S*rauta ya*gñ*a, of which an Agnish*t*ut forms part. He adds that another commentator explains the Sûtra to mean, 'or at any other sacrifice, provided that an Agnish*t*ut sacrifice be its final ceremony.' Regarding the Agnish*t*ut sacrifice, see also above, XIX, 10.

11. Yâ*gñ*avalkya III, 252.

12. Âpastamba I, 9, 24, 9; Manu XI, 88; Yâ*gñ*avalkya III, 251.

13. Âpastamba I, 9, 24, 8; Manu, Yâ*gñ*avalkya, loc. cit.

14. Âpastamba I, 9, 24, 1, 4. 'Prâk*ri*ta (normal) means natural

years; and he shall give one thousand cows and one bull.

15. For (killing) a Vai*s*ya (the same penance must be performed) during three years; and he shall give one hundred cows and one bull.

16. For (killing) a *S*ûdra (the same penance must be performed) during one year; and he shall give ten cows and one bull.

17. And the same (rule applies) if a female (has been killed) who was not in the condition (described in Sûtra 12).

18. (The penance for killing) a cow is the same as for (the murder of) a Vai*s*ya,

19. And for injuring a frog, an ichneumon, a crow, a chameleon, a musk-rat, a mouse, and a dog,

20. And for killing one thousand (small animals) that have bones,

21. Also for (killing) an ox-load of (animals) that have no bones;

(svâbhâvika), i.e. not accompanied by the carrying of the foot of a bedstead and the rest.'—Haradatta.

15. Âpastamba I, 9, 24, 2, 4.

16. Âpastamba I, 9, 24, 3, 4.

17. Âpastamba I, 9, 24, 5; Yâ*gñ*avalkya III, 269. Haradatta says that this rule refers to the expiation of the murder of a virtuous Brâhma*n*î.

18. Âpastamba I, 9, 26, 1; Manu XI, 109–116; Yâ*gñ*avalkya III, 263. Haradatta thinks that the Sûtra refers to the cow of a virtuous *S*rotriya or of a poor Brâhma*n*a who has many children.

19. Âpastamba I, 9, 25, 13. Haradatta explains dahara to mean a small mouse, but gives the meaning assigned to it in the translation as the opinion of others. He states that all the animals named must have been intentionally injured and together.

20. Manu XI, 142; Yâ*gñ*avalkya III, 275.

21. Âpastamba I, 9, 26, 2.

22. Or he may also give something for (the destruction of) each animal that has bones.

23. For (killing) a eunuch (he shall give) a load of straw and a mâsha of lead;

24. For (killing) a boar, a pot of clarified butter;

25. For (killing) a snake, a bar of iron;

26. For (killing) an unchaste woman, who is merely in name a Brâhma*n*î, a leather bag;

27. (For killing a woman who subsists) by harlotry, nothing at all.

28. For preventing that (a Brâhma*n*a) obtains a wife, food, or money, (he must) in each case (remain chaste) during a year,

29. For adultery two years,

30. (For adultery with the wife) of a *S*rotriya three years.

31. And if he has received a present (from the woman), he shall throw it away,

32. Or restore it to the giver.

33. If he has employed Vedic texts for people (with whom such intercourse is) forbidden, (he shall remain chaste for a year), provided (the portion of the Veda thus employed) contained one thousand words.

---

22. Haradatta quotes a verse showing that 'something' means eight handfuls (mush*t*i) of grain.

23. Manu XI, 134; Yâ*gñ*avalkya III, 273.

24. Manu XI, 135.

25. Manu XI, 34; Yâ*gñ*avalkya III, 273. Possibly da*nd*a, a bar, denotes here a particular measure, as a da*nd*a is said to be equal to four hastas or ninety-six aṅgulis.

26. Manu XI, 139.

29–30. Âpastamba II, 10, 27, 11.

33. Haradatta says that by the employment of Vedic texts, teaching or sacrificing is meant, but that others refer the Sûtra

34. And the same (penance must be performed) by him who extinguishes the (sacred) fires, who neglects the daily recitation of the Veda, or (who is guilty) of a minor offence (upapâtaka),

35. Also by a wife who violates her duty (to her husband): but, being guarded, she shall receive food.

36. For committing a bestial crime, excepting (the case of) a cow, (he shall offer) an oblation of clarified butter, (reciting) the Kûshmâ*nd*a texts.

Chapter XXIII.

1. They shall pour hot spirituous liquor into the mouth of a Brâhma*n*a who has drunk such liquor; he will be purified after death.

2. If he has drunk it unintentionally, (he shall drink) for three days hot milk, clarified butter, and water, and (inhale hot) air. That (penance is called the Tapta-)k*rikkh*ra. Afterwards he shall be again initiated.

3. And (the same penance must be performed) for swallowing urine, excrements, or semen,

---

to the performance of these acts in the company of, not for unworthy people.

35. Manu XI, 189; Yâ*gñ*avalkya III, 297.

36. Manu XI, 174. Regarding the Kûshmâ*nd*as, see XIX, 12.

XXIII. 1. Âpastamba I, 9, 25, 3. Haradatta remarks that other twice-born men also must perform the same penance in case they drink liquor forbidden to them, see above, II, 20 note. He also states that the offence must have been committed intentionally and repeatedly in order to justify so severe an expiation. Regarding the effect of the purification after death, see above, XX, 16.

2-3. Manu XI, 151; Yâ*gñ*avalkya III, 255; see also Âpastamba I, 9, 25, 10.

4. And (for eating) any part of a carnivorous beast, of a camel or of an ass,

5. And of tame cocks or tame pigs.

6. If he smells the fume (exhaled) by a man who has drunk spirituous liquor, (he shall) thrice restrain his breath and eat clarified butter,

7. Also, if he has been bitten by (one of the animals mentioned) above (Sûtras 4–5).

8. He who has defiled the bed of his Guru shall extend himself on a heated iron bed,

9. Or he shall embrace the red-hot iron image of a woman.

10. Or he shall tear out his organ and testicles and, holding them in his hands, walk straight towards the south-west, until he falls down dead.

11. He will be purified after death.

12. (The guilt of him who has intercourse) with the wife of a friend, a sister, a female belonging to the same family, the wife of a pupil, a daughter-in-law, or with a cow, is as great as that of (him who violates his Guru's) bed.

13. Some (declare, that the guilt of such a sinner is equal to) that of a student who breaks the vow of chastity.

14. A woman who commits adultery with a man

4–5. Manu XI, 157. 6. Manu XI, 150.

7. Manu XI, 200; Yâg*ñ*avalkya III, 277.

8–10. Âpastamba I, 9, 25, 1–2. Haradatta asserts that Guru denotes here the father alone.

12. Manu XI, 171–172; Yâg*ñ*avalkya III, 232–233.

13. 'The penance also consists in the performance of the rites obligatory on an unchaste student (see Sûtras 17–19), and that for the violation of a Guru's bed need not be performed.'—Haradatta.

14. Manu VIII, 371.

of lower caste the king shall cause to be devoured by dogs in a public place.

15. He shall cause the adulterer to be killed (also).

16. (Or he shall punish him in the manner) which has been declared (above).

17. A student who has broken the vow of chastity shall offer an ass to Nir*ri*ti on a cross-road.

18. Putting on the skin of that (ass), with the hair turned outside, and holding a red (earthen) vessel in his hands, he shall beg in seven houses, proclaiming his deed.

19. He will be purified after a year.

20. For an involuntary discharge caused by fear or sickness, or happening during sleep, and if for seven days the fire-oblations and begging have been neglected, (a student) shall make an offering of clari-

---

15. Manu VIII, 372; Yâg*ñ*avalkya II, 286; Âpastamba II, 10, 27, 9. My best MSS. read ghâtayet, 'shall cause to be killed,' instead of Professor Stenzler's khâdayet, 'shall cause to be devoured.' C. has khâdayet, but its commentary, as well as that given in the other MSS., shows that ghâtayet is the correct reading. The text of the commentary runs as follows: Anantaroktavishaye gata*h* pumân râg*ñ*â ghâtayitvyo [khâdayitavyo C.] vadhaprakâra*s*k*â*nantaram eva vasish*th*avak*a*ne dar*s*ita*h*. The passages of Vasish*th*a XXI, 1-3, which Haradatta has quoted in explanation of Sûtra 14, prescribe that the adulterer is to be burnt. Another objection to the reading khâdayet is that the word would be superfluous. If Gautama had intended to prescribe the same punishment for the adulterer as for the woman, he would simply have said pumâ*m*sam.

16. Above, i.e. XII, 2, where the mutilation of the offender has been prescribed. See also Âpastamba II, 10, 26, 20.

17-19. Âpastamba I, 9, 26, 8-9.

20. Manu II, 181, 187; Yâg*ñ*avalkya III, 278, 281. The Retasyâs are found Taittirîya Âra*n*yaka I, 30.

fied butter or (place) two pieces of fuel (in the fire) reciting the two (verses called) Retasya.

21. Let him who was asleep when the sun rose remain standing during the day, continent and fasting, and him who was asleep when the sun set (remain in the same position) during the night, reciting the Gâyatrî.

22. He who has looked at an impure (person), shall look at the sun and restrain his breath (once).

23. Let him who has eaten forbidden food [or swallowed impure substances], (fast until) his entrails are empty.

24. (In order to attain that), he must entirely abstain from food at least for three (days and) nights.

25. Or (he becomes pure) after eating during seven (days and) nights fruits that have become detached spontaneously, avoiding (all other food).

26. (If he has eaten forbidden food mentioned above) before five-toed animals, he must throw it up and eat clarified butter.

27. For abuse, speaking an untruth, and doing injury, (he shall practise) austerities for no longer period than three (days and) nights.

---

21. Âpastamba II, 5, 12, 22; Manu II, 220.

22. Manu V, 86. 'An impure person, i. e. a *Kând*âla and the like. This rule refers to a student (who sees such a person) while he recites the Veda.'—Haradatta.

23–24. Âpastamba I, 9, 27, 3–4. My copies omit amedhyaprâ*s*ane vâ, or has swallowed impure substances, and the words are not required, as another penance has been prescribed for the case above, Sûtra 3. But see also Sâmavidhâna I, 5, 13.

26. Manu XI, 161. The Sûtras referred to are XVII, 9–26.

27. Âpastamba I, 9, 26, 3. My copies read trirâtraparamam instead of trirâtram paramam. This reading, which seems pre-

28. If (the abuse) was merited, (he shall offer) burnt-oblations, reciting (the Mantras) addressed to Varu*n*a and (the hymns) revealed by Manu.

29. Some (declare, that) an untruth (spoken) at the time of marriage, during dalliance, in jest or while (one suffers severe) pain is venial.

30. But (that is) certainly not (the case) when (the untruth) concerns a Guru.

31. For if he lies in his heart only to a Guru regarding small matters even, he destroys (himself), seven descendants, and seven ancestors.

32. For intercourse with a female (of one) of the lowest castes, he shall perform a K*rikkh*ra penance during one year.

33. (For committing the same sin) undesignedly, (he shall perform the same penance) during twelve (days and) nights.

34. For connection with a woman during her courses, (he shall perform the same penance) for three (days and) nights.

Chapter XXIV.

1. A secret penance (must be performed) by him whose sin is not publicly known.

---

ferable, is also confirmed by the commentary, where the words are explained, trirâtraparatayâ pare*n*a trirâtram.

28. According to Haradatta the texts addressed to Varu*n*a are yatki*m k*edam, Taitt. Sa*m*h. III, 4, 11, 6; imam me varu*n*a, tattvâ yâmi, Taitt. Sa*m*h. II, 1, 11, 6; and ava te he*l*o, Taitt. Sa*m*h. I, 5, 11, 3. The hymns seen by Manu are Rig-veda VIII, 27–31.

29. Manu VII, 112.

32. Âpastamba I, 10, 28, 10–11. Regarding the K*rikkh*ra penance, see below, chapter XXVI.

34. Manu XI, 174; Yâ*gñ*avalkya III, 288.

XXIV. 1. Manu XI, 248; Yâ*gñ*avalkya III, 301.

2. He who desires to accept or has accepted (a gift) which ought not to be accepted, shall recite the four *Ri*k-verses (IX, 58, 1-4), (beginning) Tarat sa mandî, (standing) in water.

3. He who desires to eat forbidden food, shall scatter earth (on it).

4. Some (declare, that) he who has connection with a woman during her courses becomes pure by bathing.

5. Some (declare, that this rule holds good) in the case of (one's own) wives (only).

6. The (secret) penance for killing a learned Brâhma*n*a (is as follows): Living during ten days on milk (alone) or (on food fit for offerings), during a second (period of ten days) on clarified butter, and during a third (period of ten days) on water, par-

---

2. Manu XI, 254. 'He who has accepted or desires to accept, i. e. because no other course is possible, (a present) offered by a man that is blamable on account of the caste of the giver or on account of his deeds, or (a present) that in itself is blamable, e. g. the skin of a black-buck and the like . . . in water, i. e. according to some, standing in water that reaches to his navel; according to others, entirely immersed in water.'—Haradatta.

3. Manu loc. cit. 'Forbidden food has been described above, XVII, 8, 9. If, being unable to act otherwise, he desires to eat that, he shall throw earth, i. e. a piece of earth, (into it) and then eat it.'—Haradatta.

4. Haradatta adds that he shall bathe, dressed in his garments.

5. Haradatta adds that another commentator reads ekestrîshu, i.e. eke astrîshu, and explains the Sûtra to mean, 'Some (declare the above rule to refer also) to a bestial crime.'

6. Yâg*ñ*avalkya III, 303. According to Haradatta the complete Mantras are as follows: Lomânyâtmano mukhe m*ri*tyorâsye *g*uhomi svâhâ, nakhânyâ. m. m. â. *g*uhomi svâhâ, &c. This secret penance is apparently a milder form of that prescribed Âpastamba I, 9, 25, 12.

taking of (such food) once only each day, in the morning, and keeping his garments constantly wet, he shall (daily) offer (eight) oblations, (representing) the hair, the nails, the skin, the flesh, the blood, the sinews, the bones, (and) the marrow. The end of each (Mantra) shall be, 'I offer in the mouth of the Âtman (the Self), in the jaws of Death.'

7. Now another (penance for the murder of a Brâhma*n*a will be described):

8. The rule (as to eating and so forth), which has been declared (above, Sûtra 6, must be observed),

9. (And) he shall offer clarified butter, reciting (the sacred text Rig-veda I, 189, 2), 'O fire, do thou ferry over,' the Mahâvyâh*ri*tis, and the Kûshmâ*nd*as;

10. Or, for the murder of a Brâhma*n*a, for drinking spirituous liquor, for stealing (gold), and for the violation of a Guru's bed, he may perform that (same vow), tire himself by repeatedly stopping his breath, and recite (the hymn seen by) Aghamarsha*n*a. That is equal (in efficacy) to the final bath at a horse-sacrifice;

11. Or, repeating the Gâyatrî a thousand times, he, forsooth, purifies himself;

12. Or, thrice repeating (the hymn of) Aghamarsha*n*a while immersed in water, he is freed from all sins.

---

9. The Mahâvyâh*ri*tis are, bhû*h*, bhuva*h*, sva*h*. Regarding the Kûshmâ*nd*as, see above, XIX, 12.

10. Manu XI, 260–261; Yâ*gñ*avalkya III, 302. The vow intended is that prescribed above, Sûtras 6, 8.

11. Âpastamba I, 9, 26, 14–I, 9, 27, 1. Haradatta remarks that the performer of the penance shall live on milk and stop his breath, repeatedly stopping his breath.

Chapter XXV.

1. Now they say: 'How many (gods) does a student enter who violates the vow of chastity?'

2. (And they answer): 'His vital spirits (go to) the Maruts (winds), his strength to Indra, his eminence in sacred learning to B*ri*haspati, all the remaining parts to Agni.'

3. He kindles the fire in the night of the new moon, and offers, by way of penance, two oblations of clarified butter,

4. (Reciting these two sacred texts), 'Defiled by lust am I, defiled am I, oh Lust; to Lust svâhâ;' 'Injured by lust am I, injured am I, oh Lust; to Lust svâhâ.' (Next) he (silently) places one piece of sacred fuel (on the fire), sprinkles water round the fire, offers the Ya*gñ*avâstu (oblation), and approaching (the fire) worships it, thrice (reciting the text), 'May the waters sprinkle me.'

5. These worlds are three; in order to conquer

XXV. 1. For this and the following five Sûtras, see Taittirîya Âra*n*yaka II, 18, 1 seq.

2. 'All the remaining parts, i.e. his sight and the other organs of sense, go to Agni. Thus a student who has broken the vow of chastity becomes short-lived, weak, destitute of eminence in sacred learning, and destitute of sight, and so forth. Therefore a penance must be performed.'—Haradatta. It must, of course, be understood that the penance prescribed here, is a 'secret penance.'

3. 'He, i.e. the unchaste student, shall kindle the fire in the night of the new moon, i.e. at midnight, in the manner declared in the G*ri*hya-sûtra.'—Haradatta.

4. Haradatta says that while sprinkling water the performer shall recite the texts 'Aditi, thou hast permitted,' see Âpastamba II, 2, 3, 17 note. The Ya*gñ*avâstu oblation, which follows after the Svish*t*akr*i*t offering, is described Gobhila G*ri*hya-sûtra I, 8, 26–29.

these worlds, in order to gain mastership over these worlds, (this rite must be performed.)

6. According to some, the above (described) rite is a penance (for all hidden offences) in general, (and they say) regarding it, 'He who may be impure, as it were, shall offer burnt-oblations in this manner, and shall recite sacred texts in this manner; the fee (of the officiating priest shall be) whatever he may choose.'

7. He who has been guilty of cheating, of calumniating, of acting contrary to the rule of conduct, of eating or drinking things forbidden, of connection with a woman of the *S*ûdra caste, of an unnatural crime, and even of performing magic rites with intent (to harm his enemies), shall bathe and sprinkle himself with water, reciting the texts addressed to the Waters, or those addressed to Varu*n*a, or other purificatory texts.

8. For offences committed by speaking or thinking of forbidden things, the five Vyâh*ri*tis (must be recited).

9. Or for all (offences) he may sip water, (reciting) in the morning (the text), 'May the day and the sun purify me;' and in the evening, 'The night and Varu*n*a.'

10. Or he may offer eight pieces of sacred fuel,

---

7. Âpastamba I, 9, 26, 7. The verses addressed to the Waters are, Rv. X, 9, 1-3 = Taitt. Sa*m*h. IV, 1, 5, 1, and Taitt. Sa*m*h. V, 6, 1. Regarding those addressed to Varu*n*a, see above, XXIII, 28. As an instance of 'other purificatory texts' Haradatta quotes Taittirîya-brâhma*n*a I, 4, 8, 1.

8. Regarding the five Vyâh*ri*tis, see above, I, 51.

10. Haradatta gives the following four Mantras: Devak*ri*tasyainasovaya*g*anam asi svâhâ, 'thou art the expiation for sin com-

(reciting the texts beginning) 'Devakr*i*tasya.' By merely offering them he becomes free from all sin.

CHAPTER XXVI.

1. Now, therefore, we will describe three K*r*i*kk*h*ras (or difficult penances).

2. (During three days) he shall eat at the morning-meal food fit for offerings, and fast in the evening.

3. Next, he shall eat (food fit for offerings), during another period of three days, in the evening (only).

4. Next, during another period of three days, he shall not ask anybody (for food).

5. Next, he shall fast during another period of three days.

6. He who desires (to be purified) quickly, shall stand during the day, and sit during the night.

---

mitted by the gods,' svâhâ pit*r*ik*r*itasyainaso . . . svâhâ, manushyak*r*itasyainaso . . . svâhâ, asmatk*r*itasyainaso . . . svâhâ. But see Vâ*g*asaneyi-sa*m*hitâ VIII, 13, where eight Mantras are given, and below, XXVII, 7.

XXVI. 1. Sâmavidhâna I, 2, 1; Âpastamba I, 9, 27, 7. Haradatta states that ata*h*, 'therefore,' means 'because the K*r*i*kkh*ras cannot be performed if they have not been described,' while Sâya*n*a, on the Sâmavidhâna, asserts that it means 'because unpurified persons who are unable to offer sacrifices cannot gain heavenly bliss without performing austerities such as K*r*i*kkh*ras.' It is a remarkable fact that Haradatta does not seem to have been aware that the twenty-sixth chapter of Gautama is taken bodily from the Sâmavidhâna.

2. Sâmavidhâna I, 2, 2. 'Food fit for offerings, i.e. such as is not mixed with salt or pungent condiments.'

3-5. Sâmavidhâna I, 2, 3.

6. Sâmavidhâna I, 2, 4.

7. He shall speak the truth.

8. He shall not converse with anybody but Âryans.

9. He shall daily sing the two (Sâmans called) Raurava and Yaudhâ*g*aya.

10. He shall bathe in the morning, at noon, and in the evening, reciting the three (verses which begin) 'For ye waters are,' and he shall dry himself reciting the eight purificatory (verses which begin) 'The golden-coloured.'

11. Next (he shall offer) libations of water.

12. Adoration to him who creates self-consciousness, who creates matter, who gives gifts, who destroys (sin), who performs penance, to Punarvasu, adoration.

Adoration to him who is worthy of (offerings)

7–11. Sâmavidhâna I, 2, 5. Âryans, i.e. Brâhma*n*as, Kshatriyas, and Vai*s*yas. Regarding the Sâmans and Mantras, see notes to Burnell's edition of the Sâmavidhâna, and above, XXV, 7. Haradatta remarks that in the Taitt. Sa*m*h. (V, 6, 1) the Mantras beginning 'The golden-coloured' are ten in number, and adds that 'if in some other *S*âkhâ eight are found, those must be taken.'

12. Sâmavidhâna I, 2, 5, where, however, only four Mantras are given instead of our thirteen. The epithets given to the deity in the Sâmavidhâna can all be referred to the Sun, provided he is identified with the universal soul, while in the above Sûtra, Rudra and Indra have been introduced. It cannot be doubtful that the Sâmavidhâna gives an older and more authentic form of the prayer. My translation of the epithets, which are found in the Sâmavidhâna also, follows Sâya*n*a's gloss. Haradatta does not explain them. About Sobhya in the twelfth Mantra, which possibly might mean, 'he who dwells in a mirage, i.e. the Sa*m*sâra,' I feel doubtful. My MSS. read somya, and the Sâmavidhâna has saumya in the second Mantra. But I am unwilling to alter the word, as Professor Stenzler's reading may have been derived from a South-Indian MS., where bhya and mya do not resemble each other so much as in the Devanâgarî characters.

consisting of Muñga grass, who is worthy of (offerings of) water, who conquers wealth, to him who conquers the universe, adoration.

Adoration to him who gives success, who gives full success, who gives great success, to him who carries (all undertakings) to a successful issue, adoration.

Adoration to Rudra, the lord of cattle, the great god, the triocular, solitary, supreme lord Hari, to dread *S*arva, to Î*s*âna who carries the thunderbolt, to the fierce wearer of matted locks, adoration.

Adoration to the Sun, to Aditi's offspring, adoration.

Adoration to him whose neck is blue, to him whose throat is dark-blue, adoration.

Adoration to the black one, to the brown one, adoration.

Adoration to Indra, the first-born, the best, the ancient, to chaste Harike*s*a, adoration.

Adoration to the truthful purifier, to fire-coloured Kâma, who changes his form at pleasure, adoration.

Adoration to the brilliant one, to him whose form is brilliant, adoration.

Adoration to the fierce one, to him whose form is fierce, adoration.

Adoration to Sobhya, the beautiful, the great male, the middle male, the highest male, to the student of the Veda, adoration.

Adoration to him who wears the moon on his forehead, to him whose garment is a skin, adoration.

13. The worship of Âditya (the sun) must be performed with the same (texts).

13–17. Sâmavidhâna I, 2, 5.

14. Offerings of clarified butter (must be made with the help of) the same (texts).

15. At the end of the period of twelve days he shall boil rice and make offerings to the following deities,

16. (Viz.) to Agni svâhâ, to Soma svâhâ, to Agni and Soma (conjointly), to Indra and Agni (conjointly), to Indra, to all the gods, to Brahman, to Pra*g*âpati, (and) to Agni Svish*t*ak*ri*t.

17. Afterwards (he must feed) Brâhma*n*as.

18. By the above (rules) the Atik*rikkh*ra (or exceedingly difficult) penance has been explained.

19. (But when he performs that), he shall eat (only) as much as he can take at one (mouthful).

20. The third (K*rikkh*ra) is that where water is the (only) food, and it is called K*rikkh*râtik*rikkh*ra (or the most difficult penance).

21. He who has performed the first of these (three) becomes pure, sanctified, and worthy (to follow) the occupations (of his caste).

22. He who has performed the second is freed from all sins which he commits, excepting mortal sins (mahâpâtaka).

23. He who has performed the third, removes all guilt.

24. Now he who performs these three K*rikkh*ras becomes perfect in all the Vedas, and known to all the gods;

25. Likewise he who knows this.

---

18. Sâmavidhâna I, 2, 6.

19. Sâmavidhâna I, 2, 7; Manu XI, 214; Yâ*gñ*avalkya III, 320.

20. Sâmavidhâna I, 2, 8; Yâ*gñ*avalkya III, 321.

21–23. Sâmavidhâna I, 2, 9.

24–25. Sâmavidhâna I, 2, 10. Sarveshu vedeshu snâta*h*, 'perfect

Chapter XXVII.

1. Now, therefore, the *K*ândrâya*n*a (or lunar penance will be described).

2. The (general) rules prescribed for a K*rikkh*ra (are applicable) to that.

3. (The hair must be) shaved, in case it (is performed as) a penance.

4. He shall fast on the day preceding the full moon.

5. And (he shall offer) libations (of water), oblations of clarified butter, consecrate the sacrificial viands, and worship the moon, reciting these (*rik*as), 'Increase' (Rig-veda I, 91, 17), 'May milk be joined with thee' (Rig-veda I, 91, 18, and) 'Ever new' (Rig-veda X, 85, 19).

6. He shall offer (clarified butter), reciting the four (*rik*as beginning) 'Yad devâ devahe*d*anam,'

7. And at the end (of the offering of clarified

---

in all the Vedas,' means, literally, equal to a student who has bathed after completing the study of all the four Vedas.

XXVII. 2. The rules meant particularly are those given XXVI, 6–11.

3. 'He calls penance vrata.'—Haradatta.

5. 'The four religious acts, the first of which is the offering of libations, are to be performed with the help of the three sacred texts, the first of which begins "Increase." As the number (of the acts and of the verses) does not agree, the fire-oblations and the libations of water must be performed severally, each with one text, and the consecration (of the offerings) and the worship (of the moon must be performed with all of them) together.'—Haradatta.

6. 'He shall offer—as nothing is specified—clarified butter, with the first four *rik*as of the Anuvâka 'Yad devâ devahe*d*anam.' Counting the three mentioned above (Sûtra 5), altogether seven oblations of clarified butter must be made.'—Haradatta.

7. 'On completion of the oblations of clarified butter, he

butter he shall offer) pieces of sacred fuel, reciting (the texts beginning) 'Devakritasya.'

8. Each mouthful of food must be consecrated by the mental recitations (of one) of the following (words): Om, bhûh, bhuvah, svah, austerity, truth, fame, prosperity, vigour, refreshment, strength, lustre, soul, law, Siva.

9. Or (he may consecrate) all (of them at once, saying), Adoration svâhâ.

10. The size of a mouthful (shall be such) as not to cause a distortion of the mouth (in swallowing it).

11. The sacrificial viands are, boiled rice, food obtained by begging, ground barley, grain separated from the husk, barley-gruel, vegetables, milk, sour

shall offer pieces of sacred fuel, reciting the eight sacred texts, which begin "Devakritasya," and have been mentioned above (XXV, 10). The word "completion" (anta) is merely a confirmation of something established, because (the place of the offering) is already fixed by the place of the rule. But others explain the word "ante" to mean "at the end of the Kândrâyana." The word "and" does not agree with their (opinion).'—Haradatta.

8. Haradatta observes that on the days when the performer eats less than fifteen mouthfuls, the later mentioned texts must be left out, and that, while eating, the performer must employ the Prânâhuti Mantras (Âpastamba II, 1, 1, 2 note). He concludes by giving the following prayoga for the performance of the ceremony: 'He places all the food in his dish, and consecrates it by the texts "Increase," &c. Next he divides it into mouthfuls, and consecrates each successively with the word Om and the rest, and eats them, reciting the texts for the Prânâhutis.'

9. Haradatta states that either of the two words may be used in consecrating all the mouthfuls, but that others think, both should be used.

10. Yâgñavalkya III, 324.

11. The term 'sacrificial viands' denotes here, according to Haradatta, the food eaten by the performer, which, like that eaten by the performer of a Krikkhra, must be havishya, 'fit for an offering,'

milk, clarified butter, roots, fruits, and water; (among these) each succeeding one is preferable (to those enumerated earlier).

12. He shall eat on the day of the full moon fifteen mouthfuls, and during the dark half (of the month) daily diminish his portion by one (mouthful).

13. He shall fast on the day of the new moon, and during the bright half (of the month) daily increase (his portion) by one (mouthful).

14. According to some (the order shall be) inverted.

15. That (is called) a month, occupied by the *K*ândrâya*n*a penance.

16. He who has completed that, becomes free from sin and free from crime, and destroys all guilt.

17. He who has completed a second (month, living according to that rule), sanctifies himself, ten ancestors, and ten descendants, as well as (any) company (to which he may be invited);

18. And he who has lived for a year (according to that rule), dwells (after death) in the world of the moon.

Chapter XXVIII.

1. After the father's death let the sons divide his estate,

---

see above, XXVI, 2. Haradatta adds that, as a G*ri*hastha must not beg, the food obtained by begging must have been collected by his pupils, and that liquid food must be used for the expiation of the more serious offences.

12. Manu XI, 217–218; Yâ*gñ*avalkya III, 324–325.

14. I.e. the performer may begin with the fast on the day of the new moon.

18. Manu XI, 221; Yâ*gñ*avalkya III, 327.

XXVIII. 1. Colebrooke, Dâyabhâga II, 4; Mitâksharâ I, 2, 7;

2. Or, during his lifetime, when the mother is past child-bearing, if he desires it,

3. Or the whole (estate may go) to the first-born; (and) he shall support (the rest) as a father.

4. But in partition there is an increase of spiritual merit.

5. (The additional share) of the eldest (son consists of) a twentieth part (of the estate), a male and a female (of animals with one row of front teeth, such as cows), a carriage yoked with animals that have two rows of front teeth, (and) a bull.

6. (The additional share) of the middlemost (consists of) the one-eyed, old, hornless, and tailless animals, if there are several.

V, Digest 20; Mayûkha IV, 4, 3. Haradatta remarks that, according to Gautama, the sons alone shall divide the estate, and that the mother is not to receive a share, as other teachers, e.g. Yâgñavalkya II, 123, prescribe. Âpastamba II, 6, 13, 2; Manu IX, 104; Yâgñavalkya II, 117.

2. Colebrooke and Mayûkha loc. cit. 'Or the sons may divide the estate even during the lifetime of the father; when he desires it, i.e. by his permission. The time for such a (division is) when the mother is past child-bearing.'—Haradatta. The correctness of this interpretation of our Sûtra is corroborated by the exclusion of sons who have divided the family estate against the father's will (XV, 19) from the *S*râddha dinner. Âpastamba II, 6, 14, 1.

3. Colebrooke, Dâyabhâga III, 1, 15; Manu IX, 105.

4. Colebrooke, Dâyabhâga III, 1, 14; V, Digest 47. After division each brother has to perform the Vais*v*adeva and the other domestic ceremonies separately, while in a united family they are performed by the eldest brother. Thus a division of the family estate causes an increase of spiritual merit; see also Manu XI, 111.

5. Colebrooke, Dâyabhâga II, 37; V, Digest 47; Manu IX, 112.

6. Colebrooke ll. cit. 'And that (additional share is given), if of the one-eyed and the rest there are several, i.e. if the others also get (some).'

7. (The additional share) of the youngest (consists of) the sheep, grain, the iron (utensils), a house, a cart yoked (with oxen), and one of each kind of (other) animals.

8. All the remaining (property shall be divided) equally.

9. Or let the eldest have two shares,

10. And the rest one each.

11. Or let them each take one kind of property, (selecting), according to seniority, what they desire,

12. Ten head of cattle.

13. (But) no (one brother shall) take (ten) one-hoofed beasts or (ten) slaves.

14. (If a man has several wives) the additional

---

7. Colebrooke ll. cit. 'Avi*h* (a sheep), i.e. an animal having a fleece. The singular number (is used to denote) the species, (and the explanation is), "As many sheep as there are." For (the possession of) one would follow already from the phrase, "And one of each kind of animals." Another (commentator says), "Though the father may possess one sheep only, still it belongs to the youngest, and the phrase 'one of each kind of animals' refers to the case when there are many." . . . This (additional share is that) belonging to the youngest. (If there are more than three sons) the others obtain the share of the middlemost.'—Haradatta.

8. Colebrooke ll. cit.

9. Colebrooke, Dâyabhâga II, 37; V, Digest 51. My best copy P. leaves out this Sûtra and the next. The others read dvya*m*sî vâ pûrva*g*a*h* (not pûrva*g*asya, as Professor Stenzler reads), and explain the former word as follows, 'dvâva*m*sau dvya*m*sa*m* tadasyâstîti dvya*m*sî.' Manu IX, 117.

10. Colebrooke ll. cit.

11. Colebrooke V, Digest 68.

12. Colebrooke loc. cit. The meaning appears to be that no brother is to select more than ten head of cattle.

13. Colebrooke V, Digest 69. 'But, as has been declared above (Sûtra 11), one of each kind only. In the case of the v. l. dvipadânâm, the word pada (step) is used in the sense of the word pâda (foot).'—Haradatta.

14. Colebrooke V, Digest 58; Manu IX, 123.

share of the eldest son is one bull (in case he be born of a later-married wife);

15. (But the eldest son) being born of the first-married wife (shall have) fifteen cows and one bull;

16. Or (let the eldest son) who is born of a later-married wife (share the estate) equally with his younger (brethren born of the first-married wife).

17. Or let the special shares (be adjusted) in each class (of sons) according to their mothers.

18. A father who has no (male) issue may appoint his daughter (to raise up a son for him), presenting burnt offerings to Agni (fire) and to Pra*g*âpati (the lord of creatures), and addressing (the bridegroom with these words), 'For me be (thy male) offspring.'

19. Some declare, that (a daughter becomes) an appointed daughter solely by the intention (of the father).

20. Through fear of that (a man) should not marry a girl who has no brothers.

21. Sapi*nd*as (blood relations within six degrees), Sagotras (relations bearing a common family name), (or) those connected by descent from the same *Ri*shi

15. Colebrooke loc. cit.; Manu IX, 124.

16. Colebrooke loc. cit.

17. Colebrooke V, Digest 59. 'After having divided the estate into as many portions as there are wives who possess sons, and having united as many shares as there are sons (of each mother), let the eldest in each class (of uterine brothers) receive the additional share of one-twentieth and so forth.'—Haradatta.

18–19. Colebrooke V, Digest 225; Manu IX, 130–140.

20. Manu III, 11; Yâ*gñ*avalkya I, 53.

21. Colebrooke, Dâyabhâga XI, 6, 25; Mitâksharâ II, 1, 18; V, Digest 440. My copies as well as *G*îmûtavâhana and Vi*gñ*âne*s*vara read in the text strî vâ, 'or the wife,' instead of strî *k*a,

(vaidika gotra), and the wife shall share (the estate) of a person deceased without (male) issue (or an appointed daughter).

22. Or (the widow) may seek to raise up offspring (to her deceased husband).

23. (A son) begotten on a (widow) whose husband's brother lives, by another (relative), is excluded from inheritance.

24. A woman's separate property (goes) to her unmarried daughters, and (on failure of such) to poor (married daughters).

25. The sister's fee belongs to her uterine brothers, if her mother be dead.

26. Some (declare, that it belongs to them) even while the mother lives.

27. The heritage of not reunited (brothers) de-

'and the wife.' Still the latter seems to be the reading recognised by Haradatta, as he says, 'But the wife is joined together (samu*kk*îyate) with all the Sagotras and the rest. When the Sagotras and the rest inherit, then the wife shall inherit one share with them,' &c. Âpastamba II, 6, 14, 2; Manu IX, 187; Yâ*gñ*avalkya II, 135-136.

22. Colebrooke, Mitâksharâ II, 1, 8, where this Sûtra has, however, been combined with the preceding. See also above, XVIII, 4-8; Manu IX, 145-146, 190.

23. Colebrooke V, Digest 341; Manu IX, 144.

24. Colebrooke, Dâyabhâga IV, 2, 13; Mitâksharâ I, 3, 11; II, 2, 4; V, Digest 490; Mayûkha IV, 8, 12. See also Manu IX, 192; Yâ*gñ*avalkya II, 145.

25. Colebrooke, Dâyabhâga IV, 3, 27; V, Digest 511; Mayûkha IV, 10, 32. 'The fee, i.e. the money which at an Âsura, or an Ârsha wedding, the father has taken for giving the sister away. That goes after his (the father's) death to the uterine brothers of that sister; and that (happens) after the mother's death. But if the mother is alive (it goes) to her.'—Haradatta.

26. Colebrooke V, Digest 511.

27. Colebrooke V, Digest 424. 'The word "eldest" is used

ceased (without male issue goes) to the eldest (brother).

28. If a reunited coparcener dies (without male issue) his reunited coparcener takes the heritage.

29. A son born after partition takes exclusively (the wealth) of his father.

30. What a learned (coparcener) has acquired by his own efforts, he may (at his pleasure) withhold from his unlearned (coparceners).

31. Unlearned (coparceners) shall divide (their acquisitions) equally.

32. A legitimate son, a son begotten on the wife (by a kinsman), an adopted son, a son made, a son born secretly, and a son abandoned (by his natural parents) inherit the estate (of their fathers).

33. The son of an unmarried damsel, the son of a pregnant bride, the son of a twice-married woman, the son of an appointed daughter, a son self-given, and a son bought belong to the family (of their fathers).

34. On failure of a legitimate son or (of the)

to give an example. (The property) goes to the brothers, not to the widow, nor to the parents. That is the opinion of the venerable teacher.'—Haradatta. Yâ*gñ*avalkya II, 134.

28. Mayûkha IV, 9, 15; Manu IX, 212; Yâ*gñ*avalkya II, 138.

29. Colebrooke, Dâyabhâga VII, 3; Manu IX, 216.

30. Colebrooke, Dâyabhâga VI, 1, 17, V, Digest 355; Mayûkha IV, 7, 10; Manu IX, 206; Yâ*gñ*avalkya II, 119.

31. Colebrooke V, Digest 137; Manu IX, 205.

32-33. Colebrooke V, Digest 184; Manu IX, 166-178; Yâ*gñ*avalkya II, 128-132. My best copy P. inserts another Sûtra between this and the following one, ete tu gotrabhâ*gah*, 'but these (latter six) belong to the family (only, and do not inherit).'

34. Colebrooke V, Digest 184. 'The residue of the estate

other (five heirs) they receive a fourth (of the estate).

35. The son of a Brâhma*n*a by a Kshatriya wife, being the eldest and endowed with good qualities, shares equally (with a younger brother, born of a Brâhma*n*î);

36. (But he shall) not (obtain) the additional share of an eldest son.

37. If there are sons begotten (by a Brâhma*n*a) on wives of the Kshatriya and Vai*s*ya castes (the division of the estate between them takes place according to the same rules) as (between) the (son by a Kshatriya wife) and the son by a Brâhma*n*î.

38. And (the sons by a Kshatriya wife and by

---

goes to the Sapi*nd*as. If it is here stated that the son of an appointed daughter receives, even on failure of a legitimate son, a fourth part of the estate only, that refers to the son of an appointed daughter of lower caste, i.e. to a son who is born, when somebody makes the daughter of a wife of lower caste his appointed daughter, and does that by intent only.'—Haradatta.

35. Colebrooke V, Digest 158; Manu IX, 149–153; Yâg*ñ*avalkya II, 125. 'If the son of a Brâhma*n*a by a Kshatriya wife is endowed with good qualities and the eldest, then he shares equally with a younger son by a Brâhma*n*î. For the one possesses seniority by age and the other by caste.'—Haradatta.

36. Colebrooke loc. cit. 'What is exclusive of the additional share of the eldest, which has been declared above, Sûtra 5, (that) other (part) he shall obtain. The verb must be understood from the context. Regarding a son by a Kshatriya wife who is the eldest, but destitute of good qualities, the Mânava Dharma-*s*âstra declares (IX, 152–153), "Or (if no deduction be made)," &c.'—Haradatta. The sense in which the Sûtra has been taken above, agrees with the explanation of the Ratnâkara adduced in the Digest loc. cit., though the reading of the text followed there seems to be different.

37–38. Colebrooke V, Digest 159. In the Digest V, 160, an additional Sûtra regarding the partition between the sons of a

a Vaisya wife share in the same manner) if (they have been begotten) by a Kshatriya (father).

39. The son by a Sûdra wife even, if he be obedient like a pupil, receives a provision for maintenance (out of the estate) of a (Brâhmana) deceased without (other) male issue.

40. According to some, the son of a woman of equal caste even does not inherit, if he be living unrighteously.

41. Srotriyas shall divide the estate of a childless Brâhmana.

42. The king (shall take the property of men) of other (castes).

43. An idiot and a eunuch must be supported.

44. The (male) offspring of an idiot receives (his father's) share.

45. (Sons begotten) on women of higher castes (by men of lower castes shall be treated) like sons (begotten by a Brâhmana) on a Sûdra wife.

Vaisya by Vaisya and Sûdra wives is quoted, which, however, is not recognised by Haradatta.

39. Colebrooke V, Digest 169; Mayûkha IV, 4, 30. '(The word) of a Brâhmana must be understood (from Sûtra 35).'—Haradatta.

40. Colebrooke V, Digest 316; Âpastamba II, 6, 14, 15.

41. Colebrooke, Mitâksharâ II, 7, 3; Mayûkha IV, 8, 25. 'The expression "of a childless (Brâhmana)" includes by implication (the absence) of Sapindas and other (heirs).'—Haradatta. Srotriyas, i.e. Brâhmanas learned in the Vedas. See also Manu IX, 188.

42. Âpastamba II, 6, 14, 5.

43. Colebrooke V, Digest 335; Manu IX, 201–202; Yâgñavalkya II, 140.

44. Colebrooke loc. cit.; Manu IX, 203; Yâgñavalkya II, 141.

45. Colebrooke V, Digest 171, 335.

46. Water, (property destined for) pious uses or sacrifices, and prepared food shall not be divided;

47. Nor (shall a partition be made) of women connected (with members of the family).

48. In cases for which no rule has been given, (that course) must be followed of which at least ten (Brâhma*n*as), who are well instructed, skilled in reasoning, and free from covetousness, approve.

49. They declare, that an assembly (parishad, shall consist) at least (of) the ten following (members, viz.) four men who have completely studied the four Vedas, three men belonging to the (three) orders enumerated first, (and) three men who know (three) different (institutes of) law.

50. But on failure of them the decision of one *S*rotriya, who knows the Veda and is properly instructed (in the duties, shall be followed) in doubtful cases.

51. For such a man is incapable of (unjustly) injuring or (unjustly) favouring created beings.

52. He who knows the sacred law obtains heavenly bliss, more than (other) righteous men, on account of his knowledge of, and his adherence to it.

53. Thus the sacred law (has been explained).

---

46. Manu IX, 219. For a fuller explanation of the terms yoga and kshema, (property destined for) pious uses and sacrifices, see Colebrooke, Mitâksharâ I, 4, 23.

47. Colebrooke, Mitâksharâ I, 4, 22; V, Digest 367; Mayûkha IV, 7, 19.

49-51. Âpastamba II, 11, 29, 13-14; Manu XII, 108-113. Three men belonging to the (three) orders enumerated first, i.e. a student, a householder, and an ascetic, see above, III, 2.

Transliteration of Oriental Alphabets adopted for the Translations of the Sacred Books of the East.

CONSONANTS.	MISSIONARY ALPHABET. I Class.	II Class.	III Class.	Sanskrit.	Zend.	Pehlevi.	Persian.	Arabic.	Hebrew.	Chinese.
Gutturales.										
1 Tenuis	k	. . .	. . . .	क	𐬐	[illegible]	ک	ك	כּ	k
2 „ aspirata	kh	. . .	. . . .	ख	𐬑	[illegible]	. . .	. . .	כ	kh
3 Media	g	. . .	. . . .	ग	𐬔	[illegible]	گ	. . .	גּ	. . .
4 „ aspirata	gh	. . .	. . . .	घ	𐬖	[illegible]	. . .	. . .	ג	. . .
5 Gutturo-labialis	q	. . .	. . . .	. . .	. . . .	. . .	ق	ق	ק	. . .
6 Nasalis	ṅ (ng)	. . .	. . . .	ङ	𐬧 (ng) / 𐬣 (N)	. . .	. . .	. . .	. . .	. . .
7 Spiritus asper	h	. . .	. . . .	ह	𐬵 (𐬓 *hv*)	[illegible]	ه	ه	ה	h, hs
8 „ lenis	’	. . .	. . . .	. . .	. . . .	. . .	ا	ا	א	. . .
9 „ asper faucalis	‘h	. . .	. . . .	. . .	. . . .	. . .	ح	ح	ח	. . .
10 „ lenis faucalis	’h	. . .	. . . .	. . .	. . . .	. . .	ع	ع	ע	. . .
11 „ asper fricatus	. . .	*‘h*	. . . .	. . .	. . . .	. . .	خ	خ	ח	. . .
12 „ lenis fricatus	. . .	*’h*	. . . .	. . .	. . . .	. . .	. . .	. . .	. . .	. . .
Gutturales modificatae (palatales, &c.)										
13 Tenuis	. . .	*k*	. . . .	च	𐬗	[illegible]	چ	. . .	. . .	*k*
14 „ aspirata	. . .	*kh*	. . . .	छ	. . . .	. . .	. . .	. . .	. . .	*kh*
15 Media	. . .	*g*	. . . .	ज	𐬘	[illegible]	ج	ج	. . .	. . .
16 „ aspirata	. . .	*gh*	. . . .	झ	. . . .	. . .	غ	غ	. . .	. . .
17 „ Nasalis	. . .	*ñ*	. . . .	ञ	. . . .	. . .	. . .	. . .	. . .	. . .

CONSONANTS (*continued*).	MISSIONARY ALPHABET. I Class.	II Class.	III Class.	Sanskrit.	Zend.	Pehlevi.	Persian.	Arabic.	Hebrew.	Chinese.
18 Semivocalis	y	...	....	य	𐬫; init. [illegible]	[illegible]	ي	ي	י	y
19 Spiritus asper	...	(*ẏ*)	....	...	....	...	...	...	...	...
20 „ lenis	...	(*y̓*)	....	...	....	...	...	...	...	...
21 „ asper assibilatus	...	*s*	....	श	𐬱	[illegible]	ش	ش	...	...
22 „ lenis assibilatus	...	*z*	....	...	𐬲	[illegible]	ژ	...	...	*z*
Dentales.										
23 Tenuis	t	...	....	त	𐬙	[illegible]	ت	ت	תּ	t
24 „ aspirata	th	...	....	थ	𐬚	...	...	...	ת	th
25 „ assibilata	...	...	TH	...	....	...	ث	ث	...	...
26 Media	d	...	....	द	𐬛	[illegible]	د	د	דּ	...
27 „ aspirata	dh	...	....	ध	𐬜	...	...	...	ד	...
28 „ assibilata	...	...	DH	...	....	...	ذ	ذ	...	...
29 Nasalis	n	...	....	न	𐬥	[illegible]	ن	ن	נ	n
30 Semivocalis	l	...	....	ल	....	[illegible]	ل	ل	ל	l
31 „ mollis 1	...	*l*	....	ळ	....	...	...	...	...	...
32 „ mollis 2	...	...	L	...	....	...	...	...	...	...
33 Spiritus asper 1	s	...	....	स	𐬯	[illegible]	س (ث)	س	שׂ	s
34 „ asper 2	...	...	s (ʃ)	...	....	...	...	...	ס	...
35 „ lenis	z	...	....	...	𐬰	[illegible]	ز (ذ)	ز	ז	z
36 „ asperrimus 1	...	...	z (ʒ)	...	....	...	ص	ص	צ	ʒ, ʒh
37 „ asperrimus 2	...	...	ẓ (ʒ)	...	....	...	ض	...	...	...

Dentales modificatae (linguales, &c.)										
38 Tenuis	...	*t*	....	ट	....	...	ط	ط	ט	...
39 " aspirata	...	*th*	....	ठ	....	...	ظ	ظ	...	...
40 Media	...	*d*	....	ड	[illegible]	[illegible]	...	...	...	...
41 " aspirata	...	*dh*	....	ढ	....	...	...	ض	...	...
42 Nasalis	...	*n*	....	ण	[illegible]	...	...	...	...	...
43 Semivocalis	r	...	....	र	[illegible]	[illegible]	ر	ر	ר	...
44 " fricata	...	*r*	....	...	....	...	...	...	...	*r*
45 " diacritica	...	...	R	...	....	...	...	...	...	...
46 Spiritus asper	sh	...	....	ष	[illegible]	[illegible]	...	...	...	sh
47 " lenis	zh	...	....	...	....	...	...	...	...	...
Labiales.										
48 Tenuis	p	...	....	प	[illegible]	[illegible]	پ	...	פּ	p
49 " aspirata	ph	...	....	फ	....	...	...	...	פ	ph
50 Media	b	...	....	ब	[illegible]	[illegible]	ب	ب	בּ	...
51 " aspirata	bh	...	....	भ	....	...	...	...	ב	...
52 Tenuissima	...	*p*	....	...	....	...	...	...	...	...
53 Nasalis	m	...	....	म	[illegible]	[illegible]	م	م	מ	m
54 Semivocalis	w	...	....	...	[illegible]	...	...	...	...	w
55 " aspirata	hw	...	....	...	....	...	...	...	...	...
56 Spiritus asper	f	...	....	...	[illegible]	[illegible]	ف	ف	...	f
57 " lenis	v	...	....	व	»	[illegible]	و	و	ו	...
58 Anusvâra	...	*m*	....	अं	[illegible] ã	...	...	...	...	...
59 Visarga	...	*h*	....	अः	....	...	...	...	...	...

VOWELS.	MISSIONARY ALPHABET. I Class.	II Class.	III Class.	Sanskrit.	Zend.	Pehlevi.	Persian.	Arabic.	Hebrew.	Chinese.
1 Neutralis	0	...	....	...	....	...	...	...	ְ	ă
2 Laryngo-palatalis	ě	...	....	...	....	...	...	...	...	...
3 „ labialis	ŏ	...	....	...	....	ا fin.	...	...	...	...
4 Gutturalis brevis	a	...	....	अ	𐬀	𐬀 init.	ـَ	ـَ	ַ	a
5 „ longa	â	(a)	....	आ	𐬁	𐬀	ـَا	ـَا	ָ	â
6 Palatalis brevis	i	...	....	इ	𐬌	...	ـِ	ـِ	ִ	i
7 „ longa	î	(i)	....	ई	𐬍	ى	ـِي	ـِي	ִי	î
8 Dentalis brevis	li	...	....	ऌ	....	...	...	...	...	...
9 „ longa	lî	...	....	ॡ	....	...	...	...	...	...
10 Lingualis brevis	ri	...	....	ऋ	....	...	...	...	...	...
11 „ longa	rî	...	....	ॠ	....	...	...	...	...	...
12 Labialis brevis	u	...	....	उ	𐬎	...	ـُ	ـُ	ֻ	u
13 „ longa	û	(u)	....	ऊ	𐬏	ا	ـُو	ـُو	וּ	û
14 Gutturo-palatalis brevis	e	...	....	...	𐬆(e) 𐬇(e)	...	...	...	ֶ	e
15 „ longa	ê (ai)	(e)	....	ए	𐬉, 𐬈	ى	...	...	ֵ	ê
16 Diphthongus gutturo-palatalis	âi	(ai)	....	ऐ	....	...	ـَيْ	ـَيْ	...	âi
17 „ „	ei (ĕi)	...	....	...	....	...	...	...	...	ei, êi
18 „ „	oi (ŏu)	...	....	...	....	...	...	...	...	...
19 Gutturo-labialis brevis	o	...	....	...	𐬊	...	...	...	ָ	o
20 „ longa	ô (au)	(o)	....	ओ	𐬋	ا	...	...	וֹ	...
21 Diphthongus gutturo-labialis	âu	(au)	....	औ	𐬃𐬎 (au)	...	ـَوْ	ـَوْ	...	âu
22 „ „	eu (ĕu)	...	....	...	....	...	...	...	...	...
23 „ „	ou (ŏu)	...	....	...	....	...	...	...	...	...
24 Gutturalis fracta	ä	...	....	...	....	...	...	...	...	...
25 Palatalis fracta	ï	...	....	...	....	...	...	...	...	...
26 Labialis fracta	ü	...	....	...	....	...	...	...	...	ü
27 G[illegible]uro-labialis fracta	ö	..		...	....	...	...	...		